The Science of Psychology:
Critical Reflections

Century Psychology Series

Kenneth MacCorquodale,
Gardner Lindzey, Kenneth E. Clark
Editors

The Science of Psychology:
Critical Reflections

Edited by Duane P. Schultz

THE UNIVERSITY OF NORTH CAROLINA AT CHARLOTTE

New York

APPLETON–CENTURY–CROFTS
EDUCATIONAL DIVISION
MEREDITH CORPORATION

750-1

Library of Congress Card Number: 73–111881

PRINTED IN THE UNITED STATES OF AMERICA

390–78679–9

PREFACE

There has been increasing concern and criticism in recent years about what many consider the unsatisfactory state of the mainstream of contemporary American psychology—the behavioristically-oriented experimental psychology. The growing body of articulate critics, both behaviorist and non-behaviorist, express alarm and disaffection at the narrowness, irrelevance, and artificiality of current psychological science. Technical deficiencies in the experimental method and the often improper and inadequate statistical analyses of research data are also open to attack.

This is the tenor of the articles selected for this book. The collection is not intended as a plea for a totally new kind of psychology, nor does it call for the discarding of an experimental approach. Rather, the purpose is to call for a sharpening of the philosophy and methodology of *scientific* psychology within the framework of the conviction that the scientific approach, broadly defined, is the only fruitful approach to the study of man.

The criticisms discussed in these articles, because of their validity and increasing number, cannot be ignored, particularly by those engaged in the training of new generations of psychologists. The articles are intended to provoke discussion and dissent and, in my own courses (in history and systems of psychology as well as social psychology), have done so quite well. In our training of new psychologists we must present an awareness of psychology's weaknesses, limitations, and sources of error, as well as its more positive virtues, achievements, and strengths. Thus, we may produce more reflective, sensitive, and sophisticated students who will be able to think and experiment critically with regard to psychological issues rather than approaching the subject in a wooden, mechanical, or "cookbook" manner.

I hope that many psychologists find these interesting and provocative articles useful in their classrooms and laboratories. At both undergraduate and graduate levels, this book can be used profitably as a supplementary text in history and systems of psychology, seminars on current problems in psychology, advanced general psychology, research methods, and experimental psychology.

My greatest debt in the preparation of this book is to the authors of the reprinted articles for the stimulation provided by their ideas and for allowing me to include their work. Through their articles I have been compelled to make my own critical reflections on my discipline—an exciting, albeit disturbing, experience which I hope others will share.

I also wish to thank the publishers and copyright-holders for granting permission to reprint. The original source of the individual articles is acknowledged on the title page of each article.

I am also grateful to my wife, Sydney Ellen, for her help in preparing the manuscript, and for sharing and reinforcing my enthusiasm for this project.

Charlotte, North Carolina   D.P.S.

CONTENTS

METHODOLOGICAL ISSUES 133

INTRODUCTION

Historical analyses of the development of psychology seem to agree on the dominant characteristics of contemporary American psychology. It is said that American psychology is strongly behavioristic, functionalistic, atomistic, mechanistic, deterministic, reductionistic, and environmentalistic (e.g., Chaplin & Krawiec, Schultz, Watson[1]). The methodology of psychology is characterized by objectivity and operationism, and the experimental method remains the fundamental technique. Indeed, the use of the experimental method, as well as its vigor and rigor, seems to be definitely increasing.

Are these major characteristics likely to continue to provide the guiding framework for the psychology of tomorrow? While many psychologists contentedly agree that the discipline should remain firmly committed to the extant traditions, a small but vocal and growing minority argue that it should not, indeed must not, continue in this same path.

These voices of dissent and criticism are being increasingly heard and the opposition is coming from all levels of the psychological spectrum; from without the behaviorist camp as well as within. While differing on the specific aspects of their attacks, many of these critics seem joined by a communal concern with what they consider to be the narrow, artificial, and sterile approach of contemporary psychology and the tendency to dehumanize man and reduce him "to a larger white rat or a slower computer."[2]

These critics argue that the behavioristic orientation provides an incomplete and perhaps inaccurate picture of "human nature" because it

[1] J. P. Chaplin & T. S. Krawiec, *Systems and Theories of Psychology*, 2nd ed. (New York, Holt, Rinehart & Winston, 1968). D. P. Schultz, *A History of Modern Psychology* (New York, Academic Press, 1969). R. I. Watson, "The Historical Background for National Trends in Psychology: United States," *Journal of the History of the Behavioral Sciences*, 1965, **1**, 130–138.

[2] J. F. T. Bugental, *Challenges of Humanistic Psychology* (New York, McGraw-Hill, 1967), p. vii.

fails to deal with what is uniquely human about man. Man, they contend, is not a machine or robot neatly programmed to respond in precisely predictable ways to the stimuli in his environment. Man is not an empty organism capable of quantified reduction to *S–R* units.

Approaching the problem on a different level are those who still generally favor the behavioristic approach to psychology but are concerned with certain perceived weaknesses in the experimental method. While agreeing on the fundamental utility of the experimental approach, these critics point to specific methodological deficiencies, such as the restricted range of subject sampling (both human and animal), inadequate control of confounding subject variables, and misuses of statistical analyses of research data.

Thus, the first group of critics calls for a complete and radical change of direction and focus for psychology, while the second group calls for a sharpening of the philosophy and methodology of existing psychology.

This second point is the focus and purpose of this book: not the elimination of the experimental approach to psychology, but rather the thoughtful reflection and examination of the direction of modern psychology. The goal is to strengthen the experimental approach by rendering it more valid, more technically "correct," and more relevant to distinctly human problems. The reprinted articles suggest that there indeed seems room for improvement; that there are deficiencies and weaknesses in current scientific psychology. Only by examining the points on which the experimental approach is vulnerable can we hope to achieve a truly significant and valid science of psychology.

This book is not an explicit plea for what has been called humanistic psychology. While many of the humanists' specific criticisms coincide with those offered by some behaviorists, their alternative course of action appears rather vague and, consequently, not overly attractive, to this observer at least, at the present time. As Koch commented, the humanistic psychologists comprise "a large number of individuals who . . . would have considerable difficulty communicating with each other and who stand for nothing focal other than a feeling of disaffection from the emphases of recent American psychology."[3]

The articles in this book are sharply critical of various aspects of scientific psychology and were chosen deliberately for that purpose. The collection as a whole, however, is not intended to destroy but to reconstruct—to build a stronger *science* of psychology. The book is presented with the hope that through self-analysis this can be achieved.

---

[3] S. Koch, "Psychology and Emerging Conceptions of Knowledge as Unitary," in T. W. Wann, *Behaviorism and Phenomenology: Contrasting Bases for Modern Psychology* (Chicago, University of Chicago Press, 1964), p. 44.

THEORETICAL ISSUES

The articles in this section deal with what might properly and broadly be called the *philosophy* of psychology for they inquire into the underlying principles or assumptions within which scientific psychology operates. There seems to be an aggressive antipathy among many contemporary psychologists toward anything connected with that "unwashed" (i.e., unscientific) amorphous area known as philosophy. In its continuing effort to become more scientific, psychology since the days of Wundt has tended to disclaim any allegiance or homage to its parent discipline. It continues to react with embarrassment and hostility to the perceived awkwardness and scientific poverty of its ancestor.

Yet it cannot be denied that each movement or system of thought throughout the history of psychology was constructed upon some philosophy of man, either expressed or implied. Every form or phase of psychology has approached its study within the framework of certain assumptions about the nature of its subject matter, which assumptions serve to determine the tools, techniques, and ultimate goals of investigation.

Contemporary scientific psychology has a model or philosophy of man that influences its research means and ends. Its critics call it the "robot model of man," but all would agree that it is a positivistic, mechanistic, reductionistic model regarding man as a complex, yet understandable and manipulatable, machine.

It is the nature of this current philosophy of man and the resulting investigatory principles that are discussed in the following articles. The philosophical foundations of psychology are criticized as inadequate and obsolete and the suggestion emerges that a behavioristic psychology is not so much incorrect as "too narrow and limited to serve as a *general* or comprehensive philosophy."[1]

[1] A. H. Maslow, *The Psychology of Science* (New York, Harper & Row, 1966), p. 5.

1. Psychology as an Exercise in Paradox[1]

D. Bannister

In this paper, Dr. Bannister examines a variety of paradoxes he finds in contemporary scientific psychology. He asks the rhetorical question of whether psychology was "ever a good idea" and urges psychologists to face the issue of reflexivity in psychological thinking. His portrait of paradoxes ranges widely and touches upon a number of the personal and philosophical discomforts that are central to the theme of this book.

The psychologists' model of man, ambition to be known as scientists, mode of thinking, dull means of communication via the journal article, and false eschewing of assumptions, are a few of the issues discussed in this delightful paper; issues we will meet again in other articles.

To cope with these problems, Dr. Bannister urges psychologists to think in more loose and imaginative terms, and to discard ill-fitting theories of man, replacing them with new and more relevant ones.

This paper was originally entitled "Was Psychology Ever a Good Idea?". On reflection such a title seemed both undignified and doomladen, and was discarded. However, the subject matter of the paper still relates to this original title in the sense that what I am concerned with are some of the personal-cum-philosophical sufferings involved in being a psychologist. Not all our difficulties take the form of paradox, but many of them seem to me to stem from a central paradox in psychology, which can be outlined as follows.

All psychological theories appear to have a model man at their centre. They seem to imply, though not necessarily state, some notion of what man really is. Thus psychoanalytic theories seem to suggest that man is basically a battlefield. He is a dark cellar in which a well-bred spinster lady and a sex-crazed monkey are forever engaged in mortal combat, the struggle being refereed by a rather nervous bank clerk. Alternatively, learning theory seems to suggest that man is basically a ping-pong ball with a memory. Along these lines some types of information theory

[1] Reprinted from the *Bulletin of The British Psychological Society*, 1966, **19**, 21–26, with the permission of the author and The British Psychological Society. Lecture delivered at Ohio State University, May 1965.

hint at the idea that man is basically a digital computer constructed by someone who had run out of insulating tape.

These pictures, however, are intended specifically as pictures of men and not as portraits of psychologists. Psychologists share the privilege of scientists in being outside the range of convenience of such theories. Granted, at a joke level psychologists may argue that a particular psychoanalyst is writing a particular paper in order to sublimate his sex instinct or we may toy with the notion that a book by some learning theorist is evidence that the said learning theorist was suffering from a build-up of reactive inhibition. But in our more solemn moments we seem to prefer the paradoxical view that psychologists are explainers, predictors and experimenters, whereas the organism, God bless him, is a very different kettle of fish.

In short, we have not yet faced up to the issue of reflexivity and the need for reflexivity in psychological thinking. If we are going to make so bold as to utter such statements as "thinking is a matter of A and B and a little C," then such statements should equally subsume the thinking which led to them. If we are going to climb up onto platforms and make generalizations about human behaviour, then such generalizations should clearly explain the behaviour of climbing up onto platforms and making generalizations about human behaviour. The delight and instruction which many of us find in George Kelly's Personal Construct theory[2] derives in no small measure from the fact that it is an explicitly reflexive theory. There may be no onus on the chemist when he writes his papers on the nature of acids and alkalis to account in terms of his acid-alkali distinction for his behaviour in writing a journal paper. But psychologists are in no such fortunate position.

Turning this issue of reflexivity the other way around, I am reminded of a recurrent theme in certain types of science fiction story. The master–chemist has finally produced a bubbling green slime in his test tubes, the potential of which is great but the properties of which are mysterious. He sits alone in his laboratory, test tube in hand, brooding about what to do with the bubbling green slime. Then it slowly dawns on him that the bubbling green slime is sitting alone in the test tube brooding about what to do with him. This special nightmare of the chemist is the permanent work-a-day world of the psychologist—the bubbling green slime is always wondering what to do about you.

Psychologists, of course, are by no means the first to bother themselves with the interesting problem of what is man. Theologians, historians, and politicians, to say nothing of mothers, bartenders, and con men, have also pondered the same issue. However, psychologists are inhibited in their thinking about this problem because they have an overwhelming desire to be considered scientists. This in itself is a laudable enough ambition but I suggest that it has been rather narrowly interpreted. Many psychologists begin their thinking with one eye firmly fixed on the detail of the ultimate experiment which must be worked out, the triumphant high significance level which must emerge and the acceptable journal paper they

[2] G. A. Kelly, *The Psychology of Personal Constructs* (New York, Norton, 1955).

will eventually publish. Experiment is a consummation devoutly to be wished but it is only part of a recurring cycle and too great a preoccupation with it in the early stages of thinking totally prevents certain kinds of issue ever being postulated. A psychologist who cannot think without an analysis of variance design in the forefront of his mind is indeed in a sad state. He reminds me of a patient I once had who was quite unable to ask a girl to go to the cinema with him because he was totally preoccupied at all times with the question of how they would get on after they had eventually been married. Had Christopher Columbus, for example, possessed the mind of many modern psychologists, I am reasonably certain he would never have discovered America. To begin with, he would never have sailed because there was nothing in the literature to indicate that anything awaited him except the edge of the world. Even had he sailed, he would have set forth bearing with him the hypothesis that he was travelling to India. On having this hypothesis disconfirmed when America loomed on the horizon he would have declared the whole experiment null and void and gone back home in disgust.

A further difficulty which arises out of our burning desire to be scientists is that lacking a white coat which would prove the point beyond question, we cling fiercely to any other proof which is available. For example, we have been taught that scientists are traditionally detached, objective, and dispassionate men. In psychology this is often curiously interpreted to mean that what we must be detached from is life. Years ago I knew an English professor of psychology who was always very worried by the fact that he suspected some of his students of entering themselves for a degree in psychology because they thought that psychology might have relevance to their own personal life problems. He solved this difficulty by arranging for the first year of the degree course to be entirely devoted to a detailed study of psychophysics. He correctly hypothesized that a year with Messrs. Weber-Fechner and Company would cause the life problem students to beat a hasty retreat to some disreputable non-scientific subject leaving behind only true psychologists. I regret to say that it was several years before I realized that there was anything in the least odd about this procedure.

Part of our conception of what is a science is often so concretistic as to breed in us the illusion that scientists think in the hypothetico-deductive mould. It is surely obvious that the hypothetico-deductive method is a style for writing journal papers and that no one ever in all his born days thought in this particular manner. Scientists in all fields, I am reasonably certain, think both inductively and deductively and more than that, have frequent recourse to thought processes which can only be described as a mixture of fantasy, prayer and sheer guesswork. Only thus are new ideas generated.

Thus our primary official means of communication—the journal paper—is cast into a fictional form—the hypothetico-deductive form—and of course must be dull because dullness is an additional hallmark of science. They are, in some ways, our least adequate means of communication. For example, I was for many years unable to distil meaning from a fair number of journal papers which described to me in some detail and very impressively the work of psychologists who sought to simulate and explicate the human being by means of machine models. After years of being bewildered, I was fortunate enough to encounter one of these psychologists in a state of psychological disinhibition and motor dysrhythmia in a social context. Clinging grimly to the bar, he explained to me with passion that we psychologists who work with people are facing certain doom, since people are notoriously non-sensical and unfit subjects for scientific scrutiny. Similarly, he claimed a flight to rats will avail us naught, since the world is full of whimsical rats who sit in the middle of the maze and chew their whiskers and seem entirely unaware of the goal gradient hypothesis. However, he had solved the whole problem by simply formulating certain theories of how human beings work, then he constructed machines which were based in detail on the prescriptions derived from these theories, then he predicted from his theory to the behaviour of the machine. And on the rare occasions when his prediction was inaccurate, a little tinkering with the works would damn soon put it right. Thus after years of bewilderment in terms of journal paper communication, the whole matter became amazingly clear to me.

Some of us are perhaps courting another paradox in assuming that scientific behaviour somehow involves avoiding assumptions and sticking to data or so-called facts. Like the well-known gentleman in one of your past television programs, a policeman of some kind, we are prone to mutter, "Just want to get the facts, ma'am." A fact, of course, is merely an assumption we are too timid to surrender in a context where a large number of our brethren are equally cowardly. This paradox can be seen at its most comic proportions in the elementary textbook of psychology. Such textbooks often begin by renouncing any theoretical bias and the very title elementary is designed to suggest on some sort of reductionist basis that we are going to be down at fact level. Then the author, allegedly for reasons of convenience, neatly sets up chapters which deal with such notions as perception, memory, emotion, motivation, learning and so forth. The most obvious conclusion on gazing at such a textbook is that the very chapter headings and divisions themselves represent a highly elaborate psychological theory and several score assumptions per chapter. The division of psychological statements into such frameworks as memory, emotion, motivation, learning and so forth is in no sense a matter of convenience. These in themselves are concepts with vast implications, and the fact that they are not merely a matter of convenience can be shown by dispensing with them for a period and noting the shattering effect this has on one's psychological approach.

Experimental psychology presents one aspect of our paradox in its sharpest form. In order to behave like scientists we must construct situations in which our subjects are totally controlled, manipulated and measured. We must cut our subjects down to size. We construct situations in which they can behave as little like human beings as possible and we do this in order to allow ourselves to make statements about the nature of their humanity. I can think of no simple formula which can allow us to escape from this paradox but I think we might have the decency to acknowledge its presence. We ought not to use the curious notions of reductionism in order to try to convince ourselves that our chaining of our subjects is the ideal way to go about things. It may be that an imprisoned, miniscule man is all we are capable of studying but let us acknowledge that we do miserable experiments because we lack the imagination to do better ones, not claim that these are scientifically ideal because they are simple minded.

If we follow the logic of non-reflexive psychological theories still further we arrive in the middle of the Skinnerian fantasy world, a world in which we can be convinced that once *all* the data is safely gathered in then we can control and manipulate men in every detail. We are now faced with the paradox of puppets controlling puppets.

However, if we view the situation reflexively, we might be led to acknowledge that any notions that we can scrape together and articulate, our subjects, being men like us, may also scrape together and articulate. We may be, and I think we often are, faced with subjects who are formulating their lives in terms of a theory and framework as extensive and well abstracted as our own. This suggests a nice infinite regress or, more properly, infinite progress in which we elaborate a theory large enough to subsume them, they being armed only with the earlier more primitive theory, and they in turn rethink and subsume the experimenter and so goes the race. The mysterious creatures we are racing with in this context are, of course, ourselves. Such an infinite and unending elaboration is perhaps a depressing vista to those who aspire to a deterministic science in pursuit of the holy grail of final truth. It is, however, a comforting thought to those of us who fear unemployment and who like to think that every answer is as good as the question it generates.

At this point I solemnly insert a reference to the literature lest you should think me scientifically illiterate. Since I want a paper which will illustrate the evils of non-reflexive thinking and since I am going to be nasty about it, I have shrewdly chosen one by two Soviet psychologists, Luria and Vinogradova. I will do the best I ever can about the precise reference, which is to say that I think it was in the British Journal of Psychology and it was published around about 1957 or 1958 and I can't for the life of me remember the title. It was an experiment tackling certain semantic issues in terms of classical conditioning psychology. It showed clearly that when a conditioned response was established to certain words then this response generalised to words which resembled the key word in meaning and not to words which only resembled it in sound. I repeat, the response generalised in terms of similarity of meaning not in terms of similarity of sound. The authors of this paper (which was, incidentally, quite well received in England) were agog with wonder at this fascinating bit of new knowledge. I would, however, have dearly loved them to go reflexive and explain to me how they could have thought up the experiment or written their paper if the contrary finding had been true.

A further set of sub-paradoxes is inherent in the situation of psychologists in that we are seeking to be scientists and at the same time we would like to make a decent living out of it. I am not thinking here of the major professional and ethical issues which excite the interests of committees but of the personal issues that leap out at us if we are ever too sleepy, too drunk or too curious to keep them under control. At the simplest level most of us who recognize that our professional onward march, in this day and age, calls for an ever increasing bibliography, have sat down to write papers. Most of us have experienced the passing treacherous thought that psychology as a science would benefit greatly from the non-publication of the effort we are about to pen. Easily the most succinct statement I have ever seen on this problem occurs on page 8 of an American Psychological Association publication called *A Career in Psychology*. In two sentences they sum up the problem thus and I quote, "Some psychologists devote themselves to the discovery of new knowledge. Others are college professors." Incidentally, looking back on this classic statement, I am intrigued by the notion of discovering new knowledge. I have yet to witness this process. I have seen people *inventing* notions and then discovering sometimes to their cost where the notions led to, but I have never seen them discovering new knowledge. I suspect that the writer of that immortal phrase was hopefully implying that science is additive. But science conceived as an effort to make sense of things and guess what happens next does not seem to me to be necessarily additive. I do not think that Darwin added to Lamarck. I think that he suggested that they take the railway someplace else and leave Lamarckville to become a ghost city.

A further implication of the concept of the professional scientific psychologist is that we have the magnificent arrogance to set up as experts on people. People have been lynched for far less than this. Some folk may gaze on our fumbling attempts to sort our own personal lives and come to a conclusion that as experts on people we are phonies, bald headed barbers trying to sell hair restorers. Other folks may be so impressed by the slick flick with which we handle our tachistoscopes or the smooth way we can mutter 'proprioceptive diathesis' without stuttering that they may come to the conclusion that we really are experts on people. In which case we may be even less popular. I construe the Reformation to be, among other things, man's objection to the notion of priests as experts on people. Historically, man has proved himself capable of shedding a lot of politicians' blood because he couldn't accept the idea that politicians are experts on people who know what's best for people. I think most of us, if driven to it, would own allegiance to the statement that ultimately "I am the only expert on me." It may be, then, that for the salvation of our necks as well as our souls, we ought to take a reflexive standpoint in psychology and acknowledge that we are all partners in the same business.

After complaint should follow suggested alternatives. Since the complaints have been wide and windy, the alternatives are equally so.

If we are to move forward from some of the paradoxes in which our thinking has involved us, then I think we shall have to accept the necessity for a great deal of more loose and imaginative thinking in relation to experimental psychology than has sometimes been the case. However tight our ultimate experimentation may be, and please God it will be organized, systematic and tight, I deem it both legitimate and advisable that in the early thinking and pilot experimental stages one should think as loosely as a drunken Welsh poet or else we are not earning our keep. Occam's Razor should be used to sharpen our wits, not to whittle away our imaginations.

Finally, I would argue that we must take the problem of reflexivity seriously.

I am not arguing here that psychological theories of what man is should be directly modelled upon and simply reflect lay common sense psychological theories of what man is. The conception of a desk held by an atomic physicist is by no means similar to the common sense conception of what a desk is. However, it is perhaps significant that the atomic physicist's notion of what a desk is is a good deal more exciting, complex, and rich than the common sense notion. A hydrographer's conceptualization of water is likewise a good deal more elaborate and soaring than that held by you or me. It may be that psychology is the only science which has been able to produce concepts of its subject which are clearly more mean, more miserable, and more limited than lay concepts.

As a simple and immediate test of the value of a psychological theory, I would suggest that you examine it and if it implies that man is much less than we know him to be or more significantly if it implies that you are much less than you know yourself to be, then such a framework should be discarded.

In spite of the sense of urgency which I detect in American psychology, I would argue that we can and should take time for a great deal of such discarding and concomitantly a great deal of new invention.

2. Some Thoughts Regarding the Current Philosophy of the Behavioral Sciences[1]

Carl R. Rogers

Contemporary behavioral science occupies a unique position which Dr. Rogers describes as increasing acceptance and acclaim as a boon to mankind and at the same time as a threat to mankind. What is the nature of psychology, he asks, this psychology that "like physics, can be used to enrich or to destroy our lives"? Through discussion of his own personal feelings with regard to this question, he calls attention to the controversy within some scientists between their affinity for precision, objectivity, hypothesis-testing, and lawful relations on the one hand, and concern for the human person on the other. Noting the reinforcing effects of behavioral science on the continued dehumanization and depersonalization taking place in our culture, he calls for a reevaluation of the process and nature of knowing, and recognition of subjectivity in scientific knowledge, and of the critical importance of patterns of relationship in nature.

BEHAVIORAL SCIENCE AS A FUNDAMENTAL ISSUE

The behavioral sciences are without doubt coming into their own: there is a vastly increased amount of public acceptance and public acclaim. The behavioral sciences are now a part of the hope of the modern world. In Washington a psychologist heads up an important commission regarding international tensions. In industry there are leaders of sensitivity groups and many other types of professionals and consultants who base their work on the behavioral sciences. In personal life, the individual who is seeking help, or the group, turns to psychotherapy. There is no doubt that the behavioral sciences and their applications play a part hitherto unknown in the history of mankind. We serve many important and valued functions.

At the same time the behavioral sciences constitute one of the bugaboos of the modern world. Skinner's *Walden Two*, the most honest and straightforward account of what the present trends in the behavioral sciences would mean if applied to the social world, has received and is receiving a great deal of fearful attention. The

[1] Reprinted from the *Journal of Humanistic Psychology*, 1965, **5**, 182–194, with the permission of the author and the *Journal of Humanistic Psychology*.

subject of control of human behavior through knowledge gained in the behavioral sciences is of increasing interest to large groups of people. When Dr. Skinner and I held a dialogue in Duluth, Minnesota, in the summer of 1962, nine hundred people attended. Both Dr. Skinner and I felt that in ways perhaps unknown to us, we were touching some important nerve in the present day culture. The response and the interest were much more than a response to a dialogue between two individuals. It is quite apparent that the behavioral sciences constitute a real issue and often a real threat to many who know about them and their increasing power. It has become clear that psychology, like physics, can be used to enrich or to destroy our lives.

Since we are a boon to society, since we are growing to be a respected area of science, since we are a fearful threat to our culture, since we are a group of rapidly developing disciplines; perhaps this is a good time to consider some of our foundations. Perhaps it is a time to try to examine, at as fundamental a level as possible and in as fresh a way as possible, the presuppositions which underly our whole field of work and its relation to life and living. Perhaps we can anticipate some of the problems which in the not too distant future will face us and our society by asking ourselves some of the deeper questions. How do we know? What is "true"? What are the identifying characteristics of a scientist? What is science? What is the special nature of behavioral science?

I am well aware of my lack of qualifications for so fundamental an inquiry. I am a therapist, a student of interpersonal relationships, not a philosopher of science. But I hope I can raise some questions which will arouse discussion, questions which I believe are fundamental to our ongoing discipline.

THE CONTROVERSY AS IT EXISTS IN ME

As in many other issues which have seemed to me to be of general importance, I feel the disputes within myself. I sometimes think that if I have a contribution to make to the behavioral sciences it is that the deepest current conflicts in that field all take place in me, as well as in the more open arena of professional and scientific life and discussion. Let me try to give you some of the tensions as I feel them in myself, the tensions which have made me turn to the simple but basic questions which I have just stated.

In the first place, let me speak of me as scientist. I love the precision and the elegance of science. The simple law of the lever, that the weight times distance to the fulcrum at one end equals the weight times the distance to the fulcrum at the other end, fascinates me. This whole question of balance and leverage has intrigued me enough that I love to build large floating mobiles which in their movement and balance express some of the beauty of the law of the lever. I can lose myself in the contemplation of this elegance. One of the most exciting books I have recently read is the book by Morris Kline (1953) on *Mathematics in Western Culture*. This is actually a history of scientific discovery in Western culture, the way in which significant new knowledge has been born. I regard the natural history of our scientific development as one of the most intriguing fields I know.

I like to create hypotheses and I like to test them against hard reality. I dislike fuzzy and personal emotional statements when they are given out as general truths, even when I respect them as expressions of the person. I am fascinated when I feel that I am close to an understanding of some principle of nature, an understanding which gives an opportunity for control of natural events by getting in tune with these discovered principles. (This of course is as close as we ever come to *control* of nature. We never control it in an arbitrary sense; we simply endeavor to put ourselves in accord with its underlying principles.)

I believe that psychological science will advance along the lines of discovering the lawful order which exists in human behavior and experience—in interpersonal relationships, in learning, in perception, in those experiences denied to awareness, and other psychological events. As a psychologist I am always looking for the invariant relationship, the statement that X always precedes Y, or is related to it in some invariant manner. I am sure that if these definite relationships exist and are discoverable, they can give us a deeper understanding of psychological events.

Despite my debates with Skinner, I feel that the elucidation of the process of operant conditioning is a great contribution which we have only begun to understand and use. I have the same attitude toward other recent developments in psychology. What I am trying to say is that I have, deep within me, a feeling for science, for that relatively new invention in human history by which we have come to have a partial understanding of the awesome order in our physical and psychological universe. Consequently I value the concepts which are near and dear to the heart of the behavioral sciences. The concern with observable behavior, the casting of all variables in operational terms, the adequate testing of hypotheses, the use of increasingly sophisticated design and statistics, all have meaning to me. I try continuously in my own research to see that it is conducted in a precise fashion with adequate controls and with sophisticated research design and statistical methodology so that we are not deceiving ourselves as to the findings. I mention all these personal attitudes because, in one part of me, I definitely am a scientist.

But I am also a person. A therapist. An individual who has lived deeply in human relationships. Here I come up with some other values and views which have equally deep meaning to me.

I value the person. Of all the incredible forms of life and non-life with which I am acquainted in the universe, the individual human being seems to me to have the most exciting potential, the greatest possibilities for an expanding development, the richest capacities for self-aware living. I cannot prove that the individual is most to be valued. I can only say that my experience leads me to place a primary value on the person of the human individual.

I am well aware that other views are possible, that one can, for example, place a primary value upon society, and only a secondary value upon the individual. But only in the individual does awareness exist. Only in the individual can alternative courses of action be most deeply and consciously tested as to their enriching or destructive consequences. The whole history of mankind, it seems to me, shows a gradually increasing emphasis upon the significance and worth of each individual. I not only observe this trend. I concur in it.

As a consequence it is not surprising that I object to the process of depersonalization and dehumanization of the individual which I see in our culture. I regret that the behavioral sciences seem to me to be promoting and reinforcing this trend. I am concerned when so astute an observer as Clifton Fadiman says, in speaking of the newspapers, that "this machine [the newspaper] . . . mediates between Technological Man (of whom we are the faint foreshadowing) and the Technological Order of which we will eventually be the computable Factors" (*Holiday*, 1963). I do not look forward with anticipation to being no more than a computable factor in such an order. It appears to me that many of the modern trends would indicate that we are moving inexorably toward a world in which men will be no more than conditioned ants in a gigantic anthill. I do not appreciate this prospect.

I have come to place a high value on personal, subjective choice. My experience in therapy confirms me in the belief that such choice, made openly by an individual who is aware both of what is going on within him, and aware also of his personal environment, is highly significant. I think of the confused psychotic man whose turn toward improvement was probably best predicted when he muttered, "I don't know *what* I'm going to do, but *I'm* going to do it." In short, I believe that terms such as personal freedom, choice, purpose, goal, have profound and significant meaning. I cannot agree with the view that the behavioral sciences have made not only such terms but the concept of meaning itself, meaningless.

I turn now to some more personal, less general views, in the hope that they will help you to interpret the views of science which follow. I believe that the internal frame of reference, the subjective private world of the person, is one of the very best ways of understanding human beings. Most of our significant hypotheses, even for our research, grow out of our own private and internal world, or out of the empathic understanding of the private world of another. This personal reality-as-perceived is the source of the valuable hunches, beliefs, ideas, which prove to be fruitful. Without the creative, inner, subjective hypothesis, all the elaborate machinery of outward verification would, in my judgment, be sterile.

With less pride I must report that I feel real glee when I discover that a careful research on planaria (Best, 1963)—a highly objective research on these lowly flatworms—is scarcely understandable without the use of such terms as apathy, significant choice, rejection, desire for richness of experience. It would not concern me at all if I found that we had to allow for subjectivity even in lower forms of life.

But there are boundaries to my regard for the subjective. I find that the elaboration of the subjective alone, as in some of the more far-out existentialists, is as unacceptable to me as the rigidity of a closed, impersonal science. As I read *some* of these existential writers, I feel that here we are entering into a situation in which history is repeating itself. We have suffered enough from the dogmatism of an unscientific Freudianism which initially enlightened us and then bound us into a rigid straitjacket. I do not want to see us repeat this history with some of the newer elements of existential thinking.

I have tried to give something of this continuing dialogue within myself simply to indicate that as a person I stand in both camps—the world of the precise, hard scientist, and the world of the sensitive subjective person. I hope this may provide a background for a better understanding of some of the ideas I would like to put forth in an attempt to answer some of the naive questions which I initially raised.

HOW DO WE KNOW?

In recent years I have attempted, with the aid of colleagues and students, to think and probe more deeply into some of these issues.[2] Let me turn first to the question of "How do we know?" We are apt, when we first encounter this question, to think of some of the impressive machinery of science. The more one pursues this question, the more one is forced to realize that, in the last analysis, knowledge rests on the subjective. I *experience*; in this experiencing I *exist*; in thus existing I in some sense *know*, I have a "felt assurance." All knowledge, including all scientific knowledge, is a vast inverted pyramid resting on this tiny, personal, subjective base.

If this seems to you to be an unwarranted undercutting of the solidity of our knowledge I would simply want to say that modern philosophers of science like Polanyi reinforce this view. I think it is not too much to say that knowing, even in the hardest sciences, is a risky, uncertain, subjective leap even when it is most "objective." We do no one a service by pretending it is not this. Instead we might look with awe at the scientific, philosophical, and artistic achievements which man has been able to build upon this very shaky base of personal experience. It speaks well for the essential trustworthiness of his functioning.

If it seems hard or difficult to give up the certainty of knowing which has customarily been related to science, perhaps we should recognize that the statements I am making put a firm emphasis upon science as a *process*, rather than upon science as a result. I believe there is a great deal of evidence to indicate that in many aspects of our culture, including science, we are moving toward a process conception of all aspects of living and life. Even in the teaching of high school science as the conduct of inquiry, we are endeavoring to facilitate an understanding of science as a subjectively guided *process*. To me it appears that our security is in this process, not in the scientific results, which may at any time be contradicted.

One of the best statements of the character of knowing, and also of the true scientist, is given not by a philosopher of science but by a choreographer. Agnes

[2] First in a seminar at the Center for Advanced Study in the Behavioral Sciences, Stanford, California, 1962–3; second in a seminar of faculty and graduate students at the University of Wisconsin, in 1963; most recently in a seminar of faculty, graduate students, and scientists from other fields, at the Western Behavioral Sciences Institute, La Jolla, California, in 1964.

de Mille (1958, pp. 190-191) has this to say about the gaining of knowledge: "The moment one knows how, one begins to die a little. Living is a form of not being sure, of not knowing what next or how. And the artist before all others never entirely knows. He guesses, and he may be wrong. But then how does one know whom to befriend or, for that matter, to marry? One can't go through life on hands and knees. One leaps in the dark. For this reason creative technique reduces itself basically to a recognition and a *befriending* of one's self. 'Who am I?' the artist asks, and he devotes his entire career to answering.

"There is one clue: what moves him is his. What amuses or frightens or pleases him becomes by virtue of his emotional participation a part of his personality and history; conversely what neither moves nor involves him, what brings him no joy, can be reckoned as spurious. An artist begins to go wrong exactly at the point where he begins to pretend. But it is difficult sometimes to accept the truth. He has to learn who he in fact is, not who he would like to be, nor even who it would be expedient or profitable to be."

The parallel with truly scientific thinking is profound. The scientist trusts himself and his experiencing or, as she puts it so charmingly, "befriends" himself, as he searches for the perceptions of truth which are his, which really belong to him, which constitute his basis for taking the subjective leap. This process is beautifully illustrated by none other than Dr. B. F. Skinner (1961), in his subjective account of his process of becoming a scientist. Here his story is studded by such phrases as, "This was, of course, the kind of thing I was looking for;" "I can easily recall the excitement of;" "Of course, I was working on a basic assumption." These phrases indicate the kind of intuitive trust which he placed in his own experiencing, and the fact that it was those experiences which moved him, subjectively, that guided his scientific directions.

WHAT IS SCIENCE?

But let us turn away from these comments on the personal process of knowing, to the larger conception of science as a whole. How do we pursue truth? How do we discover new or generalized knowledge? What is it like to be a scientist? What is the essence of science? I should like to set forth a few statements as a basis for discussion.

It would appear that if I wish to become a scientist the first step is to immerse myself in the phenomena of the particular field in which I have developed an interest. The more complete the immersion, the longer it lasts, the more I love and prize the whole field, the more open I am to all the subtleties of my experiencing, the more likely I am to discover new knowledge. This means a tolerance for ambiguity and contradiction, a resistance to the need for closure. It means soaking up experience like a sponge so that it is taken in in all its complexity, with my total organism freely participating in the experiencing of the phenomena, not simply my conscious mind.

THE EMERGENCE OF A SENSE OF PATTERN

Out of this immersion in the phenomena, certain things "come to mind." I may find emerging some sense of pattern or rhythm or relationship. As I read the history of science and as I understand the thinking of men like Polanyi this subjective sense of pattern is something to be nourished, no matter how absurd such patterns may seem when scrutinized by my conscious thought. I need to recognize that my conscious thought is full of fixed constructs which may interfere with the perception of an underlying pattern. It appears that the discoverer of knowledge feels a trust in *all* his avenues of knowing, unconscious, intuitive, and conscious.

It is this intuitive sensing of a pattern which is all-important in true science. If I can lay aside rigidly held preconceptions, can forget for a moment the "truth," the clear-cut constructs already known, then the pattern may shine through more clearly. Here is an excellent statement of the attitude I am describing. "What you have to do is let go, let go every thought of your own, wipe your mind clean, fresh, innocent, newborn, sensitive as unexposed film to take up the impressions around you, and let what will come in. This is the pregnant void, the fertile state of no-mind. This is non-preconception, the beginning of discovery" (Flaherty, 1960, p. 20). This could certainly have come from a scientist. Actually, it is a statement by a gifted creator of documentary films, Frances Flaherty.

The great scientists, men like Kepler, Einstein, and others, have learned to trust this intuitive sensing. It may be clearly wrong and yet fundamentally right. For example, I have chuckled at the natives in the Caribbean who would not think of planting their crops except at the time of the new moon, when "the moon is right." All of us "know" that the moon cannot possibly affect this seed that is placed in the ground. The native is acting on a ridiculous hypothesis. Now, however, centuries after the natives formulated their adages, scientists find to their puzzlement that rainfall during the week following the new moon is significantly greater all over the world than rainfall during the other portions of the moon's cycle. In other words, the hypothesis that the moon affected the seed is as wrong as we in our superior knowledge thought that it was. But the sensing of the pattern, by natives immersed for a lifetime in the growing of crops, was correct! This accords very deeply with my belief that the human organism, when operating freely and non-defensively, is perhaps the best scientific tool in existence and is able to sense a pattern long before it can consciously formulate one.

Bronowski (1956, pp. 23, 24, 32) sees these patterns or rhythms as "hidden likenesses," that is, a similarity between two objects or events which on the surface would seem to be totally unrelated. He says, "All science is the search for unity in hidden likenesses . . . the scientist looks for order in the appearances of nature by exploring such likenesses, for order does not display itself of itself; if it can be said to be there at all it is not there for the mere looking. There is no way of pointing a finger or a camera at it; order must be discovered and in a deep sense it must be created. What we see as we see it is mere disorder. . . . We remake nature by the act of discovery in the poem or in the theorem."

One of the great mistakes in the behavioral sciences today, in my judgment, is that since our science must deal in observables—the movement of a needle on a polygraph, a mark on paper, a sound emitted, a movement of a limb, and the like —we have assumed that the pattern we sense must also have to do with observables. This is where the freely functioning human organism is confined in its operation and permitted only a distorted perception. It appears to me that a pattern when it is sensed must be perceived in its *own* terms, whether those terms are internal, ineffable, subjective and invisible, or whether they are external, tangible and visible.

If I develop some sense of pattern regarding the perceptions and visions of individuals who have taken the drug LSD, my first perception of that pattern can best be cast in terms of the visions and hallucinations (which no observer can see) rather than in terms of the emitted words, tears, groans, writhings, of the individuals involved. We need not be fearful of perceiving the pattern in terms which are natural to it. Later, in testing hypotheses, we may have to limit ourselves to observable areas, but this is a different matter.

May I sum up this point about pattern by saying that I have come to realize that all science is based on a recognition—usually prelogical, intuitive, involving all the capacities of the organism—of a dimly sensed gestalt, a hidden reality. This gestalt or pattern appears to give meaning to disconnected phenomena. The more that this total apprehension of a pattern is free from cultural values and is free from past scientific values, the more adequate it is likely to be. The more that it is based on all sensory avenues, upon unconscious directions, as well as cognitive insights, the more adequate it is likely to be. I regard this sensing of a pattern of relationships as perhaps the heart of all true science. I believe this view would be supported by Polanyi and many others in the physical sciences.

THE CHARACTERISTICS OF A FRUITFUL PATTERN

Since I have laid such stress upon this sensing of a pattern I should like to indicate some of the elements that would be likely to discriminate a significant and fruitful pattern from one that is simply an illusion or a misperception. The more that the pattern is based on some of the following elements, the more likely it is, I believe, to prove fruitful and productive in a scientific sense:

A keen and alert intelligence.

A dedicated immersion over time in a broad range of related phenomena.

A disciplined personal commitment by the scientist to his search, to finding out.

A fresh, non-defensive openness to all of the phenomena and their interrelationships. This is an openness to the field of his study, laying aside so far as possible all previous knowledge and previous conceptions, or at least holding such knowledge and concepts very lightly.

An openness to all avenues of knowledge—previous studies in the field, the insights of non-scientists, openness to the experiencing of others who are involved in the same field and a willingness to take in any bit of seemingly relevant data.

A trust in the total organismic sensing which is based on the above and which is deeper than, but includes, the cognitive perceptions.

A recognition that the beauty or elegance of the perceived pattern is at least one clue to its fruitfulness. Such phrases as "the true inner simplicity," "the intuition of rationality in nature" (phrases used, I believe, by Polanyi) indicate that beauty is one of the ways by which we judge the truth value of a sensed pattern.

The more that the pattern reveals a unity in nature, the more likely it is to be fruitful. (It should be obvious that both the beauty or elegance of the pattern and its sensing of a unity in nature can be artificial and misleading. Nonetheless it is true that all significant scientific discoveries do have these qualities of both elegance and the introduction of a hitherto unperceived unity.)

Perhaps a quotation from Dr. Polanyi (1958, p. 6) would be in order here. He says: "To say that the discovery of objective truth in science consists in the apprehension of a rationality which commands our respect and arouses our contemplative admiration; that such discovery, while using the experience of our senses as clues, transcends this experience by embracing the vision of a reality beyond the impression of our senses, a vision which speaks for itself in guiding us to an ever deeper understanding of reality—such an account of scientific procedure would be generally shrugged aside as out-dated Platonism: a piece of mystery-mongering unworthy of an enlightened age. Yet it is precisely on this conception of objectivity that I wish to insist."

PUTTING THE PATTERN TO TEST

Important as is this "vision of reality," this sensing of a pattern, it is not in itself sufficient for the discovery of new truth. The hypothesis must be put to the test. Here I would say that for me operationism, as I understand it, appears to be the most satisfactory mode of testing a hypothesis and confirming, modifying, or disconfirming it. I have a deep respect for the methodology which scientists have developed.

I do not propose to expand on this point because I believe the operational approach is fairly well understood. I will simply give an example from my own experience which could be duplicated, I am sure, in the experience of any scientist. I have made the assertion that certain describable attitudinal sets in the psychotherapist—genuineness, acceptance, a sensitive empathic understanding—are the necessary and sufficient conditions of change in the client or patient who is involved with the therapist in psychotherapy. Simply as an assertion, this has about the same status as the assertion that the moon is made of green cheese. When it is recognized that the assertion grows out of some thirty years of therapeutic experience it has a slightly better, but not greatly better, status. Unless I am willing to define these terms operationally, to design a research which will put them to test, or to encourage others to design such researches, unless the various extraneous variables are controlled, and unless the findings support the hypotheses, then we are only in the realm of pattern perception and not of confirmation.

Perhaps, however, the methodology of science and all its enormous modern sophistication is placed in a more suitable perspective if we clearly recognize that it is simply the machinery by which we try to determine whether we have deceived ourselves in the pattern which we have sensed in nature.

Even in the realm of confirmation the personal element enters in. In a recent discussion with Lancelot Whyte, the physicist who has become a historian of ideas and a philosopher of science, I was surprised to find that for him the truth value of a statement, even in science, could in the last analysis be evaluated by one criterion only. If I understood him correctly he was saying that his only criterion was as to how deeply acquainted with the phenomena, how non-defensive, how truly open to all facets of his experiencing, is the scientist who has perceived the pattern and put it to test. I realized after my conversation that if I tried to state in my own terminology the judgment of this physicist it would be that the more nearly the individual comes to being a fully functioning person (Rogers, 1963), the more trustworthy he is as a discoverer of truth.

In the behavioral sciences I think that one of our problems is that the methods of testing hypotheses come to be regarded as dogmas. These are, or should be, as unwelcome as dogmas in any other field. The rules and methods we have for testing hypotheses are creations of the scientists themselves and should be recognized as such. Thus we should realize that there is no special virtue to any one procedure. Some hypotheses can best be tested in one case. One such famous hypothesis had to do with the circulation of the blood, and the testing of it involved no statistics. Others can only be satisfactorily tested on a large population using all of the most elaborate statistical methods. Some very pioneering hypotheses should first be tested in rough ways before they are put to refined test. In all instances the method of testing should be appropriate to the hypothesis, the pattern, the "vision of reality."

Perhaps it will help us in achieving a proper perspective on our methodology if we recognize that we are always dealing with labels in our research work, never with the phenomenon itself. No one has ever seen a stimulus or a response or a reinforcement, for example, any more than we have ever seen a negative self concept. We do observe behavior which we *interpret* to be a stimulus or a response or a reinforcement to the animal or the human being, just as we can observe behaviors which seem to be reasonably interpreted as indicators of a negative self concept. But it is always true that the measures which we adopt or devise are based on external clues. We try to choose measures which bring us as close as possible to the underlying phenomena in which we are actually interested but our research methods never utilize those phenomena, only an external clue or interpretation of them. This is true in all the sciences, *especially* in the sciences we so admire as the "hard" sciences.

SOME IMPLICATIONS OF THIS VIEW FOR THE BEHAVIORAL SCIENCES

If we look at the behavioral sciences in the light of what I have been saying, certain questions come naturally to mind. Are the behavioral scientists immersing themselves in their true field of study, or are they endeavoring to work in detachment from it? I have heard much criticism in recent years of those who teach clinical psychology in the universities. The statement is often made that they are so intent on doing research in the field that they do no clinical work. But if what I have been saying is true, their only hope of doing *significant* research is to be immersed in clinical work. I think we might ask of all behavioral scientists whether they are permitting themselves to live deeply, fully, openly, in interpersonal relationships, in deep contact with individuals and the culture which helps to shape them? Or are they quickly, and sometimes fearfully, abstracting themselves from the very groundwork of their science? If so, it is unlikely that they can be very creative as scientists.

Are we creating a climate in our graduate schools and laboratories in which a confrontation with the mystery of the real in human personality and behavior can exist? Is the atmosphere such as to permit dimly perceived patterns to emerge and be tested? In the graduate departments which I know best, I would say that such a climate does not exist. We have a good environment for training technicians, but not a good climate for scientists.

Is it clear to us as behavioral scientists that our true task is to discern patterns, rhythms, relationships, which cut so deeply into the rationality of nature that the implications of our perceptions will only be fully evident many decades hence? Granted that such perceptions cannot be forced, and must emerge, is it clear that this is our central purpose? It appears to me that all too often the behavioral sciences are marked by a shallowness which bodes ill. When one small technical study is piled on top of many others, this is not science in its true sense. The effort to get two papers out of one study, the lengthening of publication lists by spurious co-authorship, thus spreading the kudos around, is too often the characteristic of our field. We seem, all too frequently, to have forgotten the nature of science.

SOME POSSIBLE CHANGES IN THE BEHAVIORAL SCIENCES

Let me bring my remarks to a close. It may seem that the statements I have been making about knowing, and science, and the behavioral sciences in particular, add very little to our present conceptions. Yet I should like to indicate some of the effects that such a view of science, particularly if imparted to our graduate students and to the younger men in the field, might have.

In the first place it would tend to do away with the fear of creative subjective speculation. As I talk with graduate students in the behavioral sciences this fear is a very deep one. It cuts them off from any significant discovery. They would be shocked by the writings of a Kepler in his mystical and fanciful searching for likenesses and patterns in nature. They do not recognize that it is out of such fanciful thinking that true science emerges. As Bronowski says (1956, pp. 22-23), "To us the analogies by which Kepler listened for the movement of the planets and the music of the spheres are far fetched. But are they more so than the wild leap by which Rutherford and Bohr found a model for the atom in, of all places, the planetary system?"

A second effect would be to place a stress on disciplined commitment, disciplined *personal* commitment, not methodology. It would be a very healthy emphasis in the behavioral sciences if we could recognize that it is the dedicated, personal search of a disciplined, open-minded individual which discovers and creates new knowledge. No refinement of laboratory or statistical method can do this.

Another effect would be that it would do away with many of the "oughts" in selecting hypotheses. For example, it is deeply imbedded in most behavioral scientists that we "ought" to be concerned only with the observables in behavior. Until recently this has tended to inhibit work on dreams, on fantasy, on creative thinking. It has made most psychologists small-calibre scientists.

Another effect would be that it would permit a free rein to phenomenological thinking in behavioral science, our effort to understand man and perhaps even the animals from the inside. It would recognize that no type of hypothesis has any special virtue in science save only in its relationship to a meaningful pattern which exists in the universe. Thus, a phenomenologically based hypothesis would have as much place in the behavioral sciences as a chemically based, genetically based, or behaviorally based hypothesis. We would develop a broader science (Rogers, 1964).

Another effect would be that it would do away with those hypotheses which are selected simply because there are tools to measure the variables involved.

Another effect would be that it would put the machinery of confirmation, the machinery of empirical testing of hypotheses, in its proper place. Method would not occupy a central place as the be-all and end-all of behavioral science.

Another effect would be that it would put the stress on meaning, not simply on statistical significance at the .01 level.

Another and more general effect would be that if the picture of science I have tried to suggest gains some general acceptance in our field, then it would give a new dignity to the science of man and to the scientist who commits himself to that field. It would keep the scientist as a human being in the picture at all times and we would recognize that science is but the lengthened shadow of dedicated human beings.

Perhaps most important of all, it would keep the subject of the investigation of the behavioral sciences in the picture as a subjective human being, not simply as a machine, not simply as a determined sequence of cause and effect. We would not be fearful of looking at man as an existing human being, to use Kierkegaard's term, with more to his life than can be compressed into a machine model. Unless we can make progress in this direction the behavioral sciences have, I fear, the capacity for becoming a threat to society more extreme and more devastating than the physical sciences have been.

REFERENCES

Best, J. B. Protopsychology. *Scientific American*, 1963, **208**(2), 54–62.

Bronowski, J. *Science and human values*. New York: Harper Torchbooks, 1956.

De Mille, Agnes B. *And promenade home*. Boston: Little, Brown, 1958. Pp. 190–191.

Fadiman, C. Party of one. *Holiday*, 1963, **34** (5), 14.

Flaherty, Frances. *The odyssey of a film-maker*. Urbana, Ill.: Beta Phi Mu, 1960.

Kline, M. *Mathematics in Western culture*. New York: Oxford University Press, 1953.

Polanyi, M. *Personal knowledge*. Chicago: University of Chicago Press, 1958.

Rogers, C. R. The concept of the fully functioning person. *Psychotherapy: Theory, Research, and Practice*, 1963, **1**(1), 17–26.

Rogers, C. R. Toward a science of the person. In T. W. Wann (Ed.), *Behaviorism and phenomenology: contrasting bases for modern psychology*. Chicago: University of Chicago Press, 1964. Pp. 109–140.

Skinner, B. F. *Cumulative record*. New York: Appleton-Century-Crofts, 1961.

3. Assumptions in Psychology[1]

Adrian Van Kaam

Contemporary developments in physics as well as phenomenology point to the inescapable conclusion that science is relatively subjective. In the light of these new developments, Dr. Van Kaam asserts that thinking in science takes place within the framework of certain basic assumptions, and that psychology is no exception.

He forcefully suggests, however, that psychologists have tended to deny the place of assumptions and subjectivity in their science, and notes the reasons for this denial. He urges a greater awareness on the part of positivistic psychologists of the basic presuppositions or assumptions used to construct their model of man. It is argued that phenomenological-existential psychologists are aware of these assumptions and therefore reflect more accurately the current notion of subjectivity in science.

Important in the development of science is the realization that science is relatively subjective. It was physicists like Planck (1949), Bohr, von Weizsaecker (1949), and Heisenberg (1944, 1954) who made man aware of this. Especially the development of quantum physics made clear that the ideal of absolute objectivity and of an absolutely objective view of the universe was a dream never to be realized. Recent discoveries taught convincingly that every so-called scientific view of the world is extremely limited. Every scientist who approaches the universe selects necessarily one out of many viewpoints which could be taken. It is essential that the scientist does not look on man and the universe in all their dimensions but that he limits himself to a selected part of the universe. This selection is based on a choice and on assumptions which are relatively subjective.

Not only the physicists but other thinkers as well realized the relative subjectivity of science. Remarkable in this context is the so-called phenomenological way of thought. The phenomenologist studies man's primary experience. This experience is more comprehensive than the conceptual knowledge which man selects later from his original experience by means of analysis. This original experience precedes clear conceptualization. It is the matrix of all partial concepts arbitrarily chosen by man. Man in his primary experience is still open to the universe. He is in contact

[1] Reprinted from the *Journal of Individual Psychology*, 1958, **14**, 22–28, with the permission of the author and the *Journal of Individual Psychology*.

with the fullness of reality in all its nuances. This experience is therefore essentially different from the scientific way of knowing. Man can only understand in a scientific way when he subjectively limits his original view. In order to be scientific he must adopt an attitude other than the open pre-scientific one. He has to change and to reduce that which was originally given in his primary experience. What are considered to be objects in science are not objects which are given as such, but which are viewed in a specific frame because man orients himself subjectively in a certain way towards reality. Naive experience does not know about the objects of science but knows people, houses, trees, birds and flowers, love, hate and anxiety.

When man determines subjectively that he will consider all these realities in a scientific way then he limits his experience of them by some subjectively created frame of reference (Husserl, 1901, 1948). They are no longer what they were. So-called exact data are rather interpretations of man's primary experience (Heidegger, 1950; Taylor, 1946). Scientific thinking foregoes primary experience instead of penetrating it. The scientific view of man and the universe is thus the result of a certain modification of the human attitude. The primary experience of the world is fenced in by science. Science modifies experience fundamentally. And it does this by means of a subjective choice by man (Minkowski, 1936).

The realization by contemporary physicists and phenomenologists that science is relatively subjective made man more aware of the fact that he always starts from certain assumptions in his scientific endeavors.

DENIAL OF ASSUMPTIONS

Psychology does not absorb easily these new realizations. Various psychologists try to escape the realization that assumptions are inevitable. Some of them profess that they consider all the views of all the schools of psychology as equally relative and that they themselves start without any assumption. But by declaring all these views to be relative the psychologist cannot escape having his own very definite view. The more this relativity of the different psychological viewpoints is stressed, the more forcefully the absolute character of one's own position in psychology reveals itself. Perhaps it could be called a superviewpoint, but nevertheless it remains a viewpoint. It offers no escape from a decisive, absolute choice of position in the understanding of man.

Others say that there are no assumptions because they cannot be proven by means of the scientific method. Even this effort to get rid of assumptions is in vain. For to declare that only these propositions of psychologists make sense which can be experimentally verified is one of the most sweeping assumptions one can think of because it contains a definite and irrevocable judgment concerning all possibilities of human knowledge and their relationship to what is knowable. There is no escape from assumptions in psychology. The psychologist of every school always makes an ultimate and absolute judgment about what is called the nature of man and about the way in which man can be understood. These assumptions of psychologists are not arrived at by psychological research. On the contrary, the assumptions of the psychologist are the point of departure for the kind of research that he will perform and for the evaluation of the results of this research (Van Melsen, 1952, 1954).

REASONS FOR THE DENIAL

It seems more difficult for the field of psychology than for other areas to assimilate the new realization that science is relatively subjective and always implies assumptions which cannot be arrived at by the scientific method itself.

The early psychologists were inclined to imitate physics. This tradition still influences many psychologists today. But what they actually know about physics are probably the optimistic tenets of the early physicists (Mach, 1942). They seem less familiar with the realizations of such physicists as mentioned at the outset. They are therefore less sensitive to the relative subjectivity of science than some of their contemporaries are.

Early psychology had to free itself from the dominance of philosophy. It was understandable that the psychologist reacted against a domineering philosophy which at that time was rationalistic and abstract. An unfortunate consequence is that many psychologists now are inclined more than other intellectuals to under-evaluate all publications which are of a more theoretical, philosophical or literary nature. This may result in a certain narrow-mindedness, an unawareness of what is transpiring on the contemporary intellectual scene. Because of this, certain psychologists may be less able to profit from the new realizations which are expressed in these other areas, concerning the nature of science.

Psychology was a relatively young science which had to prove itself. Science rightly claims a certain degree of objectivity and consistency in its methods and factual results, once the scientist has subjectively selected a small segment of reality as an object of research. It is easily understood again that the insecure psychologist of that day was inclined to over-stress his claims on objectivity. As a result of this historical condition certain psychologists today are more afraid than other scholars to admit in the light of the new realizations that assumptions are inescapable and that they are not provable by the scientific method itself.

The psychologist who believes that his assumptions and the interpretation of the outcomes of his research are absolutely objective may be inclined to construct his view of life on the basis of these findings. His science becomes his philosophy of life. This makes it more difficult for him to tolerate the realization that his scientism, as much as science itself, is finally built on assumptions which according to his feeling are not trustworthy because they are not based on results of the scientific method.

Another factor may be that certain scientists who are committed to a certain kind of minute research may have a more or less compulsive personality structure. Science in their lives may have the function of organizing reality in such a way that they feel sure that they can at least potentially measure, control and dominate the unknown. The realization that assumptions which are not experimentally demonstrable are at the base of their science could evoke anxiety. In this case the avoidance of this realization operates as a subtle defense (Maslow, 1954).

Finally the character of experimental work does not lead directly to the realization of all the implications of experimental psychology. One even has to admit that as far as the psychologist is aware of these problems it is to his advantage to bar them from his awareness as long as he is engaged in experimental research. Paying attention to assumptions during the experimentation itself would make scientific work impossible. This attitude of abstraction from the assumptions involved during experimentation extends itself easily outside the laboratory and makes the experimenter blind to the very existence of the assumptions involved.

The education of the psychologist suffers necessarily from the imperfections which characterize psychology itself. From the very beginning the student may be inclined not to take seriously certain sources of knowledge of reality such as philosophy and literature which are common to other intellectuals in his culture. At the same time he does not have the preparation that would enable him to involve himself deeply in a modern science such as physics. So he misses also the realizations that are common to the modern physicist.

AWARENESS OF ASSUMPTIONS

In spite of all this one finds an increasing number of psychologists who become aware of the fact that their research necessarily takes its departure from relatively subjective assumptions (Ansbacher & Ansbacher, 1956; Maslow, 1954; Moustakas, 1956; Rogers & Skinner, 1957). The reason is probably not that these psychologists are better acquainted with the latest results of quantum physics and the relativity of the scientific view that is one of the consequences of its recent development. Nor can it probably be explained by a deeper and more extensive knowledge of contemporary art, literature and philosophy.

How did these psychologists escape intellectual isolation? It seems that they are for the most part psychologists who are interested in the clinical area. This interest implies concern for the human person and especially for his experiential life. This genuine and lasting attention to the experience of man may lead to the realization that his relatively subjective experience is the source of all his endeavors even in science. And it is here that clinical psychology approaches the realizations of modern thinking and the perceptivity of contemporary existence. One of the results is that these psychologists tend to be more aware of assumptions and try to make them explicit.

We could in a somewhat inaccurate way draw a distinction between positivistic and phenomenological-existential psychologists. When we ask ourselves about their relative subjectivity, we may characterize this as follows. The subjectivity of the positivistic psychologist seems to be a more repressed and inaccessible, rigid and closed subjectivism. This means that he is inclined to see his relatively subjective assumptions as absolutely objective. He has a certain disdain for reflection on subjective assumptions, and even a certain fear of this reflection. This more or less repressed subjectivism tends to make him rigid and absolute regarding, for instance, the evaluation of his methods. He may, for instance, believe that quantifying methods are the only ones which are worthwhile. And because the relatively subjective basis for this belief is not open to his continual reflection he has no means to correct this attitude.

The subjectivity of the more phenomenological-existential psychologist seems to be more accessible, flexible and open. He is less inclined to believe that his assumptions are absolutely objective. He is more aware of what determines his scientific work (Rogers & Skinner, 1957). This prevents subjective influence from becoming too fixed and too rigid. It makes him more open to the subjective determinants which influence other people in psychology and other fields. He is inclined to reflect on his relatively subjective assumptions and to ask himself from time to time whether they are still tenable, whether they can be expanded or reconciled with the relatively subjective viewpoints of other men who study in one or another way the human person. He might even see the concept of science itself as a growing and changing concept. Dependent on relatively subjective assumptions, this concept takes on a different meaning and content in different periods of culture (Buytendijk, 1950).

It is clear that such an open, flexible and accessible subjectivism could be promoted in students of psychology. One could require that they write down in every research paper what their basic assumptions are. While interpreting the results, they would have to indicate clearly what the interpretation would be in the light of their own assumptions and what, in the light of the assumptions of some other prominent schools of psychology.

POSITIVISTIC VERSUS PHENOMENOLOGICAL ASSUMPTIONS

Finally one could ask, what are the assumptions of the positivistic psychologists and what are those of the phenomenologically existential ones ? It would be impossible to elaborate on this extensively in this paper. It briefly comes down to this, that the more positivistic psychologist still adheres implicitly to the two assumptions of mechanism and determinism which were characteristic of early physics. Mechanism implies a wholly quantitative theory of atoms-without-qualities (Van Melsen, 1952). This implicit assumption is more and more in contradiction with the facts discovered by the physicists. The same is true of the development in psychology. The implicit assumption that man can be understood by analyzing him into elements which are statistically the same is basically in contradiction with reality. In other words, the assumption of mechanism that all phenomena can be reduced to local change or to a change in position of intrinsically immutable particles is no longer tenable in view of the facts. But it still influences the scientific work of the positivistic psychologist. Another assumption of the early physicists, namely that of determinism, was that every situation of primordial particles at any given moment was determined by an inner law and by the situation at another moment. This assumption in its psychological form is still of great influence on the thinking of the positivistic psychologist. The physicists are far more cautious since the principle of uncertainty was formulated by Heisenberg. We call both tenets philosophical assumptions. We call them assumptions because they do not find support in strictly empirical theory. We call them philosophical because of the absoluteness with which they are held: they are applied by the positivistic mind to everything in man and in the universe.

The assumptions of phenomenological-existential psychologists are of as great a variety as those of the positivistic psychologists. The scope of our paper allows us only to refer to them negatively as the contrary of an absolute mechanism and an absolute determinism. They are the counterpart in psychology of the new assumptions of the quantum physicists and the existential philosophers. Becoming, creativity, growth, self-actualization (Ansbacher & Ansbacher, 1956; Maslow, 1954; Moustakas, 1956; Rogers & Skinner, 1957) are terms which more or less indicate in which direction these assumptions are developing.

REFERENCES

Ansbacher, H. L., & Ansbacher, Rowena R. (Eds.) *The individual psychology of Alfred Adler*. New York: Basic Books, 1956.

Buytendijk, F. J. J. *De psychologie van de roman; studies over Dostojevskij*. Utrecht, Holland: Spectrum, 1950.

Heidegger, M. *Holzwege*. Frankfurt a.M.: Klostermann, 1950.

Heisenberg, W. *Wandlungen in den Grundlagen der Naturwissenschaft*. Leipzig: Hirzel, 1944.

Heisenberg, W. Das Naturbild der heutigen Physik. In *Die Kuenste im technischen Zeitalter*. Munich: Oldenbourg, 1954.

Husserl, E. *Logische Untersuchungen; Untersuchungen zur Phaenomenologie und Theorie der Erkenntnis*. Halle: Niemeyer, 1901.

Husserl, E. *Erfahrung und Urteil*. Hamburg: Claasen & Goverts, 1948.

Mach, E. *The science of mechanics*. LaSalle, Ill.: Open Court, 1942.

Maslow, A. H. *Motivation and personality*. New York: Harper, 1954.

Minkowski, E. *Vers une cosmologie*. Paris: Aubier, 1936.

Moustakas, C. E. *The self; explorations in personal growth*. New York: Harper, 1956.

Planck, M. *Vortraege und Erinnerungen*. Stuttgart: Hirzel, 1949.

Rogers, C. R., & Skinner, B. F. Some issues concerning the control of human behavior. *Science*, 1957, **124**, 1057–1066.

Taylor, F. S. *The fourfold vision*. London: Chapman & Hall, 1946.

Van Melsen, A. G. *From atomos to atom*. Pittsburgh: Duquesne University, 1952.

Van Melsen, A. G. *The philosophy of nature*. Pittsburgh: Duquesne University, 1954.

Von Weizsaecker, C. F. *Zum Weltbild der Physik*. Stuttgart: Hirzel, 1949.

4. Philosophy Reconsidered[1]

Herman Feifel

The relationship, past and present, between psychology and philosophy, is critically examined by Dr. Feifel. He notes the early separation of these two disciplines and also the continuing attempt on the part of psychology to emulate the physical sciences. As a result, consciousness has ceased to be of interest to psychology since it is not amenable to the objective, experimental methods of study that have assumed commanding positions. However, while psychology has continued to forcefully reject philosophy, post-Newtonian physics has come to strongly interact with it. Despite this new look in physics, psychology clings to an outmoded view that causes it to be "too bewitched by methodology, analysis, and operational definition." Psychology must, Dr. Feifel urges, expand its horizons, reconsider its philosophical heritage, and develop a theory of man based not on an obsolete physical model but rather on the existential richness of full, and distinctly human, living.

There was a time, not too long ago, when psychology was considered to be a branch of philosophy—Psychology was Philosophy 5 in my undergraduate days—and philosophy was considered to be the queen and mother of sciences. Major divisions of philosophy were logic which dealt with rules of reasoning, epistemology which concerned itself with cognitive problems, and metaphysics which analyzed problems of being, the nature of reality. Affairs of matter and spirit were in the realm of metaphysics—and psychology, often called "mental philosophy," was a legitimate province of metaphysics. Proofs offered were essentially reasoning, usually not supported by empirical data, and superficial observations of selected phenomena. The history of psychology, until the latter part of the 19th century, was essentially one of reflections, some arbitrary decisions, and just plain guesswork. The leading mental philosophy was the theory of "mental faculties."

Then along came the great empirical discoveries and sweeping victories of the natural sciences. Psychology was faced with a decision: either to detach itself from

[1] Reprinted from *Psychological Reports*, 1964, **15**, 415–420, with the permission of the author and the publisher. Paper presented as part of the symposium "Philosophical Psychology," at the annual convention of the California State Psychological Association, San Francisco, December 13, 1963.

metaphysics and follow in the footsteps of the rapidly progressing empirical sciences, or remain with its free play of mind. With Wundt leading the way, psychology veered toward experimental science and began occupying itself with measurable stimuli and responses. The issue of mental faculties was junked. Questions concerning an immortal soul and its relation to a perishable body were enjoined. The subject matter of psychology became experience; its methods combined introspection, i.e., self-observations of the experiencing person and experimentation with regard to subjective phenomena. Steered by the burgeoning experimental psychophysiology and psychophysics developing in Europe, particularly Germany, American psychologists moved to declare the independence of their new science from philosophy and ethics. Experimental and objective study of behavior became the commanding posture.

The long shadow of this orientation can be seen in Galileo and Newton who were the first to systematically combine experimentation and deductive reasoning. They were also perpetrators of metaphysical distinctions with far reaching influences on man's view of the world. Galileo divided the attributes of perceived objects into two classes: the "primary qualities" of mass and extension, which he believed to be properties of objects themselves; and all other "secondary qualities," such as color, taste, smell, hotness, which he considered merely subjective sensations in the observer's mind produced by atomic particles constituting the real world. The basis he himself gave for speaking of primary qualities was their permanence. It is clear that he was actually attributing to external reality only those properties, namely, mass and velocity, with which he, as a physicist, had been able to deal successfully. In other words, he constructed a metaphysics out of a method. It was easier to get ahead in the reduction of nature to a system of mathematical equations by supposing that nothing existed outside the human mind not so reducible. The development of this viewpoint in the complete dualism of Descartes and the total materialism of Hobbes is well known—and in the French Enlightment (Laplace), it became the groundwork for a thoroughgoing naturalism and mechanism (Barbour, 1960).

Back to our more contemporary story—the history of psychology is very much one of changing of views, doctrines, and images about what to copy in the natural sciences—especially, physics. In the late 19th century, as I have indicated, this implied extension of the experimental method to subjective phenomena. For early behaviorism, it meant the use of experimental method exactly as in physics. By the late 20's there was much objective experimentation in psychology but few bodies of clearly stated predictive principles comparable to the crowning achievements of physics—Newtonian mechanics, relativity theory. Instead, experimentation sometimes seemed aimless and theoretical hypotheses were loosely related to data. Thus, the beginning 30's brought with it emulation of the natural science *theoretical* method. It is no secret that the primary source from which psychology borrowed its notion of scientific enterprise, especially at theoretical levels, was the logical positivistic philosophy of the late 20's and early 30's (Koch, 1959).

This, it was felt, would bring psychology into line with physics and mathematics. A consequence was restraint in investigating consciousness as a datum as well as neglect of the personality sector. In these domains, relatively few concrete operations could be performed, few were repeatable or public. Undoubtedly, this is a major reason why so many psychologists have failed to take an interest in the existential richness of human life. We incline to tackle those problems which yield to acceptable operations. Hence, the high promotion of areas as animal psychology and mathematical psychology—and the slim attention given to those of religion, values, selfhood—at least, in American psychology (Allport, 1955).

The influence of logical positivism upon psychology was unquestionably whole-some, in part. It was responsible for developing imposing diagnostic instruments, discrediting anecdotal data, and stimulating demand for more exacting standards of evidence. Additionally, it was responsible for more intelligible communication because of its stress on operational definition. But, it also brought stultifying effects, e.g., tending to exclude explanation in terms of inner traits, purposes, or interests. Since nothing that occurs between stimulus and response was observable, no "intervening variables" were admissible. Explanatory efforts are confined to events lying outside the organism. The pulsation of real life is muted.

Positivism, in its addiction to the physical sciences as exemplary models of all knowledge, undoubtedly expresses the powerful penchant of our time to take physical facts as real above all else. This is, after all, as Barrett (1962) has pointed out, the age of mathematical physics come to a climax with the discovery of nuclear power. It has provided us with tremendous explanatory leverage but to adopt it as a para-digm for *all* knowledge leaves unanswered the question of whether the science of man, lagging so disastrously behind the power of destruction already achieved in the physical sciences, can best be advanced by extensively imitating methods of the physical sciences. The Cartesian dualism between the cognitive and emotive, with disparagement of the latter in scientific circles, is an expression of the fragmentation of modern man. Positivism leans toward splitting the world of science and the world of man.

Ironically, while psychology sought to dissociate itself from its possessive mother philosophy, physics formed new alliances with it. While psychology had recourse to "objectivity," post-Newtonian physics increasingly operated on the basis of a field theory which, as in Heisenberg's principle of indeterminacy, recognized that the observer was part of the observational event. Likewise, while most psychologists continued to accept a Cartesian subject-object dualism which predicated that the categories of "reality" were isomorphic with those of conception and language, the natural sciences increasingly rejected the subject-object distinction. While psychologists sought "naked facts," such philosophers as Collingwood were demonstrating the inextricable intertwining of "fact and interpretation" (Douglas, 1963).

Twentieth century physics has become aware of the way in which metaphysical assumptions influence our methodology and vice versa. Naturalism is a live option but it must be defended as a philosophical viewpoint and not as a conclusion of science. Caution exists in utilizing method to determine our concept of reality.

One is reminded of the astronomer Eddington's parable of the man studying deep-sea life by means of a net of ropes of a two-inch mesh—who, afterwards, concluded "there are no fish smaller than two inches in the sea!"

I am told that the philosophy of science talked about in the psychological literature is about 25 years out-of-date—and reflects minimally, if at all, new philosophical evolvements, e.g., the liberalization which has taken place in logical positivism, and such cognate movements as neo-pragmatism and English analytic philosophy. Apparently, psychology still bases its understanding of the vital question of method on an extrinsic philosophy of science which, in some ways, is more than two decades behind the times (Koch, 1959). We psychologists have become too bewitched by methodology, analysis, and operational definition at the expense of purpose, anxiety, conditions of well-being, and redemption. Man cannot be grasped in his totality by a behavioristic psychology which excludes these from its purview.

From the earliest days of the experimental pioneers and ever since our existence as an independent science, as Koch (1959) has rightfully specified, psychology has not courageously confronted its historically constituted subject-matter. Its desire for scientific respectability has resulted in the erection, at times, of an epistemology and conceptual language which make this difficult.

The events of World War II, the challenge of racism, the defense of democratic values, and the clamor of significant social problems forced psychology to look somewhat beyond its traditional positivism. Further, the "New Look" in perception, the interest in central processes, are influencing psychologists to devaluate the hypothetico-deductive formulation as an end in itself. The consequential entrance of psychology into the bailiwick of personal conflicts involving moral issues and life-choices is also contributing toward a shift in emphasis from the *form* of theoretical formulations to their meaning and illuminative value. An increasing number of psychologists are beginning to realize that the scientific laboratories of Wundt and Titchener and their inheritors—and the Newtonian framework into which many American psychologists are still attempting to fit their phenomena, even after their hero, the physicist, has long since become involved with non-Newtonian concepts —will not do the job of encompassing the full behavior of man (MacLeod, 1957).

A vital psychology must be rooted in man, not in a mathematical physics model. We must see man not principally as a perceiving consciousness nor as an epistemological subject as do Descartes and Hume but as a human person, self-aware, involved with others, and concerned with his salvation. I do not mean to be misunderstood as pleading for return to a willful romanticism or to unreined impressionism, or as oblivious to the considerable contribution of "method." I ask, rather, for a psychology committed to purposive and striving man: one whose scope will not be made parochial by a stricturing philosophy of science; one whose concepts will not be essentially derived from methods of study but rather from the functioning of human life, embodying courage, love, tragedy, will, delight as well as reaction time, memory, maze learning, perception of form and color. Too often have we worked with portions of the human individual and tried to make a virtue of this.

The challenge is to enlarge horizons without sacrificing our gains. Hardly anyone, as Gordon Allport (1955) has observed, wants adequacy of outlook if the resulting system remains a tissue of unverifiable assumptions. But, neither can we derive satisfaction from mere accuracy if the ensuing productions are largely irrelevant to the fundamental problem of "what is man?" Certainly a major, if not the central, task of psychology is formulation of a theory of man. Recent empirical studies increasingly disclose the germaneness of personal Weltanschauung to behavior, and the idea that one's philosophy lies at the nexus of meaning, value, and personality. Explicit or not, the concept of human nature we hold guides our research directions, psychotherapeutic efforts, social conduct, international relationships.

Philosophy is, admittedly, not a revelation of the physical or metaphysical structure of the universe, of the nature of reality. It can, however, underline the predicaments, protests, and aspirations of man. Philosophy is primarily a beacon providing us with a meaning and perspective often disregarded in our worship of naked fact. John Dewey once said that "As long as we worship science and are afraid of philosophy, we shall have no great science" for philosophy is a vision of possibilities grounded on actualities but not determined by them (Hook, 1963). I do not imply that psychology is to entrust philosophy with the responsibility of mapping its future. I do assert that it is myopic to maintain that philosophic analysis is of no relevance to psychology; or that the whole scientific venture has been revealed in an outdated philosophic position to which, *horribile dictu,* too many non-Freudians have become fixated.

In summary, psychology needs to re-examine its philosophic and humanistic heritage in the context of its generic ideal of science. Granted that great verities can begin as poetic or prophetic insights, it still remains true that their views have, in fact, often been shown to be partial, conflicting, and illusory. The seed which ripens into vision may be a gift of the gods but the labor of cultivating it so that it may bear nourishing fruit is the indispensable function of arduous scientific technique. The life of science is in exploration and in the weighing of evidence (Cohen, 1953). We may end up with truths already promulgated by Shakespeare, Spinoza, Dostoevsky but this time they will not be acumen or wisdom alone but also demonstrable truths. Psychology is an arena where humanist and physicist-engineer cultures, presently insulated and at cross-purposes with one another, intersect. It may be that psychology, in helping to determine dimensions of probable truth, will hopefully diminish contentions among philosophies of man, and that a re-scrutiny of its philosophic legacy will permit it to talk and communicate more meaningfully and pertinently with the humanities and general body of human thought.

REFERENCES

Allport, G. W. *Becoming: basic considerations for a psychology of personality.* New Haven: Yale University Press, 1955.

Barbour, I. G. The methods of science and religion. In H. Shapley (Ed.), *Science ponders religion*. New York: Appleton-Century-Crofts, 1960. Pp. 196–215.

Barrett, W. Introduction. In W. Barrett & H. D. Aiken (Eds.), *Philosophy in the twentieth century*. Vol. 3. *Positivism*. New York: Random House, 1962. Pp. 3–21.

Cohen, M. R. *Reason and nature: an essay on the meaning of scientific method.* (2nd ed.) Glencoe, Ill.: Free Press, 1953.

Douglas, W. Religion. In N. L. Farberow (Ed.), *Taboo topics*. New York: Atherton Press, 1963. Pp. 80–95.

Hook, S. *The quest for being.* New York: Dell, 1963.

Koch, S. Epilogue. In S. Koch (Ed.), *Psychology: a study of a science.* Vol. 3. *Foundations of the person and the social context.* New York: McGraw-Hill, 1959. Pp. 730–788.

MacLeod, R. B. Teleology and theory of human behavior. *Science*, 1957, **125**, 477–480.

5. Philosophical Embarrassments of Psychology[1]

Herbert Feigl

In this erudite discussion, Dr. Feigl presents a strong case for the productive utility of philosophy of science when it is able to serve as critic and catalyst for both theoretical and methodological efforts in science. Such an effort in psychology is discussed in terms of several philosophical embarrassments or perplexities pertaining to psychology as a science. For example, theories so formulated that they are "irrefutable by *any* sort of evidence" constitute what he calls a methodological embarrassment. However, the most serious philosophical perplexity for psychology involves the definition of its subject matter, and the problem of subjective versus behavioral experience is pursued with fresh insights into this long-standing and much repressed issue. Modern scientific psychology, it is argued, must free itself from the constraining influences of radical empiricism of the behavioristic and operationistic variety. A more liberal attitude toward the development of scientific theory is called for.

PSYCHOLOGY AMONG THE SCIENCES

It is customary to assign to psychology a place in the system of the sciences, somewhere straddling the fence between the natural and the social sciences. This is to say that, if we first distinguish the formal sciences (i.e., pure logic and mathematics) from the empirical or factual sciences, psychology is clearly one among the latter; and in some of its divisions like psychophysics and psychophysiology, as well as in the behavioristic studies of the learning processes, psychology shares many of the characteristics of the natural sciences; it is in this respect closely akin to, and allied with, biology. But when it comes to clinical psychology, psychoanalysis, the psychology of thought, to social and anthropological psychology, the relation to the social and cultural sciences appears much closer. Possibly under the influence

[1] Reprinted in part from the *American Psychologist*, 1959, **14**, 115–128. Copyright 1959 by the American Psychological Association, and reproduced by permission of the author and the publisher. Invited Address delivered at the sixty-sixth Annual Convention of the American Psychological Association, Washington, D.C., August 31, 1958.

of certain philosophical doctrines, some psychologists (but they are a minority) still insist on a fundamental difference not only in subject matter, but also and especially in *method*, between the natural and the social sciences.

Thus it has been claimed that the natural sciences are "nomothetic" while the social sciences are "idiographic." This means that the natural sciences are supposed to concentrate on the discovery of general laws whereas the social sciences are said to concentrate on unique and individual cases and events. This seems plausible enough if one compares, e.g., theoretical physics with history. But there are idiographic natural sciences—such as descriptive astronomy, physical geography— and even such historical disciplines as paleontology. And there are clearly nomothetic social sciences such as sociology or economics. Even if you question their success in the discovery of reliable laws in these fields, the intent of the research is undeniably nomothetic. I think many of the recurrent disputes in regard to this issue can be settled by a recognition and proper allocation of the nomothetic (generalizing) and the idiographic (individualizing) components in the natural as well as the social sciences. Even if we feel that we do not have very precise and reliable theories of personality in current psychology, the very concepts which have been introduced in this discipline lend themselves to both: the description of the individual case, *and* the formulation of general regularities. These regularities may be only of a *statistical* character, but this still does not diminish their difference from individual description.

Cutting a little more deeply, there is the related alleged difference between *explaining* and *understanding*. Various schools of thought—mostly of German descent—have emphasized this as a fundamental distinction between the natural and the social sciences. To come down to specific examples, we are told that the regularities, e.g., concerning negative afterimages or concerning thresholds and limens in psychophysics, are not in any way "understandable" in the manner in which we can understand that frustration engenders aggression, that success leads to greater self-confidence, or that some given premises lead a thinker to draw a special conclusion. The role of the phenomenological approach, the importance of *empathy*, has been stressed by certain representatives of clinical psychology. It had of course also been an important tenet of Gestalt psychology. "Intuition," "insight," "understanding," and "empathy" have been key words in the strife of psychological movements. These terms are used honorifically by one party, but they are suspect (if not on the *index verborum prohibitorum*) with the other party.

But I think the dust and the heat of the disputes now are clearing away. We recognize that, especially in the psychology of human motivation, and in psychodynamics generally, empathy is an often helpful and important heuristic tool. But we realize also that empathetic judgments can go woefully wrong, no matter how strong their intuitive conviction. Empathy may be a *source* of knowledge in that it *suggests* hypotheses. But it is not self-authenticating. Objective tests alone can confirm the correctness of these "hunches." The philosophical embarrassment here arises out of a confusion between the origin and the justification of knowledge-claims. Once we distinguish between the psychological roots and the methodological validation of our judgments, there remains no fundamental difference in the type of justification legitimately applied in the natural and the social sciences. This may be recognized quickly if "understanding" is seen to rest on familiarization. Familiarity breeds intuition; but it is neither a necessary nor a sufficient condition for scientific explanation. In the more advanced physical sciences highly abstract theories possess great explanatory power, but the postulates of those theories are not in the least self-evident or intuitively convincing. They are effective premises for the sort of derivation which constitute scientific explanations. We should not feel constrained to explain the new, the surprising, or the unfamiliar exclusively on the basis of old, customary, and familiar premises. To be sure, it is pleasant if it can be done this way, but, I repeat, this is neither necessary nor sufficient for a good scientific explanation.

The phrase "clinical experience has shown . . ." is sometimes intended to disparage or discourage independent objective tests. Freud, for example, despite his respect for the scientific method and his general naturalistic outlook, was not interested in the experimental confirmation of his doctrines. But though it is admittedly difficult to test psychoanalytic hypotheses, it seems imperative at least to formulate them in such a way that an experimental confirmation or disconfirmation becomes possible. I have no particular partisan axe to grind in regard to psychoanalytic theory or any other school of thought in contemporary psychology. The philosopher of science can afford, and should sincerely attempt, to remain above the battle. After all, we philosophers operate mostly by hindsight anyway. Do not expect us to blaze many new scientific trails—those glorious times are over. Altogether too many philosophers have sold their birthright for a pot of message! (The "prophet motive" operates here! This is part of *our* embarrassment.) In view of the enormous complexity of modern scientific research, we have had to lower our level of aspiration. We are glad if we can provide a clearer understanding of the scientific enterprise. But here, I am confident, we can fulfill a useful auxiliary role; especially in collaboration with productive scientists we can serve as critics and catalysts. This is the sort of thing we have been doing at the Minnesota Center for Philosophy of Science—in connection with psychological as well as with physical theory.

After this modest advertisement I return to the issues of Understanding vs. Explaining: Hardheaded psychologists, especially those of radically behaviorist convictions, usually repudiate psychoanalytic interpretations as so much fantasy or metaphysics. But let us see whether the wheat cannot be separated from the chaff; or, if you permit a horrible shift in metaphors, whether we cannot save the baby while throwing out only the dirty bath water. As is well known, Freud himself considered his theory as "monolithic"; i.e., he did not permit his disciples to pick and choose among its postulates. Only wholesale acceptance or wholesale rejection seemed legitimate to the grand old man. But this is surely not in accordance with Freud's own procedure. On numerous occasions he revised parts of his doctrine— no doubt on the basis of clinical experience! Even from a logical point of view it must be admitted that scientific theories consist of relatively independently testable hypotheses. It is true, and has been stressed ever since Pierre Duhem and Henri Poincaré, that there are no *strictly* crucial experiments. But this is simply a logical triviality, viz., that a particular experimental finding can never establish the truth *or* the falsity of a single hypothesis which is part of a whole set of postulates. But careful experimental or statistical designs can group and regroup the to-be-tested hypotheses in such a way that the probabilities of confirmation or of disconfirmation become so significant as to be practically sufficient for the (always tentative) acceptance or rejection of a given hypothesis. As we empiricist philosophers must never forget to repeat: Scientific truth can be held only "until further notice," such notice to be given when contrary evidence crops up.

Now there are theories (and some of the Freudian doctrines are examples) which are so conceived as to be irrefutable by *any* sort of evidence. But these are the excesses of the psychoanalytic creed. When we consider the Eros-Thanatos doctrine, i.e., the attempts of explaining behavior in terms of life and death instincts, we find that it explains too much, namely, *any* conceivable type of behavior. This, far from being a virtue, vitiates the theory. Theories of this sort—I am tempted to call them manichaean—are (usually unwittingly) made immune against any conceivable test. They are proof against disproof. They constitute a *methodological* embarrassment. The history of scientific and philosophic thought offers many parallel examples. Doctrines of material substance, of an indestructible soul, of absolute space and time, the phlogiston hypothesis in early chemistry, the ether hypothesis in its comatose last ditch stand, the speculations about vital forces or entelechies in biology, etc., have all been defended in a manner that precludes even the most indirect or incomplete confirmations or disconfirmations. Closer logical analysis reveals that the factual content claimed for such doctrines and hypotheses simply does not exist. This may come about in the following ways: Some of the key terms of the doctrine may fail to have empirical significance in that they are completely severed from any and all observation bases. This in turn may be the result either of (implicit or explicit) stipulation, or it may come to pass by a process most aptly described as "whittling away" whatever empirical meaning those key terms may have had to begin with. In the case of Freud's manichaean doctrine, very much like in the case of the older formulations of the pleasure-displeasure principle in British psychology, the factual emptiness results from a slide into tautology. It is like the well known rule for weather prediction: "The weather will either remain the same or it will change." The quest for certainty, the craving for infallibility, has produced the embarrassments of *emptiness* and *circularity*. If behavior is to be explained or be predicted on the basis of Eros or Thanatos, and if the only criterion supplied for deciding which of the two to adduce is the actual conduct, then there can be no explanation or prediction at all.

It would however be grossly unfair to psychoanalytic theory if, in the light of these criticisms, we were to repudiate it altogether. There are much more substantial contributions in the theories concerning the unconcious. The mechanisms of repression and of defense, the interpretation of dreams, the psychopathology of everyday life, the explanations of neurotic behavior, etc., are in principle capable of empirical examination. But here again, tough-minded operationists and radical behaviorists have criticized the theories as metaphysical and have attempted to reduce their tenable core to empirical regularities concerning the positive or negative reinforcement of behavior.

Before I turn to a more general discussion about the nature of, and the need for, theories in psychology, there are a few remarks to be made about the notion of *evidence* in psychological explanation, interpretation, and prediction. Let us take as examples the psychoanalytic view of dreams and of free associations. As I have already mentioned, the intuitive conviction carried by some of these interpretations may by far outrun anything that a scientifically minded psychologist would grant in terms of objective probabilities. The high level of aspiration in experimental science seems to prevent acknowledgment of the cognitive significance of such weak indicators as are at the disposal of the clinical psychologist or psychoanalyst.

But if we reject these indicators as evidence, we would in all consistency have to reject likewise the clues in historical research or in detective work. Straightforward experimental procedures and even explicit statistical designs are here scarcely applicable. This is a matter of stark practical impossibility. But historical and detective methods may be quite scientific in that they consist in a careful scrutiny and critical comparison of the various items of evidence. If the historian ascribes a given painting to an individual artist of the fifteenth century, he utilizes clues of various sorts and of course holds his interpretation open to further confirmation, as well as possibly to disconfirmation, by whatever relevant evidence may be discovered later on. This is not different in principle from such reconstructions of past events as we find in geology or paleontology. To be sure, if we define the scientific character of an hypothesis in terms of a criterion of strict *predictability*, most of what goes on in historical studies of any kind would be relegated to the limbo of the unscientific or the nonscientific endeavors. But surely, this is too narrow a view of the scientific enterprise. The specific and detailed features of an island that arose out of volcanic activities, or of a canyon that was formed by erosion, could not have been predicted before these events happened. The particular shape of the devastation or the shambles produced by an earthquake are unforeseeable. The *particular* structures and functions of plants and animals as they came about in the evolution of the species will very likely remain unexplained. But the ex post facto explanation of the *gross* features of the respective results (i.e., the general features of the island, of the canyon, of the devastation, of the organisms) is perfectly legitimate.

Mutatis mutandis this may be applied to human behavior. The particular manner in which a murder or a suicide was executed would generally not have been predictable on the basis of even a fairly complete knowledge of the antecedent circumstances. Similarly, just which specific images occur in the manifest content of a dream may forever remain unpredictable. But this need not prevent a psychoanalytic interpretation of the manifest image as a symbol. Just what specific free associations will be produced in response to a certain stimulus situation may well remain equally unforeseeable. But this again does not exclude an explanation of the emitted verbal responses on the basis of assumed unconscious mental states as long as these are accessible through other independent avenues of confirmation.

The diffidence with which predictions and explanations of this type are treated by tough-minded scientists may have much to do with a fixation on the well known *deductive* model of inference. But once it is realized that the deductive model fits only some very special cases, and is applicable even to these only by way of considerable idealization, a more liberal attitude may well be accepted. There are perfectly good explanations not only in common life but also in the sciences in which the derivation of the facts or regularities to be explained from the laws and the conditions which provide the explanation is no more than *probabilistic*. Deductive necessity can be had only *more geometrico*. The classical theories of mechanics, thermodynamics, and electromagnetics were deductive systems, owing mainly to the deterministic form in which their postulates were cast. With the intrusion of probabilistic and statistical concepts even in basic physics, the deductive model must now be regarded as an ideal limit case. And in the light of pertinent scientific evidence it is highly precarious to hope for successive approximations which will take us anywhere near this limit. (Perhaps I should remark here that my previous definition of free will does not presuppose a *strict* determinism. A statistical type of causality is perfectly sufficient for the ascription of responsibility.)

The ways and means of behavior, I conclude, may not ever be more accurately predictable than probabilistically. But this is sufficient for an (equally probabilistic) type of explanation. Out of the thousands of images or words that may occur in a given situation one only actually occurs. This specific item has therefore only an extremely low probability. But in the light of psychoanalytic theory (i.e., if we could only fully spell it out) there is always a *class* of responses which is greatly more probable than the class of all alternative responses. The difficult job to be done consists in specifying the first class in terms of its defining characteristics. Here, too, we should not and need not aspire to too much precision. Classes with vague borderlines are used commonly and profitably in many sciences. Perhaps one way of getting at the defining characteristics would be by utilizing the intuitive experiences of empathizers as a first guide. After all, something very similar is done in the construction of personality and other psychological tests. Later validations can correct whatever errors are due to the original "bootstraps" procedure. Prima facie this might seem to re-establish the difference between the social and the natural sciences which I have been at pains to deny. But remembering the helpful distinction between the context of discovery and the context of justification we can recognize that criteria which have their origin in clinical intuition may later be validated objectively and scientifically. We may even be able subsequently to explain the workings of intuition.

Let me illustrate this by a story (no doubt a canard) which appeared in the newspapers a long time ago. A doctor had a dog that would bark in a peculiar way when confronted with patients who had an incipient cancer. The cancers were in such an early stage of development that they could not be detected by the usual (x-ray, etc.) methods. Just how the dog managed this marvelous feat was completely obscure. But, if one wanted to be "scientific" about it, the relative frequency of "correct" barkings could be ascertained statistically. Once it is established that this frequency is significantly above chance, then the question of how to explain this fact may be tackled. (This is, after all, the attitude many psychologists take in regard to graphology, or in regard to extrasensory perception.) I suggest that the clinical psychologist, and the empathizer generally, is his own diagnosis dog. If and only if a high "batting average" can be established, on the basis of subsequent objective evidence, is he entitled to some confidence in his diagnoses. This way of looking at the matter should satisfy even a rigorous behaviorist.

DEFINITION OF SUBJECT MATTER

This brings me to what is perhaps the most painful philosophical embarrassment of psychology: the definition of its very subject matter. As the well known saying goes: psychology first lost its soul, later its consciousness, and seems now in danger of losing its mind altogether. I know very well that the specification of psychology's subject matter is highly controversial. The disputes concerning it seem to be emotionally highly charged, if, for no other reason, then certainly because of the perennially puzzling mind-body problem. This problem is currently not fashionable, not even in pure philosophy. I think that the behaviorist revolution in psychology has much to do with this state of affairs. According to my own diagnosis, the mind-body problem has been repressed, and all sorts of defense mechanism have been developed to evade this issue which traditionally has been so closely tied up with theology, religion, and metaphysics. Powerful emotions are elicited whenever we touch questions of *Weltenschauung*. I do not flatter myself that I could desensitize many of you in the course of a few brief remarks. But perhaps I can at least suggest to you that repression of the problem merely produces troublesome symptoms—paradoxes and perplexities in this case—and that philosophical analysis can provide a helpful catharsis. Judging by recent publications in theoretical and methodological matters, the issues of introspective vs. behavioristic, of phenomenological vs. neurophysiological psychology crop up again and again, and with remarkable tenacity. The *Zeitgeist* may not be favorable for a revival of these traditional issues, but since I believe there is a genuine possibility for a constructive solution, I shall take the liberty of briefly sketching it out for you. (I must ask you to forgive the somewhat dogmatic tone of my presentation. It took me over a hundred pages in an essay (Feigl, 1958) published earlier this year to deal with the major facets of this badly tangled problem.)

If we extricate the mind-body problem from its traditional theological and metaphysical background, there remain nevertheless a number of questions which are apt to produce intellectual discomfort, if not anxiety. The central issue is this: Can we give a logically consistent and scientifically acceptable account of the relations between subjective immediate experience on the one hand and behavioral or neurophysiological processes on the other? The traditional answers are well known to you. (Psychology textbooks used to mention them at least in the introductory chapter.) They are: dualistic interactionism, psychophysiological parallelism (usually in the form of epiphenomenalism), the double aspect doctrine, and the theory of emergent evolution. The endless disputes between these different attempts at a solution of our "riddle of the universe" have been so discouraging that many thinkers—in the camps of philosophy as well as psychology—have tried to undercut the whole issue. They have tried to show that this is a pseudoproblem which need not trouble us. But, as I hope to show you, these are maneuvers of evasion. Prominent among them are phenomenalism (or neutral monism) and logical behaviorism. Characteristically, the positivist movement in more than a century of vigorous influence upon epistemology and philosophy of science has embraced sometimes the one and at other times the other of these points of view. But both phenomenalism and radical behaviorism must be accused of committing reductive fallacies. The phenomenalists reduce our concepts concerning physical objects to logical constructions out of the data of direct experience. And the logical behaviorists reduce "mentalistic" concepts (including those that refer to direct experience) to logical constructions out of the publicly observable peripheral behavior. (If we are not to spend hours on formal technicalities, I shall have to ask you to let me get by with these rather loose characterizations.) It appeared for a while that we must choose between a reductive view (of either sort) and a metaphysical solution of the mind-body problem. Metaphysical solutions are abhorred by the tough-minded scientists —though they have been tempting to the speculative philosopher. I have called them "seductive" fallacies, because they arise out of wishful thinking.

Is there no *via media* between the philosophies of the "nothing but" and the philosophy of the "something more"? My own way of thinking in these matters was dubbed by my students as "Feigelian dialectics." That is to say that I discern and recommend a constructive *synthesis* of the *thesis* of tender-minded and the *antithesis* of tough-minded thinking. (You will remember that William James, a long time ago, proposed this sort of resolution of philosophical issues. James himself, however, never found a satisfactory equilibrium. He vacillated between radical empiricism and an early form of functionalism. Perhaps I should also remark that my approach has precious little in common with either Hegelian or Marxian dialectics. I do not plead for a new logic. I use the dialectical pattern only as a means of exposition.) In short, I suggest that instead of committing ourselves to either a philosophy of the "nothing but" or of the "something more," we adopt a philosophy of the "*what's what*"! That is to say that we need not impoverish the world by absurd reductions, nor enrich it by unconfirmable projections. We may, instead, follow the lead of the scientific method: ascertaining what there is and attempting to explain and formulate it in a clear, coherent, and parsimonious manner.

More specifically, I plead for a monistic, naturalistic view of the mental and the physical, allowing for a qualified reinstatement of the introspective and phenomenological approaches; and I look to neurophysiological theory for an eventual emendation and supplementation of behavior theories. At first this may sound to you either cheaply eclectic or hopelessly programmatic, if not utopian. But there are increasing indications that such a synthesis is not only logically possible, but that it is a fruitful direction of research. To bring this closer home to you, and to make it more concrete, I would say (even at the risk of shocking part of my audience) that an approach such as Donald Hebb's *Organization of Behavior* may well supplement B. F. Skinner's *Behavior of Organisms*. (I have been wondering whether Hebb had chosen the title of his book in contrast and opposition to that of Skinner's.) Clark Hull's neurophysiological speculations, it is true, were rather idle wheels in the machinery of his system, but his basic methodological orientation at least provided a place for neurophysiological theory. Edward C. Tolman's "intervening variables" may yet turn out to be hypothetical constructs or theoretical concepts which will correspond to neurophysiological concepts in a more complete theory à la Hebb, perhaps in the not-too-distant future. Some of Kurt Lewin's field theoretical and dynamic concepts have been absorbed in Tolman's approach, and would in any case in principle be open to the same neurophysiological specification. This is, of course, in keeping with the original isomorphism doctrine, especially in the form given to it by Wolfgang Köhler. Add to this the promising contributions of Norbert Wiener, Warren McCulloch, and others, along the lines of cybernetics, and we have at least the beginnings of a theory of those intriguing teleological (i.e., goal directed and self-regulating) processes which in earlier times drove some philosophers, and even some psychologists, into a defeatist vitalism.

I realize that there are a great many empirical questions yet to be settled in this highly controversial area. But it does seem to me, at least from the vantage point of my philosophical armchair, that the doctrine of isomorphism has a good deal of experimental evidence in its favor. I think, moreover, that the doctrine has been subjected to unjustifiable criticisms by behaviorists and operationists. The reintroduction of introspection, the new concern with the phenomenal field, the clinical attention to subjective experience, the studies in social perception, etc., seem to me to indicate, not indeed a regression to an obsolete psychology, but rather an advance along the spiral (or should I say "helix"?) of the evolution of the scientific outlook.

The limitations of the introspective and phenomenological approach are realized and admitted. We are aware of the sources of error in introspective description and phenomenological-clinical observation and interpretation; and being aware, we can apply measures to correct these errors. If we refrain from fallaciously reducing subjective experience to response patterns, we may well reinstate the classical distinction between mental states and their behavioral manifestations. It is precisely because we have been cautioned by the behaviorists that we can do this with greater sophistication, and hence with a better intellectual conscience. And thinking the situation through to its logical conclusion, we may go beyond a timid psychophysiological parallelism and hold an identity theory of the mental and the physical. That is to say that the data of subjective experience are identical with certain central states of behavior theory, and thus ultimately with certain neurophysiological states. Let me indicate the logic of these identifications by way of a succinct outline.

As I diagnose one of the main motives of classical behaviorism, it was the problem of our knowledge of other minds which constituted the major philosophical embarrassment. Professional philosophers have carried on agonizing discussions over this puzzle. The admitted impossibility for one person to inspect another person's mental contents seemed to conflict with the firm beliefs of commonsense. Even if, in ordinary life or in clinical observation, we claim to apprehend fairly directly or intuitively what goes on in the other person, it was rightly maintained that this—by itself—does not constitute a justification for our assertions about other minds. The obvious gambit of using analogy arguments for such a justification seemed excluded because of a fundamental difference between this particular application of analogical reasoning from the ordinary type of analogical argument. In most ordinary cases the conclusion can be independently verified with the same directness and to the same degree of certainty as the premises of the argument. But just this is fundamentally impossible in the case of the inference to other minds. Aided and abetted by the positivists, the behaviorists insisted on a criterion of meaning according to which only objectively verifiable assertions are scientifically meaningful. Introspection as such did not seem to qualify—unless interpreted (as already suggested by John B. Watson) as a response to previous responses. The objectively certifiable behavior of organisms, along with, and in the same sense as, the processes and events in the lifeless or inorganic realm, was considered the only legitimate subject matter of science. No wonder then that behaviorism (as Max Mayer put it so strikingly in the title of his 1921 book) became "the psychology of the other one." (To be sure, there are other facets of behaviorism, such as the emphasis on the experimental method and the faith in environmentalism; but these are irrelevant in the present context.)

You may feel that since the battle of behaviorism was fought some 30 or 40 years ago, that there is no point in reviewing it today. But I surmise we might get a very different picture in a current opinion poll among psychologists. Even the positivists have mended their ways. They have liberalized their erstwhile extremely restrictive meaning criterion. That is the main reason why most of them prefer to label themselves as "logical empiricists" or "scientific empiricists." These new party designations are intended to convey the shift from verifiability to *confirmability*. That is to say that we no longer insist on complete and direct testing, but that we consider any statement as scientifically meaningful if it is at least incompletely and/or indirectly testable.

The problem of other persons' mental states thus appears in a very different light. As long as we conceive of mental states, be they our own or those of others, as part and parcel of a network of lawfully related facts, they are no longer inaccessible to confirmation, i.e., to indirect verification. The phenomenal data of one's own experience are of course susceptible to direct verification, they are open to immediate inspection. And in keeping with our commonsense convictions, we have every reason to identify these directly inspected or inspectable states with mental states imputed to us by others or, after a little scientific refinement, with the central states of modern behavior theories. What will *not* work in this connection is a purely peripheralistic behaviorism. As I have pleaded before, peripheral stimulus situations and response patterns may serve as (probabilistic) indicators of central (i.e., mental) states, but they cannot be identified with them. Even B. F. Skinner—perhaps the most consistent among the behaviorists—now has a place for something like private central states in his conceptual scheme of things. Of course this privacy is not the "absolute" privacy of the metaphysicians. It is the relative, practical privacy familiar from everyday life and admitted by any psychologist who accepts confirmability, but does not insist on direct verifiability.

The embarrassment of unanswerable questions can be avoided if we do not introduce absolutely unconfirmable entities into our theories. Such puzzles as that of the "inverted spectrum" illustrate this vividly. This ancient poser has been revived a great many times and caused innumerable philosophical headaches. The question is: Even if two subjects A and B perform equally well in thorough color discrimination tests, could they not "privately" experience different color qualities? Could there not be a systematic difference between A and B, such that A experiences, e.g., green when B experiences red, and vice versa, throughout the whole circle of pure hues? If it is further assumed that all other behavior tests, and even neurophysiological investigations do not reveal any significant individual differences between A and B, then the scientifically minded psychologist feels he can rest his case and assert that the color experiences are similar in A and B. But the metaphysician insists that there might be differences in the private experiences which remain forever and absolutely incapable of objective test.

Shall we just shrug our shoulders and give up on philosophers who make life so difficult for themselves? Perhaps we can attempt a little philosophical therapy. We might show the philosopher that he has illegitimately extended ordinary or empirical doubt and thus fallen into metaphysical doubt. Ordinary empirical doubt may occasionally be hard to settle. But if it is transformed into metaphysical doubt, then there is no conceivable way of settling it by either logical argument or by empirical demonstration. Will this cure the metaphysician? Not necessarily. He may grant that unanswerable questions should be kept out of science, but that they are a worthy subject of puzzlement for the philosopher. But if the philosopher remains forever puzzled, this is a most frustrating state of affairs even to him. Perhaps we can suggest that the philosopher's mistake consists in conceiving of color experience merely on the basis of his direct acquaintance with the qualities he experiences, that he lifts this concept artificially and arbitrarily out of the rich network of causal relations which constitutes the meaning of the concept in ordinary discourse, and even more fully so in scientific knowledge. Perhaps we can show him that on the basis of all these lawful relations his concepts of mental qualities can be recognized as denoting the very same referents that terms of behavior theory (and ultimately of physiological theory) also denote.

This view of co-reference of different terms, as I have already hinted, may well be the key to the solution of the mind-body problem. And it would thus also solve, or rather *dissolve*, the embarrassing puzzles concerning our knowledge of other minds. As long as, in the spirit of the scientific method, we require that it must in principle be possible to *give reasons* for our knowledge claims, we must never entertain knowledge claims that are entirely and absolutely divorced from, and hence unsupportable by, empirical evidence. Philosophical doubt concerning other minds is in this respect similar to philosophical doubt about the occurrence of past events. There is no logical guarantee—so the skeptic argues—that the laws of nature might not have changed from period to period, and that therefore our inferences of past events are hopelessly precarious. He might even go so far as to say that there was no past at all and that the universe originated with a bang a second ago, with all the so-called remnants (geological strata, fossils, memories, etc.). This is just as irrefutable as is solipsism, but of course just as insanely irrational. A little reflection suffices to show that the very meaning and essence of rational belief, as we understand it in common life and in science, includes most prominently the "normal" procedures of inductive and analogical inference, as well as of the hypothetico-deductive or hypothetico-probabilistic methods of theory construction.

The mind-body problem need no longer be evaded or repressed. Advances in science as well as in logical analysis have helped in freeing us from its metaphysical shudders. An explicit uncovering of the various functions of language and of the corresponding types of significance may break whatever resistance still remains against the sort of identity or co-reference view I am advocating. Language serves all sorts of purposes. It may be used for the sake of the fomulation and the communication of information. This is *cognitive* meaning. But it may also express or evoke images, emotions; and it may be used in eliciting action or in the molding of dispositions or attitudes. The alleged gulf between the qualities of the mental and the physical, I submit, are largely due to the images which we connect with the use of *physical* concepts. "How can the processes in central nervous systems or the cortex be identical with mind or subjective experience?" If you conceive the brain as that grayish mass you perceive upon opening a skull, or if you visualize the protein molecules of the nervous tissues in terms of the tinkertoy models chemistry instructors show to their classes, then it is indeed impossible to form any consistent idea of mind-body identity. But this is picture-thinking. Pictures and illustrative models are a help, heuristically or didactically. But even in basic theoretical physics such pictures are now at best regarded as an intellectual scaffolding which is to be removed once the building of knowledge has been erected. "Thou shalt not make graven images unto thee!" The proper factual content of physical theories is strictly speaking unvisualizable. It consists in the abstract conceptual formulation of the postulates which are connected by correspondence rules (usually probabilistic ones) with the observables in various domains of evidence. The description of a neural process in abstract physical terms may therefore be interpreted as referring to the very same events which may be described also in phenomenal language on the basis of introspection.

Psychological theories, such as those of molar behaviorism or those of Freudian psychodynamics, use theoretical concept which, perhaps after some revisions or refinements, may well dovetail with certain concepts of neurophysiology. I can see no objection in principle or from a *logical* point of view against the possibility of such a final identification. Any serious doubts about it must be empirical ones and concern the explicability of behavior on a neurophysiological basis. In this connection both the psychologist and the philosopher had better be cautious and await further evidence. For example, the facts of parapsychology—if indeed they are facts and not due to experimental error, hoax, or fraud—might well force upon us a thorough reconsideration of the very framework of presuppositions in psychophysiology. But there is, as far as I know, not even a glimmer as yet of an acceptable and responsible theory of these curious phenomena. As an empiricist I have at least to go through the motions of an open mind on this topic.

PROBLEMS OF THEORY CONSTRUCTION

Let me conclude this long paper with a few more explicit remarks about the problems of theory construction in psychology. The embarrassment here is a *methodological* one; and to the historian and logician of science it is familiar from parallels in the development of physics and chemistry. There have been proponents as well as opponents of theory construction both in the physical as well as in the behavioral sciences. The philosophical perplexity consists in the question: What do theories enable the scientist to do that he could not do with the aid of straightforward empirical generalizations? The two parties to this dispute are the theoreticians and the radical empiricists (we call them "dustbowl empiricists" at Minnesota). I must leave it to you to diagnose and to explain the temperamental differences between these character types; this is of course a matter for psychological or cultural-anthropological study. I will only suggest that radical empiricism has a good deal to do with the wish for intellectual security, i.e., with the desire to restrict one's extrapolations to the domain in which they have been thoroughly tested; it also has a good deal to do with the fear of the invisible and intangible. Hypothesis-phobia has often been a personality trait of positivists—that is why they are such *negativists*! The theoreticians on the other hand do not mind living dangerously. This seems commendable as long as they keep their theories open to revision. Fixation on theories is of course a frequent weakness. But rivalry, competition, and fierce criticism are the order of the day and help in the avoidance of dogmatism.

But enough of this dilettante psychology. I wish to tackle the question from a *logical* angle. This requires a little reflection upon the aims of science. If we distinguish the applied sciences, with their aims of control and guidance, from the pure or fundamental sciences, then the aim of the latter may be defined as the attainment of adequate descriptions and explanations. Prediction, vitally important in all practical applications of science, enters pure science primarily as a means of checking the adequacy of laws and theoretical assumptions. It should not be necessary to defend the distinction between description and explanation. Explanation always involves inference or derivation, deductive or probabilistic, as the case may be. Among the premises of an explanation we need at least one law-like assumption, deterministic or statistical in character. It is expedient to restrict the meaning of the word "description" to singular statements of specific facts—or to conjunctions or disjunctions thereof. This makes for a clean distinction of explanation and description.

Now, according to the radical empiricist, the cognitive, factual content of science consists in the descriptive facts and in the regularities formulated in empirical laws. Empirical laws are usually conceived as fairly directly testable functional relations (again, either deterministic or statistical) between observables. It is my impression that the radical empiricists confuse "factual content" with "cash value." The term "cash value" is not intended here in a pejorative sense. I use it merely to designate the kind of information which is eminently useful in the practical applications of scientific knowledge. I would argue, however, that in the very interest of obtaining this sort of "cash value," *theories* have become extremely helpful, and in many fields indispensable. But quite apart from the practical applications, theories have the distinct value of helping us to *understand* the world and man's place in it. Man does not live by bigger and better technologies alone! Through a sort of "heterogony of purposes" (Wundt) or through "functional autonomy" (Allport) civilized man has acquired curiosities which can be satisfied only by adequate and comprehensive explanations. Such explanations can be achieved only with the aid of theories. A good theory enables us to *derive* empirical laws—and not only those which we have already attained by simple generalization, but also others which still remain to be certified experimentally. Theories are thus not merely convenient and compendious summaries of empirical laws, they are heuristically fruitful in that they enable us to infer further, as yet untested regularities.

But right here our antitheorists ask: Suppose we had investigated all empirical regularities of a given domain, would a theory then be more than, at best, an equivalent though compressed and possibly elegant formulation of a set of empirical laws? My answer is in the negative—and for the following reasons. First of all, most of the so-called empirical laws of science are not as empirical as they appear to be. The concepts in terms of which they are formulated are rarely open to straightforward operational definition. I am referring here not only to the usual idealizations and simplifications experimental scientists apply in the formulation of empirical laws. I have in mind especially the *ceteris paribus* clauses which are often implicitly taken for granted. This is tantamount to guessing at a functional relation between certain key variables—a functional relation which would manifest itself in measurements and experiments, if it were not camouflaged by certain obfuscating variables which are not sufficiently known and hence largely beyond control. The empirical laws that psychologists confidently incorporate in their textbooks are thus not as directly testable as they are often made out to be.

Operationism, just like behaviorism or other forms of radical positivism, has had an undeniably helpful influence in the development of recent science. Untestable assumptions have been relegated to the limbo of metaphysics. But it is time to recognize that radical operationism would curtail the enterprise of science very severely indeed. Of course, "operationism" is now often understood in the much more liberal sense of a methodological attitude, insisting on clarity in regard to the rules—according to which we use our terms. And if these rules concern the observational-experimental *as well* as the logico-mathematical procedures, then "operationism" simply becomes synonymous with "good scientific method" and loses its distinctive reductionist emphasis. But the earlier more restrictive operationist ideology is not at all in agreement with the actual procedures of science.

I have anticipated the essential point here already in some of my earlier remarks. Radical operationists, very much like the logical positivists of some 20 or 30 years ago, are so fixated on direct verifiability that they never analyze the implications of (indirect and incomplete) confirmability. But just this is the essential feature of all sciences which advance beyond the observational, fact-collecting ("botanizing") stage. The radical operationist maxim "different operations, different concepts" is severely at variance with the actual manner in which the meaning of theoretical concepts is specified. The most important syntheses and unifications in science depend on the introduction of theoretical concepts through convergent avenues of specification, coming from different, often at first very heterogeneous areas of evidence.

I admit that for a while it did seem plausible to view many scientific concepts as dispositional and hence to define them by means of test operation→test result conditionals. For example, habit strength in Hullian psychology, or expectancy in Tolman's, seemed dispositional in the sense that, though direct observation is impossible (just as in the case of magnetic strength in physics), these concepts could be regarded as shorthand for certain stimulus-response or (more generally) certain empirical regularities in the sequence of test operations and test results. This procedure was formalized by R. Carnap (1936–37) in a very influential essay more than 20 years ago by the device of reduction sentences. But Carnap (1958; see also Hempel, 1958) himself has abandoned this approach, mainly for the reason that even open sets of such reduction sentences do not adequately reconstruct the actual role of theoretical concepts and their relations to the observables.

Ever since the incisive article by MacCorquodale and Meehl (1948) we at Minnesota, as well as Carnap, have found it helpful to distinguish between purely empirical dispositional concepts ("intervening variables" in the narrower sense) and hypothetical constructs (or "theoretical concepts," as they had better be called). Theoretical concepts are introduced by postulates which, as it were, define these concepts implicitly. The meaning of theoretical concepts is thus given by their place in the network of laws—the "nomological net" as we label it. The nomological net is what Einstein used to call a matter of relatively "free construction." It is anchored only in a few places in the facts of observation. Or, in less picturesque language, theories are postulate systems which derive their empirical meaning and factual reference through the correspondence rules by which the theoretical concepts are connected with certain concepts in the observation language. This allows for the empirical confirmation (or disconfirmation) of theories; it also provides for the multiple routes from various domains of evidence to the theoretical concepts; and it provides for a legitimate way in which to include statements about unobservable entities in our theories.

Since most correspondence rules are not simply explicit definitions or semantic designation rules, but rather probabilistic indicator relations, it is clear that the cognitive content of theories cannot be translated into observation statements, not even an infinite set of these. Modern physics certainly cannot be interpreted in any other way. The concepts of the atomic and the quantum theories refer to unobservables, but they are related to observables in many various areas of evidence. It seems to me that the situation in psychological theory is quite analogous. Just as in physics, we may begin with the formulation of empirical laws. But empirical laws almost always are severely limited in their range of validity. For more comprehensive integrations we have to ascend to higher levels of explanations. This usually results in corrections to be applied to the empirical laws with which we started. Molar behavior theory—and psychodynamics may be construed as part of it—is in many respects methodologically analogous to classical ("phenomenological") thermodynamics. There is clearly a good measure of explanatory power present in theories of this type. But just as physics had to rise to the next higher level of explanation by introducing the molecular theory of matter and the kinetic theory of heat, so molar behavior theory is now in the initial stages of being reduced to neurophysiology.

I realize that many psychologists feel threatened by this sort of reduction. They think that their own subject matter of research is being supplanted by another one in which they do not feel at home and which they regard as beyond the limits of psychology proper. As a philosopher of science I can afford to view these developments with equanimity. Anyone (like myself) interested in the adventure of the unification of the sciences will even welcome these interdisciplinary transgressions. But the experimental and the clinical psychologists may in any case rest assured that a tremendous amount of work remains to be done on their particular level of research. I would merely plead that neurophysiological theory may yield important fruit much sooner than many molar behaviorists seem to believe.

Space does not permit me to deal with other philosophical perplexities of psychology. There are many other embarrassments, and one can never be sure to have selected the ones that are most poignant to one's readers. The whole area of value judgments and its relations to scientific knowledge is in urgent need of thorough clarification. There are also a number of topics much closer to the issues I did discuss, and which I had to omit from this paper.

By way of an *envoi* let me say that modern psychological research and modern logical and methodological analysis may have much to offer to each other. We have made a promising start in the collaboration between creative science and critical, clarifying methodology. The time has come to emancipate ourselves from the radical empiricism of the operationists and the behaviorists. A more liberal view of the nature of scientific theory will help us more adequately and clearly to assign to psychology its proper place in the uniting sciences and to remove many of the philosophical embarrassments that have stood in the way of scientific progress.

REFERENCES

Carnap, R. Testability and meaning. Parts I–IV. *Philosophy of Science*, 1936, **3**, 419–471; 1937, **4**, 1–40.

Carnap, R. The methodological character of theoretical concepts. In *Minnesota studies in the philosophy of science.* Vol. I. Minneapolis: University of Minnesota Press, 1958. Pp. 38–76.

Feigl, H. The "mental" and the "physical." In *Minnesota studies in the philosophy of science.* Vol. II. *Concepts, theories and the mind-body problem.* Minneapolis: University of Minnesota Press, 1958. Pp. 370–497.

Hempel, C. G. The theoretician's dilemma. In *Minnesota studies in the philosophy of science.* Vol. II. *Concepts, theories and the mind-body problem.* Minneapolis: University of Minnesota Press, 1958. Pp. 37–98.

MacCorquodale, K., & Meehl, P. E. On a distinction between hypothetical constructs and intervening variables. *Psychological Review*, 1948, **55**, 95–107.

6. The Concept of Consciousness[1]

Sir Cyril Burt

Taking sharp issue with the current focus on behavior in psychology, Dr. Burt argues persuasively for the return of consciousness as a productive concept, and of introspection as a valid research technique. He provides a critical, historical overview of the ascendancy of behavior as subject matter and objective observation as technique. Theoretical issues involved in the consciousness-versus-behavior controversy are discussed and it is concluded that behaviorism, in subject matter and methodology, is inadequate since it provides an incomplete and frequently misleading picture of human behavior. Dr. Burt does not argue for the discarding of a behavioristic approach to psychology but rather for the use of *both* internal and external observation. He suggests that consciousness is of such importance to the understanding of man that it must be studied, and that it is amenable to scientific inquiry through the skilled use of introspection.

CURRENT CRITICISMS OF THE CONCEPT

"The time has come when psychology must discard all reference to consciousness, and need no longer delude itself into making mental states the object of observation; its sole task is the prediction and control of *behaviour*; and introspection can form no part of its method." Nearly half a century has passed since Watson (1913) thus proclaimed his manifesto. Today, apart from a few minor reservations, the vast majority of psychologists, both in this country and in America, still follow his lead. The result, as a cynical onlooker might be tempted to say, is that psychology, having first bargained away its soul and then gone out of its mind, seems now, as it faces an untimely end, to have lost all consciousness.

In the hope of rescuing it from the threat of extinction, I want, if I may, to enter a plea for the reinstatement of consciousness as a useful and necessary concept, and at the same time try to rehabilitate introspection as a valid scientific procedure. The natural starting-point will be a brief examination of the arguments commonly advanced in support of the opposite doctrine. They have been re-stated in up-to-date form by several American writers (see Mandler & Kessen, 1959, and refs.), and, more recently still, by Mr. Broadbent in his book on *Behaviourism* (1961).

[1] Reprinted from the *British Journal of Psychology*, 1962, **53**, 229–242, with the permission of the author and the *British Journal of Psychology*.

Watson's contentions were by no means new. But, like most revolutionaries, he recognized that, without the challenge of an all-out attack, and the emphasis imparted by somewhat sweeping overstatements, his criticisms were likely to attract but scant attention. Nor can anyone seriously doubt that much of his indictment was at that time fully justified, and that his behaviouristic methods have since produced a prolific crop of results in various fields of psychology. Nevertheless, this of itself is not enough to warrant a wholesale taboo on all introspective methods and all introspective concepts. What then are the grounds that are still put forward for these drastic prohibitions?

(1) Of those mentioned by Broadbent, the first, and the earliest in point of time, was the series of apparently insoluble controversies to which the introspective approach had given rise. "Instead of an ever-growing system of facts and generalizations," says Watson, "what introspection has engendered is merely a progressively increasing chaos of conflicting reports and speculative theories." The outcome, as James had already complained, was "not science; it is not even the hope of a science." Broadbent cites two such controversies as typical—the protracted debate between German psychologists over the possibility of imageless thought and the wrangle among American psychologists over the James-Lange theory of emotions. To psychologists in this country, impressed as they had been by Galton's work on individual differences, such diversified pronouncements seemed only natural: the error lay simply in the fact that each of the protagonists implicitly assumed that his own experience must be typical of everybody else's.

(2) The argument that one most frequently hears today seeks to go deeper, and is based on a special theory of scientific methodology. Science, it is maintained, deals only with events which are "public," that is, accessible to *any* observer. Conscious states from their very nature can be accessible (if at all) solely to the person who owns them; they are "private," and consequently "lack the certainty all scientific data should possess." What X calls his "feelings," his "sensations," and his "mental images" can be inspected by no one but X himself. All that other psychologists can observe are X's own overt responses to various stimuli—his gestures, his vocal or sub-vocal utterances, his internal visceral changes—in short, X's "behaviour." "The fallacy," says Broadbent, "in asking a man to describe the contents of his mind is that his words cannot convey directly how he feels. If I say I experience 'mixed feelings,' *nobody can prove or disprove* the accuracy of my observation. . . . This means that we must reject all concepts that are not defined by any operation."

Both these arguments are anything but conclusive. To begin with, no scientist outside the field of psychology, not even Bridgman himself, would today support the thoroughgoing doctrine of operationism propounded thirty-five years ago;[2]

---

[2] Psychologists appear to think that operationism is a creed taken over from the physical sciences: physicists regard it as a creed borrowed from psychology. "In spite of laboratory vocabulary," says an eminent physicist, "the operational viewpoint is not really a genuine product of physics; it is the echo, in the precincts of physical science, of that curious and typical American doctrine known as 'behaviourism'" (A. O'Rahilly, 1938, chap. XIV, "Operations and Concepts").

and it would be much easier to quote or construct good operational definitions for the technical terms employed by introspectionists than it would be for some of the newer concepts introduced by contemporary physicists. But this is a minor issue. What I am most anxious to challenge is the widespread assumption that, before any phenomenon can be accepted as a scientific datum, we must (like the Grand Inquisitor in *The Gondoliers*) feel "no probable possible shadow of doubt, no manner of doubt whatever" about the legitimacy of its claim: in short, that science must insist on certainty. "There is," says Broadbent, "no other way besides the behaviourist way of attaining *certain knowledge* about other men" (my italics). But not even "the behaviourist way" can achieve "certain knowledge." Nor would any branch of empirical science be justified in exacting such a guarantee. Dr. Taylor (1958) cites Newtonian astronomy. Admittedly, if we start with Newton's assumptions (e.g. with Euclidean space and the law of inverse squares), his purely mathematical conclusions can be deduced with absolute certainty; but the applicability of the assumptions to the stellar universe and the verification of the conclusions must be decided by personal observation; and no observations are infallible. In A.D. 1054 a Chinese "sky-watcher" at Peiping recorded that he had seen a new star, of such brilliance that it was visible even in daylight, flare up in a corner of the constellation that Western astronomers have christened the Bull, at the very spot where we now find that powerful radio-emitter known as the Crab Nebula (De Mailla, 1785). Since we cannot unwind the reel of time, no one today can "prove or disprove" his observation; yet every astronomer accepts it. All that an empirical science requires, or indeed can hope for, is that what an observer reports shall, when duly weighed in the light of what we can infer about his reliability as an observer or reporter, and of all the other relevant facts, seem *highly probable*.

However, the heart of the argument lies in the distinction between what is "private" and what is "public." The distinction is applied at two different levels which are usually confused. First, it is argued that a person's inner experience has to be described in words which he alone understands, i.e. in a "private" *language*. To some extent this is true. *I* know what I mean by red; but *you* cannot know what I mean by it, since my colour sensations may differ from yours. Nevertheless, though you cannot know for certain, it remains highly *probable* that, unless there is positive evidence for some rather abnormal variation in the brain and sense-organs of one or other of us, your interpretation of the word will be much the same as mine. Thus, even if the experiences are private, the *language* is public so long as it can be understood. Indeed social intercourse would be utterly impossible if a man's words did not "convey how he feels."[3]

More frequently, however, the behaviourist's distinction refers not to the language, but to the objects or events which the language describes. I and I alone, it is said, can *observe* my inner experiences. Hence, it is maintained, such experiences cannot be data for a "scientific psychology." But surely as thus interpreted the dis-

---

[3] The view that experiences as such are incommunicable seems to be derived from the early pronouncements of certain members of the so-called Viennese Circle; cf. Schlick (1918) and Carnap (1928). But I doubt whether any philosopher would today seriously support it.

tinction is based on the falsest of false antitheses. In no other branch of science would the mere fact that only one man can observe a given phenomenon be offered as a sound *a priori* reason for rejecting it forthwith. Strictly speaking, *every* first-hand observation is necessarily "private." Whether certain observations are treated as "public" turns not on their specific or intrinsic nature, but merely on the context. X is asked: can he or can he not detect a faint point of light somewhere near the centre of a dark field. He answers "Yes." If the field is the field of a 4-inch tele-scope, and the faint point of light is presumed to be one of Jupiter's smaller satel-lites, then what is observed is said to be "public." If the field is the far end of a psychologist's dark-room, and the experiment is intended to determine the subject's threshold for visual sensation, then what is observed is said to be "private." Nevertheless, when astronomers are permitted to accept such observations at their face value, why should psychologists be forbidden to do so?

The behaviourist does not wholly rule out experiments undertaken to determine such things as sensory thresholds; but he insists that the threshold shall be regarded as a threshold for "producing a reaction" not for "producing a sensation." And such experiments are sanctioned only when it is possible to make objective checks —e.g. by "a catch trial . . . to make sure that the man will always say 'I see nothing' when we show him nothing." In the case of mental images and of "feelings" (i.e., pleasure, and pain in the sense of unpleasure) we have no such means of "checking the exact boundaries between the situations which a man describes in one way (e.g. by an affirmative) and those which he describes in another (e.g. by a negative)." Here, says Broadbent, lies the "fatal weakness" of all such introspective studies.[4]

Our American contemporaries make much the same points. "What a man tells us about his emotions or sensations—whether he himself is a psychologist or not— must be viewed, not as the statement of a scientific observation, but merely as part of his total behaviour. . . . Every therapist knows that a patient's statement 'I am not angry' is *not* equivalent to the statement 'The patient is not angry'; often indeed such verbal behaviour may be used as a datum for the conclusion 'The patient *is* angry.'" Introspective statements about feelings, such as "I feel happy" or "X feels a pain," we are told, are "not statements in psychology" or "statements about genuine psychological variables." "The language of the subject and the language of psychology must be kept strictly separate." For simplicity the psy-chologist may be permitted to say a human being "sees" something; but such expressions can only be tolerated on the strict understanding that "in the language of psychology 'see' is defined according to the principle that '*S* sees *O*' means, when presented with the stimulus X, *S* reacts by saying* 'I see *O*'" (Mandler & Kessen, 1959, pp. 35f.; cf. Bergmann, 1950, pp. 485f. and Skinner, 1957). For psy-chology "*S*," the subject, thus becomes nothing more than a stimulus-response

---

[4] As we have seen, Broadbent is careful to insist that he does not for a moment wish to deny or ignore the notion that other people beside ourselves can hear, see, feel, or think: he merely holds that psychology is not the proper place to mention or discuss such inner proc-esses. His guiding principle seems to be that of Machiavelli's ideal philosopher: "Odi, vedi, e taci, se vuoi vivere saviamente."

machine: you put a stimulus in one of the slots, and out comes a packet of reactions. Meanwhile, what of the patient himself?

> In the midst of the word he was trying to say
> He has softly and suddenly vanished away;

for what appeared to be a psychical Snark turns out to be just a mechanical Boojum. But by this time it is, I think, plain that all these reservations and qualifications are little more than linguistic subterfuges. They save the behaviourist's face; but they misdirect our attention. When a patient says that he "feels a pain," or that, after an injection of morphia he "now feels happy and comfortable," or again, when a volunteer, after taking a dose of mescalin, declares that she is witnessing "a glorious panorama of colour and hears the angels sing," or after 40 μg of LSD-25 can "see half-a-dozen gigantic devils chasing a small boy with pointed tridents," surely the crucial feature about the situation is the fact (or should we say the high probability) that the persons in question really do see, hear, or feel what they describe, not that they exhibit this or that "verbal behaviour." But, it is objected, "no words can convey directly" the intrinsic nature of a man's experiences. True; but words cannot "convey directly" the intrinsic nature of anything. And if "different subjects use the same vague words to describe different experiences and describe the same experience by different names," that might be said of the pre-scientific language used by the plain man in almost every field of discussion.

However, when psychologists like Myers or McDougall spoke of introspection, they were not thinking of the incidental remarks made by patients to the therapist, but of the reports of skilled and practised observers, trained to use a special technique and equipped with a special scientific terminology—the so-called *systematische Selbstbeobachtung* developed by Wundt and his co-workers in the psychological laboratory. The words and phrases which Watson and other behaviourists would have us abjure—sensation, after-image, memory-image, feeling, and the like—were used in a technical and somewhat Pickwickian sense, rigorously defined by explicit interpretations. The objection that subjective terms are "by their very nature obscure, elusive, and ambiguous" has been grossly magnified. Most students find the words that Watson wishes to ban far more intelligible than his own circumlocutions or the recondite phraseology coined by later behaviourists—"sign-gestalt-expectations," "demanded type of means-or-goal," and so on—even when these are scrupulously defined. Few readers would want their favourite novelist to translate his "subjective nomenclature" into a behaviouristic idiom; and all that the introspective psychologist seeks to do is to apply the scientist's techniques to the novelist's material, and refine and standardize the novelist's improvised vocabulary.

(3) But it seems clear from various incidental remarks that the most powerful motive influencing the champions of behaviourism in their selection of concepts has its roots in certain tacit assumptions about what kind of concepts are admissible in other natural sciences. The smear-word which Watson most frequently applies when he wishes to deny or deprecate some particular concept is "unscientific";

and in deciding what is and what is not "scientific" his criteria are plainly derived from his early training in the physical and biological sciences as they were understood towards the close of the nineteenth century. Psychologists who talked of consciousness and conscious states were, so he contended, "professing to discover something immaterial and wholly outside the world of natural phenomena." That world, it was supposed, was essentially a mechanical system, made up of material particles and inexorably governed by a few simple causal laws. Into such a scheme Procrustes himself could not fit the concepts of the introspectionist—concepts such as "will" or "purpose" which claim to produce effects in defiance of causation, or such as "sensations" and "images" which produce no causal effects at all and whose own causal origin is wrapped in mystery. Accordingly, like Milton's fallen angel, Watson is firmly resolved

> To exclude
> All spiritual substance by a corporeal bar.

The theory that ensues has all the appeal of a trim, tidy, easily intelligible system, with everything all neatly buttoned up. But unfortunately relativity and quantum theory have meanwhile undermined the whole structure. Today no reputable scientist accepts its oversimplified assumptions. And the physicist himself is the first to emphasize that the schemes he constructs are neither final nor complete: they are models that symbolize reality, not photographs that reproduce it.[5]

(4) There is, however, a small but growing band of behaviourists, who now incline to accept this newer standpoint. They prefer to rest their creed on a fundamental principle of methodology which throughout the twentieth century has played an effective part in the formulation of physical as well as of psychological theories—namely, what psychologists call the principle of parsimony and logicians have nicknamed Occam's Razor. As ordinarily stated, it maintains that the number of basic concepts and assumptions should be reduced to the barest minimum. Russell has extolled it as "the supreme maxim in scientific philosophizing." "Minimizing axioms" has long been a guiding precept with mathematical and geometrical theorists; and the practical appeal of the Newtonian system, particularly as re-shaped by the mathematical physicists of the eighteenth and nineteenth centuries, arose largely from the ingenious way it succeeded in embracing a vast and varied mass of observable phenomena in a single deductive scheme derived from an amazingly small array of fundamental concepts and axiomatic "laws."

In the field of psychology the most ambitious achievement attained by the application of this methodological principle has been the deductive system outlined by Clark Hull (1952). Yet he himself has recorded how unexpectedly difficult he found it to keep his final list of concepts and postulates down to a plausible minimum. One of his later formulations contains at least eighteen postulates and as many as

---

[5] In support of this pronouncement one could cite passages from almost any contemporary physicist—Heisenberg, Schrödinger, Whittaker, Bohr; but I suppose the most recent and authoritative is that of the past President of the Royal Society (Hinshelwood, 1961; cf. also Burt, 1958).

eighty-six definitions, while the number of theorems deduced from them, and empirically verified, is so far comparatively small. And, since Hull published his last and most comprehensive scheme, the tendency of his behaviouristic successors has been to multiply rather than to reduce the number of their basic concepts.

In my view the attempt to construct a comprehensive and coherent axiomatic system, derived from a minimum list of concepts and postulates, is something that can be reasonably undertaken only when the science in question has, like mathematics or mechanics, arrived at a highly developed stage. Otherwise it almost inevitably leaves out too much. The general trend of modern research, even in sciences which, like astronomy and physics, were once thought to be ripe for a systematic formulation of this kind, has been to reveal an unexpected richness and variety in the universe; and surely the study of human life is likely to be the most complex of all scientific disciplines.

I submit then that none of the behaviourists' arguments really prove what they set out to prove. As a working methodology the cautionary principles advocated by the pioneers of the movement are admirable, particularly in reference to those special fields of research in which they were predominantly interested. But to put them forward dogmatically as an *a priori* limitation to which all psychological theories must in future conform is wholly unjustified and already threatens to block the further advance of psychological inquiry. I am all for a kind of psychological passport officer, who shall scrutinize the credentials of the vast crowd of popular concepts, which, more than in any other science, are apt to intrude from the common discussions of everyday life. But the behaviourist's criteria seem to me as unfair as they are old-fashioned.

However, if anyone proposes, as I have done, to allow the re-entrance of words like "consciousness," which appear in no other scientific vocabulary, it is incumbent on him first of all to explain precisely what he understands by such terms.

THE PROBLEMS OF CONSCIOUSNESS

The Nature of Consciousness. Some years before Watson commenced his onslaught on the concept of consciousness, William James published an essay entitled "Does Consciousness Exist?" (1902). He reached the surprising conclusion that it does not. But throughout his discussion he takes it for granted that the word "consciousness" denotes a special kind of *substance*, or, as he termed it, a "stuff." That indeed had been the tacit assumption of most of the older psychologists, including not only those whom James attacked, but James himself in his earlier writings. Occasionally, however, the term was interpreted as the name either of some specific activity or *process*, or of a specific property or *attribute*, of some particular substance, e.g. of the individual organism or of the material brain. And certainly, even though we reject James's own alternative, there can be little doubt that all these earlier interpretations present insuperable difficulties and have proved to be untenable.

Modern scientific arguments are no longer couched solely in terms of substances and their properties or processes; they also include the category of *relations*. And the view I myself have put forward (Burt, 1960 and refs.) is that consciousness in all its forms necessarily implies a specific relation between (*a*) someone or something who is said to be conscious and (*b*) something else which he, she, or it is said to be conscious *of*. When, for instance, I "see" a rose or "smell" its scent, when I "hear" a noise or "feel" a pain, the verbs that I use really designate various instances of a unique kind of relation for which the most convenient name is perhaps "awareness." It is a two-term relation; but, as in so many cases, the nature of the terms is somewhat elusive. Since the relation is asymmetrical, we need a different label for each. Let us provisionally dub them the "subject" and the "object," respectively. In the examples cited the "subject" is indicated by the pronoun "I"—a word which may denote either what would commonly be called my "self" or my "mind," or what the physiologist would call my "brain," or possibly just the passing thought: its precise character is a matter for psychological examination. The "object" of the awareness seems in some cases to be a physical "object," i.e. a "thing," or at least a part of its surface, as when I see a red tomato or a silver spoon; in other cases, as when I feel pain from pricking myself with a pin, the mental object seems to be caused *by* the physical object rather than to form part *of* it. However, my purpose at the moment is not to discuss the problems of perception or the soundness of the sense-datum theory (on that see Burt, 1961*a*), but merely to insist that what confronts us is in all such cases a specific type of relation.

There are only two ways in which the psychologist can avoid introducing some such concept: first, to deny or deliberately ignore its existence, as Watson and the earlier behaviourists decided to do—a procedure so flagrantly inadequate that no competent writer today seems prepared to defend it; or secondly, to reduce all statements containing the word "consciousness" (or one of its many synonyms) to statements containing some more familiar type of relation. Explicitly or implicitly the notion of "reduction" is widely adopted in recent psychological writings (cf. Bergmann, 1954, Hempel, 1952, Mandler & Kessen, 1959, especially pp. 114 and refs.); but the notion itself is seldom clearly or satisfactorily defined. By way of definition I suggest the following. If a proposition X is validly reducible to a proposition A, then (i) propositions of class A must be on a lower epistemological plane than those of class X in the sense that they involve fewer concepts, and (ii) X must be logically equivalent to A in the sense that (*a*) X entails A and (*b*) A entails X.

In the attempt to reduce propositions about consciousness in this way, a wide variety of alternative relations have been put forward—causation, ownership, resemblance or correspondence, representation or symbolization, the relation of part to whole, a temporal relation such as "compresence," and even spatial relations such as "contact." In the end, however, each of these reductions seems to issue in much the same type of fallacy. Among psychologists and physiologists the favourite device is a reduction to the relation of causation. A "subjective statement" such as "I see a red glow from the fire" implies (so it is said quite rightly) an "objective statement" such as "That fire causes a red glow." The behaviourist usually prefers a rather more elaborate translation, e.g. "The stimulus, fire, causes me to react with an observable and distinctive type of behaviour—a particular movement or a particular verbal response." It is then assumed that these causal propositions provide a complete description of the situation, or at least as complete a description as a psychologist is entitled to demand. The crucial test is to reverse the implication. Does the statement "That fire causes a red glow" (or any of these other versions) really imply "I see a red glow"? Plainly it does not; some further assertion is needed.

Among contemporary philosophers the commonest mode of reduction is that proposed by Russell and most clearly described by Ayer (1954a, pp. 122f.). "To begin with," he writes, "we do not accept the realist analysis of our sensations in terms of subject, act, and object. . . . We do not deny that a given sense-content can be legitimately said to be experienced by a particular subject; but this *relation of being experienced* by a particular subject is to be analysed in terms of the relation of sense-contents to one another. . . . Accordingly, we define a sense-content not as the *object*, but as *part of* a sense-experience; and from this it follows that the existence of a sense-content always entails the existence of a sense-experience." Later he changes the name, and speaks of a relation of *belonging*. When you or I say "experience" this or that sense-content, all that we imply (so one gathers) is that this and other sense-contents "belong to the sense-history of the same *self*"—a phrase which is interpreted to mean "all such sense-experiences contain organic sense-contents which are elements of the same *body*."

Now, to begin with, the notion that the "elements" of which the "body" is composed are "sense-contents" is one which only a convinced phenomenalist could accept: it would scarcely be endorsed by the ordinary physiologist. And the change to the notion of "belonging" is a little puzzling. Since it is said to designate a "symmetrical relation," it must apparently mean, not "being a part of which the sense-history constitutes the whole," but "being a part of some more general whole of which the organic sense-contents are *also* a part." Let us then apply the same test as before. "I see a brown dog" may plausibly be said to imply "There is a brown, dog-shaped 'content' which is part of a wider whole that includes the further 'contents' specified by the theory"; but quite obviously this alternative proposition does not of itself imply "I see a dog."

However, most writers who have used the word "belonging" intend it to designate the relation of possession or "ownership." Now in popular parlance we frequently use such expressions as "I *have* a pain in my finger," where the verb "have" could be taken to mean "I (that is my body) *possess* a pain." But a phrase like "I have a red glow" cannot possibly be used in this fashion. The reason is plain. This idiomatic use of "have" is only permissible where the following noun itself implies some kind of relation. We can speak of "having a meal" or "a wash," because the nouns themselves imply the actions of eating or of washing, and such actions involve relations. Similarly the word "pain" connotes something that is consciously felt. But with other types of noun we are obliged to insert a word which explicitly indicates some sort of consciousness: we are therefore forced to say "I have the *sensation* of a red glow." Ayer himself in this context always speaks of "*sense* contents." Thus the equivalence of the two types of relation is really effected by covertly transferring the notion of consciousness from the word which explicitly describes the *relation* in the first statement to the word which implicitly describes the *relatum* in the second.[6]

After all, consciousness in the sense of "being aware of" is essentially a form of knowledge.[7] Indeed it is the most fundamental form of knowledge: without it observation, which every scientist including the behaviourist automatically postulates, would be impossible. When I am aware of a red glow over there, I know that something is (or at least seems to be) over there, and I also know its distinctive nature, namely, that it is a glowing red. Since knowing is neither a substance nor an attribute, the only logical category under which we can subsume it is that of relation. Hence to deny that there is such a relation between the knower (i.e., me) and the known (i.e., the red glow) is tantamount to denying the very possibility of knowledge. Indeed, it lands us in the self-contradictory situation of saying "I know that I can never know."

The arguments that I have used in refuting the attempt to reduce the relation of awareness to a relation of causation, or of part-and-whole, or of belonging, can be used of all the other modes of reduction that have at one time or another been proposed. And, to clinch the matter, we may note that, as Russell (1921, p. 76) rightly points out, "we are not only aware of things, we are often aware of being aware of them." Should anyone ask whether I am sure that I see a red glow, I can confidently reply, not only that I am seeing it, but also that I *know* that I am seeing it. I conclude then that the concept of consciousness in the sense of an irreducible relation of awareness is a concept that we can neither exclude nor exchange, if, as psychologists, we are to give an adequate account of human life and behaviour.

Now it is not difficult to show by carrying the analysis a few stages further that

[6] In a later publication Ayer (1954b) recognizes that it is difficult to avoid defining the phrase "sense content" or "sense datum" without introducing some transitive verb like "seeing," "hearing," etc., which implies the relational notion of awareness. Accordingly he suggests that we should interpret it by saying it denotes something that "appears"; and by this (so he presently explains) he means "something that is sensibly present." But this substitution of an adverb for a verb no more eliminates the reference to a relation of awareness than the substitution of the phrase "temporally subsequent" would eliminate the reference to a relation of time. We only talk of something "appearing" when we think of it as actually or hypothetically appearing "*to* someone," where the preposition now indicates the relation. The relational view of consciousness has been criticized both by Russell (who formerly accepted it) and more recently by Ryle—but solely as part of the sense-datum theory. Since I do not accept that theory, their objections are largely irrelevant. I have, however, discussed them elsewhere (Burt, 1960, 1961b).

[7] Some writers have denied that awareness can legitimately be regarded as a form of knowledge; but that is only because they deliberately define the term "knowledge" so that awareness is excluded. The dictionaries, however, all recognize the sense I have adopted, as well as the more special sense of "knowing that." As has often been pointed out, the English verb "know" does duty for what in other languages—Greek, Latin, German, French, and Welsh—is expressed by two or more different verbs. It was indeed largely to avoid the side-issues that are raised by using the simpler but more ambiguous word "know" that the earlier introspectionists substituted the somewhat pedantic term "cognize" or "cognition" to denote the more comprehensive concept.

immediate awareness is by no means the only species of cognitive relation: knowing in the sense of *savoir* is a different type of relation from knowing in the sense of *connaître*. Older psychologists used also to include such processes as remembering, imagining, judging, and inferring under the same generic heading. Moreover, it may be plausibly argued that there are other genera of conscious relation besides the cognitive: there are, for instance, "affective" relations such as being pleased with, and "conative" relations such as wanting or desiring. Situations in which one or more of these conscious relations occur differ profoundly from those studied in the physical sciences. Such situations therefore must be studied in and for themselves. When so studied, they display certain regularities, and are in some measure predictable. Hence their investigation is plainly a task for science, and the appropriate science will naturally be what has traditionally been termed psychology.

THE NEED FOR INTROSPECTION

In the investigations I have just mentioned four main groups of problems seem to be involved: first, the nature of the various conscious relations; secondly, the nature of the proximate objects of such relations—i.e., what some writers have termed the "contents" of consciousness; thirdly, the relation of these objects to physical objects; and finally, the nature of the subject of these relations—whether, for example, we are to think of that subject as a material organism or brain, as an immaterial mind or "psychic factor" (to use Broad's expression), or as some joint or composite entity. To investigate these various problems would scarcely be possible without employing that particular type of observation known as "introspection." Introspection is necessary, not only because it brings new questions to the fore, but also because it alone can supply much of the observational data needed to answer them. However, as many psychologists of a younger generation have entered the field since introspective methods fell into disrepute, it seems desirable to justify their revival by citing a few illustrative instances, and then endeavouring to rebut the commoner objections.

To begin with, most of our detailed knowledge about the psychology of sensation, at least so far as man is concerned, was discovered by experimental studies in which introspective methods were systematically employed. Many of the results— notably the sensory thresholds—could doubtless have been reached, a little deviously, by purely behaviouristic techniques. Yet I question whether anyone would have thought of examining such problems had it not been for the introspective interest in the subject—the interest of the painter, for example, in problems of colour vision, and of the musician in those of sound. And there are many unexpected facts which could never have been established by procedures that barred all forms of introspection—e.g. the curious fact that a mixture of red, green, and blue will produce a pure white, or that the fusion of two stereoscopic pictures gives rise to the extraordinary sensation of solidity or depth, not to mention the so-called phi-phenomenon and the many other phenomena embraced by the term Gestalt.

The most striking discoveries that we can lay to the credit of introspective methods are those relating to mental imagery—particularly the wide differences between individuals in the types of imagery to which they are prone. Watson himself was almost completely destitute of concrete imagery, and did most of his thinking by dint of what he calls "implicit speech." Quite illogically he inferred that all other people must do their thinking in the same fashion—by "abridged or incipient movements of the tongue and larynx, often too slight to be detectable even by the most delicate instrumental devices" (Watson, 1931). And when we turn to investigate mental processes on their higher and more complex levels—notably those of creative and of logical thinking—we find the use of introspective methods still more illuminating.

There are no doubt many areas of research—for instance, those of animal psychology—where such techniques are out of the question, and where introspective terms may prove misleading. Nor would I deny that even in human psychology much may be learnt by treating man as just another animal or even as a mere electrochemical machine. Nevertheless, human beings are neither rats nor robots. And where "internal" self-observation is available as an adjunct to the "external" observation of overt behaviour, the marriage of the two is bound to be far more fruitful than the adoption of either to the exclusion of the other.

But science is more than the sheer accumulation of facts and problems. The theoretical psychologist wants to understand behaviour; the practical psychologist to forecast and direct it. As Watson (1919) puts it, scientific psychology has two aims—"to predict human activity with reasonable certainty and to formulate principles whereby human activities can be guided and controlled." Let us then accept his own criteria, and consider how far the introspective study of conscious processes is likely to assist these aims. Once again, space will permit only a cursory glance at a few of the more typical examples.

When I have to report on a child referred for examination as a potential delinquent or neurotic, I should be quite unable to offer any trustworthy prognosis after merely observing his behaviour and noting his "verbal responses." My first step is to gain some insight into his private thoughts and emotions. These I infer and interpret partly on the basis of my own self-observation and partly from the results of comparable observations on other children. The more fully the child himself is able to introspect, the easier it is to secure revealing clues as to his conscious and unconscious motivations. And the value of such an approach is clearly demonstrated by the follow-up results obtained from different clinics. For much the same reason it is almost impossible to direct or control the activities of children or young people with genuine understanding unless we adopt introspective methods and introspective concepts. The study of mental imagery, for instance, turns out to be of great practical as well as theoretical importance—notably in educational and vocational guidance. The most striking instance perhaps is to be found in remedial work on disability in reading (for details see Burt, 1962a).

The rule that all introspective terms must be expunged from the vocabulary of "objective psychology" has played havoc with the interpretation of mental tests and mental factors. In the early days of such research no investigator would have claimed that some new test or factor really measured this or that particular ability, until he had first checked his conclusion by securing introspections from his subjects. Today such identifications are commonly made simply on the basis of some hypothetical preconception—often quite differently by different interpreters. And in almost every field of cognitive psychology—in the study of colourblindness, of sensitivity to noise, of artistic creativity and musical appreciation, of the processes of thought and reasoning, to pick but a few of the most recent examples—this obsessive psychophobia leads to the most far-fetched and misleading periphrases merely to express what are essentially psychical characteristics in purely behaviouristic terms. It is, however, on the motivational side rather than the intellectual that the gulf between the introspective method and a strict behaviourist approach is most conspicuous. "Will," "purpose," "conation," these are the concepts which Watson singled out for his most ruthless attacks. Instead we must "substitute mechanical explanations for the meaningless jargon of affective and conative processes," and hold fast to the view that man is "an assembled organic machine."

"If you think we are waxworks," said Tweedledum to Alice, "you ought to pay." And Watson has to pay a heavy price for his strict adherence to mechanistic principles. It makes nonsense of every form of applied psychology. Educational psychology, vocational psychology, criminology, and psychotherapy—all become impossible if we are to look upon men and women, patients and pupils, as mere automata, devoid alike of reason and feeling. Even in laboratory research on animal behaviour it has become necessary to discard the original restrictions; and it is largely around these motivational problems that the controversies between later behaviourists have revolved. Little by little, however, some of the younger members of the school have ventured to reintroduce a few basic concepts reminiscent of the discredited introspectionist psychology, usually disguised by new names or fresh descriptions. The traditional notion of willing, wanting, or striving—"conation," in short—is rechristened "drive"; a "purpose" appears as a "goal"; and instead of the old pleasure–pain principle—the "algedonic" law—we have a "law of effect." We are forbidden to say the "satisfaction" we feel at the success which has attended a particular action increases the probability that the action will be repeated; but we are allowed to say that "the nervous process resulting from a 'reward' tends to 'reinforce' the nervous process which issued in the reward."

The object of these heroic circumlocutions is, so we are told, to abolish terms implying "occult notions, such as perception, pleasure, purpose, or conscious state," and to replace them by interpretations that "imply nothing more than the mechanical operation of physical causes and effects." But the futility of the attempt is patent. The hypothetical "nervous processes" or "excitations" which the interpretation presupposes are far more "occult" than the conscious states whose mention is taboo'd. After all, feelings of satisfaction and the like are things that everybody can observe; no one has ever observed the alleged nervous processes that are put in their place, nor has anyone the slightest idea of what they are like, how they can be identified, or indeed whether they really exist.

SUMMARY AND CONCLUSIONS

I conclude then that behaviourism, both in its original or "naïve" form and in its later or "sophisticated" forms (to use Boring's convenient labels), has proved untenable. As a principle of methodology—particularly in certain specialized fields, such as animal psychology—the behaviourist approach has suggested useful experimental techniques and produced valuable results; but as a basis for a general theory of human experience it is hopelessly inadequate. The need to reintroduce the concept of consciousness seems inescapable. It is quite untrue to declare, as Watson does, that the introspectionist "never tells us what consciousness is, but merely puts things into it by assumption." The phenomena of consciousness are not doctrinal assumptions; they are undeniable facts which everyone can verify. In its most conspicuous form—that of direct awareness—consciousness is a unique relation; it constitutes the basis of all observation, including the observations of the behaviourist himself. And the immediate objects of this awareness—the so-called "contents" of consciousness—are the things we know with the highest degree of certitude.

The behaviourists' chief objection to descriptions and explanations involving a reference to the processes and contents of consciousness is that, even if we concede their existence, such processes and contents are from their very nature "private" or "subjective." However, as we have seen, the popular antithesis between subjective and objective, between what is "private" and what is "public," turns out, when closely examined, to be at once ambiguous and misleading. What is commonly said to be "public" is known solely "by description" (as the logician puts it), i.e., inferentially; and the "private" experiences of other persons are knowable in precisely the same way. Indeed, as modern physicists like Bohr and Heisenberg are the first to assure us, "all the raw material of our knowledge consists of conscious events in the lives of separate observers."

The behaviourist, as we have seen, goes on to argue that, for purposes of scientific study, what are usually regarded as mental events can always be reduced without remainder to terms of physical events—"responses of the organism such as can be described in the universal language of natural science." By "responses," it would appear, the behaviourist originally meant gross bodily movements such as make up what we should ordinarily call behaviour. With this limited interpretation, however, the proposed reduction is plainly impossible. We need to know what intervenes between the stimulus and the subsequent response; and here, so I have argued, introspection yields the most important clues. To avoid introspective concepts, however, later behaviourists preferred to postulate, in addition to "overt" or "explicit" responses ("macroscopic behaviour," as I have termed it), certain types of "internal" or "implicit" response—including under this phrase the molecular or submolecular processes of the brain or nervous system ("microscopic behaviour"). But, even if we could demonstrate that there was in every case a complete one-to-one concomitance between conscious processes and the corresponding nervous processes, we still could not *identify* conscious processes with their neural counterparts. We should still require a set of psychophysical laws stating how, in the various cases, the two were in fact correlated.

In order to study how the various phenomena of consciousness are related to physical processes introspection is essential. Nevertheless, since behaviour and experience are both influenced by unconscious as well as by conscious processes, introspection alone is not enough. The arguments advanced by behaviourists to condemn introspective techniques and terminology have no doubt served a useful purpose by drawing attention to their occasional misuse and their inevitable limitations; but they fail to justify any sweeping prohibition. The proposal of later behaviourists to permit introspective phraseology as part of the subject's "verbal behaviour" while excluding it from the language of "scientific psychology" misses the vital point of the subject's report; and such a convention makes it meaningless to ask whether the subject is speaking the truth and impossible to discover what he really intends to assert.

The common complaint that "the efforts of the earlier introspectionists produced nothing but controversy and confusion" is thus a reason not for abandoning introspection, but for greater skill in its use. Rightly understood, self-observation differs in no essential respect from other modes of observation. And even if introspection confronts us with a series of baffling problems, it has also shown that conscious processes exhibit certain regularities, and obey certain laws. It has already revealed a number of suggestive generalizations—some connecting conscious events with physical causes and with physical consequences, others connecting conscious events with one another. The phenomena of consciousness are thus clearly amenable to scientific research; and they are surely of sufficient interest and importance to deserve systematic study in and for themselves. Such a study (as the behaviourist himself reminds us) is undertaken by no other science. It should therefore form the most distinctive feature of the psychologist's task.

I conclude then that observation of self and observation of others are both indispensable. Unless we study our own inner consciousness we cannot fully understand the behaviour of others; and unless we observe others we cannot fully understand our own.

> Willst du dich selber erkennen, so sieh wie die andern es treiben;
> Willst du die andern verstehn, blick' in dein eigenes Herz.[8]

REFERENCES

Ayer, A. J. *Language, truth, and logic.* (10th ed.) London: Gollancz, 1954*a*.

Ayer, A. J. *Philosophical essays.* London: Macmillan, 1954*b*.

Bergmann, G. Semantics. In V. Ferm (Ed.), *A history of philosophical systems.* New York: Philosophical Library, 1950.

[8] "If you want to get to know yourself, then look how the others behave. If it is the others you want to understand, then look into your own heart." (Editor's translation).

Bergmann, G. Sense and nonsense in operationism. *Scientific Monthly of New York*, 1954, **59**, 140–148.

Broadbent, D. E. *Behaviourism*. London: Eyre and Spottiswoode, 1961.

Burt, C. Quantum theory and the principle of indeterminacy. *British Journal of Statistical Psychology*, 1958, **11**, 77–93.

Burt, C. The concept of mind. *Journal of Psychological Research*, 1960, **1**, 1–11.

Burt, C. The structure of the mind. *British Journal of Statistical Psychology*, 1961a, **14**, 145–170.

Burt, C. The psychology of perception. *British Journal of Statistical Psychology*, 1961b, **14**, 173–180.

Burt, C. *Mental and scholastic tests*. (4th ed.) London: Staples Press, 1962a.

Burt, C. The sense datum theory. *British Journal of Statistical Psychology*, 1962b, **15**, 138–164.

Carnap, R. *Der Logische Aufbau der Welt*. Berlin: Engelmann, 1928.

De Mailla, Moyria. *Annales de l'Empire Chinois traduits de Tong-Kien-Kang-Mou*. Paris: Alcan, 1785.

Hempel, C. G. Fundamentals of concept formation in empirical science. In *International encyclopaedia of unified science*. Vol. 2. Chicago: University of Chicago Press, 1952.

Hinshelwood, Sir Cyril. *The vision of nature*. Cambridge: University Press, 1961.

Hull, C. *A behavior system*. New Haven: Yale University Press, 1952.

James, W. *Essays in radical empiricism*. New York: Macmillan, 1902.

Mandler, G., & Kessen, W. *The language of psychology*. New York: John Wiley, 1959.

O'Rahilly, A. *Electromagnetics: a discussion of fundamentals*. London: Longmans, Green and Co., 1938.

Rivers, W. H. R. *Instinct and the unconscious*. Cambridge: University Press, 1920.

Russell, B. A. W. *The analysis of mind*. London: Allen and Unwin, 1921.

Schlick, M. *Allgemeine Erkenntnislehre*. Berlin: Engelmann, 1918.

Skinner, B. F. *Verbal behavior*. New York: Appleton, 1957.

Taylor, J. G. Experimental design. *British Journal of Psychology*, 1958, **49**, 106–116.

Watson, J. B. Psychology as the behaviorist views it. *Psychological Review*, 1913, **20**, 158–167.

Watson, J. B. *Psychology from the standpoint of a behaviorist*. Philadelphia: Lippincott, 1919.

Watson, J. B. *Behaviorism*. (2nd ed.) London: Kegan Paul, Trench, Trubner and Co., 1931.

7. Behavior: Datum or Abstraction[1]

Rolland H. Waters

The proper definition of psychology's subject matter is the topic of the late Dr. Waters's provocative essay, and he begins by taking issue with current textbook assertions that this subject matter is behavior. He suggests that the term, behavior, is not defined adequately and, as a result, is discussed in ambiguous fashion. He feels that the behavior studied in psychology should be clearly distinguished from the behavior of animals, machines, or stars as studied in zoology, physics, or astronomy. Certain distinguishing attributes characterizing behavior in psychology, including spontaneity or autonomy, persistence, variability, and docility, are discussed. Dr. Waters argues that a clear analogy can be drawn between the psychologists' study of behavior and the physicists' study of heat or light in that both refer to something abstracted from what is being observed. Viewed in this way, behavior is a class of activities possessing the above-listed attributes and hence is an abstraction rather than a datum.

The problem of the subject matter of psychology and its implications has recently taken on renewed interest (Johnson, 1956; McClelland, 1955; Nuttin, 1955). This may be because of the reference to studies of the rat as appropriate for a rodentology but not for a psychology of human behavior. But another reason may be that contemporary textbook writers give insufficient attention to the problem of defining and delimiting psychology's field of study. This is reflected in the uncritical assertion that the subject matter of psychology is behavior, a term which is then characteristically left undefined and, hence, ambiguous. An example from a current textbook illustrates the situation. The writer says:

If you ask almost any psychologist to define his subject, the chances are that he will say, "*The study of behavior.*" He takes it for granted, of course, that you know he is talking about human and animal behavior, not the behavior of stars or machines or atoms . . . [If one asks] why is psychology the study of behavior? the answer is . . . straightforward. You can study only what you can observe, and behavior is the only

[1] Reprinted from the *American Psychologist*, 1958, **13**, 278–282. Copyright 1958 by the American Psychological Association, and reproduced by permission of Mrs. Rolland H. Waters and the publisher. Address of the President at the Annual Meeting of the Florida State Psychological Association, Miami Beach, Florida, May 3, 1957.

aspect of a person that is observable. We know very well that there are events going on within a person—events that can be called "thought," "feelings," or more generally, "mental activities." We can and do make fairly trustworthy inferences about these events, but we always make them from the way a person behaves. It is what he says, does, and writes that we as scientists can observe and record. Hence it is only behavior that we can study. A person who cannot talk, write, move a muscle, or behave in some way might very well have a "mind," "thoughts," and "feelings," but we could never know what they were, because we would have no access to them. These inner processes are brought to light only through a person's behavior. That is why we say psychology is the study of behavior (Morgan, 1956, p. 3).[2]

This statement raises a series of questions. What is the meaning of the term "behavior"? Is the term appropriately applied to the movements of machines, stars, and atoms? How would an animal have to behave to be a star? Or a machine to be human? How are we to know that "he is talking about human and animal behavior, not the behavior of stars or machines or atoms?" The last question requires some criterion by which we can distinguish the movements of atoms from those of the human individual. Is this criterion *external* to the movements themselves, such as being exhibited by living things? If so, what about plants? Are their movements to be described as "behavior"? Does this external criterion limit the applicability of the term "behavior" to living animal forms? Then does "behavior" include all the movements and activities carried out by the animal or only certain specified activities, activities that exhibit certain characteristics? If this latter is true, then the criterion must be an internal one, that is, one based on the intrinsic or inherent features of the various acts performed. Such an internal criterion is not described. But unless we know what these differentiating characteristics are, I doubt our ability to distinguish between the "behavior" of man, animal, plants, stars, machines, or atoms.

Again the author says:

We know very well that there are events going on within a person—events that can be called "thoughts," "feelings," or more generally, "mental activities."

Now when he, by implication at least, asserts that "you cannot observe these events within a person," does he mean that you, as experimenter, cannot observe them in another, as subject, or does he mean they cannot be observed by either experimenter or subject? If the latter, how can he accept their existence without question? If the former, what is the justification for accepting the subject's behavior as an index of their existence? I would agree that their presence in the experimental subject is, in part, inferential and based, as he tells us, on the character of the subject's responses. However, our belief in the *existence* of such processes is certainly *not* based only on responses we observe. Such a belief is based on our observations of those processes taking place within ourselves. If what we call "behavior" is only a partial basis for accepting their existence, must we not once more ask for

[2] Quotation reprinted by permission from *Introduction to Psychology* by C. T. Morgan. Copyright, 1956. McGraw-Hill Book Company.

the differentiating characteristics of those activities which we can class as "behavior"? Is it not also legitimate to ask: What is the status of these inner processes? Do they not, in their own right, possess those characteristics which justify their being included, along with other activities, in the class "behavior"?

This illustration should be sufficient indication of the need for a definition of the term, behavior, when used to refer to the subject matter of psychology. Such a definition should specify those characteristics of psychology's "behavior" that set it off or serve to differentiate it from the physicist's "behavior of atoms," the botanist's "behavior of plants," the astronomer's "behavior of the stars," and similar usages. The definition must be broad enough to include within its scope three classes of events: the movements of the organism through space, his manipulative and adaptive responses, all of which may be referred to as molar in nature; the subjectively reported, experiential processes; and the neurophysiological activities occurring in conjunction with the molar and experiential processes. Finally, such a definition or, perhaps better, such a conception of behavior must provide *Lebensraum* not only for the comparative psychologist but for the phenomenologist, the clinician, the sensory and physiological psychologist, the experimentalist, the theoretician, and all the rest.

We are all familiar with the statement Woodworth credits to some "wag" to the effect that psychology first lost its soul, then its mind, then consciousness, but that, strangely enough, it still behaves. This characterization is supposed to be descriptive of the change in the subject matter, or content, of psychology throughout its history. We can readily think of a similar characterization of psychology's methodology. For example, the mind has been exorcized, mesmerized, hypnotized, analyzed, psychoanalyzed, cauterized, and is now being tranquilized. It's a wonder the poor thing has survived!

Along with these shifts in content and method there has been a change in the kind of laboratory subject employed. Thus, as substitutes for the adult human individual, we are accustomed to find psychologists using children, the ape, the monkey, the dog, cat, rat, pig, pigeon, hamster, fish, porpoise, paramoecium, and the ant lion in his investigations.

Psychology has thus had a curious and interesting history with respect to its subject matter, its correlated methodologies, and experimental subjects. It started with the conception of a dualism between an immaterial substance, spirit, soul, or mind, and a material substance, matter or body. Then came the first division of labor among the original philosopher-scientists. The study of the changes and phenomena of material things was given over to one group who became the physicists, chemists, physiologists, and neurophysiologists of our day. The study of the phenomena of immaterial substance was taken on by another group from whom we present-day psychologists trace our line of descent. But there is an important point to notice in the present context. The first group claimed to be studying matter; the second, the soul. Matter for the first, soul for the second, was the underlying reality manifesting itself in the phenomena under investigation.

From this early beginning, and we shall now confine ourselves to psychology, the above series of changes were rung on this object of study. The soul was found to be heavily freighted with theological connotations and hence was abandoned by the psychologist. This occurred in spite of the stand taken by Aristotle who, according to McDougall,

. . . rejected the traditional notion of the soul, and regarded it rather as the sum of the vital functions . . . to say that a thing possessed a soul was for him but a convenient way of saying that it exhibited some or all of these peculiarities (peculiarities that distinguish living beings from inert things)(McDougall, 1912, p. 12).

Following the rejection of the term, soul, as an adequate designation or label for the subject matter of psychology, the term, mind, was introduced. But this term was too reminiscent of the soul as an active agent, an entity or substance that carried on its activities "behind the scenes" as it were, and hence did not serve as a satisfactory name for that which could actually be brought into the laboratory. At best it could only be used as a class name for all the concrete "thoughts and feelings" that could be empirically observed. Mind thus lost favor, and the term, consciousness, was introduced in its place. This concept in its turn was discarded and for much the same reason. To paraphrase James's statement made with reference to the Transcendental Ego: mind and consciousness turned out to be but "cheap and nasty editions of the soul" (James, 1890, p. 365). Thus, we come finally to the "modern" notion, at least it is as modern as Aristotle, that the proper subject matter of psychology is behavior. And is there now evidence that this term is being rejected, although for what reason is not clear, by the phenomenologists?

These changes imply a shifting conception of the essential nature of psychology's subject matter. This is not necessarily so. It might as easily be argued that the true nature of that subject matter has not changed. There has been a change in emphasis, a shift in the relative value placed upon different components of this subject matter, or, if you will, a broadening in some respects; but all this gives belated recognition of the fact that no basic change in the conception of psychology's subject matter has taken place. The verbal tag or label attached to that subject matter has changed. But the successive changes in this label reflect only a continuing attempt on the part of psychologists to arrive at a better descriptive term for that which they abstract from the data at hand.

Thus the fundamental reason for the rejection of soul, mind, and consciousness was the fact that, as conceptions abstracted from the raw data, they took on the status of entities, of obscure agencies determining behavior. And this sort of construct was out of harmony with the developing scientific temper of the time. They were not discarded because they were looked upon simply as names for a given class of phenomena. In this respect they might have been discarded later when the emphasis on psychology's data shifted to what was called behavior. Perhaps the longevity of this term, behavior, is due to the fact that it cannot be easily conceived of as an agent or entity. It remains simply a term referring to a group of phenomena. In any other sense it is in no better logical status than was Wundt's "consciousness" or Titchener's "mind."

As we all know, McDougall, for all his being described as a purposivist and interactionist, was the first to use the term, behavior, in the title of a textbook in psychology. True enough he, as did the man who spat out his first drink of beer, regretted it ever afterward. This regret, for McDougall, stemmed from the fact that behaviorism denied the validity of introspection as a method and hence ignored data which were available to the psychologist through this source. McDougall was thus led to modify his 1912 definition of psychology, as ". . . the positive science of behaviour of living things" (McDougall, 1912, p. 19), in such a way as to leave the psychologist room for the use of ". . . the observed facts of experience, facts of his own experience observed introspectively and facts of others' experience described and recorded by them (McDougall, 1923, p. 38).

There are few of us who would disagree with the formal definition of psychology as the positive and empirical science of behavior, providing, of course, that the meaning of behavior can be agreed upon. We will return to this question in a moment. More of us would hesitate to accept introspection as a method on a par with objective observation. In a recent historical review, however, Boring (1953) says that "introspection is still with us, doing business under various aliases, of which *verbal report* is one." He enumerates other places in which the method is used:

. . . the sensory experience of psychophysics, the phenomenal data of Gestalt psychology, the symbolic processes and intervening variables employed by various behaviorists, the ideas, the manifest wishes, the hallucinations, delusions, and emotions of patients and neurotic subjects, and the many mentalistic concepts which social psychology uses.

In this sense, and in some one or more of these areas, who of us does not use that method of observation? But what is it that we are observing or that the subjects of our experiments are observing? Are they states of consciousness, of a consciousness that is wholly separate, distinct, and independent of bodily activities taking place at the same time? In other words, when we make such use of introspection, are we still operating under a dualistic point of view that has been with us throughout our history? Are we, as Boring seems to be saying in his historical review, simply using the verbal reports, the language responses, as well as behavioral responses as the basis for making consciousness "an inferred construct, a concept as inferential as any of the other psychologist's realities" (McDougall, 1912, p. 187)? May it not be that in the introspective or verbal reports, we are being given an account of the components of an act or bit of behavior that we can not know in any other way? In any other way, that is, except through something the subject, human or animal, does or says? When the clinician observes, either by reading or hearing, what the client sees in the Rorschach Test, when the physiological psychologist observes a human subject discriminating between two brightness values, or a comparative psychologist sees the rat doing the same task, the three of us immediately assume that these several reactions, linguistic or grossly behavioral, are telling us something about what is taking place beyond our ken, simultaneously and as part and parcel of the behavioral manifestations that can be observed from the outside and by an independent observer. In other words, we base our inferences of the inner, subjective side of the activity on these outer, objective components of the act. We need these reports, these revelations of the subjective components of the act, to achieve an understanding of the entire act. We need them even more when the external components of the performance are either absent or present in such a manner as not to be open to our own observation. This is the situation when reasoning, thinking, subtle affective, attitudinal, and motivational processes are under examination and study. True, were we clever enough, we assume that instrumental means would reveal that minute neurophysiological and muscular events were likewise taking place. But lacking these instrumental devices, or even with them, the verbal report or some other aspect of the subject's behavior would be necessary to make our knowledge of the entire performance sure. True enough, the subject's verbal report may not be accurate, they may mislead the investigator, but just so may the handshake or complimentary statement be mistakenly interpreted by the recipient.

This seems to me to be the point at which Titchener, and possibly Boring, have missed something important. The dualism between consciousness or mental process and bodily activity was so deeply entrenched in their thinking that they did not see what introspective observation and theory plainly revealed: that the activity of the organism was not properly divisible into two or three distinct parts, but that the parts constituted a single unitary performance. This unit presented certain phenomena that were observable by an external observer and other phenomena that were observable only by the subject himself.

The act that psychology studies is a unitary act. It is not made up of different kinds of reality that run in parallel lines or courses or that interact with each other. No, the act is a complex totality, composed of elements, parts, or phases of which some are open to the observation of an outsider, with or without instruments, and some can be observed only by the subject and reported in linguistic or other expressive movements. Whether the act is a sensory discrimination, a perceptual reaction, a flight of fancy, or a laborious act of reasoning, these components are present within and through it. It is because of this complexity that we need and use, as Boring has so clearly shown, both objective and subjective observation. Both approaches are necessary if we are to arrive at an understanding of the act or bit of behavior we are examining.

Of course it is true that both approaches are not open to us if there is not a common language between subject and experimenter. Some may seize upon this fact and argue that there is no place in psychology for comparative or animal work since the lack of a common language is here obvious. But remember that the subject's report may not be perfectly correlated with the inner side of his behavior—and the human animal is the only animal we know that may deliberately attempt to mislead the experimenter. Predictions of behavior can be made even though we are not in a position to know all the details of that act. I can predict that my car will start when I twist the key, although I know nothing about the operation of the carburetor or its ignition system. The comparative psychologist must grant that what the subjective side of the animal's behavior may be is unknown to him. But this does not prevent most of us from engaging in a bit of judicious anthropomorphizing.

But now we must come to some conclusion to the question with which we started. What is this "behavior" that the psychologist studies? Can we formulate a conception of behavior, the subject matter of psychology, that will be acceptable to our modern temper? Presumably such a conception should utilize only those criteria that can be referred to behavior itself. That is, the conception should be delineated in terms of the essential properties of behavior and not in terms of some extra-behavioral characteristics. For these criteria or attributes which characterize an act as behavior, I favor the following, with grateful acknowledgment to Mc-Dougall, Carr, Tolman, and others who have contributed them: The term *behavior* refers to those activities which exhibit (*a*) spontaneity or autonomy, that is, that are not always or completely controlled by conditions external to the organism itself, (*b*) persistence, (*c*) variability, and (*d*) docility. I would be quite willing to add a fifth characteristic, purpose, but do not do so for two reasons. First, purpose is implied, in any reasonable sense, in the four given; and, second, it might be misunderstood as involving an objectionable brand of teleology.

These, then, are the characteristics, properties, or attributes of those activities that form the subject matter of psychology, that is, behavior. Must they all be present in any given instance, or will the presence of one alone mark the action as behavior? Neither situation may hold. The earmarks need not be present simultaneously, nor does the presence of one alone justify our classifying the act as behavior. In the latter instance, I would argue that somewhere along the line, in the history of the act, the other earmarks have been exhibited. Thus the question might be raised as to the docility of a well learned or habitual performance. To settle such an issue we would ask: "Has the early history of this act exhibited docility?" If so, and to that extent, it qualifies as a bit of behavior. And so we would proceed to apply these criteria to all those actions or activities that present themselves as candidates for psychological study. Those failing to meet the criteria would be excluded; those meeting them would be included.

When I submitted the title for these comments, I proposed to discuss the following question: Does the term "behavior" as used in psychological jargon refer to something we observe, examine, and manipulate in the laboratory or to something abstracted from the observed phenomena? When the subject, or client, responds to an experimental or interview situation, is this response—whether it be partly overt, partly covert, objective or subjective—a bit of behavior; or is it an activity or response possessing characteristics which justify its being a member of a class of phenomena to which the term "behavior" refers?

An analogy may help. The physicist notes and records the readings on his thermometer, his voltmeter, or his pressure gauge. Were we to ask him what he is studying, would he say that he was studying the variation in the readings these instruments exhibit or would he say that he is studying heat, electricity, light, and so on? I think he would say the latter and then add that these terms are the class names or labels for particular groups of phenomena. Any given phenomenon is assigned to this or that category in terms of the characteristics that are held in common with other members of the class.

My contention is that psychology's "behavior" is analogous to the physicist's heat, that the psychologist uses the term to refer to a class of activities that possess certain characteristics, those referred to by the criteria outlined above. This means that "behavior" is an abstraction, not a datum. The data are the specific responses exhibited by the human or animal subject. Some of these specific responses can be classed as "behavior" for and by the psychologist; others presumably exist that do not belong to that class and hence are not data for psychology.

I think that what I am suggesting is not particularly novel in any way. Throughout its history, psychology has continually used such terms as mind, consciousness, adaptation, or adjustive activities to refer to its subject matter. And has not this usage always implied an abstracting of common characteristics from the specific and concrete activities studied? In a more restricted area, are not such terms as learning, retention, intelligence, aptitude, one's perception of his "self," and a host of other terms used in this abstract sense?

REFERENCES

Boring, E. G. A history of introspection. *Psychological Bulletin*, 1953, **50**, 169–189.

James, W. *Principles of psychology*. Vol. I. New York: Holt, 1890.

Johnson, E. On readmitting the mind. *American Psychologist*, 1956, **11**, 712–714.

McClelland, D. C. The psychology of mental content reconsidered. *Psychological Review*, 1955, **62**, 297–302.

McDougall, W. *Psychology: the study of behavior*. New York: Holt, 1912.

McDougall, W. *Outline of psychology*. New York: Scribner's, 1923.

Morgan, C. T. *Introduction to psychology*. New York: McGraw-Hill, 1956.

Nuttin, J. Consciousness, behavior, and personality. *Psychological Review*, 1955, **62**, 349–355.

8. The Nature of the
Human Data Source in Psychology[1]

Duane P. Schultz

The following article discusses the nature and role of the human subject in the historical development of psychology from structuralism to the current neo-behavioristic era. It is suggested that there is reason for alarm about the nature of the human subject, the ways in which he is used, and the validity of the data he supplies. The role and task of the human subject has changed as psychology has progressed, but his status or image as a mechanical, passively responding object has remained unchanged.

This view of subject-as-object is no longer meaningful when considered in the light of current thinking in physics and philosophy of science which recognizes the subjectivity of all knowledge and the fusing of observer and observed in the very act of observing. For philosophical as well as empirical considerations, new methods of research must be developed to make more valid and realistic use of subjects. The subject must be recognized as an acting participant in the research process and not as a mechanical responder to stimuli.

An important though often neglected aspect of contemporary psychology is the source of most of our data—the human subject. Beyond the somewhat mechanical process of securing subjects and "running" them (a significant way of describing what psychologists do with them), little consideration seems to be given to the nature or role of the subject as a source of data and, indeed, as our prototype of man in general. It has been suggested that psychologists today "have long since lost sight of the fact that their experimental subjects are, after all, people" (Sanford, 1965, p. 192).

Our subjects are human beings, however, and not just passive responders to stimuli, although the latter has been assumed to be the case since the earliest days of scientific psychology. The subjects come to our laboratories with fears and anxieties, curiosity and eagerness, hostility and belligerence, and respond not just to the experimental situation as the experimenter has manipulated it, but rather to the situation as they perceive it. And their perception is influenced by a host of variables from both within and without the laboratory, many of which are beyond the control of the experimenter.[2]

In an imaginary letter (Jourard, 1968), *S* asks *E*:

> Did you ever stop to think that your articles, and the textbooks you write, the theories you spin—all based on your data (my disclosures to you)—may actually be a tissue of lies and half-truths (my lies and half-truths) or a joke I've played on you because I don't like you or trust you? That should give you cause for some concern (p. 11).

There is ample reason for concern and alarm in psychology today about the nature of the human subject, the ways in which he is used, and the validity of the data he supplies. On both empirical and philosophical grounds, it is time to re-examine the nature of the human data source in psychology. This discussion will cover the subject in early scientific psychology and his changed role with the advent of behaviorism. It will be argued that although the subject's role and task changed as psychology progressed, his nature or image has remained constant throughout, and that this image is obsolete in that it fails to reflect current thinking in physics and philosophy of science.

THE SUBJECT IN EARLY PSYCHOLOGY: STRUCTURALISM

Those subjects (or, more properly, observers) who participated in the introspective research of Wundt and Titchener differed in several respects from the subjects of today. First, they were either psychologists themselves or psychologists-in-training (graduate students). As such, they were probably highly motivated in their roles as observers, as one would have had to be to perform the complex and time-consuming introspections required in that era. They were well trained for their task, having undergone long apprenticeships, and knew what to look for and what errors to avoid. Boring (1953) noted that observers in the Leipzig reaction experiments were required to perform some 10,000 introspective reactions before they were considered capable of providing data worthy of publication. Thus, the early subjects were highly skilled and motivated to pursue what Titchener called the "hard introspective labor."

It is interesting that the observers during this introspective era were sometimes referred to in journal articles as "reagents," which may be defined as any substance which, from its capacity for certain reactions, is used in detecting, examining, or measuring other substances (*Webster's New Collegiate Dictionary*, 1958, p. 704). The use of this term suggests that a subject was considered to be of the nature

[2] These influencing variables are discussed by Kelman, Orne, and Rosenthal in the section "Research with Human Subjects."

of a chemical reagent: a constant which will elicit an invariant reaction from any substance or process to which it might be applied. This might imply that subjects were thought of as rather like recording instruments, objectively noting the characteristics of their target of observation. This "machine view" of observers was noted by Titchener (1912) when he spoke of the technique of observing becoming mechanized through training and practice, so that observation was not a conscious process. In speaking of this mechanism of habit, Titchener quoted Wundt as saying that *"In his attention to the phenomena under observation,* the observer in psychology, no less than the observer in physics, *completely forgets to give subjective attention to the state of observing"* (1912, p. 443).

Thus we have an objective and detached observing mechanism who reports to the experimenter on the processes observed. The phenomena under consideration, the elemental contents of consciousness, were considered to be independent of and separate from the observer. The observer and observed were thus discrete entities.

Could anyone be a reagent? Did everyone have this invariant capacity for certain reactions? The structuralists' answer was initially negative. Titchener (1895*b*) quoted Wundt as saying:

there are individuals who are entirely incapable of any steady concentration of the attention, and who will therefore never make trustworthy [reagents]. That should not be surprising. It is not everyone who has the capacity for astronomical or physical observation; and it is not to be expected either that everyone is endowed with the gifts requisite for psychological experimentation (p. 507).

Binet (1894) also noted that "the aptitude for introspection is not given to everyone; some possess it in high degree; these are the born psychologists" (p. 18).

It was thought, then, that there was a "disposition" (as Titchener called it) for psychological research. Precisely what constituted this disposition was never made explicit beyond describing it as specific habits, attitudes, and "characteristics of mind." Presumably, however, a master-introspectionist would recognize this ability.

By 1912, perhaps due to a shortage of "born psychologists," Titchener modified this requirement of a disposition for introspection, noting that "any normal person, coming to the task with goodwill and application, may understand and acquire [it]" (p. 446). Thus, a person could be trained to properly introspect. This training, Titchener argued, was similar to the kind of training required for reliable observations in biology or physics. In addition to the proper training, introspection required that the observers be in good health, free from anxiety and worry, and comfortable in their surroundings at the time of observation.

It was suggested that a subject was considered a constant eliciting an invariant reaction. If this were true, then the research findings must have resulted in satisfyingly consistent data with no extreme scores to cause dismay. But surely Titchener's reagents, no matter how well trained and mechanized, could not have all produced highly similar reactions, considering the subjective nature of their task.

It seems that they did not, but let us quote from Titchener on this point of data consistency.

In his famous reaction time debate with James Mark Baldwin (1895–1896), Titchener noted that "The only results ruled out are those which are wholly irregular and inconstant" (1895*b*, p. 507). In one research report he noted that "Seven participants in this investigation were found to be incapable of reacting with any degree of constancy: their results were therefore not employed" (1895*a*, p. 75). Thus, out of ten reagents in this particular study, seven gave inconsistent results, but the remaining three consistent reagents (no doubt "born psychologists") gave highly similar reaction times and so constituted the findings.

Small wonder that Baldwin engaged in such an active debate! In commenting on another Titchener study, in which the results of six out of nine reagents were ruled out, Baldwin asked:

If one-third of mankind are to be taken to prove that a result is a universal principle, the rest being deliberately excluded because they cannot get the result that the one-third do, then what conclusions could not be proved in well-managed psychological laboratories? (1896, p. 82).

A CHANGE WITH FUNCTIONALISM

Baldwin favored the use of untrained and unpracticed observers and the Titchener-Baldwin debate centering on the kinds of subjects to be used was really a debate between the older structuralist position and the newer American spirit of functionalism. Wundt and Titchener searched for general laws of the human mind and so the existence of individual differences among the reagents was, to them, a source of annoyance to be eliminated rather than investigated.

The functionalist spirit or attitude was able to accommodate the notion of individual differences; indeed, it fostered an active psychology of individual differences under the aggressive leadership of James McKeen Cattell. The functionalists were interested in studying the minds of untrained observers and so could turn to naive subjects from the college and general populations. Earlier, a precursor of functional psychology, Sir Francis Galton, used naive subjects from the general population in his famous Anthropometric Laboratory—and these subjects even paid for the privilege of being tested.

Thus, the functionalists' concern with individual differences brought about a change in the kind of human subject studied, from the trained and well-practiced professional of Titchener to the untrained and naive amateur of Cattell and other functionalists.

There was another change taking place also and that had to do with the decline of introspection with an attendant shift in the role of the human subject from observer to the one (or thing) observed. In the early years of this century, dissatisfaction was being expressed over introspection in this country (except, of course, at Cornell). For example, G. Stanley Hall wrote in 1910: "formerly everyone supposed that self-observation . . . was the oracle and muse of philosophic studies. Now, however, . . . it is coming to be seen that this method gives us access to but a very small part of the soul " (p. 621). Hall urged the use of objective natural science methods involving the description of what we observe in others.

Even before John B. Watson and his behaviorist manifesto of 1913, there was a decided leaning among many American psychologists toward greater objectivity. At the functionalist base at the University of Chicago, much research was conducted in the early 1900s without recourse to introspection. Many of the subjects used in these studies were those most readily available—the graduate and undergraduate students.

BEHAVIORISM: A NEW ROLE FOR SUBJECTS

Completing with a sharp finality the move away from introspection (of the classical variety) and toward the more exclusive use of experimental observation of behavior was, of course, behaviorism. And it was this that brought about the total change of role of the human subject.

In classical introspection, the reagent was the observer and the observed at the same time. It was the reagent who observed the subject matter— his own conscious experience. As Boring (1953) commented, the observer "has the responsibility for the correctness of his descriptions of conscious data" (p. 184). The observer, then, had a very important and responsible position in the experimental procedure. The experimenter set up the conditions and recorded the observations of the observer.

With behaviorism, this situation changed completely for Titchener's observer became Watson's subject. In other words, with behaviorism, the true observer is the experimenter who observes the responses of the subject to the conditions the experimenter has set up. Thus, the human subject was demoted in status—he no longer observed, he merely behaved and became the object of observation. And almost anyone can behave—children, the mentally ill, animals, and even the college sophomore!

THE UNCHANGED IMAGE: SUBJECT-AS-OBJECT

It is suggested that throughout the history of scientific psychology, from the introspective era to the current neo-behavioristic climate, the image of the human subject has been that of inanimate object. The model of man adopted by the psychology of Wundt was quite naturally that of the prevailing climate of thought induced by the mechanistic philosophers. Man was (and still is) considered to be an organic machine. In the Newtonian world view, the image of the universe as a great machine was extended to man and the concepts of determinism and mechanistic causation were applied to human nature. As a consequence of this machine model of man, the subject in psychology "becomes nothing more than a stimulus-response machine: you put a stimulus in one of the slots, and out comes a packet of reactions" (Burt, 1962, p. 232).

One aspect of Newtonian classical physics of particular relevance to our discussion is the notion that nature constituted a unique reality independent of man. An important consequence of this was the assumption that nature was objectively observable and independent of the observer. There developed a dichotomy between man and nature, inner world and outer world, observer and the observed. The observer is detached, distant, and aloof from what is being observed be it the physical universe, the contents of consciousness, or behavioral responses.

This observer-observed dichotomy, together with the tendency to view our subjects as mechanical inanimate objects to be poked, prodded, manipulated and measured, causes the experimenter-subject dyad to be of the order of Buber's I-It relationship. The relationship is not that of person-to-person but rather of person-to-thing with its attendant tendencies of domination, manipulation, and control.

Thus, when an experimenter is observing a human subject in the laboratory, he is dealing with some *thing* which is "not human, not personal, something independent of . . . the perceiver." The observer is alien to his subject, "uncomprehending and without sympathy and identification" (Maslow, 1966, p. 49). In the same vein, Clark Hull suggested that we consider "the behaving organism as a completely self-maintaining robot, constructed of materials as unlike ourselves as may be" (1943, p. 27).

Viewed in this manner, the sophomore in our modern laboratory is not a person, not an individual, but merely an object—and only a sample object at that.

A POSSIBLE NEW DIRECTION

This highly objective, detached, and aloof spectator observation (by E) of a machine-like object (S) would be commendable, indeed necessary, if the underlying assumptions, *i.e.*, the Newtonian machine view of the universe and the consequent behaviorist machine view of man, were valid. But physics many years ago discarded this mechanical view as several of the previous articles in this section have amply demonstrated. Physics now recognizes the ultimate subjectivity of all that which we would call objective, and that the very act of observing nature disturbs it, thus distorting or changing reality.

One important implication of this is the closing of the gap between the observer and the observed, and the change of focus of scientific inquiry from an independent and objectively knowable universe to man's observation of the universe. No longer the detached observer, the modern scientist is now cast in the role of participant-observer. The process of observation becomes an interaction, with contributions coming from both sides of the observational transaction. There is no longer an independent fact and independent observer but rather an interaction and integration of the two in an observation. The observer and the observed are no longer considered as being separable.

Complete and total objectivity, then, is now seen as illusory for it is recognized that "as human beings, we must inevitably see the universe from a centre lying within ourselves. Any attempt rigorously to eliminate our human perspective from our picture of the world must lead to absurdity" (Polanyi, 1958, p. 3).

Psychology, with its history of emulating physics, continues to cling to an antiquated model: "as the mechanistic viewpoint has been found to be inadequate for the full comprehension of inorganic matter and natural events, it is a fortiori inadequate for the understanding of human nature and human events" (Matson, 1964, p. 155). If and when psychology absorbs the newer physics of subjectivity, of uncertainty, of participation in observation, then it must institute a thorough methodological and conceptual reorientation and develop a new image of man.

As the articles in this section demonstrate, there are signs of a growing disaffection with the behaviorists' machine model and the consequent dehumanization of man. New lines of thought with regard to the valid and realistic use of human subjects are appearing in the literature.

These suggested changes are seen as necessary not only on the philosophical grounds already discussed, but also on empirical grounds. The reference here is to the growing body of data which suggest that subjects are well aware of our attempts at deceiving them in the laboratory (Argyris, 1968; Kelman, 1967; Orne, 1962; Riecken, 1962; Schultz, 1969), and that they consequently do not believe what we tell them (with good reason). Further, subjects tend to respond in ways designed to please the experimenter if they like him, or to "foul up" the experimenter if they don't like him or are unhappy at being required to serve as subjects.

The important point is that the subject responds in accordance with his attitude toward and perception of the situation, which means that he is not simply a passive responder to the situation, although this is the assumption usually made. He is an active participant in it and this very activity changes the nature of the situation for him. His world, then, is not simply what the experimenter defines and presents to him. No matter how thoroughly we attempt to control and standardize the experimental situation, it is, in fact, neither controlled nor standardized to the subject. The resulting situation is one that is not intended and, more importantly, not known to the experimenter, and one that will vary among subjects. That some change in our image and use of the human subject is necessary seems an inescapable conclusion.

Let us examine two recently proposed experimental approaches in the light of these considerations.

One approach, suggested by Brown (1965) and Kelman (1967), among others, is that of role-playing. Instead of deliberately concealing the nature and purpose of the experiment, these would be explained to the subject and his cooperation sought. The intent is for the subject to directly and actively involve himself in the experiment, and to conscientiously participate in the experimental task. In this approach, the subject hopefully would have a more positive attitude toward the experiment and the experimenter if he felt that he was sharing with the experimenter in a collaborative endeavor rather than being used as a guinea pig.

This technique eliminates the questionable practice of deception which, as we have seen, is frequently ineffective. The subject, in role-playing, is not considered as merely a mechanical responder to stimuli but is much more of an acting participant. How effectively subjects will role-play, of course, may depend on a number of variables including the degree of intrinsic interest of the task, the face validity of the instructions, and the subject's perception of and attitude toward the experimenter. Of course, the latter point is also a serious problem in current research techniques.

Role-playing would seem to offer two advantages: the elimination of deception and the involvement of the subject as more of a direct participant in the data collection. It must be remembered that the subject is a direct and influencing participant in data collection whether we recognize or like it. Such being the case, it would seem appropriate to make active use of this participation rather than to pretend that it does not exist.

Another approach, suggested by Jourard (1968), involves the conducting of experiments with a mutual self-disclosure between the experimenter and the subject. Instead of the impersonal, detached, and distrustful relationship that is now often the case, Jourard suggests a greater openness and mutual knowing in the experimenter-subject dyad. The subject would be encouraged to report what the stimuli and his behavioral responses really mean to him. The experimenter, in turn, would explain what he thinks the subject's responses mean, and the subject asked to respond. Thus, both experimenter and subject would be open and revealing to one another.

This approach, too, eliminates the problem of deception and it involves the subject as an active participant and collaborator, perhaps even more fully than role-playing. It might be suggested, however, that the subject's degree of self-disclosure and openness would depend in large measure on the "personality" of the experimenter and that this factor could influence the subject's responses more than the independent variables involved in the experiment. Of course, the subject's perception of and attitude toward the experimenter affects his behavior in contemporary research, but this influence of the experimenter would seem to be greater when he is more intrusive and interacting in the experiment.

Of less importance, but still a consideration, is the fact that such an approach would be tremendously time-consuming in experiments requiring relatively large numbers of subjects. Further, it would be difficult to adapt this technique to group research involving interaction and intermember influence.

These reservations notwithstanding, the technique is an interesting one and does offer certain advantages including the potential for changing "the status of the subject from that of an anonymous *object* of our study to the status of a *person*, a fellow seeker, a *collaborator* in our enterprise" (Jourard, 1968, p. 25). Jourard and his students are performing very imaginative research to investigate the technique.

Both of these approaches have several points in common. They eliminate deception and "require us to *use* the subject's motivation to cooperate rather than to bypass it; they may even call for increasing the sophistication of potential subjects, rather than maintaining their naiveté" (Kelman, 1967, p. 10). They both involve the subject as an active participant in the research process (which he always was) rather than assuming him to be an inanimate, mechanical responder to stimuli (which he *never* was).

For the various reasons discussed herein, it seems imperative that psychology adopt a more realistic image of the human subject—one that reflects and incorporates both the newer thinking in philosophy of science and the results of our own research on research. If we are able to cast off our prejudices and long-ingrained habits of thought and practice in research, we might even advance to the point of discovering "what everyone else already knows, that one can usually understand a person's behavior much better if one tries to find out what he thought of the experiment and decided to do about it" (Farber, 1963, p. 187). Perhaps, then, the best way of investigating the nature of man is to ask him.

REFERENCES

Argyris, C. Some unintended consequences of rigorous research. *Psychological Bulletin*, 1968, **70**, 185–197.

Baldwin, J. M. The "type-theory" of reaction. *Mind*, 1896, **5**, 81–90.

Binet, A. *Introduction à la psychologie expérimentale.* 1894.

Boring, E. G. A history of introspection. *Psychological Bulletin*, 1953, **50**, 169–189.

Brown, R. *Social psychology.* New York: Free Press, 1965.

Burt, C. The concept of consciousness. *British Journal of Psychology*, 1962, **53**, 229–242.

Farber, I. E. The things people say to themselves. *American Psychologist*, 1963, **18**, 185–197.

Hall, G. S. A children's institute. *Harper's Monthly Magazine*, 1910, cxx.

Hull, C. L. *Principles of behavior.* New York: Appleton-Century-Crofts, 1943.

Jourard, S. M. *Disclosing man to himself.* Princeton, N. J.: Van Nostrand, 1968.

Kelman, H. C. Human use of human subjects: the problem of deception in social psychological experiments. *Psychological Bulletin*, 1967, **67**, 1–11.

Maslow, A. H. *The psychology of science.* New York: Harper & Row, 1966.

Matson, F. W. *The broken image.* New York: George Braziller, 1964.

Orne, M. T. On the social psychology of the psychological experiment: with particular reference to demand characteristics and their implications. *American Psychologist*, 1962, **17**, 776–783.

Polanyi, M. *Personal knowledge.* Chicago: University of Chicago Press, 1958.

Riecken, H. W. A program for research on experiments in social psychology. In N. Washburne (Ed.), *Decisions, values and groups.* Vol. II. New York: Pergamon Press, 1962. Pp. 25–41.

Sanford, N. Will psychologists study human problems? *American Psychologist*, 1965, **20**, 192–202.

Schultz, D. P. The human subject in psychological research. *Psychological Bulletin*, 1969, **72**, 214-228.

Titchener, E. B. Simple reactions. *Mind*, 1895a, **4**, 74–81.
Titchener, E. B. The type-theory of the simple reaction. *Mind*, 1895b, **4**, 506–514.
Titchener, E. B. Prolegomena to a study of introspection. *American Journal of Psychology*, 1912, **23**, 427–448.
Watson, J. B. Psychology as the behaviorist views it. *Psychological Review*, 1913, **20**, 158–177.
Webster's New Collegiate Dictionary. Springfield, Mass.: G. & C. Merriam, 1958.

9. Operationism as Methodology[1]

Robert Plutchik

One of the more important components of the philosophical framework of scientific psychology is the principle of operationism. In his comprehensive article, Dr. Plutchik discusses the several varieties of operationism that have developed out of psychology's modification of Bridgman's original concept. Although operationism has been influential in psychology, Dr. Plutchik notes that the concept has met with much highly vocal criticism since its initial appearance. In summarizing this wide-ranging criticism, he discusses problems such as generality, equivalence of operations, reductionism, and infinite regress. The conclusion is drawn that operationism falls short of adequacy and that there are other more useful means of defining concepts at the various stages in the development of a science.

The doctrine of "operationism" formulated by Bridgman (1927) has caught the imagination of psychologists and has gradually come to dominate most psychological discussions of philosophy of science and the meaning of concepts. It has been claimed that operationism will insure against "hazy, ambiguous and contradictory notions," and will cure the "notable instability of psychology" (Stevens, 1935, p. 323). In the 1945 Symposium on Operationism, five of the six participants were clearly in favor of it while only one was opposed.

Since that time, however, there have been many reactions to this doctrine, some of which have been quite harsh in their judgment of its value. A sociologist writes that "the operational definition, as here discussed, is an obstacle to scientific advance because of its exclusion of criticism" (Adler, 1947, p. 442). It is also claimed that operationism does not answer the basic question of when an operation is pertinent to a problem, or whether operations can be selected in completely arbitrary ways (Ginsberg, 1955). Pratt (1945, p. 268) adds that "it would be unfortunate indeed if the effect of operationism in psychology were to place a stamp of approval on certain limited fields of research in which hypotheses can be neatly formulated

[1] Reprinted from *Behavioral Science*, 1963, **8**, 234–241, with the permission of the author and *Behavioral Science*. The author wishes to thank Father Joseph Dorff for critically reading the manuscript and for his comments.

in the language of the older sciences, and to look askance at the wide open spaces in which concepts are fluid and vague and sometimes nonsense." And Skinner (1945, p. 294) has noted that "the confusion which seems to have arisen from a principle which is supposed to eliminate confusion is discouraging."

The reason for such varied reactions to this doctrine may be related not only to the content as formulated by Bridgman but also the various modifications it has gone through at the hands of psychological theorists. It is quite possible that the critics are reacting to things quite different from those originally intended.

That this is indeed the case can be illustrated by reference to the various (non-operational) definitions and explications of operationism that have appeared in the literature.

THE VARIETIES OF OPERATIONISM

Bridgman's (1927) own ideas may be summarized by the following propositions:

1. The concept is synonymous with the corresponding set of operations. "The concept of length involves as much as and nothing more than the set of operations by which length is determined" (p. 5).

2. The definition of a concept should not be in terms of its properties but in terms rather of actual operations.

3. "The true meaning of a term is to be found by observing what a man does with it, not by what he says about it" (p. 7).

4. All our knowledge must be relative to the operations selected to measure our scientific concepts. "If we have more than one set of operations, we have more than one concept" (p. 10).

In Bridgman's later writings he added two other important notions, to wit: a concept may be defined not only in terms of physical operations used to measure it but also in terms of mental or paper-and-pencil operations (Bridgman, 1950); and, secondly, that "operational analysis is mostly restricted to questions of meaning and as such can have only partial congruence with the universe of experimental method" (Bridgman, 1945, p. 248).

Stevens' (1939) view of operationism is put in a different way: ". . . the propositions of science have empirical significance only when their truth can be demonstrated by a set of concrete operations" (p. 222). In this conception, operations are thought of, not simply as ways of measuring concepts, as by Bridgman, but rather as ways of proving or disproving propositions. This view should be clearly distinguished from Bridgman's, for the problem of verification is one on which contemporary philosophers of science are far from unanimous.

Another definition of operationism is attributable to Skinner (1945): "Operationism may be defined as the practice of talking about (1) one's observations, (2) the manipulational and calculational procedures involved in making them, (3) the logical and mathematical steps which intervene between earlier and later statements, and (4) nothing else" (p. 270). He also adds, "Operationism is not regarded as a new theory or mode of definition" (p. 270).

It should be evident that this statement, although in the general pragmatic tradition, is different from Bridgman's conception of operationism. The key issue involved in Skinner's definition concerns what is to be meant by "one's observations." Does the physicist "observe" electric fields and electrons or does he observe dials? Does the psychologist "observe" answers on a test of intelligence? The problem of how one goes from pointer readings to concepts still exists. In commenting on Skinner's definition, Benjamin (1955, p. 55) writes: "... to use the term in this highly general sense would immediately make all scientists operationists, since one could hardly conceive of any entity entering into scientific consideration which is not either observational or inferred from something observational."

A sociologist who has written extensively on operationism has presented his interpretation of it in the following statements: "The only way of defining anything objectively is in terms of the operations involved." He also writes that by using "overt behavior of some sort, such as pointing to an object, or going through the operations which we use the new terms to designate . . . [we] avoid becoming involved in insoluble metaphysical questions of ultimate reality" (Lundberg, 1939, p. 25).

This view is much closer to that of Bridgman although it makes explicit the idea that by proper methods of defining concepts all the age-old metaphysical problems of science will be solved or eliminated at one sweep. It thus implies a right to be called a full-fledged philosophy of science.

In contrast to this view is one developed by Feigl, the philosopher who participated in the 1945 Symposium on Operationism. He wrote: "Operationism is not a system of philosophy. It is not a technique for the formation of concepts or theories. It will not by itself produce scientific results. These are brought about by the labor and ingenuity of the researchers. Operationism is, rather, a set of regulative or critical standards" (1945, p. 258).

One final point will be made about the varieties of operationism. Israel and Goldstein (1944) gather a good deal of evidence to show that psychologists have tended to interpret Bridgman's views of meaning, not so much in terms of the operations needed to *measure* a concept but rather in terms of the operations needed to *produce* a phenomenon. Thus "drive" might be defined by the length of time an animal is kept away from food rather than in terms of the behavior of a hungry animal. Now, although this may be a valid way of defining a concept, it should be recognized that it is not the same way that Bridgman chose to define physical concepts. Still other varieties of operationism are described by Benjamin (1955) and by Newbury (1953).

These illustrations indicate that the word "operationism" does not define any one clearly specified body of doctrine. Although there is a general pragmatic flavor to most of the discussions of this topic, the specific things meant by the term vary widely and thus make any critique only partially applicable.

CRITIQUE OF THE OPERATIONIST POSITION

Since the appearance of Bridgman's book, there have been many criticisms of his viewpoint, some by philosophers, some by physicists, and some by sociologists and psychologists. The following remarks represent, essentially, a summary of the various criticisms which have been made of the operationist position. The basic point of departure will be the writings of Bridgman, and thus, it is possible that not all criticisms apply to all the varieties of operationism described in the preceding section.

Measurement Presupposes a Concept

Expressions such as, "intelligence is what an intelligence test measures," have often been used to illustrate an operational definition of a concept. That this is a highly inadequate way of defining can be exemplified by an illustration given by Adler (1947). He defines what he calls "The C_N Test" by the answers to a series of questions:

"1. How many hours did you sleep last night? ———
2. Estimate the length of your nose in inches and multiply by 2.
3. Do you like fried liver? (Mark 1 for Yes and —1 for No.)
4. How many feet are there in a yard? ———
5. Estimate the number of glasses of ginger ale the inventor of this test drank while inventing it.

Add the above items. The sum is your crude C_N score. Take the test daily at the same hour as long as you can. Then calculate your refined C_N rate by . . ." (p. 439).

It is obvious that such a test is pure nonsense regardless of the statistical formulas used or methodological refinements involved in the statement of items or categories of analysis. The statement that "C_N is what the test measures" is completely unsatisfactory on the two grounds that we are unable to form any meaningful concept of it, and that all criticism is excluded since "The test measures C_N and C_N is what the test measures." It is also clear that an infinite number of such "tests" can be formed in this arbitrary way. Operationism provides no basis for distinguishing between meaningful and meaningless concepts defined by such measurements.

Before we can adequately measure anything we need to know, at least in general, what we want to find out, even if there is some vagueness to our concept. Science develops its measuring tools, typically, by a series of successive approximations in which the concept gradually achieves greater precision, the ambiguities are eliminated, and the relations between the concept and other concepts are more clearly formulated. Observation and measurement presuppose things with properties as well as previous theory. We never start from operations.

The fact that measurement presupposes a concept is illustrated by Prentice (1946) in a discussion of the controversy over "continuity versus non-continuity" theories of learning. He points out that "the term 'hypothesis' is misleading when it has been defined to mean a kind of behavior. If hypotheses in rats were what they are in man, the hypothesis would necessarily *precede* the behavior which indicated its presence, and lack of that behavior could not disprove the existence of the hypothesis. . . . We are still without operations which can define 'noticing the stimulus cues' or 'having a (symbolic) hypothesis' in animals but the concepts are surely not meaningless . . ." (p. 248).

Not only does measurement presuppose a concept but the concept is usually broader than the particular method used to measure it. This is what makes it possible for "habit strength" to be measured by rate of learning, errors made, probability of response, trials to reach a criterion, etc. It occurs, not uncommonly, that two or three measures of the same concept do not correlate well. Operationism provides no basis for selecting between operations which ostensibly measure the same thing or for evaluating the relative value of measurements.

The Problem of Generality

Pfannenstill (1951), Peters (1951), and Benjamin (1955) all have pointed to the problem of generality of concepts raised by the operational view of definition. They ask whether operationism does not make all general concepts impossible since even the smallest variation in the procedures of measurement implies a new concept. Bridgman himself has noted that yardsticks and triangulation measure two different kinds of "length." But does this not also imply that "length" as measured by a steel ruler is different from that measured by a wooden ruler, or by a micrometer, etc.; and that in the same sense, "heat" is different when measured by a mercury thermometer, an alcohol thermometer, a thermocouple, or a thermistor ?

Such variations in procedure are commonplace in science, and yet it is generally believed that these different procedures or operations are designed to measure the same concept. It is also recognized that certain sources of error may operate for one measuring procedure that do not operate for another. These sources of error are gradually discovered and eliminated and the different measurement procedures converge to produce a single consistent answer. In the measurement of temperature the differential expansion rates of different substances used as thermometers provided some sources of error which were increasingly understood and taken into account. Finally, temperature as defined by the Kelvin scale became measurable by the use of general physical laws which were independent of the specific properties relating to the expansion of substances.

Similarly, the charge on the electron and the velocity of light have both been measured in a variety of ways, with increasing convergence of results. An astronomer working in the recently developed field of radio astronomy has written: "By the use of a variety of techniques, and with everlasting emphasis on high precision in the measurement of positions, we may count on slow future progress . . ." (Bok, 1955, p. 338).

Operationism would imply that the use of many different methods to determine the properties of the synapse means that many different and unrelated concepts are being studied. This, of course, is contrary to the spirit of the whole series of observations made in connection with this problem. If there are many independent operational definitions, how is it possible to arrive at general constructs? The fact is that most scientists are interested in finding general explanations and general concepts that will account for a large number of apparently isolated or unrelated observations in terms of a small number of terms or constructs. Operationism, literally interpreted, would move science in the opposite direction, greatly increasing the number of unrelated concepts and actually providing a new concept for each new observation. Such a situation would make scientific teaching and prediction almost impossible.

This problem of generality of concept has been recognized by some of the operationists and an answer has been attempted: generalization can occur in terms of the equivalence of results of operations. But this solution leads to another problem.

The Problem of Equivalence of Operations

Bridgman has pointed out that two operations may be said to be equivalent if they lead to the same numerical results. Thus, since tape measurement and triangulation produce the same outcome in all terrestrial applications they therefore refer to the same concept, even though we must be prepared to abandon this notion of equivalent concepts when and if the two methods of measurement do not produce the same numerical results. This may seem like a perfectly valid procedure, but it is a direct denial of the basic operational principle, since if concepts are to be defined by operations, and the operation is of primary significance, then the concept cannot *also* be defined by the equivalence of numerical results obtained by using different operations. "This argument detaches the concept of quantitative value from its operational meaning and gives it the status of an absolute property which transcends the methods by which it was determined. It is a mistake, therefore, to regard two constructs as the same because they bear the same numerical designation. ... Equivalence among operations demands a point of reference outside of the operations themselves" (Israel, 1945, p. 260).

Thus, this attempt to fit operationism to the actual practices of scientists actually leads to a contradiction in that the basic definition of a concept in terms only of operations is superseded by something which is not an operation, to wit, a numerical equivalence of results.

There is one other problem involved in this context. If two procedures provide the same outcome in measurement of a phenomenon, then the operationist may conclude that the same concept is being measured by the different methods. If, however, the two operations do not lead to the same equivalent outcome then the temptation is strong simply to conclude that two different concepts are being measured which may have nothing to do with one another. This is in contrast to asking: *Why don't the two numerical results agree?* The exploration of discrepancies, observed in the course of experimentation, has often, in the history of science, led to important discoveries and advances, and a strict following of the operationist view may prevent potentially fruitful questions from being asked and may impede the discovery of new phenomena.

The Problem of Error

The fact that in actual scientific practice there are often several ways of measuring a given phenomenon poses several problems for the operationist. One has already been mentioned, i.e., the problem of equivalence of operations, but a second question which arises is the question of whether one measure is in some sense "better" than any other. To be able to judge the relative value of measurements or of operations requires criteria beyond the operations themselves. If a concept is nothing but an operation, then how can we talk about being mistaken or about making errors? If "heat" stands for certain measurement procedures, then there is no sense in talking of better ways of measuring it or of being mistaken in such measures. Similarly, from a definition such as "intelligence is what IQ tests measure," one cannot construct a new test or judge how good the old one is (Ginsberg, 1955).

One of the facts of science is a continuous tendency to modify existing methods of measurement so that certain properties can be evaluated with greater and greater precision. New instruments and new designs are continuously being developed, and yet we do not identify the concept being measured with the measurement procedure or instrument being used. If we did, then improvements and changes of method would produce new concepts, which they generally do not do. Over the past half century, skin resistance, or GSR, has been measured with dozens of different instruments, circuits, designs, and procedures, and although many of these operations have had various sources of bias associated with them, the common element which binds all this research together is the fact that the particular concept "skin resistance" is being measured. As science develops the sources of error are gradually eliminated. Operationism has never adequately taken into consideration this problem of the improvement of measuring procedures and the elimination of error. Feigl (1945) has pointed out that thermometers and IQ tests did not arise in a historical vacuum but that there were repeated redefinitions. "It makes perfectly good sense to ask whether a mercury thermometer measures temperature adequately" (p. 255). The same, of course, may be asked of psychological measurements.

The Problem of Infinite Regress

In the 1945 Symposium on Operationism the question was raised of whether operationism leads to an infinite regress: that is, since a concept is defined by the operations used to measure it, how will the operations themselves be defined? It is clear that it would be possible to define operationally each of the words used in a particular definition, but these new operational definitions would need to be defined operationally also, ad infinitum.

The only answer given in the Symposium is that we stop operationally defining when we use terms that everyone pretty much understands. Although this is a practical kind of solution necessitated by the impossible situation, it is not logically consistent with the tenets of operationism which, when carried through consistently, lead to an infinite regress.

The Problem of Theoretical Terms

The criticisms raised against operationism under this general heading are of three sorts: (1) very few terms have in fact been operationally defined; (2) some theoretical terms *cannot* be operationally defined; and (3) some terms can be operationally defined which are not usually thought to be included in the scientific universe of discourse.

Considering the first point, it has been noted that there is actually a dearth of illustrations in the literature of operational definitions of terms, and that the few examples usually given such as "Intelligence is what the intelligence test tests" are not fair samples of the terminology of psychologists (Peters, 1951). Very few, if any, attempts have been made to define operationally such currently used terms as "field," "synapse," "emotion," "cognitive map," "Oedipus complex," "drive," "superego," etc. Almost none of the terms in any dictionary of psychology are defined operationally. This may mean either that it is very difficult to give an operational definition of a concept or that there is not much value in doing so. In the light of the criticisms of operationism that have been presented it is more than likely that the latter suggestion is true.

That there are some meaningful concepts which are not operationally definable is also clear. Many of the terms used in science refer to ideal states such as perfect gases, point masses, frictionless engines, instantaneous velocities, etc., which represent the limiting condition of an infinite series of approximations. Mathematical concepts used in science also often refer to conditions not realizable in the actual world; this is illustrated by the concepts of the calculus which use notions relating to infinity. In addition to this, there are concepts employed in science which cannot be measured by currently available techniques, for example, the earth's core, the neurophysiological basis of memory, the fossil link between man and the higher primates, etc. These concepts are not meaningless or invalid (Ginsberg, 1955).

In relation to the third point it may be said that the way operationist thinking has developed, it is possible to "operationally define" almost all the terms of our language, even those usually called metaphysical. Operationists have extended the term to include "paper-and-pencil," "mental," and "logico-mathematical" operations, which dilutes operationism to such a degree that almost anything a scientist does to get knowledge can be included. Even a metaphysician uses mental operations, and "God" and the "soul" can be deduced from certain postulates (Ginsberg, 1955). Feigl also notes (1945) that such a broad definition of operation can be applied to the speculations of theology and metaphysics. If this is the case, operationism cannot discriminate between meaningful and meaningless concepts, as has sometimes been claimed. This was also seen in the illustration given earlier of the C_N test which is patently nonsense and yet operationally definable. It is not the case that operationism can avoid or solve metaphysical questions of ultimate reality.

The Problem of Reductionism

There has been a tendency on the part of some operationist writers to imply that the use of operational definitions will enable psychologists to avoid theoretical terms in their analyses or at least those theoretical terms that are not firmly anchored in observables. This opinion is not shared by other writers dealing with the philosophy of science.

Braithwaite (1955, p. 80), for example, has claimed that "the theoretical terms of a science are not explicitly definable, but instead are implicitly defined by the way in which they function in a calculus representing a scientific deductive system. . . . On this view, to say that theoretical concepts exist is to assert the truth of the theory in which they occur." In a similar vein Craig (1956, p. 52) writes, "Empirical significance attaches to an entire framework of assertions or beliefs, and to individual expressions or concepts only indirectly by means of that framework. . . . Empirical significance seems to be a matter of degree."

This view is further supported by Quine (1953, p. 41) who writes: "The dogma of reductionism survives in the supposition that each statement, taken in isolation from its fellows, can admit of confirmation or infirmation at all. My counter-suggestion . . . is that our statements about the external world face the tribunal of sense experience not individually but only as a corporate body. . . . The unit of empirical significance is the whole of science."

The problem of whether to reduce observations to simple descriptive summarizing terms or to theoretical terms actually has a long history (Plutchik, 1954). For example, although the famous scientists Mach and Ostwald rejected the atomic theory in physics and chemistry, yet in time the atomic theory, with the host of unobserved theoretical terms it brought, came to dominate the thinking of physical scientists.

To the extent that these views cited above are valid, then operational definitions of single theoretical terms are of relatively little value. In the mathematically developed sciences, theoretical concepts are often introduced by postulation as undefined primitive terms which get their meaning only within the total framework. This is also true in the parts of psychology which are more mathematically developed.

CONCLUSIONS

In this paper, an attempt has been made to re-examine some of the issues involved in the operationist position. The conclusion reached was that the classical version of operationism is inadequate on one or more grounds.

Is this conclusion a reason for despair? Is there any adequate alternative to operationism? The answer is simple and affirmative. Scientists introduce concepts into the scientific language by a variety of procedures. Without elaborating on these in detail (or being exhaustive), terms may be defined by: *nominal* definitions (equating symbols), *ostensive* definitions (pointing at), *real* definitions (listing properties), *conditional* definitions (stating sufficient conditions), or *postulational* definitions (as in mathematical models). The stage of development of a given area of science generally determines which of these will be most often used. Psychologists will continue to use any and all of these definitional procedures in their quest for knowledge and understanding.

Pratt (1945) has noted that "most experimental work is preceded by a period of picking and choosing among various problems, a period of vague speculations, of casting up of half-formed hypotheses, of trial and error thinking, etc. Little help can or should be expected from operationism in this period" (p. 269). In their actual practice, scientists seek *theoretically fruitful* concepts rather than ones which are operationally definable. Peters (1951) concludes: "Too much pre-occupation with method often distracts people from the necessity for fertile hypotheses" (p. 61). Psychologists could well take these admonitions to heart.

REFERENCES

Adler, F. Operational definitions in sociology. *American Journal of Sociology*, 1947, **52**, 438–444.

Benjamin, A. C. *Operationism*. Springfield, Ill.: Charles C. Thomas, 1955.

Bok, B. J. New science of radio astronomy. *Scientific Monthly*, 1955, **80**, 333–345.

Braithwaite, R. B. *Scientific explanation*. New York: Cambridge University Press, 1955.

Bridgman, P. W. *The logic of modern physics*. New York: Macmillan, 1927.

Bridgman, P. W. Some general principles of operational analysis. *Psychological Review*, 1945, **52**, 246–249.

Bridgman, P. W. *Reflections of a physicist*. New York: Philosophical Library, 1950.

Craig, W. Replacement of auxiliary expressions. *Philosophical Review*, 1956, **65**, 38–55.

Feigl, H. Operationism and scientific method. *Psychological Review*, 1945, **52**, 250–259.

Ginsberg, A. Operational definitions and theories. *Journal of General Psychology*, 1955, **52**, 223–248.

Israel, H. E. Two difficulties in operational thinking. *Psychological Review*, 1945, **52**, 260–261.

Israel, H., & Goldstein, B. Operationism in psychology. *Psychological Review*, 1944, **51**, 177–188.

Lundberg, G. A. *Foundations of sociology*. New York: Macmillan, 1939.

Newbury, E. Philosophic assumptions in operational psychology. *Journal of Psychology*, 1953, **35**, 371–378.

Peters, R. Observationalism in psychology. *Mind*, 1951, **60**, 43–61.

Pfannenstill, B. A critical analysis of operational definitions. *Theoria*, 1951, **17**, 193–209.

Plutchik, R. Further remarks on the hypothetical construct. *Journal of Psychology*, 1954, **37**, 59–64.

Pratt, C. C. Operationism in psychology. *Psychological Review*, 1945, **52**, 262–269.

Prentice, W. C. H. Operationism and psychological theory: a note. *Psychological Review*, 1946, **53**, 247–249.

Quine, W. V. O. *From a logical point of view*. Cambridge, Mass.: Harvard University Press, 1953.

Skinner, B. F. The operational analysis of psychological terms. *Psychological Review*, 1945, **52**, 270–277.

Stevens, S. S. The operational basis of psychology. *American Journal of Psychology*, 1935, **47**, 517–527.

Stevens, S. S. Psychology and the science of science. *Psychological Bulletin*, 1939, **36**, 221–263.

Symposium on operationism. *Psychological Review*, 1945, **52**, 241–294.

10. On the Need for Relativism[1]

Jerome Kagan

Dr. Kagan characterizes the psychology of the first half of the twentieth century as possessing an authoritarian temperament, "absolutistic, outer directed, and intolerant of ambiguity." Noting the trend away from such an absolute point of view and toward a more relativistic attitude in biology and physics, he feels that psychology should follow this lead and recognize that human behavior, too, is ambiguous. Further, he suggests that theoretical constructs in psychology be defined in relativistic terms that consider the internal state and belief structure of the individual organism, and not the external stimulus events alone. Two problem areas in psychology, the concept of self and the learning process, are discussed within such a framework. Psychology, it is argued, must develop a relativistic orientation including new techniques of investigation and measurement, and greater tolerance for the ambiguous.

The psychology of the first half of this century was absolutistic, outer directed, and intolerant of ambiguity. When a college student carries this unholy trio of traits he is called authoritarian, and such has been the temperament of the behavioral sciences. But the era of authoritarian psychology may be nearing its dotage, and the decades ahead may nurture a discipline that is relativistic, oriented to internal processes, and accepting of the idea that behavior is necessarily ambiguous.

Like her elder sisters, psychology began her dialogue with nature using a vocabulary of absolutes. Stimulus, response, rejection, affection, emotion, reward, and punishment were labels for classes of phenomena that were believed to have a fixed reality. We believed we could write a definition of these constructs that would fix them permanently and allow us to know them unequivocally at any time in any place.

Less than 75 years ago biology began to drift from the constraints of an absolute view of events and processes when she acknowledged that the fate of a small slice

[1] Reprinted from the *American Psychologist*, 1967, **22**, 131–142. Copyright 1967 by the American Psychological Association, and reproduced by permission of the author and the publisher. Preparation of this paper was supported in part by research Grant MH-8792 from the National Institute of Mental Health, United States Public Health Service. This paper is an abridged version of a lecture presented at the Educational Testing Service, Princeton, New Jersey, January 1966.

of ectodermal tissue depended on whether it was placed near the area of the eye or the toe. Acceptance of the simple notion that whether an object moves or not depends on where you are standing is a little over a half century old in a science that has 5 centuries of formalization. With physics as the referent in time, one might expect a relativistic attitude to influence psychology by the latter part of the twenty-third century. But philosophical upheavals in one science catalyze change in other disciplines and one can see signs of budding relativism in the intellectual foundations of the social sciences.

The basic theme of this paper turns on the need for more relativistic definitions of selected theoretical constructs. "Relativistic" refers to a definition in which context and the state of the individual are part of the defining statement. Relativism does not preclude the development of operational definitions, but makes that task more difficult. Nineteenth-century physics viewed mass as an absolute value; twentieth-century physics made the definition of mass relative to the speed of light. Similarly, some of psychology's popular constructs have to be defined in relation to the state and belief structure of the organism, rather than in terms of an invariant set of external events. Closely related to this need is the suggestion that some of the energy devoted to a search for absolute, stimulus characteristics of reinforcement be redirected to a search for the determinants of attention in the individual.

It is neither possible nor wise to assign responsibility to one person or event for major changes in conceptual posture, but Helson's recent book on adaptation-level theory (Helson, 1964), Schachter's (Schachter & Singer, 1962) hypothesis concerning the cognitive basis of affects, and Hernández-Peón's demonstration of the neuro-physiological bases of selective attention (Hernández-Peón, Scherrer, & Jouvet, 1956) are contemporary stimulants for a relativistic view of psychological phenomena.

Three messages are implicit in the work of these men.

1. If a stimulus is to be regarded as an event to which a subject responds or is likely to respond then it is impossible to describe a stimulus without describing simultaneously the expectancy, and preparation of the organism for that stimulus. Effective stimuli must be distinct from the person's original adaptation level. Contrast and distinctiveness, which are relative, are part and parcel of the definition of a stimulus.

2. The failure of one individual to respond to an event that is an effective stimulus for a second individual is not always the result of central selection after all the information is in, but can be due to various forms of peripheral inhibition. Some stimuli within inches of the face do not ever reach the interpretive cortex and, therefore, do not exist psychologically.

3. Man reacts less to the objective quality of external stimuli than he does to categorizations of those stimuli.

These new generalizations strip the phrase "physical stimulus" of much of its power and certainty, and transfer the scepter of control—in man, at least—to cognitive interpretations. *Contrast, cognitively interpreted, becomes an important key to understanding the incentives for human behavior.* Since contrast depends so intimately on context and expectancy, it must be defined relativistically.

The issue of relativism can be discussed in many contexts. Many existing constructs are already defined in terms of contextual relations. The concept of authority
only has meaning if there are fiefs to rule. The role of father has no meaning without
a child. The concept of noun, verb, or adjective is defined by context—by the
relation of the word to other constituents. We shall consider in some detail the ways
in which a relativistic orientation touches two other issues in psychology: the
learning of self-descriptive statements (the hoary idea of the self-concept), and,
even more fundamentally, some of the mechanisms that define the learning process.

THE CONCEPT OF THE SELF

The development and establishment of a self-concept is often framed in absolute
terms. The classic form of the statement assumes that direct social reinforcements
and identification models have fixed, invariant effects on the child. Praise and love
from valued caretakers are assumed to lead the child to develop positive self-
evaluations; whereas, criticism and rejection presumably cause self-derogatory
beliefs. The presumed cause-effect sequences imply that there is a something—a
definable set of behaviors—that can be labeled social rejection, and that the essence
of these rejecting acts leads to invariant changes in the self-concept of the child.
Let us examine the concept of rejection under higher magnification.

The concept of rejection—peer or parental—has been biased toward an absolute
definition. Witness the enormous degree of commonality in conceptualization of this
concept by investigators who have studied a mother's behavior with her child
(Baldwin, Kalhorn, & Breese, 1945; Becker, 1964; Kagan & Moss, 1962; Schaefer,
1959; Schaefer & Bayley, 1963; Sears, Maccoby, & Levin, 1957). These investigators typically decide that harsh physical punishment and absence of social contact
or physical affection are the essential indexes of an attitude called maternal rejection. It would be close to impossible for an American rater to categorize a mother
as high on both harsh beating of her child and on a loving attitude. A conventionally
trained psychologist observing a mother who did not talk to her child for 5 hours
would probably view the mother as rejecting. This may be a high form of pro-
vincialism. Alfred Baldwin[2] reports that in the rural areas of northern Norway,
where homes are 5 to 10 miles apart, and the population constant for generations,
one often sees maternal behaviors which an American observer would regard as
pathognomonically rejecting in an American mother. The Norwegian mother sees
her 4-year-old sitting in the doorway blocking the passage to the next room. She
does not ask him to move, but bends down, silently picks him up and moves him
away before she passes into the next room. Our middle-class observer would be
tempted to view this indifference as a sign of dislike. However, most mothers in this
Arctic outpost behave this way and the children do not behave the way rejected
children should by our current theoretical propositions.

[2] Personal communication.

An uneducated Negro mother from North Carolina typically slaps her 4-year-old across the face when he does not come to the table on time. The intensity of the mother's act tempts our observer to conclude that the mother hates, or at best, does not like her child. However, during a half-hour conversation the mother says she loves her child and wants to guarantee that he does not grow up to be a bad boy or a delinquent. And she believes firmly that physical punishment is the most effective way to socialize him. Now her behavior seems to be issued in the service of affection rather than hate. Determination of whether a parent is rejecting or not cannot be answered by focusing primarily on the behaviors of the parents. Rejection is not a fixed, invariant quality of behavior qua behavior. Like pleasure, pain, or beauty, rejection is in the mind of the rejectee. It is a belief held by the child; not an action by a parent.

We must acknowledge, first, a discontinuity in the meaning of an acceptance-rejection dimension before drawing further implications. We must distinguish between the child prior to 30 or 36 months of age, before he symbolically evaluates the actions of others, and the child thereafter.

We require, first, a concept to deal with the child's belief of his value in the eyes of others. The child of 4 or 5 years is conceptually mature enough to have recognized that certain resources parents possess are difficult for the child to obtain. He views these resources as sacrifices and interprets their receipt as signs that the parents value him. The child constructs a tote board of the differential value of parental gifts—be they psychological or material. The value of the gift depends on its scarcity. A $10.00 toy from a busy executive father is not a valued resource; the same toy from a father out of work is much valued. The value depends on the child's personal weightings. This position would lead to solipsism were it not for the fact that most parents are essentially narcissistic and do not readily give the child long periods of uninterrupted companionship. Thus, most children place high premium on this act. Similarly, parents are generally reluctant to proffer unusually expensive gifts to children, and this act acquires value for most youngsters. Finally, the child learns from the public media that physical affection means positive evaluation and he is persuaded to assign premium worth to this set of acts. There is, therefore, some uniformity across children in a culture in the evaluation of parental acts. But the anchor point lies within the child, not with the particular parental behaviors.

This definition of acceptance or rejection is not appropriate during the opening years. The 1-year-old does not place differential symbolic worth on varied parental acts, and their psychological significance derives from the overt responses they elicit and strengthen. A heavy dose of vocalization and smiling to an infant is traditionally regarded as indicative of maternal affection and acceptance. This bias exists because we have accepted the myth that "affection" is the essential nutrient that produces socially adjusted children, adolescents, and adults. The bias maintains itself because we observe a positive association between degree of parental smiling and laughing to the infant and prosocial behavior in the child during the early years. The responses of smiling, laughing, and approaching people are learned in the opening months of life on the basis of standard conditioning principles. This conclusion is supported by the work of Rheingold and Gewirtz (1959) and Brackbill (1958). However, phenotypically similar behaviors in a 10- or 20-year-old may have a different set of antecedents. The argument that different definitions of rejection-acceptance must be written for the pre- and postsymbolic child gains persuasive power from the fact that there are no data indicating that degree of prosocial behavior in the child is stable from 6 months to 16 years. Indeed, the longitudinal material from the Fels Research Institute study of behavior stability (Kagan & Moss, 1962) showed no evidence of any relation between joy or anxiety in the presence of adults during the first 2–3 years of life and phenotypically similar behaviors at 6, 12, or 24 years of age. The child behaviors that are presumed, by theory, to be the consequences of low or high parental rejection do not show stability from infancy through adolescence. This may be because the childhood responses, though phenotypically similar to the adult acts, may be acquired and maintained through different experiences at different periods.

It seems reasonable to suggest, therefore, that different theoretical words are necessary for the following three classes of phenomena: (*a*) an attitude on the part of the parent, (*b*) the quality and frequency of acts of parental care and social stimulation directed toward the infant, and (*c*) a child's assessment of his value in the eyes of another. All three classes are currently viewed as of the same cloth. The latter meaning of "rejection" (i.e., a belief held by a child) is obviously relativistic for it grows out of different experiences in different children.

SELF-DESCRIPTIVE LABELS

Let us probe further into the ideas surrounding the learning of self-evaluation statements, beyond the belief, "I am not valued." The notion of a self-concept has a long and spotted history and although it has masqueraded by many names in different theoretical costumes, its intrinsic meaning has changed only a little. A child presumably learns self-descriptive statements whose contents touch the salient attributes of the culture. The mechanisms classically invoked to explain how these attributes are learned have stressed the invariant effects of direct social reinforcement and identification. The girl who is told she is attractive, annoying, or inventive, comes to believe these appellations and to apply these qualifiers to herself. We have assumed that the laws governing the learning of self-descriptive labels resemble the learning of other verbal habits with frequency and contiguity of events being the shapers of the habit. Identification as a source of self-labels involves a different mechanism, but retains an absolutistic frame of reference. The child assumes that he shares attributes with particular models. If the model is viewed as subject to violent rages, the child concludes that he, too, shares this tendency.

Theory and data persuade us to retain some faith in these propositions. But relativistic factors also seem to sculpt the acquisition of self-descriptive labels, for the child evaluates himself on many psychological dimensions by inferring his rank order from a delineated reference group. The 10-year–old does not have absolute measuring rods to help him decide how bright, handsome, or likeable he is. He naturally and spontaneously uses his immediate peer group as the reference for these evaluations. An immediate corollary of this statement is that the child's evaluation is dependent upon the size and psychological quality of the reference group, and cannot be defined absolutely. Specifically, the larger the peer group, the less likely a child will conclude he is high in the rank order, the less likely he will decide he is unusually smart, handsome, or capable of leadership. Consider two boys with IQs of 130 and similar intellectual profiles. One lives in a small town, the other in a large city. It is likely that the former child will be the most competent in his peer group while the latter is likely to regard himself as fifth or sixth best. This difference in perceived rank order has obvious action consequences since we acknowledge that expectancies govern behavior. In sum, aspects of the self-descriptive process appear to develop in relativistic soil.

LEARNING AND ATTENTION

A second issue that touches relativistic definitions deals with a shift from external definitions of reinforcement—that is, reward or pleasure—to definitions that are based more directly on internal processes involving the concept of attention. Failure to understand the nature of learning is one of the major intellectual frustrations for many psychologists. The query, "What is learning?" has the same profound ring as the question, "What is a gene?" had a decade ago. Our biological colleagues have recently had a major insight while psychology is still searching. The murky question, "What is learning?" usually reduces to an attempt to discover the laws relating stimuli, pain, and pleasure, on the one hand, with habit acquisition and performance, on the other. Pain, pleasure, and reinforcement, are usually defined in terms of events that are external to the organism and have an invariant flavor. Miller (1951) suggested that reinforcement was isomorphic with stimulus reduction; Leuba (1955) argued for an optimal level of stimulation, but both implied that there was a level that could be specified and measured. We should like to argue first that sources of pleasure and, therefore of reinforcement, are often relative, and second, that the essence of learning is more dependent on attentional involvement by the learner than on specific qualities of particular external events.

The joint ideas that man is a pleasure seeker and that one can designate specific forms of stimulation as sources of pleasure are central postulates in every man's theory of behavior. Yet we find confusion when we seek a definition of pleasure. The fact that man begins life with a small core set of capacities for experience that he wishes to repeat cannot be disputed. This is a pragmatic view of pleasure and we can add a dash of phenomenology to bolster the intuitive validity of this point of view. A sweet taste and a light touch in selected places are usually pleasant. Recently, we have added an important new source of pleasure. It is better to say we have rediscovered a source of pleasure, for Herbert Spencer was a nineteenth-century progenitor of the idea that *change in stimulation* is a source of pleasure for rats, cats, monkeys, or men. But, change is short-lived, quickly digested, and transformed to monotony. Popping up in front of an infant and saying peek-a-boo is pleasant for a 3-month-old infant for about 15 minutes, for a 10-month-old infant for 3 minutes and for a 30-month-old child, a few seconds. This pleasant experience, like most events that elicit' their repetition a few times before dying, is usually conceptualized as a change in stimulation. The source of the pleasure is sought in the environment. Why should change in external stimulation be pleasant? The understanding of pleasure and reinforcement in man is difficult enough without having to worry about infrahuman considerations. Let us restrict the argument to the human. The human is a cognitive creature who is attempting to put structure or create schema for incoming stimulation. A schema is a representation of an external pattern; much as an artist's illustration is a representation of an event. A schema for a visual pattern is a partial and somewhat distorted version of what the photograph would be. Consider the usefulness of the following hypothesis:

The creation of a schema for an event is one major source of pleasure. When one can predict an event perfectly, the schema is formed. As long as prediction is not perfect the schema is not yet formed. The peek-a-boo game works for 15 minutes with a 12-week-old for it takes him that long to be able to predict the event—the "peek-a-boo." Charlesworth (1965) has demonstrated the reinforcing value of "uncertainty" in an experiment in which the peek-a-boo face appeared either in the same locus every trial, alternated between two loci, or appeared randomly in one of two loci. The children persisted in searching for the face for a much longer time under the random condition than under the other two conditions. The random presentation was reinforcing for a longer period of time, not because it possessed a more optimum level of external stimulation than the other reinforcement schedules, but because it took longer for the child to create a schema for the random presentation and the process of creating a schema is a source of pleasure.

Consider another sign of pleasure beside persistence in issuing a particular response. Display of a smile or laugh is a good index of pleasure. Indeed, Tomkins' (1962) scheme for affect demands that pleasure be experienced if these responses appear. Consider two studies that bear on the relation between pleasure and the creation of schema. In our laboratory during the last 2 years, we have seen the same infants at 4, 8, and 13 months of age and have shown them a variety of visual patterns representative of human faces and human forms. In one episode, the 4-month-old infants are shown achromatic slides of a photograph of a regular male face, a schematic outline of a male face, and two disarranged, disordered faces. The frequency of occurrence of smiling to the photograph of the regular face is over *twice* the frequency observed to the regular schematic face—although looking time is identical—and over *four times* the frequency shown to the disordered faces. In another, more realistic episode, the 4-month-old infants see a regular, flesh-colored sculptured face in three dimensions and a distorted version of that face in which the eyes, nose and mouth are rearranged. At 4 months of age the occurrence of smiling to the regular face is over three times the frequency displayed to the distorted version, but looking time is identical. There are two interpretations of this difference (Kagan, Henker, Hen-Tov, Levine, & Lewis, 1966). One explanation argues that the mother's face has become a secondary reward; the regular face stands for pleasure because it has been associated with care and affection from the mother. As a result, it elicits more smiles. An alternative interpretation is that the smile response has become conditioned to the human face via reciprocal contact between mother and infant. A third interpretation, not necessarily exclusive of these, is that the smile can be elicited when the infant matches stimulus to schema—when he has an "aha" reaction; when he makes a cognitive discovery. The 4-month-old infant is cognitively close to establishing a relatively firm schema of a human face. When a regular representation of a face is presented to him there is a short period during which the stimulus is assimilated to the schema and then after several seconds, a smile may occur. The smile is released following the perceptual recognition of the face, and reflects the assimilation of the stimulus to the infant's schema—a small, but significant act of creation. This hypothesis is supported by the fact that the typical latency between the onset of looking at the regular face (in the 4-month-old) and the onset of smiling is about 3 to 5 seconds. The smile usually does not occur immediately but only after the infant has studied the stimulus. If one sees this phenomenon live, it is difficult to avoid the conclusion that the smile is released following an act of perceptual recognition.

Additional data on these and other children at 8 months of age support this idea. At 8 months, frequency of smiling to both the regular and distorted faces is *reduced dramatically*, indicating that smiling does not covary with the reward value of the face. The face presumably has acquired more reward value by 8 months than it had at 4 months. However, the face is now a much firmer schema and recognition of it is immediate. There is no effortful act of recognition necessary for most infants. As a result, smiling is less likely to occur. Although smiling is much less frequent at 8 than 4 months to all faces, the frequency of smiling to the distorted face now *equals* the frequency displayed to the regular face. We interpret this to mean that the distorted face is sufficiently similar to the child's schema of a regular face that it can be recognized as such.

The pattern of occurrence of cardiac deceleration to the regular and distorted three-dimensional faces furnishes the strongest support for this argument. A cardiac deceleration of about 8 to 10 beats often accompanies attention to selected incoming visual stimuli in adults, school-age children, and infants. Moreover, the deceleration tends to be maximal when the stimuli are not overly familiar or completely novel, but are of intermediate familiarity. One hypothesis maintains that a large deceleration is most likely to occur when an act of perceptual recognition occurs, when the organism has a cognitive surprise. Let us assume that there is one trial for which this type of reaction occurs with maximal magnitude. If one examines the one stimulus presentation (out of a total of 16 trials) that produces the largest cardiac deceleration, a lawful change occurs between 4 and 8 months of age. At 4 months of age more of the infants showed their largest deceleration to the regular face (45% of the group: $n = 52$) than to the scrambled (34%), no eyes (11%), or blank faces (10%). At 8 months, the majority of the infants ($n = 52$) showed their largest deceleration to the scrambled face (50% to scrambled versus 21% to regular face). This difference is interpreted to mean that the scrambled face now assumes a similar position on the assimilation continuum that the regular face did 16 weeks earlier.

At 13 months of age these infants are shown six three-dimensional representations of a male human form and a free form matched for area, coloration, and texture with the human form. The stimuli include a faithful representation of a regular man, that same man with his head placed between his legs, the same man with all limbs and head collaged in an unusual and scrambled pattern, the man's body with a mule's head, and the mule's head on the man's body, the man's body with three identical heads, and a free form. The distribution of smiles to these stimuli is leptokurtic, with over 70% of all the smiles occurring to the animal head on the human body and the three-headed man, forms that were moderate transformations of the regular man, and stimuli that required active assimilation. The free form and the scrambled man rarely elicited smiles from these infants. These stimuli are too difficult to assimilate to the schema of a human form possessed by a 13-month-old infant. It is interesting to note that the regular human form sometimes elicited the verbal response "daddy" or a hand waving from the child. These instrumental social reactions typically did not occur to the transformations. The occurrence of cardiac deceleration to these patterns agrees with this hypothesis. At 13 months of age, the man with his head between his legs, the man with the animal head, or the three-headed man, each elicited the largest cardiac decelerations more frequently than the regular man, the scrambled man, or the free form ($p < .05$ for each comparison). Thus, large cardiac decelerations and smiles were most likely to occur to stimuli that seemed to require tiny, quiet cognitive discoveries—miniaturized versions of Archimedes' "Eureka."

It appears that the act of matching stimulus to schema when the match is close but not yet perfect is a dynamic event. Stimuli that deviate a critical amount from the child's schema for a pattern are capable of eliciting an active process of recognition, and this process behaves as if it were a source of pleasure. Stimuli that are easily assimilable or too difficult to assimilate do not elicit these reactions.

A recent study by Edward Zigler[3] adds important support to the notion that the smile indicates the pleasure of an assimilation. Children in Grades 2, 3, 4, and 5 looked at cartoons that required little or no reading. The children were asked to explain the cartoon while an observer coded the spontaneous occurrence of laughing and smiling while the children were studying the cartoons. It should come as no surprise that verbal comprehension of the cartoons increased in a linear fashion with age. But laughing and smiling increased through Grade 4 and then declined markedly among the fifth-grade children. The fifth graders understood the cartoons too well. There was no gap between stimulus and schema and no smiling. Sixteen-

---

[3] Unpublished paper; personal communication.

week-old infants and 8-year-old children smile spontaneously at events that seem to have one thing in common—the event is a partial match to an existing schema and an active process of recognitory assimilation must occur.

The fact that a moderate amount of mismatch between event and schema is one source of pleasure demands the conclusion that it is not always possible to say that a specific event will always be a source of pleasure. The organism's state and structure must be in the equation. This conclusion parallels the current interest in complexity and information uncertainty. The psychologist with an information-theory prejudice classifies a stimulus as uncertain and often assumes that he does not have to be too concerned with the attributes of the viewer. This error of the absolute resembles the nineteenth-century error in physics and biology. This is not a titillating or pedantic, philosophical issue. Psychology rests on a motive-reinforcement foundation which regards pleasure and pain as pivotal ideas in the grand theory. These constructs have tended to generate absolute definitions. We have been obsessed with finding a fixed and invariant characterization of pleasure, pain, and reinforcement. Melzack & Wall (1965) point out that although the empirical data do not support the notion of a fixed place in the brain that mediates pain, many scientists resist shedding this comfortable idea. Olds' (1958, 1962) discovery of brain reinforcing areas has generated excitement because many of us want to believe that pleasure has a fixed and absolute locus. The suspicious element in this discovery of pleasure spots is that there is no habituation of responses maintained by electrical stimulation to hypothalamic or septal nuclei, and minimal resistance to extinction of habits acquired via this event. Yet, every source of pleasure known to phenomenal man does satiate—for awhile or forever—and habits that lead to pleasant events do persist for awhile after the pleasure is gone. These observations are troubling and additional inquiry is necessary if we are to decide whether these cells are indeed the bed where pleasure lies.

We are convinced that contiguity alone does not always lead to learning. Something must ordinarily be added to contiguity in order to produce a new bond. Psychology has chosen to call this extra added mysterious something reinforcement, much like eighteenth-century chemists chose to label their unknown substance phlogiston. If one examines the variety of external events that go by the name of reinforcement it soon becomes clear that this word is infamously inexact. A shock to an animal's paw is a reinforcement, a verbal chastisement is a reinforcement, an examiner's smile is a reinforcement, a pellet of food is a reinforcement, and a sigh indicating tension reduction after watching a killer caught in a Hitchcock movie is a reinforcement. These events have little, if any, phenotypic similarity. What then, do they have in common? For if they have nothing in common it is misleading to call them by the same name. Learning theorists have acknowledged their failure to supply an independent a priori definition of reinforcement and the definition they use is purely pragmatic. A reinforcement is anything that helps learning. And so, we ask: What has to be added to contiguity in order to obtain learning? A good candidate for the missing ingredient is the phrase "attentional involvement." Let us consider again the events called reinforcements: a shock, food, a smile, each of these acts to attract the attention of the organism to some agent or object. They capture the organism's attention and maybe that is why they facilitate learning. Consider the idea that what makes an event reinforcing is the fact that it (*a*) elicits the organism's attention to the feedback from the response he has just made and to the mosaic of stimuli in the learning situation and (*b*) acts as an incentive for a subsequent response. The latter quality is what ties the word "reinforcement" to the concepts of motivation and need, but much learning occurs without the obvious presence of motives or needs. Ask any satiated adult to attend carefully and remember the bond syzygy-aardvark. It is likely that learning will occur in one trial. It is not unreasonable to argue that a critical component of events that have historically been called reinforcement is their ability to attract the organism's attention. They have been distinctive cues in a context; they have been events discrepant from the individual's adaptation level. If attention is acknowledged as critical in new mental acquisitions it is appropriate to ask if attention is also bedded in relativistic soil. The answer appears to be "Yes." The dramatic experiments of Hernández-Peón and his colleagues (1956) are persuasive in indicating that attention investment may not be distributed to many channels at once. One has to know the state of the organism. Knowledge of the organism's distribution of attention in a learning situation may clarify many controversial theoretical polemics that range from imprinting in chickens to emotion in college undergraduates. For example, comparative psychologists quarrel about which set of external conditions allow imprinting to occur with maximal effect. Some say the decoy should move; others argue that the young chick should move; still others urge that the decoy be brightly colored (e.g., Bateson, 1964*a*, 1964*b*; Hess, 1959; Klopfer, 1965; Thompson & Dubanoski, 1964). The quarrel centers around the use of phenotypically different observable conditions. Perhaps all these suggestions are valid. Moving the decoy, or active following by the infant chick, or a distinctively colored decoy all maximize the organism's level of attention to the decoy. The genotypic event may remain the same across all of these manipulations.

A similar interpretation can be imposed on Held's (1965) recent hypothesis concerning the development of space and pattern perception. Held controlled the visual experience of pairs of kittens. The only exposure to light was limited to a few hours a day when one kitten was placed in a gondola and moved around by an active, free kitten in an arena whose walls were painted in vertical stripes. After 30 hours of such experience each kitten was tested. The free kitten showed appropriate visual reactions. It blinked when an object approached; it put up its paws to avoid collision when carried near to a surface; it avoided the deep side of a visual cliff. The passive passenger kitten did not show these normal reactions. Why? Held, focusing on the obvious external variable of activity versus no activity, concludes that the sensory feedback accompanying movement is necessary to develop visual-motor control. This conclusion rests on the assumption that the passive kitten sitting in the gondola was attending to the stripes on the wall as intently as the free walking kitten. This assumption may be gratuitous. If the passive kitten were staring blankly—as many human infants do—then one would not expect these animals to develop normal perceptual structures. This interpretation may not be better, but it has a different flavor than the one suggested by Held.

A final example of the central role of attention is seen in Aronfreed's (1964, 1965) recent work on the learning of self-critical comments. Aronfreed states that the learning of a self-critical comment proceeds best if the child is first punished and then hears a social agent speak the self-critical statement. He interprets this result in drive reduction language. However, suppose one asks which sequence is most likely to maximize a child's attention to the adult's comment—Punish first and then speak to the child? Or speak first and then punish? The former sequence should be more effective. The punishment is a violation of what the child expects from a strange adult and recruits the child's attention to the adult. The child is primed to listen to the self-critical commendation and thus more likely to learn it.

Distinctiveness of Cues

The above examples suggest that the organism's distribution of attention is a critical process that should guide our search for the bases of many diverse phenomena. One of the critical bases for recruitment of attention pivots on the idea of distinctiveness of the signal. Jakobson and Halle (1956) argue that the chronology of acquisition of phonemes proceeds according to a principle of distinctive elements. Distinctive elements capture the child's attention and give direction to the order of learning.

The importance of *relative distinctiveness of cues* finds an interesting illustration in the concept of affect. The concept of emotion has lived through three distinct eras in modern times. The pre-Jamesian assumed the sequence was: stimulus event —cognition—visceral response. James interchanged events two and three and said that the visceral afferent feedback occurred before the cognition. But Cannon quieted Jamesian ideas until Schachter's ingenious studies and catching explanations suggested that the individual experiences a puzzling set of visceral afferent sensations and integrates them cognitively. The language integration of visceral feelings, cognition, and context is an affect. This imaginative suggestion may be maximally valid for Western adults but perhaps minimally appropriate for children because of a developmental change in the relative distinctiveness of visceral cues.

Let us share a small set of assumptions before we proceed with the argument. Aside from pain and its surrogates, the major psychological elicitors of unpleasant visceral afferent sensations are violations of expectancies (uncertainty); anticipation of receiving or losing a desired goal; anticipation of seeing or losing a nurturant person; blocking of goal attainment; and anticipation of harm to the integrity of the body. Each of these event situations becomes conditioned to visceral afferent feedback early in life. These events—or conditioned stimuli—are salient and maximally distinctive for children and affect words are attached to the events, not primarily to the visceral afferent sensations. Thus, the 6-year-old says he is mad because mother did not let him watch television; he says he is sad because the cat died; he says he is happy because he just received a prized toy. Affect words are labels for a set

of external events. With development, individuals—with the help of social institutions—learn to protect themselves against most of the unpleasant sources of visceral
afferent feedback—against the apocalyptic horsemen of uncertainty, loss of nurturance, goal blocking, and bodily harm. Moreover, they erect defenses against recognizing these events. They defend against recognition that they are confused, rejected,
unable to attain a goal, or afraid. Thus, when events occur that are, in fact, representations of these situations, the events are not salient or distinctive and are not
labeled. However, the conditioned visceral afferent sensations do occur, as they
always have in the past. In the adult, the visceral afferent sensations become more
distinctive or salient; whereas, for the child, the external events were salient and
distinctive. The adult provides us with the situation Schachter and his colleagues
have described. The adult often has visceral afferent sensations but cannot decide
why he has them or what they mean. So he scans and searches the immediate past
and context and decides that he is happy, sad, alienated, uncommitted, or in love.
The essence of this argument is that for the child the external event is more distinctive than the visceral afferent sensations and the affect word is applied to external
events. In the adult, the visceral afferent sensations are relatively more distinctive
and the affect words are more often applied to them.

The personality differences ascribed to children in different ordinal positions
are the result, in part, of differences in relative distinctiveness of social agents. For
the firstborn, the adult is the distinctive stimulus to whom to attend; for the second
born the older sibling has distinctive value and competes for the attention of the
younger child. Only children lie alone for long periods of uninterrupted play. A
parent who enters the room and speaks to the infant is necessarily a distinctive
stimulus. For a fifth born whose four older siblings continually poke, fuss, and
vocalize into the crib, the caretaking adult, is, of necessity, less distinctive and, as a
result, less attention will be paid to the adult. The importance of distinctiveness
with respect to adaptation level engages the heated controversy surrounding the role
of stimulus enrichment with infants and young children from deprived milieux.
The pouring on of visual, auditory, and tactile stimulation willy-nilly should be
less effective than a single distinctive stimulus presented in a context of quiet so it
will be discrepant from the infant's adaptation level. If one takes this hypothesis
seriously, a palpable change in enrichment strategies is implied. The theme of this
change involves a shifting from a concern with increasing absolute level of stimulation to focusing on distinctiveness of stimulation. Culturally disadvantaged children
are not deprived of stimulation; they are deprived of distinctive stimulation.

The early learning of sex role standards and the dramatic concern of school
children with sex differences and their own sex role identity becomes reasonable when
one considers that the differences between the sexes are highly distinctive. Voice,
size, posture, dress, and usual locus of behavior are distinctive attributes that focus
the child's attention on them.

One of the reasons why the relation between tutor and learner is important is that
some tutors elicit greater attention than others. They are more distinctive. Those of
us who contend that learning will be facilitated if the child is identified with or

wants to identify with a tutor believe that one of the bases for the facilitation is the greater attention that is directed at a model with whom the child wishes to identify. A recent experiment touches on this issue.

The hypothesis can be simply stated. An individual will attend more closely to an initial stranger with whom he feels he shares attributes than to a stranger with whom he feels he does not share attributes, other things equal. The former model is more distinctive, for a typical adult ordinarily feels he does not share basic personality traits with most of the strangers that he meets. The subjects in this study were 56 Radcliffe freshmen and sophomores preselected for the following pair of traits. One group, the academics, were rated by four judges—all roommates —as being intensely involved in studies much more than they were in dating, clubs, or social activities. The second group, the social types, were rated as being much more involved in dating and social activities than they were in courses or grades. No subject was admitted into the study unless all four judges agreed that she fit one of these groups.

Each subject was seen individually by a Radcliffe senior, and told that each was participating in a study of creativity. The subject was told that Radcliffe seniors had written poems and that two of the poets were selected by the Harvard faculty as being the best candidates. The faculty could not decide which girl was the more creative and the student was going to be asked to judge the creativity of each of two poems that the girls had written. The subjects were told that creativity is independent of IQ for bright people and they were told that since the faculty knew the personality traits of the girls, the student would be given that information also. The experimenter then described one of the poets as an academic grind and the other as a social activist. Each subject listened to two different girls recite two different poems on a tape. Order of presentation and voice of the reader were counterbalanced in an appropriate design. After the two poems were read the subject was asked for a verbatim recall of each poem, asked to judge its creativity, and finally, asked which girl she felt most similar to. Incidentally, over 95% of the subjects said they felt more similar to the model that they indeed matched in reality. Results supported the original hypothesis. Recall was best when a girl listened to a communicator with whom she shared personality traits. The academic subjects recalled more of the poem when it was read by the academic model than by the social model; whereas, the social subjects recalled more of the poem when it was read by the social model than the academic model. This study indicates that an individual will pay more attention to a model who possesses similar personality attributes, than to one who is not similar to the subject. Distinctiveness of tutor is enhanced by a perceived relation between learner and tutor.

Myths and superstitions are established around the kind of experimental manipulations teachers or psychologists should perform in order to maximize the probability that learning will occur. When one focuses on the kind of manipulation—providing a model, giving a reinforcement, labeling the situation, punishing without delay—there is a strong push to establish superstitions about how behavioral change is produced. Recipes are written and adopted. If one believes, on the other hand, that a critical level of attention to incoming information is the essential variable, then one is free to mix up manipulations, to keep the recipe open, as long as one centers the subject's attention on the new material.

The most speculative prediction from this general argument is that behavioral therapy techniques will work for some symptoms—for about 20 years. A violation of an expectancy is a distinctive stimulus that attracts attention. The use of operant shaping techniques to alleviate phobias is a dramatic violation of an expectancy for both child and adult, and attention is magnetized and focused on the therapeutic agent and his paraphernalia. As a result, learning is facilitated. But each day's use of this strategy may bring its demise closer. In time, a large segment of the populace will have adapted to this event; it will be a surprise no more and its attention getting and therapeutic value will be attenuated. Much of the power of psychoanalytic techniques began to wane when the therapist's secrets became public knowledge. If therapy is accomplished by teaching new responses, and if the learning of new responses is most likely to occur when attention to the teacher is maximal, it is safe to expect that we may need a new strategy of teaching patients new tricks by about 1984.

Let us weave the threads closer in an attempt at final closure. The psychology of the first half of this century was the product of a defensively sudden rupture from philosophy to natural science. The young discipline needed roots, and like a child, attached itself to an absolute description of nature, much as a 5-year-old clings to an absolute conception of morality. We now approach the latency years and can afford to relax and learn something from developments in our sister sciences. The message implicit in the recent work in psychology, biology, and physics contains a directive to abandon absolutism in selected theoretical areas. Conceptual ideas for mental processes must be invented, and this task demands a relativistic orientation. Learning is one of the central problems in psychology and understanding of the mechanisms of learning requires elucidation and measurement of the concept of attention. Existing data indicate that attention is under the control of distinctive stimuli and distinctiveness depends intimately on adaptation level of subject and context, and cannot be designated in absolute terms.

These comments are not to be regarded as a plea to return to undisciplined philosophical introspection. Psychology does possess some beginning clues as to how it might begin to measure elusive, relative concepts like "attention." Autonomic variables such as cardiac and respiratory rate appear to be useful indexes, and careful studies of subtle motor discharge patterns may provide initial operational bases for this construct.

Neurophysiologists have been conceptualizing their data in terms of attention distribution for several years, and they are uncovering some unusually provocative phenomena. For example, amplitude of evoked potentials from the association areas of the cortex are beginning to be regarded as a partial index of attention. Thompson and Shaw (1965) recorded evoked potentials from the association area of the cat's cortex—the middle suprasylvian gyrus—to a click, a light, or a shock to the forepaw. After they established base level response to each of these "standard" stimuli, the investigators presented these standard stimuli when the cat was active or when novel stimuli were introduced. The novel events were a rat in a bell jar, an air jet, or a growling sound. The results were unequivocal. Any one of these novel stimuli or activity by the cat produced reduced cortical evoked responses to the click, light, or shock. The authors suggest that the "amplitude of the evoked responses are inversely proportional to attention to a particular event [p. 338]." Psychology is beginning to develop promising strategies of measurement for the murky concept of attention and should begin to focus its theorizing and burgeoning measurement technology on variables having to do with the state of the organism, not just the quality of the external stimulus. The latter events can be currently objectified with greater elegance, but the former events seem to be of more significance. Mannheim once chastised the social sciences for seeming to be obsessed with studying what they could measure without error, rather than measuring what they thought to be important with the highest precision possible. It is threatening to abandon the security of the doctrine of absolutism of the stimulus event. Such a reorientation demands new measurement procedures, novel strategies of inquiry, and a greater tolerance for ambiguity. But let us direct our inquiry to where the pot of gold seems to shimmer and not fear to venture out from cozy laboratories where well-practiced habits have persuaded us to rationalize a faith in absolute monarchy.

REFERENCES

Aronfreed, J. The origin of self criticism. *Psychological Review*, 1964, **71**, 193–218.

Aronfreed, J. Internalized behavioral suppression and the timing of social punishment. *Journal of Personality and Social Psychology*, 1965, **1**, 3–16.

Baldwin, A. L., Kalhorn, J., & Breese, F. H. Patterns of parent behavior. *Psychological Monographs*, 1945, **58**(3, Whole No. 268).

Bateson, P. P. G. Changes in chicks' responses to novel moving objects over the sensitive period for imprinting. *Animal Behavior*, 1964a, **12**, 479–489.

Bateson, P. P. G. Relation between conspicuousness of stimuli and their effectiveness in the imprinting situation. *Journal of Comparative and Physiological Psychology*, 1964b, **58**, 407–411.

Becker, W. C. Consequences of different kinds of parental discipline. In M. L. Hoffman & L. W. Hoffman (Eds.), *Review of child development research*. Vol. 1. New York: Russell Sage Foundation, 1964. Pp. 169–208.

Brackbill, Y. Extinction of the smiling response in infants as a function of reinforcement schedule. *Child Development*, 1958, **29**, 115–124.

Charlesworth, W. R. Persistence of orienting and attending behavior in young infants as a function of stimulus uncertainty. Paper presented at the meeting of the Society for Research in Child Development, Minneapolis, March 1965.

Held, R. Plasticity in sensory motor systems. *Scientific American*, 1965, **213**(5), 84–94.

Helson, H. *Adaptation level theory: an experimental and systematic approach to behavior*. New York: Harper & Row, 1964.

Hernández-Peón, R., Scherrer, H., & Jouvet, M. Modification of electrical activity in cochlear nucleus during attention in unanesthetized cats. *Science*, 1956, **123**, 331–332.

Hess, E. H. Two conditions limiting critical age for imprinting. *Journal of Comparative and Physiological Psychology*, 1959, **52**, 515–518.

Jakobson, R., & Halle, M. *Fundamentals of language*. The Hague: Mouton, 1956.

Kagan, J., Henker, B. A., Hen-Tov, A., Levine, J., & Lewis, M. Infants' differential reactions to familiar and distorted faces. *Child Development*, 1966, **37**, 519–532.

Kagan, J., & Moss, H. A. *Birth to maturity*. New York: Wiley, 1962.

Klopfer, P. H. Imprinting: a reassessment. *Science*, 1965, **147**, 302–303.

Leuba, C. Toward some integration of learning theories: the concept of optimal stimulation. *Psychological Reports*, 1955, **1**, 27–33.

Melzack, R., & Wall, P. D. Pain mechanisms: a new theory. *Science*, 1965, **150**, 971–979.

Miller, N. E. Learnable drives and rewards. In S. S. Stevens (Ed.), *Handbook of experimental psychology*. New York: Wiley, 1951. Pp. 435–472.

Olds, J. Self stimulation of the brain. *Science*, 1958, **127**, 315–324.

Olds, J. Hypothalamic substrates of reward. *Physiological Review*, 1962, **42**, 554–604.

Rheingold, H., Gewirtz, J. L., & Ross, H. Social conditioning of vocalizations in the infant. *Journal of Comparative and Physiological Psychology*, 1959, **52**, 68–73.

Schachter, S., & Singer, J. E. Cognitive, social and physiological determinants of emotional states. *Psychological Review*, 1962, **69**, 379–399.

Schaefer, E. S. A circumplex model for maternal behavior. *Journal of Abnormal and Social Psychology*, 1959, **59**, 226–235.

Schaefer, E. S., & Bayley, N. Maternal behavior, child behavior and their inter-correlations from infancy through adolescence. *Monographs of the Society for Research in Child Development*, 1963, **28**, No. 87.

Sears, R. R., Maccoby, E. E., & Levin, H. *Patterns of child rearing*. New York: Row, Peterson, 1957.

Thompson, R. F., & Shaw, J. A. Behavioral correlates of evoked activity recorded from association areas of the cerebral cortex. *Journal of Comparative and Physiological Psychology*, 1965, **60**, 329–339.

Thompson, W. R., & Dubanoski, R. A. Imprinting and the law of effort. *Animal Behavior*, 1964, **12**, 213–218.

Tomkins, S. S. *Affect imagery consciousness*. Vol. 1. *The positive affects*. New York: Springer, 1962.

11. Psychological Science Versus the Science-Humanism Antinomy: Intimations of a Significant Science of Man[1]

Sigmund Koch

Dr. Koch focuses on the wide gap between the scientific and humanistic explorers of man and takes scientific psychology to task for being "more concerned with being a science than with courageous and self-determining confrontation of its historically constituted subject matter." The image of man presented by psychology is incomplete, he contends, although psychology is the one science that approaches and overlaps the humanities and could, therefore, be an effective third force serving to unite science and humanism. He feels psychologists should be developing humanistic sensitivities, while at the same time retaining appropriate scientific attitudes and skills. Psychology should take the lead in exploring the relationship between science and the humanities; a relationship with much potential relevance for the understanding of the human condition.

I am going to engage a problem for which I have feeble intellectual tools. It relates to an issue that if not yet a *cause célèbre* seems on the way to becoming so—that concerning the relations between science and the humanities. If my tools for this task are feeble, I claim some extenuation merely from the fact that I am a psychologist. Little that my field has done during its brief history as an independent science could equip me for work on the present question. Moreover, the climate of my field has not been such as to develop any sensibility in humanistic domains. Indeed, if there ever was such sensitivity, its suppression, starvation, and eventual atrophy seems to have been a necessary condition for Guild membership.

[1] Reprinted from the *American Psychologist*, 1961, **16**, 629–639. Copyright 1961 by the American Psychological Association, and reproduced by permission of the author and the publisher. A Division 1 invited address given at the American Psychological Association Annual Convention, Chicago, September 5, 1960.

The reason I speak on this theme is that sooner or later someone from my field *must*. The situation is becoming embarrassing. Physicist-philosophers have addressed the theme. Physicist-literary critics have not been silent. Physicist-novelists have joined the issue. Physicist-administrators have not gone unheard. Sociologists have spoken. From the other side of the fence, historians, literary critics, and philosophers have been vocal. And more and more stridently there have of course been the educators, politicians, and last, but not least, military men. Psychologists have been strangely silent. That in itself is a fact worth pondering.

Against a silence so charged, anything one says must sound explosive. One might thus just as well speak with utter abandon from the start. I will state my main thesis boldly right now.

In any consideration of the science-humanities antinomy, the position of psychology must be given special, if not central, attention. In any assessment of the actual relations—similarities, differences, interpenetrations—of the work of science and of the humanities, psychological questions and modes of analysis must almost as a matter of definition be paramount. In any creative redefinition of the relations between science and the humanities, in any readjustment of the images, lay or technical, of these two great areas of the human cognitive adventure, which might more justly and precisely convey the essential unity of knowledge, psychological questions are again paramount. If psychology is to live up to the purview of its very definition, then it *must* be that science whose problems lie closest to those of the humanities; indeed, it must be that area in which the problems of the sciences, as traditionally conceived, and the humanities intersect. Relative to the present divisive situation in the world of knowledge, psychology, then, might be seen as a third force. It *could* be seen as a third force whose ranks, when they arrive in no man's land in sufficient numbers, would fill up the gap separating the contenders and reveal all three forces for what they really are: detachments from the same army which had forgotten that there was a common enemy.

Note the shift from the descriptive to the normative in the last paragraph. As I have already hinted, far from having been such a "third force," psychology (and the social sciences—my remarks will concentrate on psychology, but hold as well for the social sciences) in the twentieth century has perhaps done more to solidify, sharpen, perpetuate, thus obfuscate, the division between science and the humanities than any other "force" in the culture. It has sold to man an image of life as being nastier and more brutish, if longer, than any that Hobbes could have entertained—an image which could leave to the humanist only the role of idle *voyeur* peering tenderly into a sewer.

Among the brute facts that must be faced are these: Ever since its stipulation into existence as an independent science, psychology has been far more concerned with being a science than with courageous and self-determining confrontation of its historically constituted subject matter. Its history has been largely a matter of emulating the methods, forms, symbols of the established sciences, especially physics. In so doing, there has been an inevitable tendency to retreat from broad and intensely significant ranges of its subject matter, and to form rationales for so doing which could only invite further retreat. There has thus been, at least until very recently, an ever widening estrangement between the scientific makers of human science and the humanistic explorers of the content of man. Indeed, in its search for scientific respectability, psychology has erected a widely shared epistemology, and a conceptual language which render virtually impossible the exploration of the content of man in a differentiated way. So deeply engrained are these latter in the sensibilities of inquirers that even those who seek to study subtle or complex human phenomena are badly handicapped.

When phenomena of the sort that might concern the humanist *are* approached, a drab and sodden "middlebrowism" prevails. Humanists who stumble upon the results of such efforts are likely to feel revulsion. Perhaps fortunately they are unlikely so to stumble, in that scientific or academic psychology (exclusive of the psychiatric disciplines) has had only slight *direct* effect upon the culture at large. This fact of minimal direct representation in the culture is in itself significant. On the other hand, the indirect effects on the culture are I think profound.

With only a few exceptions, major twentieth century psychologists have had limited background in the humanities and, what is worse, limited sensibilities at esthetic levels and even as savorers of experience. The psychology of esthetics has practically not existed in the twentieth century. Psychology seems not even to have had its due share of individuals who have made significant independent contributions in humanistic areas. I can think of only one living psychologist who has, but of several living *physicists*.

Having observed that psychology must be a third force and then that throughout its history it has done little other than create the need for one, it is now only fair that I consider a number of matters which might reduce the stress between these observations. I begin by itemizing—to save time, summarily and dogmatically— some signs that something that could become a third force may be shaping up in psychology. Then, more positively, I (*a*) address a specific, though general, problem of a sort which psychology must engage in preparing to approach questions of joint import to the humanities and itself, and finally, (*b*) consider certain aspects of psychology's role in any effective redefinition of the relations between science and the humanities, and certain consequences thereof for problems of education in general and in psychology.

Of the factors predisposing psychology to confront problems of humanistic import, the first is indigenous; the second, though compelling, is indirect.

1. Psychology, after a long interval of imaging its ends and means on the model of physics, as interpreted and mediated by logical positivism, operationism, neo-pragmatism, and related movements, seems ready, perhaps for the first time in its history, to rise to its problems in free and *sui generis* ways. Simplistic theories of correct scientific conduct no longer occasion monolithic conformity. Behaviorist epistemology is under stress; neobehaviorism on the defensive; while neo-neo-behaviorism enfolds itself in a womb of its own manufacture. There is a strongly increased interest in perception and central process, even on the part of S-R theorists: in fact a tendency for the central area of psychological interest to shift from

learning to perception. There is a marked, if as yet unfocused, disposition on the part of *even* fundamental psychologists to readdress human phenomena and to readmit questions having experiential reference. Along with such changes, there is a marked devaluation of hypothetico-deductive formalization as an end in itself, and a shift of emphasis from the *form* of theoretical formulations to their meaning, empirical adequacy, and even illumination value. These and many cognate changes are conspicuous in the general literature and emerge with special force from the pages of *Psychology: A Study of a Science*. I have summarized the complex of changes to which I here allude in the "Epilogue" to Study I (Koch, 1959) of that enterprise, and happily offer that reference in exchange for the extensive development of the present assertions that might here be desirable.

Such changes *could* liberate psychology for the engagement of problems of direct humanistic concern. Though not tantamount to actual progress on such problems, the change of atmosphere is so marked as to betoken deep dissatisfaction with recent and traditional constrictions upon the range of research, even on the part of those fundamental psychologists whose purity is as the driven snow. The unrest has in fact led to a broadening of the range of problems investigated within more or less conventional terms and a diversification of the systematic and conceptual options that have been asserted.

2. Coincident and interrelated with these signs are others. An important set is provided by the changing image of the nature of science projected by the philosophy of science and by certain elements in the scientific community at large. These trends, uneven and disorderly, but pointing up and condoning a thoroughgoing pluralism of ends and means in science, are sure to influence the future direction of psychology. The picture I have in mind here is an enormously complex movement within recent scholarly culture—indeed one which has done much to prepare the grounds for the present general interest in exploring, and perhaps recentering, the relations between science and the humanities. I refer to such diverse matters as the weakening grip of logical positivism and related analytic philosophies; the relegitimation of metaphysics; the recognition of substantial areas of mootness in many problems of scientific method (e.g., the nature of definition, of "interpretation," of mathematics itself) which had been considered solved. Moreover, men like Bronowski, Polanyi, and others have at least begun to show that science, especially at theoretical levels, involves creative processes which no formalism can reduce to rule, processes in fact not dissimilar to those mediating the activity of poets, artists, historians, and other residents on the other side of the barricades. Such developments have been remarkably slow to register on psychology. For instance, the philosophy of science still talked in psychological literature is approximately 20 years out of date. But such developments are *beginning* to influence psychology.

I have said that psychology (and social science) has constructed a language which renders virtually impossible a differentiated exploration of the content of man. Such a constraint upon the very possibility of a sensitive analysis of experience is precisely what has kept psychology away from questions that could be of concern to the humanist. The humanist, I fear, has no particular reason for regretting this loss.

Psychology, however, *must*, in that if the awesome range of its subject matter be the functioning of organisms, there is no sound basis for it to defect at precisely that point at which such functioning becomes most interesting and, by the judgment of civilization, valued. As an illustration of the type of constraint that must be loosened if psychology is to effect contact with phenomena of import to the humanities (and thus itself), I should like to consider some issues pertaining to the analysis of motivation.

This illustration will demonstrate, I think, that major psychological problems cannot be embraced except in terms of levels of experiential sensitivity commonly cultivated, in the past, only in the humanities. It shows, further, that when such embracement *does* occur, psychology can begin to say things which are relevant to the humanities and indeed can reveal itself to the humanist as an ally. Again, I think that this illustration will make clear that we need a new kind of psychologist who fuses a scientific temperament with a humanistic sensibility, and perhaps a subspecies of humanist with a similar admixture of traits.

A few years ago, I suggested some ideas concerning what I consider an essential rephrasing of certain motivational phenomena. There is no reason why they should have been especially difficult. Yet they have proven so slippery to psychologists, and even to myself at times, that there seems no alternative but to refer this to the immense power of those schematisms which at some rock-bottom level regulate psychological thought.

My point of departure was something like the following. In the common sense epistemology of the West, there has long been a tendency to phrase all behavior and sequences thereof in goal directed terms: to refer behavior in all instances to ends, or end-states, which are believed to restore some lack, deficiency, or deprivation in the organism. I have called this deeply embedded presumption a kind of rough-and-ready "instrumentalism" which forever and always places action into an "in order to" context. In this common sense theory, behavior is uniformly assumed predictable and intelligible when the form "X does Y in order to . . ." is completed. In many instances in practical life it is possible to fill in this form in a predictively useful way. Often, however, a readily identifiable referent for the end-term is not available. In such cases we assume that the form must hold, and so we hypothesize or invent an end-term which may or may not turn out to be predictively trivial and empty. For instance, X does Y in order to be happy, punish himself, be peaceful, potent, respected, titillated, excited, playful, or wise.

Precisely this common sense framework—syntax if you will—has been carried over into the *technical* theories of motivation of the modern period, of which there have been bewilderingly many. In the technical theories, the central assumption is that action is always initiated, directed, or sustained by an inferred internal state called variously a motive, drive, need, tension system, whatnot, and terminated by attainment of a situation which removes, diminishes, "satisfies," or in any other fashion alleviates that state. The model is essentially one of disequilibrium-equilibrium restoral and each of the many "theories of motivation" proposes a different imagery for thinking and talking about the model and the criterial circumstances or end-state under which such disequilibria are reduced or removed. Matters are rendered pat and tidy in the various theories by the assumption that all action can be apportioned to (*a*) a limited number of biologically given, end determining systems (considered denumerable, but rarely specified past the point of a few "e.g.'s" like hunger and sex), and (*b*) learned modifications and derivatives of these systems variously called second-order or acquired motives, drives, etc.

My proposal, I think, is a quite simple one. In essence, it points up the limitations of referring *all* action to extrinsic, end determining systems, as just specified; it challenges the fidelity to fact and the fruitfulness of so doing. At the most primitive level it says: if you look about you, even in the most superficial way, you will see that all behavior is *not* goal directed, does not fall into an "in order to" context. In this connection, I have presented (Koch, 1956) a fairly detailed descriptive phenomenology of a characteristic sequence of "creative" behavior, which shows that if this state of high productive motivation be seen by the person as related to an extrinsic end (e.g., approval, material reward, etc.), the state becomes disrupted to an extent corresponding to the activity of so seeing. If, on the other hand, some blanket motive of the sort that certain theories reserve for such circumstances, like anxiety, is hypothesized, one can only say that the presence of anxiety in any reportable sense seems only to disrupt this creative state, and in precise proportion to the degree of anxiety.

If such states seem rare and tenuous, suppose we think of a single daily round and ask ourselves whether *everything* that we do falls into some clearcut "in order to" context. Will we not discover a rather surprising fraction of the day to be spent in such ways as "doodling," tapping out rhythms, being the owners of perseverating melodies, nonsense rhymes, "irrelevant" memory episodes; noting the attractiveness of a woman, the fetching quality of a small child, the charm of a shadow pattern on the wall, the loveliness of a familiar object in a particular distribution of light; looking at the picture over our desk, or out of the window; feeling disturbed at someone's tie, repelled by a face, entranced by a voice; telling jokes, idly conversing, reading a novel, playing the piano, adjusting the wrong position of a picture or a vase, gardening. Yet *goal directedness* is presumably the *fact* on which virtually all of modern motivational theory is based.

The answer of the motivational theorist is immediate. He has of course himself noticed certain facts of the same order. Indeed, much of motivational theory is given to the elaboration of detailed hypothetical rationales for such facts, and these the theorists will have neatly prepackaged for immediate delivery. I will not detain the discussion by unwrapping these packages, but merely guess at a few of the contents. There will be some containing the principle of "irrelevant drive"; others, "displacement" and other substitutional relations. An extraordinarily large package will contain freely postulated motives with corresponding postulated end-states, as, e.g., "exploratory drive" and its satiation, "curiosity drive" and its satisfaction, perceptual drives, esthetic drives, play drives, not to mention that vast new complement of needs for achievement, self-realization, growth, and even "pleasurable tension." Another parcel will contain the principle of secondary reinforcement or some variant thereof like subgoal learning, secondary cathexis, etc. Another will provide a convenient set of learning principles which can be unwrapped whenever one wishes to make plausible the possibility that some acquired drive (e.g., anxiety, social approval) which one arbitrarily assigns to a bit of seemingly unmotivated behavior, *could* have been learned. Another contains the principle of functional autonomy. There are indeed a sufficient number of packages to make possible the handling of any presumed negative instance in *several* ways. Why skimp?

The answer to all this is certainly obvious. The very multiplication of these packages as more and more facts of the "in and for itself" variety are acknowledged, makes the original analysis, which was prized for its economy and generality, increasingly cumbersome. But more importantly, it begins to get clear that the *search* for generality consisted in slicing behavior to a very arbitrary scheme—the result was a mock generality which started with inadequate categories and then sought rectification through more and more ad hoc specifications. In the end, even the apparent economy is lost and so largely is sense. Worst of all, much of the research which continues to get done in terms of the standard model, the problems that are raised, the phenomenal analysis that takes place, become senseless. To take but one conspicuous example, it should never have taken the amount of research that it has to establish (and *still* not to the satisfaction of all) that the drive reduction hypothesis is inadequate.

The positive part of my proposal would commence with an analysis of what seems involved in behavior which is phenomenally of an "in and for itself" variety as opposed to clear-cut instances of the "in order to" sort of thing. Take "play" to start with. I would resent being told that at any time I had a generalized need for *play* per se. I do not like to think of myself as that diffuse. I never liked cards. Nor even chess. And indeed my present girth is fairly solid testimony to the fact that I never had an insistent urge for the idle agitation of my musculature. My play "needs," or activity "needs," etc., have been such that if described with any precision at all, we soon find ourselves outside the *idiom* of "needs." I have been *drawn towards* certain specific activities which—because they fall into no obvious context of gainful employ, biological necessity, or jockeying for social reward, etc.—could be *called* play. But I have been drawn to these activities, and not others, because (among other reasons) they "contain," "afford," "generate" specific properties or relations in my experience towards which I am adient. *I like these particular activities because they are the particular kinds of activities they are*—not because they reduce my "play drive," or are conducive towards my well-being (often they are not), or my status (some of them make me look quite ludicrous), or my virility pride (some are quite girlish).

Do I like them, then, by virtue of nothing? *On the contrary*, I like them by virtue of something far more *definite*, "real," if you will, than anything that could be phrased in the extrinsic mode. Each one I like because of *specific* properties or relations immanent, intrinsic within the given action. Or better, the properties and relations *are* the "liking" (that, too, is a terribly promiscuous word). Such properties and relations in any on-going activity are no doubt dated instances of aspects of neural process which occur each over a family of conditions. Similar properties or relations would be produced (other factors constant) the next time I engage in the given activity. And no doubt there are families of activities which share similar properties and relations of the sort I am trying to describe. Thus there may be a certain consonance (by no means an absolute one) about the *kinds* of "play" activities that I like. But more importantly, properties or relations of the same or similar sorts may be generated within activity contexts that would be classified in ways quite other than play: eating, esthetic experience, sexual activities, problem solving, etc.

I call such properties or relations "value properties," and the (hypothetical) aspects of neural process which generate them, "value determining properties." Value or value determining properties to which an organism is adient, I call "positive"; those to which the organism is abient, "negative." Adience and abience of organisms are controlled by value determining properties (or by extension, value properties) of the different signs.

It can be instructive to consider from the point of view just adumbrated any of the types of "in and for itself" activity to which it is common gratuitously to impute extrinsic, end determining systems with their corresponding end-states. Thus for instance, one can only wince at the current tendency to talk about such things as "curiosity drives," "exploratory drives," "sensory drives," "perceptual drives," etc. as if the "activities" which are held to "satisfy" each of these "drives" (if indeed they are distinct) were just so much undifferentiated neutral pap that came by the yard. I am inclined to think that even the experimental monkeys who learn discrimination problems for the sole reward of being allowed visual access to their environments from their otherwise enclosed quarters, are being maligned when it is suggested that what their "drive" leads them to seek is "visual stimulation." Could it not be that even for the monkeys there are sights they might prefer not to see? Be this as it may, when explanations of this order are extended, say, to visually mediated esthetic activities in man, the reduction to a pap-like basis of particulate experiences to which many human beings attribute intense (and differentiated) values, can only be held grotesque.

To make such points graphic and further to clarify the notion of "value properties," it may be well to take the hypothetical instance of a person looking at a painting. I will quote a passage (Koch, 1956) in which I once introduced the notion through such an example.

> X looks at a painting for five minutes, and we ask, "Why?" The grammar of extrinsic determination will generate a lush supply of answers. X looks in order to satisfy a need for aesthetic experience. X looks in order to derive pleasure. X looks because the picture happens to contain Napoleon and because he has a strong drive to dominate. X looks because "paintings" are learned reducers of anxiety. . . . Answers of this order have only two common properties: they all refer the behavior to an extrinsic, end-determining system, *and* they contain very little, if *any* information.
>   . . .
> A psychologically naive person who *can* respond to paintings would say that an

important part of the story—the essential part—has been omitted. . . . Such a person would say that *if* the conditions of our example presuppose that X is really looking at the painting *as* a painting, the painting will produce a differentiated process in X which is correlated with the act of viewing. That fact that X continues to view the painting or shows "adience" towards it in other ways is equivalent to the fact that this process occurs. X may report on this process only in very general terms ("interesting," "lovely," "pleasurable"), or he *may* be able to specify certain qualities of the experience by virtue of which he is "held" by the painting.

. . . Suppose we assume that there are certain immanent qualities and relations within the process which are specifically responsible for any evidence of "adience" which X displays. Call these "value-determining properties." We can then, with full tautological sanction, say that X looks at the painting for five minutes because it produces a process characterized by certain value-determining properties. This statement, of course, is an empty form—but note immediately that it is not necessarily more empty than calling behavior, say, "drive-reducing." It now becomes an empirical question as to *what* such value-determining properties, intrinsic to the viewing of paintings, may be, either for X or for populations of viewers.

Though it is extraordinarily difficult to answer such questions, it is by no means impossible. The degree of agreement in aesthetic responsiveness and valuation among individuals of . . . varied environmental background but of comparable sensitivity and intelligence is very remarkable indeed (pp. 73–74).

It becomes important now to note that even in cases where the equilibrium model seems distinctly to fit, it may still yield an extraordinarily crass specification of the activities involved and either overlook their subtle, and often more consequential, aspects, or phrase them in a highly misleading way. Thus, for instance—though I do not have time for the analysis of the large class of activities imputed to so extensively studied a drive as hunger—I know of no account which gives adequate attention to the facts that in civilized cultures cooking is an art form, and that the discriminating ingestion of food is a form of connoisseurship. There is no reason in principle why value properties (or classes thereof) of the sort intrinsic to eating processes may not yield to increasingly accurate identification. Further, though we should not prejudge such matters, it is possible that certain of the value properties intrinsic to eating processes may be of the same order as, or in some way analogous to, value properties involved, say, in visual art-produced processes.

Because these ideas are often found difficult, let us take the case of another activity-class which can be acceptably, but only very loosely, phrased in a language of extrinsic determination: sexual activity. On this topic, the twentieth century has seen a vast liberation of curiosity, scientific and otherwise. Yet the textbook picture of sex, human sex, as a tension relievable by orgasm—a kind of tickle mounting to a pain which is then cataclysmically alleviated—is hardly ever questioned at theoretical levels (at least in academic psychology). When it is, it is likely to be in some such way as to consider the remarkable possibility that some forms of "excitement" (e.g., mounting preclimactic "tension") may themselves be pleasurable, and this may be cited, say, as a difficulty for the drive reduction theory, but not for some other drive theory, say some form of neohedonism like "affective arousal," which recognizes that the transition from some pleasure to more pleasure may be reinforcing. But our view would stress that sexual activity is a complex sequence with a rich potential for value properties; for ordered, creatively discoverable combinations, patterns, structures of value properties, which are immanent in the detailed quiddities of sexual action. Sexual experience, like certain other experiential contexts, offers a potential for art and artifice not unnoticed in the history of literature, fictional and confess. "al, but rarely even distantly mirrored in the technical *conceptualizations*. (The technical *data language* is another matter, but even here the "fineness" of the units of analysis involved in much empirical work is aptly symbolized by Kinsey's chief dependent variable, namely, the "outlet" and frequencies thereof.) The vast involvement with this theme at private, literary, and technical levels, has produced little towards a precise specification of experiential value properties, certainly none particularly useful at scientific levels.

Sex, eating behavior, activities written off to curiosity, play, perceptual drives, creative behavior, etc., are contexts each with a vast potential for the "discovery" and creative reassemblage of *symphonies* of value properties. Doubtless each such context offers a potential for differential ranges of value properties, but it is highly likely that there is marked overlap among such ranges. Indeed, formal or relational similarities in experiences that "belong" to quite different contexts of this sort suggest that Nature sets a fairly modest limitation on the number of "fundamental" value properties implicated in activity. There is much reason to believe, from the protocols of experientially sensitive and articulate people, as well as from the observation of behavior, that certain of the value properties intrinsic to such varied contexts of events as the "perception" of (and directed behavior towards) a picture, a poem, of a "problem," whether scientific, mathematical, or personal, of a "puzzle" in and for itself, are of an analogous order and in some sense overlap. And as we have just tried to show, it is reasonable to believe that the so-called consummatory aspects of hunger or of sex "contain" relational qualities not dissimilar to some of the value properties immanent in "complex" activities like those listed in the last sentence.

Once the detailed phenomena of directed behavior are rephrased in terms of intrinsic value properties, it becomes possible to reinspect the extrinsic language of drives and the like, and determine what utility it might actually contain. For *some* behaviors clearly are brought to an end or are otherwise altered by consummations, and organisms clearly show both restless *and* directed activities in the absence of the relevant consummatory objects. Questions about the relations between what one might call extrinsic and intrinsic grammar for the optimal phrasing of motivational phenomena are among the most important for the future of motivational theory.

Whatever is viable in the drive language is, of course, based in the first instance on "organizations" of activity sequences which converge on a common end-state. Each such organization, if veridical, would permit differential (but overlapping) ranges of value properties to "come into play." No doubt *primary* organizations of this sort, when veridical, are related to deviations of internal physiological states, the readjustments of which play a role in the adaptive economy. When such deviations are present, it is probable that certain value properties, or ranges thereof, are given especial salience and effectiveness with respect to the detailed moment-to-moment control of directed behavior. That all activities, however, must be contingent on such deviation-states, on the face of it seems absurd. Behavior will often be directed by value properties which have nothing to do with gross organizations of this sort, and which may in fact conflict with the adjustment of the concurrent deviation. Much of what is called "learned motivation" will consist not in "modifications of primary drives"—whatever that can mean—but rather in the building up of expectations and expectation-chains which terminate in anticipated processes with value properties. Whatever might be meant by the learned drives would be built up as systems of anticipation of value property constellations and sequences.

This, however, is not the place to develop whatever exists of the more detailed aspects of the formulation. The purpose was to suggest a line of thought which might bring psychology into contact with phenomena of fundamental concern both to itself and to the humanities. If I have established the barest possibility of such a development, that is all I could have wished.

You will now wish from me concrete illustrations of the "value properties" which I have talked about with such indirection. Your wish is unfair. Much as I would like to oblige, I cannot accomplish, in passing, what several thousand years of human, humanistic, and scientific analysis has failed to do. In the case of visual art-produced experience, the typical kinds of things that the estheticians, articulate artists, and art critics have been able to come up with in millenia of analysis, have been such global discriminations as harmony, symmetry, order, "significant form," "dynamic tension," "unity in variety," the "ratio of order to complexity," etc. By "value properties" I have in mind far more specific relational attributes of experience. They could, to borrow a cue from Gibson, be contingent upon subtle relational invariants in arrays of stimulation, as distributed over space and cumulated over time. They are almost certainly related to what Gibson would call "high order variables of stimulation" and are themselves high order relational variables within experience. The isolation of such value properties will not be accomplished within any specifiable time limit, will require learning to use language in new ways, and will require most of all the efforts of many individuals of exceptional and specialized sensitivity in significant areas of experience.

What, in effect, I am doing is merely drawing attention to certain particulate phenomena which all of us "know" are there. We have never *directly* set ourselves the problem of isolating and precisely delineating such phenomena. There are many reasons for this, some implicit in our common-sense conceptual categories and even the structure of our language, and others related to the fleeting character and extraordinary embeddedness of these "phenomena" in the flux of our experience. As I have just said, to approach these matters, we will have to learn to attach language to experience with a new kind of specificity. We will have to arrive at a highly differentiated set of metaphors, each of which is isomorphic with a significant relational aspect of experiential process, and learn to use these *intersubjectively*—

i.e., so as to achieve reliability of communication among groups having relevant sensitivity, but not necessarily esoteric levels thereof.

Such a system of metaphors must thus be *teachable*, and to achieve this as well as their initial "isolation," we must depend on all available knowledge, method, and technical lore of *perception psychology*. Experimental technique deriving from psychophysical method in the broadest sense must be tapped, as must knowledge and method concerning sensory mechanisms, neurophysiology of perception, perceptual learning, etc.

The great advances within psychology to date—and these must not be under-estimated by humanists or anyone else—have been in the domain of discovering the pitfalls involved in any attempt to isolate functionally significant units or vari-ables determining organismic action and experience, and in methods for coping with, compensating for, circumventing these pitfalls. If the humanist complains that many of the variables thus far isolated and studied by psychology seem to him insignificant, that is nothing to the point. Some substantial core of the experimental analysis, statistical compensation, environmental "input" control, and control or measure-ment of background variables within the organism emerging from this work has quite general significance for the analysis of organismic systems, whatever the "units" of analysis, problems, or hypotheses that are entertained. That is the real contribution of psychology to modern culture—of which laymen and humanists alike have never been apprized.

Recently the British physicist-novelist, C. P. Snow, has stirred much discussion by virtue of a distinction that he makes between "two cultures"—the "scientific" and the "traditional" or "literary-intellectual"—which he sees as almost completely insulated one from the other and at cross purposes.[2] He finds this a blight on the world intellectually, but he is more concerned with practical consequences that may in fact threaten the future of the world, in that he feels that the ruling establishment, which (in England at least) receives a purely humanistic education, must become increasingly incapable of wise decisions without an understanding of science. His proposed solution for this—not an unradical one for England, where the undeniable charm of its archaic educational forms can instill vast defensive passions—is that the curriculum be diversified, that science be gotten into humanities programs, and vice versa. Snow, of course, is dealing with a pressing practical problem and, in light of the educational traditionalism in England, he is not to be criticized for posing so limited a solution. But it seems to me to be indeed so limited as to be almost beside the point.

No fertile integration or even interplay between science and the humanities can come about—either in individual minds or in the scholarly community as a whole—merely by juxtaposing scientific and humanistic subject matters in the same

---

[2] In his provocative anatomy of the two cultures (Snow, 1959), it is clear that by the "traditional" he has broadly in mind the humanistic culture, while by the "scientific" he means specifically the physicist-engineer culture. He leaves psychology and social science out of the picture and thereby, I think, effects a serious distortion. For, one of the unique features of psychology is precisely that this is an area at which the two cultures must be in contact.

curriculum. Snow, for instance, complains that at a literary gathering he attended, not a single individual proved to have knowledge of the second law of thermo-dynamics. Had they been taught this information at Cambridge, I doubt that they would have found it particularly titillating. What is needed is not merely more joint education in these two great divisions of subject matter, but a *new and more significant mode* of education which will present them in such a way as to reveal their relatedness and represent human knowledge for the organic thing that it is.

But such a proposal must remain largely empty until we know *what kind* of "organic thing" knowledge is, know this precisely and in detail. Only then can the ideologies and images of science and the humanities be adjusted in such a way as to reduce the arbitrary gap that still exists; only then could such ideologies and images find their place within a single more inclusive organization. *Such* changes would of course automatically be reflected in education and *only then* could we expect to see once more in the world a type of individual who has not been with us since the nineteenth century: the scientist-humanist (or, of course, humanist-scientist). He will not of course be the same such individual as that of the nineteenth century, just as the nineteenth century version was not the same as that of the Enlightenment or the Renaissance. He will be highly specialized (the present differentiation of knowledge demands this of its scholars), but whether his work falls into an area allocated to science or a humanity, he will have deeply within him a sense of its relations to whatever areas are actually *relata*, however they be named. He will also have a sense of the relatedness of all inquiry and be not ignorant of, or uninterested in, at least a few of the things that exist across the gulf that so effectively separated his recent forebears.

But all this is contingent on the prior exploration of relations between science and the humanities, no easy task when assayed for its dimension away from the conference table. Returning to our major theme, it is psychology which, as third force, must take the lead. This is not to be seen as altruism, still less as imperialism. Its subject matter leaves it no choice. It can only blame itself for having elected to be the empirical science of the functioning of intact organisms, including intact human ones, in all of its forms. It is trapped. Even if, say, it defensively held that esthetic experience were illusory, it would still have to prove this, thus study and account for esthetic experience.

My discussion of value properties was but one illustration of a context in which rapprochement with matters of humanistic concern (and with humanists) could not only augment knowledge in valuable ways, but lead to a surer understanding of its organization. There are many other connections in which psychology must play an important, if not central, part in getting the nature of man's knowledge, and thus its texture, into better focus. This of course is tantamount to saying that psychology may have a central responsibility in helping put the ideology and image of science into finer correspondence with its actual content. I should like to mention in passing one especially vital context in which psychology could contribute to such an end.

I have in mind the need for effective psychological analysis of the nature of language, especially certain of the relevant problems like those of definition, meaningfulness, and meaning, which have too long been left in the hands of philosophers of science and, to some extent, linguists (which latter group to the best of my knowledge seems to have pretty much side-stepped them). The philosopher of science regards these as problems in epistemology and treats them mainly in terms of that tradition. It is, incidentally, my growing conviction that many problems still allocated to epistemology will receive little further clarification until they are recognized for the psychological problems they are.

The relevance of questions of definition and meaning to the present issue is this: most dichotomies advanced as between science and the humanities depend fundamentally on the assumption that they use "concepts" and "terms" of disparate type, that they seek differing "explanations" (or modes thereof), and that they generate different modes of meaning. If this is so, then an adequate analysis of language should have something to say about whether and to what extent such differences exist. If one begins with the premise (which everyones admits) that scientific language develops as a specialization of the natural language, and recognizes further that the natural language is what humanists use when they use language, then a psychological analysis of the functioning of natural language could well be instructive.

I have recently become interested in such matters and am amazed at what a bit of preliminary thinking seems to reveal. If we look at the problem of definition, for instance, psychologically, we immediately see that a definition, if apprehended by a recipient, must result in a process of perceptual learning and that what is learned is the discrimination of the properties, relations, or system thereof, which the definer wishes to designate by the term. This clearly means that definition, at bottom, is a *perceptual training process* and that everything that we know about the *conditions* of perceptual training and learning must apply to the analysis of definition. Adding to this a few obvious circumstances concerning the genesis and status of words in the natural language—circumstances that can be inferred from a study of something no more esoteric than dictionaries—quite a few matters take on a new light. It emerges, for instance, that contrary to what we were once told by logical positivists and others, no natural language and no scientific one of any richness can be regarded as organized into logical levels such that all terms are reducible to, or definable upon, a common (and usually, as the story goes, extremely restricted) definition base. On the contrary, if we want to pinpoint with a term any reasonably subtle, embedded, or delicately "contoured" relation or property, we must often, if using verbal means of definition, build up our defining expression from words that are *just as*, or even more ,"rarified" (remote from the presumptive definition base) as the one at issue. Moreover, for defining abstract or subtle concepts, or ones based on "new" discriminations, we will have to go outside of language and relate the term to a carefully controlled "perceptual display" (as it were) far more often than any logical positivist, especially of an older day, would care to admit.

Such findings, if they are that, are related to others at considerable variance with our lore and strictures concerning our *own* definitions in psychological discourse. Thus one thing that eventuates is the utter irrationality of expecting that all terms will be understood and used with equal nicety by all people in a scientific field (even with a "competent investigator" clause thrown in), depending only on the adequacy of the "operational" definitions. More generally, it becomes clear that in science, as in the humanities, communication (and in the first instance, observation) must depend on the ability to make certain specialized discriminations, which in turn depends on the individual's learned "backlog" of discriminations, *and* on special perceptual sensitivities. Universality of communication (relative to given language communities) therefore is achievable *neither* in science nor the humanities, and unless we want to disenfranchise the "advance fringe" ideas of the best minds in science —at the phase when communication can be accomplished only among a scattering of individuals—we will have to accept it that science cannot in principle be differentiated from the humanities on that basis.

Considerations of the order just adduced suggest that in each field of science and, of course, the humanities, there will necessarily be a plurality of language communities consisting in each case of individuals owning differential stocks of learned discriminations and differentially specialized discriminative capacities. Typically there will be also a vertical stratification of sublanguage communities within the same area of a given science, each corresponding to groups of individuals who have learned to make, or are capable of making, discriminations of different degrees of fineness. Suppose we call a certain criterial overlap of learned discriminations and special discriminative capacities, as among a number of individuals, a discrimination pool. We can then say that a language community (or subcommunity) of whatever size is characterized by a specified discrimination pool. Since in psychology *problems concerning any range of human endeavor or experience can be the object of study*, a unique feature of psychology is that it must premise its research on discrimination pools each of which overlaps to some definite extent with the discrimination pools in all of those widely ranged human areas. Thus a special demand upon psychology is that it contain a more widely diversified, and probably larger, collection of language communities than any other department of knowledge currently institutionalized. Among these must be groups of individuals whose specialized perceptual sensitivities overlap with humanists' in each of the areas in which humanistic endeavors are pursued. That is a large requirement. Where it is not met, no humanistic work of any import can be done. It is grotesque to suppose that someone totally devoid of the special discriminations and sensitivities of the artist could do meaningful psychological work in that field; similarly that an illiterate could contribute to the psychology of language or of literature.

Our brief comments on language have thus pointed up the difficulties that must be overcome if psychology is to move into its responsibility as "third force." It is clear that psychology needs many individuals having sensitivities overlapping with those of the humanist. Yet the same individuals must, in the first instance, have the special aptitudes and sensitivities—whatever they be—which equip them for *scientific* modes of analysis! For reasons foreshadowed in our remarks concerning education, it cannot expect them in even remotely adequate numbers. The absolute number of such individuals turned out by the culture at large is in itself pathetically small. Such individuals in general are not attracted to psychology, in that the very sensitivities at issue are what preclude their interest.

The emergence of a third force can at best be expected to be painfully slow and contingent on considerable skill with the bootstrap. So-called "recruitment" philosophies which currently see the ideal candidate as a kind of *Übermensch* in theoretical physics and carpentry at once, will of course have to be redefined, but not *derigorized*. If anything, the requirement will be more stringent, not less. That such a requirement will be met by few is no fatal objection. As with all requirements, compromise will continue to be the general rule. Of greater importance is that psychology be so imaged as to convey the need, the possibility, and the importance of work in areas of humanistic import. This may bring to us some of the individuals having the requisite combination of aptitudes, who now bypass us because of their uncongeniality towards the current image. Most important, we must work towards those more general educational changes at all levels which might increase the absolute number of such individuals in the culture at large.

Feeble and gradual as such a "program" may seem, the stakes are very high. For what has hardly been in the picture except by innuendo so far, has been the world outside the cloisters. Despite the "creativity" fad, and despite the recent spate of social criticism which has made organization men, lonely crowds, affluent societies, ex-urbanites, and their ilk seminar topics at every shopping center, the gentle process of dehumanization which twentieth century man has so cosily accepted continues unabated. Indeed, the truly frightening fact is that so much of the social criticism itself reproduces, at second remove, the qualities of the object criticized. Take the "beatnik" whose devastating critique of an inarticulate society is to form a cult of absolute inarticulateness.

The reduction of man to his present dimension need not be temporary. When the ability to differentiate among experiences is lost, experience is lost. When the perception of differential values as they inhere in the quiddities of experience and action is lost, then value is lost. Nothing says that these things need return. In this homogenization of experience, the recent images of science and of the humanities have played a profound part. The newer outgrowths of science—psychology and the social sciences—which, had they pursued their appropriate subject matter, could have helped resolve knowledge into its proper spectrum, turned away from that subject matter. Rejecting the first force from which all knowledge had germinated, they became camp followers of that second force called "science," or at least their image of that force. Have they the courage to become the third force that could some day cause the end of armies?

REFERENCES

Koch, S. Behavior as "intrinsically" regulated: work notes towards a pre-theory of phenomena called "motivational." In M. R. Jones (Ed.), *Current theory and research in motivation*. Vol. 4. Lincoln: University of Nebraska Press, 1956. Pp. 42–86.

Koch, S. Epilogue to study I. In S. Koch (Ed.), *Psychology: a study of a science*. Vol. 3. New York: McGraw-Hill, 1959. Pp. 729–788.

Snow, C. P. *The two cultures and the scientific revolution*. New York: Cambridge University Press, 1959.

METHODOLOGICAL ISSUES

As noted earlier, the experimental method is a *sine qua non* of scientific psychology and there is every reason to believe that its use is increasing in frequency as well as importance. Research findings constitute a major role in psychology today as reference to the burgeoning journals will attest. An important part of the training for both graduate and undergraduate students deals with research techniques and practices including the collection, analysis, and reporting of data. A major goal of graduate schools is the production of psychologists well versed in at least the technical aspects of research, in the hope that they will contribute to the growing storehouse of data.

But what of the quality and validity of psychological research? A number of psychologists would agree with David Bakan who suggests that "there is a crisis in research in psychology. Though enormous resources are being expended for psychological research, the yield of new and significant information concerning the nature of the human psyche is relatively small in comparison."[1] Not only is the meaningfulness of our research questioned, but also the technical correctness of the experimental method as used in psychology.

The articles in this section examine several phases of the research endeavor: choosing the problem; securing subjects; collecting, analyzing, and reporting the data. While deficiencies, limitations, and errors are noted, none of the authors suggests discarding the experimental method because it falls short of perfection.

It is important to remember that "the demonstration of error marks an advanced stage of a science. All scientific inquiry is subject to error, and it is far better to be aware of this, to study the sources in an attempt to

[1] D. Bakan, *On Method* (San Francisco, Jossey-Bass, 1967), p. xii.

reduce it, and to estimate the magnitude of such errors in our findings, than to be ignorant of the errors concealed in the data." [2]

Further, the very technique used to identify sources of error in the experimental method has been, in most cases, the experimental method itself. Such self-corrective procedures are certainly in the highest tradition of science.

[2] H. H. Hyman, *Interviewing in Social Research* (Chicago, University of Chicago Press, 1954), p. 4.

CHOICE OF THE
RESEARCH PROBLEM

The first step in any research undertaking is that of delimiting the problem or area to be investigated. The step is an obvious one but the actual process of decision is often difficult, particularly for the neophyte researcher. Without much prior research experience or a possible commitment to a problem area, the would-be researcher frequently finds his interests vague and the realm of possibilities for research overwhelming. The seasoned researcher, particularly one highly motivated and self-disciplined, often finds himself in just the opposite situation: not enough time to pursue his myriad research ideas.

Whatever the status and experience of the researcher, however, a variety of factors are operative in influencing his choice of a particular topic or problem, as the following two articles will demonstrate.

12. The Choice of the Problem[1]

Wilse B. Webb

Because of the great complexity and expense of much current psychological research, Dr. Webb feels that guidelines are needed to help not only researchers, but also teachers of research, thesis advisers, funding agencies, and all others concerned with research, in their choice of a problem. Since the personal and financial investment in research is of such enormous proportions, the topic or problem area must be chosen with great care. Dr. Webb presents and discusses what he considers the six reasons for conducting an experiment: "curiosity, confirmability, compassion, cost, cupidity, and conformability." While these reasons alone can lead to a good, though perhaps pedestrian, research problem, three further criteria—knowledge, dissatisfaction, and generalizability—are posited that lead to a study of more critical and enduring quality.

The matter of how to judge the goodness or badness of a result, particularly when this result is a theoretical formulation, has received considerable attention in recent years. Today in psychology, such decisions are increasingly necessary. Our subject matter has become quite boundless: muscle twitches and wars, the sound of porpoises and problems of space, the aesthetic qualities of tones and sick minds, psychophysics and labor turnover. The range of organisms involved in the studies of these problems extends from pigeons to people, from amoeba to social groups. Further the techniques of measurement have been honed and sharpened by electronic tubes, computing machines, mathematical niceties, and imaginative testing procedures. Too often, in this lush environment, we as researchers may find after some months of toil and research that our findings, although in accord with nature and beautifully simple, are utterly petty and we ourselves are no longer interested in them much less anyone else being interested.

This problem of carefully selecting and evaluating a problem does not involve the

[1] Reprinted from the *American Psychologist*, 1961, **16**, 223–227. Copyright 1961 by the American Psychological Association, and reproduced by permission of the author and the publisher. An abridged version of the Presidential Address to the Southern Society for Philosophy and Psychology given at the fifty-second Annual Meeting in Biloxi, Mississippi, April 15, 1960.

researcher alone. In our complex beehive of today, this is a question for the teacher of research, the thesis and dissertation director, the research director of laboratories or programs, and the dispensers of research funds—in a small way, department chairmen and deans, and in a large way, the guardians of the coffers of foundations and government agencies.

We are not without criteria, of course. Either implicitly or explicitly we seek justification for what we do. Certainly when grants are involved we seek for some reasons to justify the getting or the giving of money. For our consideration, I have rummaged around and turned up six widely used bases for doing an experiment: curiosity, confirmability, compassion, cost, cupidity, and conformability—or, more simply, "Am I interested," "Can I get the answer," "Will it help," "How much will it cost," "What's the payola," "Is everyone else doing it?"

I believe you will find that these are the things that enter our minds when we evaluate a student's problem, dispense a sum of research money, or decide to put ourselves to work. To anticipate myself, however, I will try to establish the fact that these bases, used alone or in combination although perhaps correlated positively with a "successful" piece of research, will probably have a zero or even negative correlation with a "valuable" piece of research.

Before proceeding to examine these criteria, however, let me introduce a clarifying footnote. Although I am concerned about selecting a problem beyond the routine and "successful" experiment—and here I shall use completely indiscriminately (with apologies to the philosophers) such terms as "good," "valued," "enduring," "worthwhile"—I do not wish to disparage the necessary place of routine experiments, i.e., well conducted experiments which fill in and extend those more creative ones. I think that even the most cursory consideration of the history of science reveals that the "original" or the "important" experiment almost inevitably pushes out from routine work that has preceded it and is further dependent upon the supportive routine experiments for their fruition into the field. Most definitely, I would contend that it is far more important to do a routine experiment than no experiment at all.

But back to the problem before us: Are our reasons for experimenting sufficient guidelines to decide about experiments? The first of these, *curiosity*, is the grand old man of reasons for experimentation and hence, justification for our experimentation. In the days when knighthood was in flower, this was the most familiar emblem on the scientist's shield. It was enough to seek an answer to "I wonder what would happen if . . . ." This was sometimes formalized with the dignified phrase, "knowledge for knowledge's sake."

Today this is not a strong base of operation. Perhaps costs have outmoded whimsey; perhaps the glare of the public stage has made us too self-conscious for such a charming urge. Or, perhaps more forebodingly, we are less curious—or, perhaps a combination of these has made curiosity less defensible. More critically, when we look more closely at this justification for doing, or proposing to do an experiment, it does not turn out to be one. Clearly a person can be curious about valuable things, trivial things, absurd things, or evil things. I think we would all find it a little difficult to judge the relative merits of two pieces of completed research by trying to decide which of the two experimenters was the most curious. Perhaps wisely, then, it seems more and more difficult to convince deans or directors of research, or dispensers of funds that a problem is worth investigating because we, personally, happened to be puzzled by it.

The criterion of *confirmability* as a criterion of worthiness of the pursuit of a topic has two sides: a philosophic one and a pragmatic one. Philosophically, this criterion reached its glory in the '30s and '40s when the voice of a logical positivist was heard throughout the land. In no uncertain terms, they told us that the criterion for a problem was "that the question asked could be answered." On the pragmatic side, this criterion is interpreted to mean: "Pick variables which are likely to be statistically significant." Undoubtedly, the philosophical point of view has done much to clear up our experimental work by hacking through a jungle of undefined and ambiguous terms. From the pragmatic point of view, this has been a much valued criterion for the graduate student with several kids and who must finish his thesis or dissertation to get out and start earning a living. However, it is just this criterion that may be voted the most likely to result in a pedestrian problem. It demands problems which have easily measurable variables and clearly stated influences. It discourages the exploration of new, complex, or mysterious areas. To exercise this criterion alone would force one to choose an experiment of measuring age as related to strength of grip on the handle of the dynamometer against exploring variables associated with happiness. Both may be quite worthwhile, but the latter has less of a chance of being approached so long as we exercise the criterion of confirmability alone.

The problem of *costs* must enter into considerations of undertaking an experiment. In the real, live world, determining the value of a thing is very simple. Find out how much it costs. Clearly, anything that costs a lot is very valuable. A car or house which costs more than another car or another house is naturally worth more. One pays for what one gets and one gets what one pays for. This thinking carries over into the world of scientific affairs. Space probes are obviously important because they cost a lot; a project which can get a large grant must be a good one or else it would not cost so much.

Certainly this is very faulty reasoning. That methodologies differ in their costs is quite obvious; the more expensive the methodology, the more valuable and important the activity is not a direct derivative. Einstein undoubtedly used less equipment than his dentist but we may suspect that Einstein attacked the more valuable problem. Departments of Philosophy are far less expensive than Departments of Veterinary Medicine but I do not believe them to be necessarily less valuable.

It is quite true that when a large sum of money is expended on a particular project that some decisions have been made that the desirability or the value of that project justifies the expenditure of this large sum. Money may serve as a crude index of where to look for decision bases that justify large expenditures but cannot serve as judgment bases themselves. If a person says, "To do this piece of research will cost x amount of money and will occupy x amount of my life," he has merely brought his problem into focus and has raised the critical question more clearly, i.e., is such an expenditure worth it? He has not solved the problem of how valuable his experiment is, but raised the question—some other criterion must be sought for an answer to that question.

A somewhat new criterion has entered into thinking today: *compassion.* As we have moved into the applied world, this rather new criterion has come into increasing use—at least this seems true of psychology. A person asks himself as he begins an experiment, "Will the results make things better?" and implicitly assumes that an affirmative answer will make his experiment or his project more valuable. The problem then is assessed in terms of its solutions or answers resulting in a patient's improvement, a reduction in prejudice, a happier or a healthier world, etc. A variation on this question, as it is asked in the market place and in some of the other sciences directly, is in a slightly cruder form: "Will this be useful; what service will this finding perform?"

H. G. Wells has a comment on this guideline for performance in his book *Meanwhile*:

The disease of cancer will be banished from life by calm, unhurrying, persistent men and women working with every shiver of feeling controlled and suppressed in hospitals and in laboratories. . . . Pity never made a good doctor, love never made a good poet, desire for service never made a discovery.

In one sense of the word, this criterion is a form of the old, applied vs. basic issue that plagues all sciences that live with one foot in technology and the other foot in theory. I cannot begin to resolve this issue here. I can, however, I believe, say this: it is quite possible for a piece of research undertaken in compassion or for utility to be quite valuable, enduring, well thought of, etc. It is also quite possible that it be trivial, superficial, limited, useless, etc. The same may be said for any given piece of basic research in which utility or compassion was never an issue. I am not one who believes that because a piece of research has no relevant use, it then by definition is valuable; or that a finding because it is useful is worthless. If these statements may be granted, it would appear then that some more fundamental criteria must be applied.

Cupidity is a variation on the criterion of compassion. Here, however, the "pay-off" is not for others but for oneself. Very simply the research is evaluated in terms of whether it will get one a promotion, favorable publicity, peer applause. Well, sometimes, undoubtedly what is good for you is good for others, and hence of general value.

However, the contrary is just as likely to be true: namely, what is good for you is not necessarily good for others at all. For example, making the natural assumptions that deans cannot read and department chairmen do not, the greater the number of papers, then the greater the probability of promotion. This results in a whirling mass of fragmented, little, anything printables to be constantly turned out instead of mature, integrated, programmatic articles. In being good to yourself you have done little or no good for others. The most casual recall would suggest that the impelling motives behind most significant advances in thought have not been cupidity, rather to the contrary such advances seemed to be more "selfless" than "selfish."

The last of my "useful" criteria is that of *conformity*. In these days of togetherness, it is not at all surprising to find conformity and its cousin, comfortableness, serving as guidelines for determining the should or should not of experimentation. We mean, by conformity, the choice of the currently popular problem, i.e., one within an ongoing and popular system, for example, operant conditioning, statistical learning theory; or a currently popular area of investigation, for example, sensory deprivation, or the Taylor Manifest Anxiety Scale.

As with all of our preceding criteria for deciding about a research project, conformity clearly has its merits. It would be foolish to turn one's back on new methods or a recent breakthrough of ideas which have been developed and certainly the interactive stimulation of mutual efforts in the same area are helpful factors in research. These, however, seem to be more means than ends to be sought for. One must be cautioned against becoming overenamored by the availability of a method at the expense of thoughtfulness or being charmed by the social benefits of working in an active area at the expense of the scientific implications of such work. More simply, some things that a lot of people are doing are quite worthwhile, and some are quite ridiculous.

Unfortunately, however, the assiduous cultivation of all these virtuous goals may still, it would seem, even in combination result in the most pedestrian of problems. We must then search further for means of assuring ourselves that the problem is a good one. The usual criteria do not seem to answer.

I am going to say that there are three fundamentals which form the basis for good experiments or good problems. None of these are new. By disclaiming originality, however, I can claim that they are profound and that their presence or absence makes a significant effect in the value of the problem to an individual. Two of these are characteristics of the person, and one of the problem. The most common tags for my trio are: knowledge, dissatisfaction, and generalizability. The first two of these, of course, refer to the individual himself and the third to the problem itself.

I think that there is very general agreement that one can only work effectively in an area when he has a thorough understanding of this general area of concern. It is quite often that the significant finding comes from a fusion of quite a number of simple studies or a perception of gaps in the detailed findings or the methodologies and procedures of others. I am quite sure that the vaunted, creative insight of the scientist occurs more frequently within a thorough knowledge of one's area than as a bolt from the blue.

In a quite mechanical sense, a failure to obtain all knowledge possible about one's problem area is to fail to profit from the errors of thought of the past, if they be errors, or the knowledges obtained, if such knowledges are correct. Either represents an arrogance of a witless kind. Moreover, in this very practical sense, unless these backgrounds are well assessed by the worker, one may find oneself both discovering a most well-known discovery and be in the embarrassing position of arriving at the party dressed in full regalia a day late. Or perhaps, more tragic for the world of ideas, such a person without knowledge may remain unheard, being incapable of gaining the attention of competent workers through an ineptitude of expression or lack of relation to the field.

Secondly, however, to avoid the sins of conformity, suggested previously—for specialized knowledge groups can become more ingroupish than a band of teenagers —a healthy opposition must be present. I have designated this as dissatisfaction. Other terms to be used are skepticism, negativism, or perhaps more charmingly, iconoclasm.

It is, of course, quite possible that I am very wrong in emphasizing the necessity of an opposing set to the existent knowledges and methodologies in one's time. Clearly the most convenient position would be to invoke the concept of "genius" or "insight," leading to important problems as a result of broad surveys of the literature, or efficiency in employing procedures. This, however, would hardly be useful as a guideline. One can hardly suggest to a person that they strain and have an insight, or try hard and be a genius.

There is, on the other hand, considerable empirical evidence, or at least examples, to substantiate the fact that original discoveries contain an element of active revolution. Skipping lightly through psychological history, we can point to Helmholtz' classical rate of nerve conduction experiments which flew in the face of established knowledge about immediate conductivity, Freud defied the reign of conscious thought, Watson negated mentalism, Köhler set against the tide of trial and error learning, in recent times Harlow has spoken not so much for positive adient motivation as against avoidant motives as the prime mover of man.

Logically, and psychologically (and happily they conjoin occasionally) this seems to make good sense. A significant research problem is a creative act. One can hardly be creative if one is avidly listening to the voice of others. We have good evidence from such experimentations as the Luchin's jar experiments that developed sets can clearly block solutions to problems. More simply, if one agrees with everything that everyone else says, one's role is automatically limited to feeding the fires, applauding the words or, at best, carrying the word. None of these are actions that lead to truly important research activities.

We may have, however, great knowledge and object quite violently to the items of this knowledge and proceed to conduct small experiments to substantiate our objections and still be doing little more than picking at a pimple on the face of one's science, to use a vulgar analogy. A further critical requirement must be recognized— a critical requirement that is most difficult to capture in words: to be an important result, one's findings require "extensity." Another word used here is that one's results must be generalizable. Poincaré, in his *Methods of Science*, states most clearly the reasoning underlying this requirement:

What, then, is a good experiment? It is that which informs us of something besides an isolated fact. It is that which enables us to foresee, i.e., that which enables us to generalize. . . . Circumstances under which one has worked will never reproduce themselves all at once. The observed action then will never recur. The only thing that can be affirmed is that under analogous circumstances, analogous action is produced.

A further quotation from the same book amplifies this point of view:

. . . it is needful that each of our thoughts be as useful as possible and this is why a law will be the more precious the more general it is. This shows us how we should choose. The most interesting facts are those which may serve many times.

Very simply, this boils down to being able to evaluate the probable consequence of your findings with the question which goes something like this: "In how many and what kind of specific circumstances will the relationships or rules that hold in this experiment hold in such other instances?" If the answer to this is only in instances almost exactly replicable of this particular circumstance, the rules that we obtain are likely to be of little consequence. If, however, the rule applies to what apparently is a vast heterogeneity of events in time and space, in varieties of species and surrounds, this rule is likely to have great value. Stated otherwise, the extent to which our variables and situations are unique and rare in contrast to universal and common largely determines the extent to which the findings are likely to be considered trivial or tremendous in their implications.

My summary can be quite simple:

Research today is both complex and costly. Guidelines are needed to sort among these complexities to enhance our chances of a sound investment, be this personal, financial, or temporal.

Six criteria may be, and often are, applied to judge a project's "success" potential: curiosity, confirmability, cost, compassion, cupidity, and conformability. There is probably a good probability that studies meeting the guidelines will "pay off" in some form of coinage—perhaps small change.

However, for a study to be an enduring and critical one for the history of ideas or to enter into that stream, three further items seem involved:

1. You must know thoroughly the body of research and the techniques of experimentation which are related to a given problem area. Naivete may be a source of joy in an artistic field but is not the case in valued research efforts.

2. You should be able to disbelieve, be dissatisfied with, or deny the knowledge that you have. (This is no paradox in relation to our first statement. Recognize that the first requirement is propaedeutic to this one. This is an active, not a passive state; this is to know and then know differently, rather than a know-nothing state.) Valued research seems to grow from dissatisfactions with the way things are, rather than agreeable perpetuation of present ways of proceeding.

3. You should, very simply, look for the forest beyond the tree, test the generality of your proposed finding. If your finding is referent to a rat in a particular maze, a patient on a particular couch, or a refined statistical difference, then that rat, that patient, or a captive statistician may listen to you. This would be a skimpy and disappointing audience to my way of thinking.

It is quite likely that we cannot all become geniuses. We can at least try to be less trivial. Learn as much as we can, believe in new ways, seek as great extensity in our variables as we can.

13. Cultural Determinants of Psychological Research Values[1]

Henry Winthrop

Dr. Winthrop focuses on some of the constraining or biasing factors capable of influencing the psychologist's choice of research problems. One major factor is the cultural climate or context (including all of the cultural values and taboos accepted and enforced by his culture) within which the researcher works. Several examples are presented of researchers from different countries who formed different hypotheses about the same research question and drew different conclusions from the same results, all due to their cultural frame of reference. In an extended discussion, Dr. Winthrop probes the influence of cultural values on the interpretation or resolution of the nature-nurture controversy.

The type of problem an investigator sets himself is often conditioned by a cultural frame of reference and at the same time by some of the prevailing values which are implicitly and uncritically accepted by the culture. Since a culture has a *lebenstyl* of its own, it may slant the type of problem chosen by the investigator and weight the type of outcome he expects. In a very real sense the cultural and frequently a subcultural frame of reference may actually determine both the form and the content of an investigator's null hypothesis. To illustrate the point, consider a Russian and an American investigator, both of whom may wish to study farm morale as a function, respectively, of the communist and democratic ways of life. Having developed, let us say, an identical scale for the measurement of *farm morale*, each studies the change in morale scores as a function of increasing size of farm, using a series of successful farms of different size. The variation in size may, of course, refer to acreage or farm population, or both. We shall assume that in both investigations, both variables were involved. The American investigator's null hypothesis might be that there is no difference in morale as a function of *increasing individuality*, interpreting the magnitude of individuality to be directly proportional to farm size. The Russian investigator's null hypothesis is likely to be that there is no difference in

[1] Reprinted in part from *The Journal of Social Psychology*, 1961, **53**, 255–269, with the permission of the author and The Journal Press.

morale as a function of "togetherness," interpreting the magnitude of "together-ness" to be directly proportional to farm size. It is right here, at the beginning of the investigation, when assumptions are being made uncritically, that the cultural bias takes its toll, for the American investigator who bends with the bias of his culture would probably be inclined to accept the unexamined notion that *individuality* can express itself in terms of the entrepreneurial ambition to concentrate land, labor, and capital in one's own hands. The Russian investigator, just as susceptible to distortion by cultural bias, would be inclined to see similar concentrations as an expression of collective, Communist mentality and outlook, indicating a sense of community or Gemeinschaft, as opposed to untempered capitalistic pre-Marxian individuality.

Assuming that both investigators obtain the same results so that the null hypothesis is rejected, the first will draw the conclusion that success at farming is a function of individuality, the second that it is a function of "togetherness," in both cases reflecting cultural bias. The design and the assumptions would admittedly be faulty, for what both investigations would have in common is a set of sample situa-tions exhibiting an increasing concentration of technology, and if morale is de-pendent upon success and the latter in turn upon concentration of agricultural technology per capita and per acre, then the initial formulations of the investigations, properly speaking, are faulty. Nevertheless, even if our illustration for this reason leaves much to be desired, our point still stands, for we suspect that some investiga-tors of both nationalities would be prone to make such an error precisely in the degree to which they would be motivated by such cultural bias.

Perhaps a humorous comment from Bertrand Russell would be more appro-priate in this same connection, although I regret that I have long since lost the source of this quotation. Russell comments as follows.

The manner in which animals learn has been much studied in recent years, with a great deal of patient observation and experiment. Certain results have been obtained as regards the kind of problems that have been investigated, but on general principles, there is still much controversy. One may say broadly that all the animals that have been carefully observed have behaved so as to confirm the philosophy in which the observer believed before his observation began. Nay, more, they have all displayed the national characteristics of the observer. Animals studied by Americans rush about frantically, with an incredible display of hustle and pep, and at last achieve the desired result by chance. Animals observed by Germans sit still and think, and at last evolve the solution out of their inner consciousness . . .

And, presumably Russell might have added, the animals observed by an English-man do not waste time looking about for a satisfactory solution but eventually muddle through, while those observed by a Russian solve their problems by the application of orthodox proletarian ideology with, I suppose, eminently satisfactory dialectical results.

To the plain man, such as the present writer, the situation is discouraging. I observe, however, that the type of problem which a man naturally sets to an animal depends upon his own philosophy, and that this probably accounts for the differences in results. The animal responds to one type of problem in one way and to another in another; therefore the results obtained by different investigators, though different, are not incompatible . . .

Russell's quip is not without some basis in reality. One evidence of it is well known to most psychologists. They are familiar with the fact that the cultural climate of continental psychology has been more conducive to approaching a problem in verstehende and personalistic terms and in terms of *la vie interieure* than the American cultural climate with its obsessive desire to make a break with the "mentalistic" pattern, even at times at the cost of seeming to deny the need to deal scientifically with events of the inner life. On the other hand, it is the Black Box approach which is more congenial to many American psychologists and a good many investigators in English-speaking countries who are strong adherents of the British empirical tradition. Such an approach is part of the cultural bias which has come down to us both from the giants of British philosophy, like Hobbes, Locke, and Hume, and British associationists in psychology, like Hartley. A fundamental bias present in the Black Box approach and which is too infrequently emphasized, is a penchant for simplicity in explanation. Too often it is felt that if a simple explanation will work, then that explanation must be the true one. Since a Black Box approach achieves a tremendous oversimplification by neglecting the existence and contributory functions of unobserved perceptual organization, the derived simplicity may prove *ultimately* to be deceptive. It should be obvious, however, that a Black Box approach, no matter how successful it proves to be over a substantial period of time, may sooner or later reach the limits of its explanatory and predictive power, for Nature has clearly provided man and the vertebrates with a central, nervous system and neuromuscular processes for participation in types of behavior to which they are surely necessary, even if not sufficient. This is a point of view which perhaps can be shared by centrists, interbehaviorists, organismic psychologists, and transactionalists, alike. Sooner or later behavior to which these central structures are maximally relevant will be investigated and the Black Box approach is likely to prove decreasingly relevant as such behavior becomes pinpointed. The virtues and the limitations of the Black Box approach have been ably and rather briefly described by Ashby (1958). Whether a Black Box approach will be adequate for the roles played by feeling, sympathy, empathy, motivation, directive values, all forms of cognitive patterning and similar considerations, remains to be seen. In fact limitations on the Black Box approach are recognized even within cybernetic theory when we say that central structures and their functions can be deduced from protocol data *up to an isomorphism*, that is to say, our deductions are successful only where a new system (and its behavior) can be shown to be a member of a class of systems whose internal structures and functions are already well understood, or whose behavior, at least, is fairly similar. Our point here, however, is to note that the Black Box approach does reflect a cultural bias and a professional value in the form of preference for a given research bias, regardless of the eventual degree of success which that research bias may achieve.

Often, however, the setting of a professional problem is less subtly dependent upon the Zeitgeist. Experiments in conformity behavior, such as those performed by Asch, yield results which unquestionably suggest group influence as a major factor. In an other-oriented culture like ours, such results may be frequent. Would we have gotten them from an experimental group of arch-individualists? No one knows until we have a valid, measuring device for individuality and have repeated experiments of this sort upon high scorers in that attribute. If we did not, perhaps we should have to conclude that Asch had paid insufficient attention to the personality variable. On the other hand, in a culture which encouraged fierce individuality, *failure* to get such results would be *likewise* due to social conditioning. The investigator in an individualist culture would be forced to conclude that conformity to the culture is operative here too, but it is conformity to the ideal of fierce independence of judgment. The standard deviation of judgments of line length in retrials would, in such a case, be likely to increase. Our point, however, in all of this is that the decision to investigate problems of this type, reflects, I believe, an implicit preference for investigating behavior determined by socially built-in habits of a sort which are not generally admired in a critical context. There are, of course, many other problem specialties of interest to the social psychologist, which, I am convinced, would betray a set of values if the roots of the investigator's interests could be probed deeply enough. In fact one would be hard put to defend the proposition that the choice of problem made by an investigator is a haphazard affair. Familiarity with one's colleagues makes it abundantly clear that most psychologists have vested values in the problems they choose for investigation and often vested interests in the outcome. Who among us is not familiar with the psychologist who pounces gleefully upon the hoped-for outcome when it is obtained and who strains vigorously for an explanation which will leave the issue in doubt if the outcome is not in the expected direction? I do not say that the average social psychologist functions like the average lawyer, and sets out to prove what he has already decided is right. I do say, however, that at times he strains somewhat at his explanations, influenced without doubt by his phenomenal bias with all the values which that bias carries in its train.

Often too, implicit in the investigator's activity is a rejection of those socially conditioned values whose influence he measures and explores. Education, reading, thought, intellectual honesty, and the *values of that subculture formed by the intelligentsia*, merge and produce a contempt for an uncritical conformity which is never expressed in public and only occasionally in private to one's trusted friends and associates. Here, however, we tread on dangerous ground for the average social psychologist will resist, in the psychoanalytic sense of the term "resist," the imputation of hostility towards the behavioral mechanisms investigated. For a variety of reasons he does not want the anticathexis which energizes this type of exploration, either to be recognized for what it is, opposition to cultural trends, or to be seen as a strong, motivational basis underlying his research. Even the fact that one tells oneself that one is dispassionately interested in the truth, cannot disguise the implicit act of rejection which thoroughgoing, careful, and detailed research, implies, if the pursuit of truth, though the Heavens fall, is accompanied by an underlying contempt for social cant, hypocrisy, and buncombe. This is perhaps as it should be. This critical anticathexis plays, however, more of a role with the historian, economist, and sociologist than with the social psychologist, which is perhaps why the latter is as yet looked upon with less suspicion than the preceding three. Those who stand to lose by a naked revelation of the truth are generally more aware of the investigator's value bias than he frequently is himself, or would care to admit. If, however, professional, financial, social, and cultural ostracism are to be avoided, the fiction must be maintained that the investigator's choice is purely dispassionate and purely disinterested. In any case I think a close analysis, depth or otherwise, will generally reveal the quicksands of value which have swallowed the investigator and determined his choice of problem for investigation.

In all honesty, however, a change that seems to be rather new in these parlous times and which perhaps may be associated with the rise of ex-Senator McCarthy, has recently been reported. The psychologist, insofar as he may be an *intellectual*, appears to have gone underground. Seeman (1958) reports that the academic intellectual now despises the label "intellectual" because of its bad flavor in the community. He quotes one academic interviewee as follows:

One consequence of anti-intellectualism is for some intellectuals to deny that they are intellectuals. This is a behavioral denial; it's part of the psychological revolution, the adjustment trend. . . . The pressure to be well-adjusted is high, and so he becomes non-intellectual and begins to deny in some respects that he is an intellectual. . . .

Seeman then adds his own impression of all the interviews:

The evidence in the interviews indicates that the retreat from membership is a substantial one and takes many forms. Indeed, one of the real surprises, during the course of these interviews, was the rarity of real acceptance of intellectual status. This non-acceptance is revealed in several ways. First, there is the frequency with which this freely offered remark appears: "Intellectuals, I hate the word!" Second, there are the direct denials to the question, "Do you consider yourself an intellectual?" A complete listing of the protocol responses on this point would reveal a quite consistent, though subtly varied, pattern of maneuvering, all aimed at being counted out—the kind of "Who, me?" response one gets from the obviously guilty (p. 31).

Having a depressing sense of their social marginality, largely because the value-systems they espouse run counter to those of the general population, Seeman finds that intellectuals "adopt, without serious efforts to build a reasoned self-portrait, an essentially negative, minority view of themselves and to find, in addition, some plausible ground for believing that this failure in self-conception is not independent of role performance." If this change among social and behavioral scientists should lead to a transvaluation of the value-systems of academic intellectuals, then, indeed, Benda's (1955) "betrayal of the intellectuals" will have begun its American premiere. However, the self-consciousness which Seeman reports should make it abundantly clear that the investigator, whether an "intellectual" or not, possesses value-systems towards which the community is sensitive, even if he is not. Only when the community betrays its hostility is the investigator likely to make obvious the role which values play in research and even then—to judge by Seeman's data—more so by denying these are his values or by openly repudiating them.

Occasionally the psychologist reveals those values which consciously underly his choice of problems. He may do this by activities not directly connected with his research work. If the relationship is pointed out to him, he may be the first to deny vehemently the connection. Yet the inference may be painfully apparent. Other psychologists are quite unafraid to make their values explicit and the degree to which these values shape their research. Skinner is one of these and we can be grateful for his honesty. Consider Skinner's *Walden Two*. Here we see the psychologist exhibiting a concern for the condition of man and constructing a possible community free from the uninformed speculations concerning the development of human behavior, which characterize what Mannheim (1936) calls the liberal-humanitarian, Utopian mentality. Applying the concept of *operant conditioning* in which an organism operates upon its environment, in contrast to Pavlovian conditioning in which the environment operates upon the organism, Skinner has tried to spell out the meaning of some of his procedures for efforts at human reconstruction. For Skinner one may move towards an ideal, intentional community by encouraging the development of what he calls *positive reinforcement*. This would be equivalent to rewarding that behavior socially, and thereby making its reappearance more probable, which we believe will promote a human condition in which, to borrow a phrase from H. G. Wells, we shall have "men like Gods." We are asked to avoid the use of *negative reinforcement* or *aversive conditioning*, involving stimuli which human subjects do not like and which traditionally they will work to avoid. Most cultures are socially cemented, largely though not wholly, through the punitive use of aversive institutional and social behavior. To some extent, of course, some social behavior is both uncomfortable and disliked, though not necessarily punitive. *Walden Two* presents a picture of a Utopian community built upon positive reinforcement, a community which promotes a sense of what the humanist calls "freedom," that is, doing what we like to do.

Underlying the Skinnerian approach is the conviction that there is no *basic, human nature*. Human nature, as we know it today, is the product of positive and negative reinforcement, of punishment and benign emotional conditioning. Skinner is convinced that the maximum use of positive reinforcement and the minimum use of negative reinforcement, will maximize freedom and minimize neurosis and anxiety. It will ensure adequate social interest and morale. With these psychological approaches an intentional, Utopian community encouraging art, science, crafts and play, rest and relaxation, and satisfying social relationships, and which discourages the growth of material and intangible deficits of every sort, can move into a future of infinite promise for human growth, potentiality, and creativity. These are, in effect, the points made by Frazier, the hero and creator of *Walden Two*. Here Skinner is taking pains to reveal the relationship between the problems of psychological interest to him and those values he holds which he seeks to project into the future. It must be admitted that most, if not all, these values would be almost universally shared in the Western world, but that is not the point. The point is that clearly there is a definite relationship between Skinner's values and his choice of research activities. There are two flies in the ointment, however. One is the fact that *not all* the values mentioned in *Walden Two* are universally well-received. The other is that even if they were, how do we get the Devil presently to release his share. This, of course, is a practical problem and its discussion is not a proper part of the present context. Theologians would probably not be too sympathetic to Skinner on the grounds that he neglects the problem of evil and Original Sin. Psychoanalysts would probably feel that he underestimates the force of the id-orientations which, of course, is merely psychological jargon for the traditionally more venerated phrase, Original Sin.

Another example of a psychologist whose choices of problems and values seem to be distinctly related, is Gardner Murphy (1958). Murphy sees the progress of science as heralding one of three possibilities:

(*a*) An international authoritarian system based upon a world hierarchical concentration of power and the channeling of human sentiment through gratification of power and prestige . . . (*b*) a world system having a degree of centralization of scientific investigation, technology and the arts, with carefully studied rules for the preservation of soft-spots—local areas of individual freedom of the scientist to conduct experiments which have no place in anyone's federally conceived plan . . . a sort of loose-jointed authoritaria . . . and (*c*) a world state, or system of states, based upon free competition of ideas in the sciences, in the arts, and elsewhere, and free competition, so to speak, between the various institutions of society.

Inasmuch as Murphy is extremely interested in what he calls our "third human nature," the creative aspects of man, and inasmuch as he chooses to emphasize scientific findings which stress the attributes of this third nature, he plumps for a society which will promote those values he holds to be necessary, namely, social planning under relatively democratic, political institutions.

Finally let us discuss to some extent the manner in which the nature-nurture controversy furnishes a good deal of evidence of the degree to which the values of psychologists line up along the lines of sentiment. I do not want to commit myself here to one or another emphasis in this controversy, nor do I wish to commit myself to the conviction that the joint play of both hereditarian and environmentalistic forces will probably in the long run yield the best account of human behavior. Some evidence can be brought forward on either side of this hoary controversy, some evidence is available to indicate the obvious interplay of both factors though with differing emphasis and some of the evidence brought forward in support of one side or the other, is ambiguous. Many experimental designs are shoddy. Often significant variables are omitted or suppressor variables neglected. For these reasons a well-crystalized position is inappropriate. However, most American psychologists, regardless of supporting evidence for the various possible positions already mentioned, are strongly inclined towards an environmentalistic approach and will prefer to account for as much behavior as possible in terms of learning theory. The degree to which some psychologists may be driven by the environmentalistic daemon is, at times, appalling, and when one of the more uncompromising partisans finds himself bottled up logically, his subsequent behavior may vary from the farcical to the religious. I knew one psychologist who, when stumped by facts or logic, or both, which were making it impossible to ascribe any but an hereditarian explanation to certain types of behavior, unlocked the door for himself by the simple expedient of calling the behavior, "biological," and asserting that he was only interested in "psychological" behavior. When pressed for a definition of terms he delivered the following syllogism. "Only biological behavior is inherited. If any kind of behavior is inheritable, it must be biological. Ergo, psychological behavior is strictly learned." He failed to see that he was employing a tautologous definition of psychological behavior, namely, one that was equivalent to stating trivially that "learned behavior is learned behavior." In addition he failed to see that he was employing an arbitrary exclusion principle of his own, namely, an implicit decision to rule out heritable behavior from the province of research for psychologists. These farcical defenses were the product of a "will to believe" which was more than a match for the corresponding bigotries of a dyed-in-the-wool hereditarian. At other times some of the psychological advocates of a true environmentalistic religion, turn red when pressed, fly into a stifled rage and refuse to discuss the matter any further. No greater betrayal of the fact that a deeply held sentiment or value has been scratched, could be produced. Lest I give aid and comfort to the enemy, however, let me say that I have heard even more obtuse and unregenerate defensive arguments from hereditarians.

What is not always well recognized is the degree to which the environmentalist sentiment is part of the Zeitgeist. Under the influence of the British empiricists and the Enlightenment thinkers, the founding fathers and some of our colonial leaders, introduced into our early national outlook the strong faith that similarities in education and environmental opportunities, could produce similarities in the talents among men. These sentiments, introduced long before the advent of a science of genetics, were reinforced by the opportunities open to all sorts of oppressed peoples who sought refuge in the New World from the tyrannies of the Old or who merely sought their fortunes here. Opportunities which arose in the conquest of a lush continent, and success in attaining religious freedom, wealth, or education, all of which would have been permanently denied by the more rigid class structures of the Old World, spread the conviction that *potentially* one man was as good as another. The enveloping quality of this outlook is driven home forcibly by any careful reader who saturates himself in De Tocqueville (1956). This conviction, aided and abetted by the faith in the possibilities of universal education in a democracy, gave to all forms of environmentalism an easy headway socially, culturally, and pedagogically. It did not take long, particularly with the rise of behavioristic influences in psychology, for the deep and abiding faith in the all-powerfulness of the environment, to take root, doubly so as theory in the behavioral sciences sought to break the shackles of a hereditarianism concerning human subjects, which was more an article of faith or an expression of individual and class snobbery, than anything else. For many decades now the environmentalist bias has been dominant in academic circles. Some behavioral scientists maintain it as a result of objective research and a dispassionate acquaintance with the relevant literature. Others have imbibed it with their academic mother's milk, so to speak, adopting the theoretical coloring and sentiments of their academic progenitors and mentors, but doing the problem little justice in intellectual depth and doing the writings of geneticists, particularly in human genetics, even less. The ranks of environmentalist partisans have been swelled the last four or five decades by those influenced by cultural residues which stress heredity and social stratification. Intelligent and curious overachieving sons and daughters of underprivileged, immigrant groups, learned to value the environmentalistic articles of faith deeply, as compensation for the social snobbery and discrimination to which they and their parents were exposed, while some found in it, at the same time, an analgesic against a half-admitted sense of shame over the illiteracy of as yet unassimilated parents. All the preceding and many other factors besides, cannot begin to exhaust the social and psychological determinants of the environmentalistic *weltanschauung* as it became more and more a value by which to guide and adjust individual effort.

It should be clear to the reader that an exhaustive analysis of the social and psychological factors which induce one to favor a strictly environmentalist bias, may be quite varied. The most respectable basis for a nurture position is, of course, clearly an objective, dispassionate acquaintance with the relevant literature and an honest conviction that the weight of the evidence and of argument is in favor of all behavior as a product of simple or complex forms of learning. In this form the position is *without bias*. In the form of a bias, the factors contributing to it are too numerous to mention. Among the most usual of these factors are probably the following: (*a*) A sense of intellectual inferiority, which can be explained away by attributing one's capacities to the accidents of chance, at the same time asserting that men are equipotential in abilities but that they develop these abilities unequally due to differences in interests. (*b*) A well-developed envy which begrudges talent or personability to others and declares that there, but for the accident of social conditioning, go I. (*c*) A vague feeling that the assertion of hereditary determinants of behavior is a cryptic form of mentalism. (*d*) The liberal bias that hereditarians are probably socially and politically reactionary, a bias explored by Pastore (1949). (*e*) An extremist, counter-swing against both the popular but uninformed tendency to explain behavior too readily in hereditary terms and the tendency of social snobs and some of the well-placed rich to do the same. The reader can undoubtedly furnish other contributing factors for himself.

It is necessary to employ the *sub rosa* thinking we have indulged in here only because we wish to indicate that, *for some psychologists*, the strong stand they take on nurture has its roots less in scientific interests with which they are burdened than in cultural determinants and bias which they have accepted uncritically. This in no way indicates that the proponents of a nurture position are in error. The history of science may eventually award them the palm. The rectitude of their position, once demonstrated, will rest, however, on scientific grounds rather than on reflected cultural values.

For our purposes, however, it is important to note that the manifestation of an environmentalistic bias may become the equivalent of a professional value which has become so deeply rooted as to constitute a sentiment in Pareto's (1935) sense of this term. It often drives certain psychologists to write textbooks which strain to find an environmentalistic explanation for almost all behavioral findings, both human and infra-human. This strain takes several forms. One of these is to note that, although an interpretation of an experiment may be made in hereditarian terms, it is also possible to furnish an environmentalistic hypothesis which will account for the same findings. This is a perfectly legitimate procedure, provided we keep the following considerations in mind. (*a*) We must recognize that *many different environmentalistic hypotheses* can be provided which would constitute *ad hoc* explanations of the findings in a great many controversial contexts, while by contrast, the hereditarian is rather limited theoretically if he seeks to provide a genetic explanation of the same results, and even more limited in terms of methodology, data and experimental design, (*b*) An environmentalistic hypothesis may be plausible but if no *experimentum crucis* has been performed to confirm it, this should be strongly pointed out to the reader on the grounds that *a plausible explanation is not necessarily an actual one*. (*c*) Hereditarians in psychology are bottled up because of the fact that, although they may be able to report statistical evidence which would be necessary if hereditary factors played a role in certain kinds of behavior, this does not mean that such evidence is sufficient, precisely for the reason mentioned already, namely, that various environmentalistic hypotheses may account for the same evidence. (*d*) Hereditarians are in an ambiguous position because even when the evidence is of the type necessary, nevertheless, even assuming a given hereditary hypothesis to be true, there are certain difficulties intrinsic to a hereditarian position. Let me mention only three of these. First, hereditarians rarely, if ever, provide a mechanism to explain the manner in which a given gene pattern determines such differences in somatic structure as may be proved relevant to the behavior in question. Second, they rarely can actually state the relevant somatic differences due to the influence of genes, which are relevant to the behavior. Third, they rarely can explain how somatic differences, presumably genetically determined, can mediate such crucial differences in behavior as are unaccountable for in terms of learning or perception. These considerations are usually stressed by environmentalists who, a fortiori, see in these very difficulties a weakness of the hereditarian position. It is true that these are difficulties for genetics, in its present state of technology and theory, but the difficulties are not to be interpreted as considerations which rule out the hereditarian hypotheses. Yet so great is the role played by sentiment among some behavioral scientists that these difficulties are treated as tantamount to ruling genetic hypotheses out of court. The result is that the more extreme partisans of the environmentalistic approach, treat themselves to a field day, and, perhaps unintentionally, take advantage of the highly unstructured atmosphere in which the nature-nurture controversy flourishes. The worst offenses of the environmentalists in this connection are first, the provision of environmentalistic explanations, while often remaining relatively indifferent to the actual performance of an experiment which will confirm the appropriateness of that explanation, and second, the willingness to let the sentiment towards nurtural explanations determine, at times, incredibly tortured explanations.

There is nothing in all the foregoing which should be construed as in any sense invalidating the strength of the environmentalist position, its good sense or its reasonableness. That position may in the end prove to be the only tenable one. All we have sought to do here is to emphasize the degree to which the behavioral scientist's values and sentiments, as a result of cultural and subcultural biases, may determine weak, difficult, or illegitimate defenses or offensives. Such defenses and offensives are often put forward even when the opposition knows better, methodologically speaking. They are frequently residues and derivations in Pareto's sense, impressively advanced under the cover of value commitments, a professional terminology, and a methodological sophistication. The worst that such a criticism implies is that if they are seen in this light, they may be considerably strengthened.

REFERENCES

Ashby, W. R. General systems theory as a new discipline. In L. Von Bertalanffy & A. Rapaport (Eds.), *General systems yearbook of the Society for General Systems Research.* Vol. III. Ann Arbor: Society for General Systems Research, 1958. Pp. 259.

Benda, J. *The betrayal of the intellectuals.* Boston: Beacon Press, 1955. Pp. 188.

De Tocqueville, A. *Democracy in America.* (Abridged ed.) New York: Mentor Books, 1956. Pp. 317.

Mannheim, R. *Ideology and utopia.* New York: Harcourt, Brace, 1936. Pp. 354.

Murphy, G. *Human potentialities.* New York: Basic Books, 1958. Pp. 340.

Pareto, V. *The mind and society.* 4 vols. (Ed., A. Livingston) New York: Harcourt, Brace, 1935.

Pastore, N. *Nature-nurture controversy.* New York: King's Crown Press, 1949. Pp. 213.

Seeman, M. The intellectual and the language of minorities. *American Journal of Sociology,* 1958, **64**, 25–35.

RESEARCH WITH HUMAN SUBJECTS

The human subject is the source of most of the data in psychology today, as he has been throughout psychology's history. The nature and responsibility of the human subject, however, has undergone drastic changes since the beginning of scientific psychology. As previously discussed,[1] subjects in the early laboratories of the introspectionists were highly trained and skilled to observe their subject matter and report on their observations. With the development of behaviorism, the highly skilled observer was replaced by the naive, untrained object of observation. Thus, today's subject does not observe but rather behaves or responds to the conditions of an experiment and his response is observed, recorded, and interpreted by the experimenter.

In recent years, as part of the growing body of psychological research into the nature of psychological research, the human subject has come under experimental scrutiny. As a point of historical interest, it is noted that many of these same problems were discussed at length as far back as 1933 in an article by Saul Rosenzweig, "The Experimental Situation as a Psychological Problem."[2] Apparently, criticism of the experimental method was not compatible with the dominant mood, the Zeitgeist, in psychology at that time as it is today.

The following articles examine various aspects of this very important element in the research process—the human subject.

[1] See D. P. Schultz, *The Nature of the Human Data Source in Psychology*, pp. 77–86.
[2] *Psychological Review*, 1933, **40**, 337–354.

14. Subject Selection Bias in Psychological Research[1]

Reginald Smart

Dr. Smart empirically inquires into the biases that may be operative in selecting human subjects for research in psychology. Are our research findings based primarily on the college student as has so often been alleged ? By examining two years of each of two major journals, Dr. Smart answers this question by presenting the percentages of subjects in various categories: college students; pre-college students; special adult groups; and samples of the general population. His results have disturbing implications for contemporary psychology. He discusses the limitations placed on psychology's research findings by the heavy reliance on college student subjects and suggests some resolutions of these problems.

On several occasions recently (Bitterman, 1960; Beach, 1960) comparative psychologists have been taken to task for their preoccupation with the rat as an experimental animal. It has rarely been considered that a similar preoccupation with selected types of subjects plagues research in human psychology. An old saw around psychology departments used to be that "social psychology is really the social psychology of the college sophomore." Evidence to support this assertion has never been gathered in any systematic way, nor has it ever been considered that perhaps most of our psychological "knowledge" (social and non-social) is derived *primarily* from studies of college sophomores. The main purpose of this note is to examine the types of bias operating in the selection of subjects for psychological research. A second purpose is to examine the effects of this bias on the generality and significance of some of the findings in areas where the bias is most striking.

Superficial reading of almost any psychological journal conveys the impression that the only people of real interest to psychologists are college students and, primarily, college students enrolled in introductory psychology courses. They seem to be far the most popular subjects for psychological research in any area. In order to clarify and expand this impression the two largest A.P.A. journals reporting

[1] Reprinted from the *Canadian Psychologist*, 1966, **7a**, 115–121, by permission of the author and the Canadian Psychological Association.

research with human non-psychiatric groups were examined. Every article in Volumes 64–67 of the Journal of Abnormal and Social Psychology (1962–4) and in Volumes 65–68 of the Journal of Experimental Psychology (1963–4) was examined for information concerning the type of subjects used. For both journals, subjects were classified into introductory psychology students, other college student groups, high school, public school, pre-school, special adult groups, and samples from the general population.

Only those articles in the J.A.S.P. concerned with non-psychiatric groups were examined. These were classified as to content area into: Social, Personality and Attitudes, Perception, Verbal Conditioning and Verbal Learning, Non-Verbal Learning, and Other (including problem solving and emotion).

The data, for J.A.S.P., on types of subjects employed in different psychological areas are shown in Table 14-1. It can be seen that almost a third (32.25%) of the studies reported used students enrolled in Introductory Psychology and that nearly three out of four (73%) used college students. Many of the latter were also enrolled in psychology courses. A few used high school and public school groups but, surprisingly, only 2 out of 342 used samples of the general population. Special adult groups not sampling the general population were more common (9.4%) but still a small minority. All of this betrays a tremendous emphasis on the college population and an almost total neglect of non-school populations. Apparently, there is little concern with the need to establish findings in widely representative adult populations and over-emphasis on specialized, intact, groups. It is worth noting, as well, that only one or two of these studies were directly concerned with the "psychology" of college students; most *sought* to establish general propositions of seemingly wide generality.

During this study it also became clear that there is a selection in terms of sex, with male students predominating. Papers employing only males ($n = 115$) greatly outnumbered ($P < .001$) those employing only females ($n = 37$).[2] It seems, then, that current social and personality research is predominately research on *male* college students enrolled in psychology. The college population, itself, is not even sampled adequately. In addition, there is a striking neglect of samples representing the general adult populations, or of samples representing particular sectors of that population.

Papers published in the J.E.P. display an even greater enslavement to the college student as the subject for human experimentation. The relevant data are shown in Table 14-2 with papers classified into the content areas: Sensation and Perception, Classical Conditioning and Discrimination Learning, Verbal Learning, Concept Formation, and "Other" (including chiefly problem solving, emotion, and perceptual–motor skills). More than 8 out of 10 papers (85.7%) in the J.E.P. employed college students. Again, non-school and adult non-college populations are ignored; no area except sensation and perception makes even token use of adult non-college populations. It is astonishing to note that 73 out of 80 studies in verbal

---

[2] Many papers in the J.A.S.P. ($n = 190$) used males and females combined but there appeared to be little difference in the proportions of males and females in studies employing both sexes.

TABLE 14-1

Frequency of Subjects Used in Papers in Various Content Areas—Journal of Abnormal and Social Psychology, Vols. 65–68, 1963–4.

TYPE OF SUBJECT

Area	Introductory Psychology	Other College Groups	High School Students	Public School Students	Pre-School Students	Sample of General Population	Special Adult Groups	Totals
Social	31	24	4	10	7	0	14	90
Personality and Attitudes	44	65	5	22	0	2	13	151
Perception	27	29	1	7	0	0	5	69
Verbal Conditioning and Verbal Learning	3	12	0	1	1	0	0	17
Non-Verbal Learning	3	5	0	0	0	0	0	8
Other	2	5	0	0	0	0	0	7
Totals	110	140	10	40	8	2	32	342
Percent	32.2	40.9	2.9	11.7	2.3	.6	9.4	100

TABLE 14-2

Frequency of Subjects Used in Papers in Various Content Areas—Journal of Experimental Psychology, Vols. 65–68, 1963–4.

TYPE OF SUBJECT

Area	Introductory Psychology	Other College Groups	High School Students	Public School Students	Pre-School Students	Sample of General Population	Special Adult Groups	Totals
Sensation and Perception	35	73	2	9	0	0	15	134
Classical Conditioning and Discrimination Learning	32	12	0	0	1	0	1	46
Verbal Learning and Verbal Conditioning	43	30	1	4	0	0	2	80
Concept Formation	7	4	0	0	0	0	0	11
Other	10	12	1	2	1	0	4	30
Totals	127	131	4	15	2	0	22	301
Percent	42.2	43.5	1.3	5.0	.7	0	7.3	100

learning used college students—a group selected for their verbal ability. Unbelievably, not a single study involved a sampling of the general population. As with the J.A.S.P., an over-representation ($P < .001$) of papers with only males ($n = 67$) compared to those with only females ($n = 18$) was found. It is clear that even the more basic and "purer" psychological research areas, as represented by the J.E.P., are suffused with research on the male college student and on few other groups. Just how "basic" and "pure" this research can be with such highly selected subjects is an important question. [3]

It might be thought that subject selection bias is peculiar only to the J.E.P. and J.A.S.P. However, less extensive examinations of other journals (e.g. Psychol. Rep.; Amer. J. Psychol.; J. Comp. Physiol. Psychol.) provide essentially the same results. College students are preferred by about 4 to 1 in every journal reporting research with adults. Research on children is covered well by several journals (e.g. Child Develop.; J. Genetic Psychol. etc.), but with the exception of geriatric studies, research on non-student adult groups is almost never reported in journals. There appears to be no journal reporting psychological research on broad samples of the adult population.

The selection of college students as the prime research subject has a number of important consequences for psychological research. For example, about 80% of this research is being performed with only that 6.3% of the adult population which gets to college. [4] This discrepancy may become less striking as the college boom increases in size. Nevertheless, it is clear that college students, however numerous, on intellectual grounds alone will never be representative of the total adult population. We know, now, that college students differ from the non-college population in a wide variety of characteristics crucially important to many aspects of psychology. The Atkinson studies of student resources (Fleming, 1958) indicated that high school students entering university were superior to those not entering university in reading ability, mathematical skills and a variety of verbal skills.

Another of these characteristics is age—most of our psychological research is being done with a very young group (age 18–24) when it is well known that such characteristics as intelligence (Wechsler, 1958; Norman and Daley, 1959), social behaviour (Gollin, 1958; Schaie, 1959; Smith, 1960), and learning ability (Broadbent and Heron, 1962; Shephard, Abbey, and Humphries, 1962; Nyssen and Crahay, 1960; Wimer, 1960), change substantially with age. Such students are probably at the peak of their learning and intellectual abilities and this could mean that many findings in learning, especially verbal learning, could be special to the college student with limited applicability to other groups. Some might argue that only the

---

[3] [Editor's footnote.] Surveys of the same journals for the period 1966–1967 reveal a frequency of subject bias highly similar to that found by Smart. His study showed that 73.1% of the studies in the J.A.S.P. (1963–1964) used college students while the later survey (using the *Journal of Personality and Social Psychology*) revealed that 70.2% of the studies used college students. Dealing with the J.E.P., Smart reported that 85.7% of the studies used college students compared with 83.7% in 1966–1967.

[4] An estimate for Canada derived from Census of Canada, 1961, Bulletin 1, 3–6, 29–10, 1963.

speed of learning would be different in the college population, and that the general principles of learning would be the same in any group. However the college student is selected for verbal learning ability and we have little evidence that this is a trivial consideration. We have little indication that the public school graduate or high school drop-out learns according to the same principles, because the question has never been investigated.

A further problem is that the college student population contains more upper class and middle class and fewer lower class persons than the general population (Fleming, 1958). This has multiple implications for social and personality research since variables such as intelligence, child rearing practices, social skills, etc., vary with social class. Numerous personality characteristics such as insecurity, feelings of rejection (Mitchell, 1957), dominance, nurturance, affiliative tendencies, and aggressiveness (Meehlman and Fleming, 1963) are also known to be related to social class in school population.

These arguments are merely intended to establish the premise that college students are an improper focus for psychological research purporting to describe human behaviour rather than to challenge the validity of the findings. Many of the research findings with college students exclusively are probably special to them and of unknown universality. How do we know that the majority of our research on social processes, attitudes, verbal learning, and personality is doing any more than exploring the vicissitudes of the present (male) college population? The answer must be that we do not know at present and that as long as we limit ourselves to college population we never will.

We also have some indications that verbal reinforcers have different reward values in various social classes. Zigler and Kanzer (1962) found that, with lower class children, praise reinforcers were more effective than those emphasizing correctness, whereas "correctness" reinforcers were more effective with middle class children. Also, Hoffman, Mitsos and Protz (1958) found that performance rose steadily with financial reward in lower class high school students, whereas many middle class students, under financial reward, experienced anxiety which interfered with performance increases. These studies tend to suggest that the basic parameters of learning in lower and middle class persons might be wholly different. Exactly what generality many of our verbal learning findings with college students have for non-college groups would be difficult to say.

No one would assert that human psychologists are interested primarily in the behaviour of the male college student any more than that the comparative psychologists are interested solely in the rat's behaviour. However, the male college student has become the white rat of human experimentation, to be studied ad nauseam and shouldering out most other types of subjects. College students are employed so extensively chiefly because of opportunistic reasons. In most university settings they are a captive group of willing subjects anxious to please instructors or to complete course requirements by participating in faculty research. Widespread exploitation of this source of subjects has important drawbacks which should lead psychologists to doubt whether they really know what is going on, psychologically, in the big world beyond the university. Many of these drawbacks could be overcome if efforts were more often made to sample from the non-college population. This could be accomplished simply by establishing large panels of volunteer subjects from the surrounding area, local industries, or large clerical concerns. If this were done human psychologists might well be surprised to find that some of the accepted principles of human psychology require extensive modification, just as the comparative psychologists have found (Bitterman, 1960) that some principles derived from rat experimentation had to be modified when other non-human species were studied.

REFERENCES

Beach, F. A. Experimental investigations of species—specific behavior. *American Psychologist*, 1960, **15**, 1–18.

Bitterman, M. E. Toward a comparative psychology of learning. *American Psychologist*, 1960, **15**, 704–712.

Broadbent, D. E., & Heron, Alistair. Effects of a subsidiary task on performance involving immediate memory by younger and older men. *Journal of Psychology*, 1962, **53**, 189–198.

Fleming, W. G. *Atkinson study of utilization of student resources*. Toronto: Ontario College of Education, 1958.

Gollin, E. S. Organizational characteristics of social judgment. A developmental investigation. *Journal of Personality*, 1958, **26**, 139–154.

Hoffman, M. L., Mitsos, S. B., & Protz, R. E. Striving, social class and test anxiety. *Journal of Abnormal and Social Psychology*, 1958, **56**, 401–403.

Meehlman, Mary R., & Fleming, J. E. Social stratification and some personality variables. *Journal of General Psychology*, 1963, **69**, 3–10.

Mitchell, J. V. The identification of items in the California Test of Personality that differentiate between high and low socioeconomic status at the fifth and seventh grade levels. *Journal of Educational Research*, 1957, **51**, 241–250.

Norman, R. D., & Daley, M. F. Senescent changes in intellectual ability among superior older women. *Journal of Gerontology*, 1959, **14**, 457–464.

Nyssen, Renie, & Crahay, S. Etude des capacités de définition et d'évocation des mots en fonction de l'age. *Acta Psychologica*, 1960, **17**, 1–22.

Schaie, K. W. The effect of age on a scale of social responsibility. *Journal of Social Psychology*, 1959, **50**, 221–224.

Shephard, A. H., Abbey, D. S., & Humphries, M. Age and sex in relation to perceptual motor performance on several control-display relations on the T.C.C. *Perceptual and Motor Skills*, 1962, **14**, 103–118.

Smith, A. J. A developmental study of group processes. *Journal of Genetic Psychology*, 1960, **97**, 29–30.

Wechsler, D. *The measurement and appraisal of adult intelligence*. Baltimore: Williams and Wilkins, 1958.

Wimer, R. E. Age differences in incidental and intentional learning. *Journal of Gerontology*, 1960, **15**, 79–82.

Zigler, E., & Kanzer, P. The effectiveness of two classes of verbal reinforcement on the performance of lower and middle class children. *Journal of Personality*, 1962, **30**, 157–163.

15. The Volunteer Subject[1]

Robert Rosenthal

Many of the subjects used in psychological research are those who have volunteered to participate. In the following thorough review of the literature, Dr. Rosenthal examines the act of volunteering and the characteristics of those who do volunteer. He feels that volunteering for an experiment is not a random event but rather a function of several factors, including the situation in which volunteers are solicited, the kinds of tasks involved, and the subjective probability of being favorably evaluated. Personal characteristics that may differentiate volunteers from non-volunteers are noted, and the implications of voluntcer-nonvolunteer differences are discussed in terms of representativeness and experimental outcomes.

INTRODUCTION

McNemar wisely said "The existing science of human behavior is largely the science of the behavior of sophomores" (1946, p. 333). Whether a useful, comprehensive science of human behavior can be based upon our knowledge of sophomores would seem to be an empirical question of great importance. Our concern in the following pages is, however, more narrow. Do we, in fact, have a science even of sophomores? To a great extent we may have a science of those sophomores who are enrolled in psychology courses and who volunteer to participate in given psychological experiments.

The widespread practice of requiring students in various psychology courses to participate in a certain number of hours' worth of experiments may in some cases permit the generalization of research findings at least to psychology students enrolled in certain courses. In many cases, however, even this generalization may be unwarranted. Frequently the psychology student, while required to serve as S in psychological research, has a choice of which experiment to participate in. Do

[1] Reprinted from *Human Relations*, 1965, **18**, 389–406, with the permission of the author and the Plenum Publishing Company, Ltd. Preparation of this paper was facilitated by research grants (G–17685, G–24826, and GS–177) from the Division of Social Sciences of the National Science Foundation. Special thanks are due to Ray C. Mulry for bibliographical assistance.

brighter (or duller) students sign up for learning experiments or at least for experiments that are labeled "learning"? Do better (or more poorly) adjusted students sign up for experiments labeled as personality experiments? Do better (or more poorly) coordinated students sign up for motor skills studies? The answers to these types of question and, more importantly, whether they make a difference, are also empirical matters.

Psychologists have concerned themselves a good deal with the problem of the volunteer *S*. Evidence for this concern will be found in the following pages, where we will find a fair number of attempts to learn something of the act of volunteering and of the differences between volunteers and non-volunteers. Further evidence for this concern can be found, too, in the frequent statements made with pride in the psychological literature of recent vintage that "the subjects employed in this experiment were non-volunteers." The discipline of mathematical statistics, that good consultant to the discipline of psychology, has concerned itself with the volunteer problem (e.g. Cochran, Mosteller & Tukey, 1953). Evidence for this concern can be found in the fact that we now know a good bit about the implications for statistical procedures and inference of having drawn a sample of volunteers (Bell, 1961). Generally, the concern over the volunteer problem has had as its goal the reduction of the non-representativeness of volunteer samples in order to increase the generality of research findings (e.g. Locke, 1954; Hyman & Sheatsley, 1954). The magnitude of the potential biasing effect of volunteer samples is clearly illustrated in a report[2] that, at a large university, rates of volunteering varied from 10 to 100 per cent. Within the same course, different recruiters going to different sections of the course obtained volunteering rates anywhere from 50 to 100 per cent.

Our special purposes here will be first to organize and conceptualize whatever may be substantively known about the act of volunteering and the more enduring personal attributes of volunteers compared with non-volunteers. Subsequently we shall examine the implications of our analysis for the representativeness of research findings and for the possible effects on experimental outcomes.

THE ACT OF VOLUNTEERING

Offering one's services as a subject in a psychological experiment is not a random event. The act of volunteering has as great a reliability as many widely used tests of personality. Martin and Marcuse (1958), employing several experimental situations, found the reliabilities of the act of volunteering for any given experiment to range from .67 to .97.

Volunteering is not, of course, independent of either the task for which volunteering is solicited or the situation in which the request is made. Understandably enough, Staples and Walters (1961) found that *S*s who had been threatened with electric shocks were less willing to volunteer for subsequent experiments involving

---

[2] John R. P. French, Jr., personal communication, 19 August 1963.

the use of shock. Nor was it too surprising to find that rates of volunteering might be increased by making the alternative to volunteering rather unattractive. Conversely, rates of volunteering could be decreased by making the alternative to volunteering more attractive (Blake, Berkowitz, Bellamy & Mouton, 1956). Rates of volunteering could also be manipulated by varying the intensity of the request to participate as well as the perception of the likelihood that others in a similar situation did or would volunteer (Rosenbaum & Blake, 1955; Rosenbaum, 1956; Schachter & Hall, 1952). It would seem likely, too, that Ss would volunteer more readily for an E they knew well than for one less well or not at all known to them. At least in the area of survey research this does seem to be the case (Norman, 1948; Wallin, 1949). Norman also concluded that there was a general trend for higher prestige survey originators to obtain better participation rates.

Responding to a mail questionnaire is undoubtedly different from volunteering for participation in a psychological experiment (Bell, 1961). Yet there are likely to be phenomenological similarities. In both cases the prospective data-provider, be he "subject" or "respondent," is asked to make a commitment of time for the serious purposes of the data-collector. In both cases, too, there may be an explicit request for candor, and almost certainly there will be an implicit request for it. Perhaps most important, in both cases, the data-provider recognizes that his participation will make the data-collector wiser about him without making him wiser about the data-collector. Within the context of the psychological experiment, Riecken (1962) has referred to this as the "one sided distribution of information." On the basis of this uneven distribution of information the S or respondent is likely to feel an uneven distribution of *legitimate negative evaluation*. On the basis of what the S or respondent does or says, the data-collector may evaluate him as maladjusted, stupid, unemployed, or lower class, any of which might be enough to prevent someone from volunteering for either surveys or experiments. The data-provider, on the other hand, can, and often does, negatively evaluate the data-collector. He can call him, his task, or his questionnaire inept, stupid, banal, and the like, but hardly with any great feeling of confidence that this evaluation is really accurate; the data-collector, after all, has a plan for the use of his data, and the subject or respondent usually does not know this plan, though he is aware that a plan exists. He is, therefore, in a poor position to evaluate the data-collector's performance, and he is likely to know it.

Riecken (1962) has postulated that one of an experimental S's major aims in the experimental interaction is to "put his best foot forward." It follows from this and from what we have said earlier that, in both surveys and experiments, prospective respondents or Ss are more likely to volunteer or respond when there is an increase in their subjective probability of being evaluated more favorably. And so it seems to be—a finding based primarily upon studies of non-responders in survey research studies. Edgerton, Britt, and Norman (1947) found that winners of contests responded most helpfully to follow-up questionnaires, whereas losers responded least. Their interpretation of greater interest in the subject on the part of the winner group does not by itself seem entirely convincing. Contest winners have the secure assurance that they did win, and they are being asked to respond, very likely, in their winner role. Contest losers, on the other hand, have the less happy assurance that they were losers and perhaps would be further evaluated as such. These same authors (1947) convincingly demonstrated the consistency of their results by summarizing work which showed, for example, that: parents of delinquent boys were more likely to answer questionnaires about them if they had nicer things to say about them; college professors holding minor and temporary appointments were less likely to reply usefully to questionnaires; teachers who had no radios replied less promptly to questionnaires about the use of radios in the classroom than did teachers who had radios; patrons of commercial airlines more promptly returned questionnaires about airline usage than did non-patrons; college graduates replied more often and more promptly to college follow-up questionnaires than did drop-outs. Norman (1948) cited evidence that technical and science graduates replied less promptly to questionnaires if they were unemployed, or employed outside the field in which they had been trained. Locke (1954) found married respondents more willing to be interviewed about marital adjustment than divorced respondents. None of these findings argues against the interest hypothesis advanced by Edgerton, Britt, and Norman (1947), and, indeed, they cite additional evidence, not reported here, which seems to be most simply interpreted as showing that greater interest in a topic leads to higher response rates. Nevertheless, on the basis of the empirical findings presented and on the basis of Riecken's (1962) and our own analysis, we postulate that: One major variable contributing to the decision to volunteer to participate in either an experiment or a survey is the subjective probability of subsequently being favorably evaluated by the investigator. It would seem trite but necessary to add that this formulation requires more direct empirical test.

CHARACTERISTICS OF VOLUNTEERS

We have already considered some characteristics of those who respond more readily to a request to participate in behavioral research. These characteristics have, by and large, been specifically related to the source and nature of the request for participation and do not seem to be stable and enduring characteristics serving to differentiate volunteers from non-volunteers. We shall now consider fairly exhaustively these potentially more stable attributes of volunteers.

Sex

In two survey research projects and in a social psychological experiment, Belson (1960), Wallin (1949), and Schachter and Hall (1952) all found no difference between men and women in their willingness to participate as *S*s. Two studies have dealt with characteristics of experimental *S*s who fail to keep their experimental appointments. Frey and Becker (1958) found no sex differences between *S*s who notify their *E* that they will be unable to keep an experimental appointment and those who do not notify their *E* of their impending absence. Since these workers claim that those *S*s who simply fail to appear can very rarely be rescheduled, their characteristics are likely to be the characteristics of non-volunteers, and determined ones at that. Though this study argues against a sex difference in volunteering, at least indirectly, the entire experimental sample was composed of extreme scorers on a test of introversion-extraversion. Furthermore, no comparison was given of either group of no-shows with the parent population from which the experimental samples were drawn. Leipold and James (1962) compared characteristics of those *S*s who failed to appear for a psychological experiment with characteristics of those who did appear. Their total group of shows and no-shows was a random sample of introductory psychology students who had simply been requested to appear in order to satisfy a course requirement. Considering the no-show student again as a determined non-volunteer, and the appearing student as volunteerlike in finding his way into an experiment, these workers confirmed Frey and Becker's finding of no sex difference associated with volunteering or nonvolunteering. A sad footnote to these results is provided by the fact that about half of Frey and Becker's no-shows notified their *E*s of their forthcoming absence whereas only one of Leipold and James's 39 no-shows so demeaned himself.

London (1961), too, found almost identical rates of simple willingness to participate in a psychological experiment among men and women, this time in an experiment involving hypnosis. He did find, however, that among those who said they were "very eager" to participate there were many more men than women. More men than women, too, are willing to volunteer for electric shocks (Howe, 1960), and for Kinsey-type interviews dealing with sex attitudes or behavior (Siegman, 1956; Martin & Marcuse, 1958). London interpreted his finding for the hypnosis research situation as a reflection of the girls' greater fear of loss of control. A more parsimonious interpretation, which takes London's finding into account as well as the findings of Howe, Siegman, and Martin and Marcuse, may be that being "very eager" to be hypnotized and being willing to be Kinsey-interviewed or electrically shocked are indications of a somewhat generalized unconventionality associated culturally with males for certain types of situation. It has been shown, and will be discussed in detail later, that more unconventional students do, in fact, volunteer more for psychological research, defining unconventionality in a variety of ways. For more run-of-the-mine type experiments, this sex-linked unconventionality would not be so relevant to volunteering, an interpretation which is not too inconsistent with findings by Himelstein (1956) and Schubert (1960). Both these workers found that, for experiments unspecified for their *S*s, females volunteered significantly more than males.

The likelihood of sex by experimental-situation interaction effects is maintained by a further finding of Martin and Marcuse (1958). To requests for volunteers for experiments in learning, personality, and hypnosis, girls tend to respond more in each case, although none of the differences could be judged statistically significant. It should be added that these authors did not ask their potential hypnosis *S*s whether they were "very eager."

Finally, we need to remind ourselves of Coffin's (1941) caution that any obtained sex differences in behavioral research may be a function of the sex of *E*. Thus we may wonder, along with Coffin and Martin and Marcuse, about (i) the differential effects on volunteer rates among male and female *S*s of being confronted with a male vs. a female Kinsey interviewer; and (ii) the differential effects on eagerness to be hypnotized of being confronted with a male vs. a female hypnotist.

Related to the sex effect on differential volunteering rates are the findings of Rosen (1951) and Schubert (1960). Both workers found males who showed greater femininity of interests to be more likely to volunteer for psychological experiments.

Birth Order

Stemming from the work of Schachter (1959) there has been increasing interest in birth order as a useful independent variable in social psychological research. Only two studies were found relating birth order to volunteering for psychological research participation, though we may predict that others will follow. Capra and Dittes (1962), working with a student sample in which first-borns were significantly over-represented, found 36 per cent of first-borns volunteering for a small group experiment. Among later-borns, only 18 per cent volunteered, a difference significant at the .05 level. A subsequent study by Weiss, Wolf, and Wiltsey (1963) served to restrict the generality of any association between birth order and volunteering. They found this relationship to depend upon the recruitment technique. When a ranking of preferences was employed, first-borns more often volunteered for a group experiment. However, when a simple yes-no technique was employed, first-borns volunteered relatively *less* for group than for individual or isolation experiments. Should subsequent work clarify the nature of the relationship between birth order and volunteering, Schachter's work would suggest that such a relationship might be mediated by the greater sociability of first-borns. It is this variable to which we now turn.

Sociability

London, Cooper, and Johnson (1961) found a slight tendency for more serious volunteers to be more sociable as defined by the California Psychological Inventory. Schubert (1960) also found volunteers to score as somewhat more sociable, using a different paper-and-pencil test definition of sociability (MMPI). Martin and Marcuse (1957), employing the Bernreuter, found for their female volunteers for a hypnosis experiment significantly higher sociability scores than for their non-volunteers, but no difference on the related variable of extraversion. In general, it seems that volunteers may be a more sociable group than non-volunteers. A possible exception to these generally consistent findings, however, is suggested by the work of Frey and Becker (1958). Among those no-show *S*s who more closely resembled volunteers, these workers found less sociability (Guilford scale) than among those no-show subjects who seemed rather to be determined non-volunteers. Interpretation of these findings is rendered difficult, however, by (i) the fact that theirs was not meant to be a direct study of volunteer characteristics, and (ii) the extremeness of all their subjects' scores on a sociability-relevant variable: introversion-extraversion.

Anxiety

Our understanding of the relationship between Ss' anxiety and the volunteering response suffers not so much from lack of data as from lack of consistency. Some studies reveal volunteers to be more anxious than non-volunteers, some suggest that they are less anxious, and still others find no differences in this respect.

There were no apparent systematic differences in the types of experiment for which participation was requested between those workers who found volunteers more anxious and those who found them less anxious.

Scheier (1959), utilizing the IPAT questionnaires, found volunteers to be less anxious than non-volunteers; and Himelstein (1956), employing the TMAS, found a trend in the same direction, though his differences were not judged statistically significant. Heilizer (1960), Howe (1960), and Siegman (1956) found no statistically significant differences in the levels of TMAS anxiety of volunteer and non-volunteer Ss. Both Rosen (1951) and Schubert (1960), however, found volunteers scoring higher on anxiety as defined by the MMPI-Pt scale. It might be tempting to summarize these findings by saying that differences in anxiety level between volunteers and non-volunteers cancel out to no difference at all. Though this might simplify our interpretation, it would be a little like taking two relatively unlikely events on opposite ends of a continuum (say feast and famine or drought and flood) and concluding that two usual events had occurred. Two other studies are relevant here and may provide a clue to the interpretation of the inconsistent findings reported.

Leipold and James (1962) compared those Ss who failed to appear for an experiment with those who did appear on level of anxiety (TMAS) separately for each sex, after finding a significant interaction effect of sex and showing up for the experiment. They found no difference in anxiety level among female Ss, but the male Ss who failed to appear (the determined non-volunteers) were significantly more anxious people than those who appeared and therefore were more representative of those males who find their way into the role of subject of a psychological experiment. Martin and Marcuse (1958) also found volunteering Ss to differ in anxiety level (TMAS) from non-volunteers, this time as a function of the type of experiment for which volunteering had been requested. Their volunteers were higher in anxiety than their non-volunteers for an experiment in personality. No differences (that held for both male and female subjects) were found between volunteers and non-volunteers for experiments in hypnosis, learning, or attitudes about sex. However, males volunteering for a hypnosis experiment were less anxious than male non-volunteers. This difference was not found for female Ss. The Martin and Marcuse data, while providing further contradictory evidence, suggest that future studies of anxiety may resolve these contradictory findings by considering the likelihood of significant interaction effects of sex of S and type of experiment for which volunteers are solicited upon the differences in anxiety level obtained between volunteers and non-volunteers.

Need for Social Approval

Marlowe and Crowne (1961) found Ss with greater needs for social approval as measured by their social desirability scale (M-C SD) reporting greater willingness to serve again as volunteers in an excruciatingly dull task. Consistent with this finding was that of Leipold and James (1962) that males who failed to appear for their experimental appointments tended to score lower on the same social desirability scale. Crowne (1961) has described high scorers on the M-C SD scale as more intropunitive than extrapunitive, making relevant to our present discussion a finding by Riggs and Kaess (1955). These workers, using Kaess's College Situation Test, found volunteers to be more intropunitive than extrapunitive, a finding which seems to fit into our sparsely stranded nomological net relating need for social approval to the act of volunteering for a psychological experiment.

Conformity

Strickland and Crowne (1962) have shown that high scorers on M-C SD conform more in an Asch-type situation. Since scores on M-C SD correlate positively with both volunteering and conformity, we might reasonably predict a positive correlation between volunteering and Asch-type conformity. Foster (1961) found such a relationship among his male Ss but not among his female Ss, for whom this relationship was in fact reversed. In any case, neither of these correlations was judged statistically significant. Inconsistent, if only indirectly, with the trend found by Foster was Newman's (1957) finding that male volunteers strongly tended to be more autonomous than male non-volunteers, and Martin and Marcuse's (1957) finding that male volunteers were more dominant as defined by the Bernreuter. Lubin, Levitt, and Zuckerman (1962) found their female respondents to differ from non-respondents to a questionnaire. Respondents were lower in dominance and autonomy relative to their scores on deference, succorance, and abasement. The test employed here was the Edwards Personal Preference Schedule. However, Frye and Adams (1959), employing the same instrument, found no personality difference between (male and female) volunteers and non-volunteers for an experiment in social psychology. At least for the variety of measures of "conformity" employed, no general conclusions about their relationship to the volunteering response seem warranted.

Age

Participants in survey research studies tend to be younger than non-participants, as shown by Wallin (1949). In addition, earlier compliers with a request to complete a questionnaire tend to be younger than later compliers (Abeles, Iscoe & Brown, 1954–55). Volunteers for personality research were found to be younger than non-volunteers by Newman (1957), who also demonstrated that, at least among females, variability of age of volunteers is a function of the type of experiment for which participation is solicited. Rosen (1951) found younger females to volunteer more than older females, but no such relationship held for male *S*s. We may have somewhat greater confidence in summarizing the relationship of age to volunteering than is warranted for some of the other variables discussed in this section. Volunteers tend to be younger than non-volunteers, especially among female *S*s.

Intelligence

Here we shall include not only intelligence-test differences between volunteers and non-volunteers, but comparisons on the related variables of motor skill, grades, education, and serious-mindedness as well. Martin and Marcuse (1957, 1958) reported that their volunteers earned higher scores on a standard test of intelligence (ACE), a finding supported by Edgerton, Britt, and Norman (1947) in their review of several survey research studies. Brower's (1948) data showed volunteers to perform a difficult motor task with greater speed and fewer errors than a group of *S*s who were forced to participate. For simpler motor tasks, performance differences were less clear cut. Leipold and James (1962) found that those *S*s who showed up for an experiment to which they had been assigned were earning somewhat higher grades in introductory psychology than those who did not show up. The trend they found was greater for female than for male *S*s. Similarly, Abeles, Iscoe, and Brown (1954–55) reported higher grades earned by those who complied more promptly with a request to participate in a questionnaire study. Rosen (1951), on the other hand, did not find a difference in respect of grades earned between volunteers and non-volunteers for psychological experiments. He did find, however, that female volunteers were more serious-minded than female non-volunteers. If we may consider not belonging to a fraternity as a mark of serious-mindedness among college students, data obtained by Abeles *et al.* support Rosen's finding of greater serious-mindedness among volunteers. Riggs and Kaess (1955) found volunteers to show more introversive thinking (Guilford scale) than non-volunteers. These last three findings we may interpret as differences in intellectuality of interest if not in ability. Finally, Wallin (1949) reported that participants in his survey research study were better educated than those who chose not to participate.

Overall, the evidence suggests that, in comparison with non-volunteers, volunteers are likely to be brighter, as defined by standard tests of intelligence; to perform better in a difficult motor task; to be earning higher grades if college students; and to be somewhat better educated.

Authoritarianism

Rosen (1951) found volunteers for psychological studies to be less fascist-minded (F) than non-volunteers; and Martin and Marcuse (1957) found volunteers for an experiment in hypnosis to score as less ethnocentric (E) than non-volunteers. This finding was particularly true for their male subjects. Consistent with these findings was that of Wallin (1949), whose survey participants were more politically and socially liberal than the non-participants.

Conventionality

A number of studies have found that volunteers for a Kinsey type of personal interview tend to be more unconventional than non-volunteers in either their sexual behavior or their attitudes (Maslow, 1942; Maslow and Sakoda, 1952; Siegman, 1956). In order to determine whether this relative unconventionality of volunteers is specific to the Kinsey-type situation, we should need to know whether these same volunteers would be more likely than non-volunteers to participate in other types of psychological studies. Further, it would be helpful if we knew whether groups matched on sexual conventionality, but differing in other types of conventionality, showed different rates of volunteering for a Kinsey-type interview.

More general evidence for the role of conventionality in predicting volunteering comes from Rosen (1951), who found volunteers to be less conventional than non-volunteers. Wallin (1949), however, did not find a difference in conventionality between his survey respondents and the non-respondents. Some indirect evidence is available bearing on the question of volunteering as a function of general unconventionality. The Pd scale of the MMPI is often clinically regarded as reflecting dissatisfaction with societal conventions, and higher scorers may be regarded as less conventional than lower scorers. Both London et al. (1961) and Schubert (1960) found volunteers for different types of experiments to be more unconventional by this definition. These same workers further found volunteers to score higher on the F scale of the MMPI, which reflects a willingness to admit to unconventional experiences. The Lie scale of the MMPI taps primness and propriety, and high scorers may be regarded as more conventional than low scorers. Although Heilizer (1960) found no Lie-scale differences between volunteers and non-volunteers, Schubert (1960) found volunteers to score lower.

It seems to be generally true that volunteers for a variety of psychological studies tend to be more unconventional than their non-volunteering counterparts. Of a dozen relevant bits of evidence, ten are consistent with this formulation and only two are not. These two inconsistent bits of evidence seem less weakening of our conclusion by virtue of the fact that they find no differences between volunteers and non-volunteers in this respect, rather than differences in the opposite direction. In general, these findings have been found to occur with both male and female Ss. There is, however, some evidence which should caution us to look for possible interaction effects of sex of S with the relationship of conventionality to volunteering. London et al. (1961) concluded that, at least for hypnosis experiments, girls who volunteer may be significantly more interested in the novel and the unusual, whereas for boys this relationship seems less likely. Under the heading of conformity we have already mentioned a finding that may bear out London et al. This was Foster's (1961) finding that the relationship between conformity and volunteering was in the opposite direction for boys as compared with girls. Although his finding did not reach statistical significance, it has theoretical significance for us here when viewed in the light of the results of London *et al.*

Arousal-seeking

Schubert (1960) postulated that volunteering is a function of a trait he called arousal-seeking. Evidence for this relationship came from the fact that his volunteers for a "psychological experiment" reported greater coffee-drinking and caffeine pill-taking in comparison with non-volunteers, as well as from differences in scores between volunteers and non-volunteers on various scales of the MMPI which might be considered consistent with his hypothesis. Those MMPI characteristics he found associated with greater volunteering were generally also found by London *et al.* (1961), with one important exception. The Hypomanic (Ma) scale of the MMPI was found by Schubert to correlate positively with volunteering. Since the implied hyperactivity of high Ma scorers is consistent with the trait of arousal-seeking, this finding strengthened Schubert's hypothesis. London *et al.*, however, found a negative relationship between the Ma-scale scores and volunteering for a hypnosis experiment, a result that appears damaging to the generality of the arousal-seeking hypothesis. Riggs and Kaess (1955) found that volunteers were more characterized by cycloid emotionality, consistent perhaps with the MMPI Ma scale. As mentioned earlier in our discussion of conventionality, London *et al.* did find a tendency that seems to be related to arousal-seeking among their female volunteers. Since scores on the Ma scale do not appear to be consistently predictive of volunteering, and since caffeine pill-taking may as easily be interpreted as an attribute of "unconventionality" as of arousal-seeking, it would seem that it might be possible to subsume Schubert's findings under the variable of conventionality. Schubert's contribution to this area of inquiry is noteworthy for its empirically-oriented attempt to establish a specific microtheory of volunteering for psychological experiments in general.

Psychopathology and Adjustment

We shall consider here some variables that have been related to global definitions of psychological adjustment or pathology. While some of the variables with which we dealt earlier have been related to such global views of adjustment, our discussion of them was intended to carry no special implications bearing on *S*s' "adjustment." Thus in discussing anxiety as a variable we have not meant to imply that higher anxiety was related to maladjustment; indeed, within the range of scores considered, the converse might be equally true.

Self-esteem is usually regarded as a correlate if not a definition of good adjustment. Maslow (1942) and Maslow and Sakoda (1952) reported that volunteers for interviews concerning the respondents' sex behavior showed greater self-esteem (but not greater security) as measured by Maslow's tests than did non-volunteers. This trend tended to be reversed when students from a more advanced psychology class served as *S*s. Siegman (1956), employing his own test, found no such differences at all. Newman (1957) found male volunteers to be less variable in degree of self-actualization than male non-volunteers, whereas his female volunteers showed greater variability than his female non-volunteers. If we can accept his self-actualization variable as a measure of adjustment, it would suggest that curvilinear and opposite relationships might exist between adjustment and volunteering for a psychological experiment as a function of sex of volunteer. Thus whereas the best and the least well adjusted males may be less likely to volunteer than moderately well adjusted males, the best and the least well adjusted females may be more likely to volunteer than the moderately well adjusted females.

London *et al.* (1961) concluded that those *S*s who volunteered for hypnosis experiments in order to serve science (rather than for novelty) were a psychologically more stable or "upright" group as defined by 16 Pf. Rosen (1951) found his volunteers to be more psychologically-minded (e.g. F-scale scores) and to admit more readily to feelings of anxiety and inadequacy (MMPI). It is difficult to decide whether we should therefore consider volunteers better or worse adjusted than non-volunteers. In clinical lore these feelings are ostensibly "bad" to have, but, on the other hand, knowing you have them gives you an adjustive edge.

In the area of medical research, Richards (1960) found projective test differences between those who volunteered to take Mescaline and those who did not. The investigator could not determine, however, which group was the better adjusted. In a sample drawn by Lasagna and von Felsinger (1954), volunteers for medical research seemed to be relatively poorly adjusted. For the area of medical research, finally, Pollin and Perlin (1958) and Perlin, Pollin, and Butler (1958) concluded that the greater the intrinsic motivation of a subject to volunteer for the role of normal control, the greater the likelihood of psychopathology. This does seem to be the clearest evidence of a relationship between volunteering and psychopathology we have yet encountered. Two circumstances should be taken into account, however, in evaluating this finding. First is the notorious unreliability of psychiatric diagnosis, and second is the fact that the medical research studies included in our discussion may differ qualitatively from the more usual psychological studies we have been considering.

On the basis of the evidence presented we may propose that the nature of the relationship between volunteering and adjustment, while essentially unknown, may be a function of the task for which volunteers are solicited, and may be differentially curvilinear as a function of sex of *S*.

Sociological Variables

Insufficient data are available to warrant much discussion of such variables as social and economic status, religious affiliation, marital status, and regional factors in the determination of volunteering behavior. Although Belson (1960) reported

higher social class *S*s to volunteer more, Rosen (1951) found the opposite relationship among his female college *S*s. Rosen found few other sociological variables
to make much difference. Wallin's (1949) data are in partial agreement except
that for his survey situation he did find religious affiliation a relevant predictor
variable. For a Kinsey-type interview, Siegman (1956) reported higher volunteering
rates in an eastern compared with a western university, whereas Edgerton, Britt,
and Norman (1947) cite a possibly contradictory finding of rural background being
associated with greater volunteering. It seems wisest to forgo discussion of these
findings at this stage of our knowledge except perhaps to raise again the issue that
the nature of the relationship between sociological variables and volunteering may
be a function of both subject and task variables.

OVERVIEW OF POPULATIONS INVESTIGATED

Before summarizing what it is we may know and what it is we surely do not
know about differentiating characteristics of volunteers for psychological studies, we
must examine the populations that we have been discussing. All the studies referred
to have sampled from populations of subjects, from populations of situations,
tasks, and contexts, and from populations of personal characteristics and various
measures of these characteristics (Brunswik, 1956).

Subject Samples

All of the requests to participate in a psychological experiment have been made
of college students. Even many of the requests to participate in a survey by answering
questionnaire items have employed samples of this population. As far as the study
of volunteer characteristics is concerned, McNemar's criticism that the science of
human behavior is largely the science of the behavior of sophomores has excellent
grounds. Those studies which sampled from other populations, such as teachers,
parents, householders, and magazine subscribers, were invariably survey research
studies. From the standpoint of representativeness in the design of experiments this
may be undesirable, but it does no damage to our purpose here since our interest
is in the college student as the human guinea pig most frequently used by psychological researchers.

Task Samples

More serious is the nonuniformity of situations, tasks, and contexts sampled by
the various studies we have discussed. The tasks for which volunteering has been
requested have included survey questionnaires, Kinsey-type interviews, medical
control studies, and, more specifically, psychological experiments focused on group
interaction, hypnosis, learning, personality, perception, and pain. Unfortunately,
very few studies have employed more than one task for which to solicit volunteers,

so that little is known about the effects of the specific task either on the rate of volunteering to undertake it or on the nature of the relationship between volunteering and the personal characteristics of volunteers. Newman (1957) did employ more than one task in his study. His Ss were asked to volunteer for both a personality and a perception experiment, but he found no systematic effect of these two tasks on the relationships between the variables he investigated and the act of volunteering. Martin and Marcuse (1958) employed four tasks for which volunteering was requested. They found greater differences between volunteers and non-volunteers for their hypnosis experiment than were found between the two groups for experiments in learning, attitudes to sex, and personality. Of these last three experimental situations, the personality study situation tended to reveal somewhat more personality differences between volunteers and non-volunteers than were found in the other two situations. Those differences that did emerge from the more differentiating tasks did not seem to be particularly related conceptually to the differential nature of the tasks for which volunteering had been requested. These findings should warn us, however, that any of the characteristics of volunteers we have discussed may be a function of the particular situation for which volunteering had been requested.

Since it would be desirable to be able to speak about characteristics of volunteers for a "generalized" psychological experiment, a special effort was made to find studies wherein the request for volunteers was quite non-specific. Several of the studies discussed met this specification (e.g. Himelstein, 1956; Leipold and James, 1962; Schubert, 1960). In these studies, requests were simply for participation in an unspecified psychological experiment. Comparison of the characteristics of volunteers for this more general situation with differentiating characteristics obtained for other task requests again revealed no systematic differences.

Attribute Samples

We have discussed virtually all the attributes of volunteers for psychological experiments which differentiate them from non-volunteers of which we are aware. For organizational and heuristic purposes, however, we have grouped these together under a smaller number of headings. Decisions to group any variables under a given heading were made on the basis of empirically established and/or conceptually meaningful relationships.

It should be further noted that, within any heading, such as *anxiety*, several different operational definitions may have been employed. Thus we have discussed anxiety as defined by the Taylor Manifest Anxiety Scale as well as by the Pt scale of the MMPI. Intelligence has been defined by several tests of intellectual ability. This practice has been necessary to our discussion in view of the limited number of studies employing identical operational definitions of any variables excepting age, birth order, and sex. This necessity, however, is not unmixed with virtue. If, in spite of differences of operational definition, the variables serve to predict the act of volunteering, we can feel greater confidence in the construct underlying the varying definitions and in its relevance to the predictive and conceptual task at hand.

SUMMARY OF VOLUNTEER CHARACTERISTICS

For the purpose of summarizing our analysis of the data bearing on characteristics that differentiate volunteers from non-volunteers for psychological studies, we have placed each characteristic or attribute into one of two groups. One of these groups contains those variables in respect of which we have some confidence that they are indeed relevant to the act of volunteering. To the second group we have allocated the variables in respect of which such confidence is lacking. Our confidence is operationally inspired by three or more supporting findings and the absence of any completely contradictory findings. Our summary is in the form of statements of relationships, comparing volunteers with non-volunteers, in roughly descending order of confidence within each group.

I. *Statements Warranting Some Confidence*

1. Volunteers tend to manifest greater intellectual ability, intellectual interest, and intellectual motivation.
2. Volunteers tend to be more unconventional.
3. Volunteers, particularly females, tend to be younger.
4. Volunteers tend to be less authoritarian.
5. Volunteers tend to manifest greater need for social approval.
6. Volunteers tend to be more sociable.

II. *Statements Warranting Little Confidence*

7. Volunteers tend to be more feminine in interests when the experiment is routine, but more masculine when the experiment is unusual.
8. Volunteers tend to have a greater need for arousal.
9. Volunteers tend more often to be first-born children.
10. Volunteers tend to be less anxious when male but more anxious when female.
11. Volunteers tend more often to be moderately well or poorly adjusted when male, and better or worse than moderately well adjusted when female.
12. Volunteers tend to be less conforming when male but more conforming when female.

Obviously the variables listed need further investigation, particularly those in our second group. The situation would seem especially to call for the use of factor-analytic and multiple-regression techniques. One particularly troublesome question arises from examination of the internal consistency of the variables listed in Group I. There we see that volunteers tend to be more unconventional than non-volunteers, yet to manifest a greater need for approval. On the basis of Crowne's (1961) discussion of the need for approval variable, this is quite unexpected and nomologically nettling.

IMPLICATIONS OF VOLUNTEER CHARACTERISTICS

For Representativeness

One conclusion seems eminently tenable from our analysis. In any given psychological experiment the chances are very good indeed that a sample of volunteer Ss will differ appreciably from the unsampled non-volunteers. Let us examine some of the implications of this conclusion. One that is rather well known is the limitation placed on subsequent statistical procedures and inference by the violation of the requirement of random sampling. This problem is discussed in basic texts in sampling theory and is mentioned by some of the workers we have had occasion to cite earlier (Cochran, Mosteller & Tukey, 1953).

Granted that volunteers are never a random sample of the population from which they were recruited, and further granting that a given sample of volunteers differs on a number of important dimensions from a sample of non-volunteers, we still do not know whether volunteer status actually makes a difference or not. It is entirely possible that in a given experiment the performance of the volunteer Ss would not differ at all from the performance of the unsampled non-volunteers if these had actually been recruited for the experiment (Lasagna and von Felsinger, 1954). The point is that substantively we have little idea of the effect of using volunteer Ss. Needed are series of investigations, covering a variety of tasks and situations, for which volunteers are solicited but both volunteers and non-volunteers are actually used, in order to determine in what type of study the use of volunteers actually makes a difference, what kind of difference, and how much of a difference. Once we know something about these questions, we can enjoy the convenience of volunteer Ss with better scientific conscience. In the meantime the best we can do is to hypothesize what the effects of volunteer characteristics might be on any given line of inquiry.

As an example of this kind of hypothesizing we can take the much analyzed Kinsey-type study of sexual behavior. We have already seen how volunteers for this type of study tend to have unconventional attitudes about sexuality and may in addition behave in sexually unconventional ways. This tendency, as has been frequently pointed out, may have had grave effects on the outcome of Kinsey-type studies, leading to population estimates of sexual behavior seriously biased in the unconventional direction. The extent of this type of bias could probably be partially assessed over a population of college students among whom the non-volunteers could be turned into "volunteers" in order to estimate the effect on data outcome of initial volunteering vs. non-volunteering. Clearly, such a study would be less feasible among a population of householders who stood to gain no course credit or instructor's approval from changing their status of non-volunteer to volunteer.

Far fewer data are available for most other areas of psychological inquiry. Greene (1937) showed that precision in discrimination tasks was related to the nature of S's type of personal adjustment and to his intelligence. Since volunteers may differ from non-volunteers in adjustment and, even more likely, in intelligence, experiments utilizing discrimination tasks might well be affected by volunteer characteristics. One might speculate, too, about the effect on the standardization of a new intelligence test where the normative sample volunteered for the task, in view of our rather consistent finding that volunteers are brighter than non-volunteers.

For Experimental Outcomes

For the situations described, the effect of using volunteer samples would be to change the average performance obtained from a sample of Ss. In most psychological studies that manipulate an independent variable, interest is not centered on such statistics as the mean but rather on the significance of a difference between means which can be attributed to the operation of the independent variable. If a sample of volunteers is drawn and divided into an experimental and a control group for differential treatment, can the fact of their volunteer status serve to alter the significance of any obtained difference between the means of the two groups? Unfortunately we have no definitive empirical answer to this question but we can readily envision an affirmative response.[3] Consider an experiment to test the effects of an independent variable on gregariousness. If volunteers are indeed more sociable than non-volunteers, the untreated control Ss may show a high enough level of gregariousness to result in the treatment's being adjudged ineffective when, with a less restricted range of sociability of Ss, the treatment might well have been judged as leading to a statistically significant difference between the means. To cite an example leading to the opposite type of error, let us consider an experiment using female Ss in which some dependent variable is observed as a function of good and poor psychological adjustment. If female volunteers are more variable than non-volunteers on the dimension of adjustment, comparing Ss in the top and bottom 27 per cent for adjustment level on the dependent variable might lead to a greater "treatment" effect than would have been obtained with a sample of non-volunteers.

GENERAL SUMMARY AND CONCLUSIONS

To McNemar's statement that ours is a science of sophomores, we have added the question of whether we might not lack even this degree of generality in our science. The volunteer status of many who serve as Ss in psychological research is a fact of life to be reckoned with. Our purpose here has been to organize and conceptualize our substantive knowledge about the act of volunteering and the more

[3] Dittes's (1961) finding that lessened acceptance by peers affected first-borns' but not later-borns' behavior is a most relevant example to the extent that we can be sure that first-borns find their way into group experiments reliably more often than later-borns.

stable characteristics of those more likely to find their way into the role of *S* in psychological research.

The act of volunteering was viewed as a non-random event, determined in part by more general situational variables and in part by more specific personal attributes of the person asked to participate in psychological research as *S*. More general situational variables postulated as increasing the likelihood of volunteering responses included the following:

1. Having only a relatively less attractive alternative to volunteering.
2. Increasing the intensity of the request to volunteer.
3. Increasing the perception that others in a similar situation would volunteer.
4. Increasing acquaintanceship with, the perceived prestige of, and liking for, the experimenter.
5. Having greater intrinsic interest in the subject-matter being investigated.
6. Increasing the subjective probability of subsequently being favorably evaluated or not unfavorably evaluated by the experimenter.

Primarily on the basis of studies conducted with college student populations in a variety of experimental situations, it was postulated that those personal attributes likely to be associated with a greater degree of volunteering included the following:

1. Greater intellectual ability, interest, and motivation.
2. Greater unconventionality.
3. Lower age.
4. Less authoritarianism.
5. Greater need for social approval.
6. Greater sociability.

Personal attributes investigated but resulting in only equivocal relationships to the likelihood of volunteering included the variables of sex, birth order, need for arousal, anxiety, adjustment, conformity, and various sociological variables. For all the personal attributes investigated, but particularly for those related more equivocally to the likelihood of volunteering, the direction of the relationship may often be a function of recruitment-situational variables.

The implications of characteristics differentially associated with volunteering and non-volunteering were considered from the frequently discussed standpoint of non-representativeness and from the less frequently discussed standpoint of implications for experimental outcomes in terms of inferential errors of the first and of the second kind.

REFERENCES

Abeles, N., Iscoe, I., & Brown, W. F. Some factors influencing the random sampling of college students. *Public Opinion Quarterly*, 1954–1955, **18**, 419–423.
Bell, C. R. Psychological versus sociological variables in studies of volunteer bias in surveys. *Journal of Applied Psychology*, 1961, **45**, 80–85.

Belson, W. A. Volunteer bias in test room groups. *Public Opinion Quarterly*, 1960, **24**, 115–126.

Blake, R. R., Berkowitz, H., Bellamy, R. Q., & Mouton, Jane S. Volunteering as an avoidance act. *Journal of Abnormal and Social Psychology*, 1956, **53**, 154–156.

Brower, D. The role of incentive in psychological research. *Journal of General Psychology*, 1948, **39**, 145–147.

Brunswik, E. *Perception and the representative design of psychological experiments.* Berkeley, Calif.: University of California Press, 1956.

Capra, P. C., & Dittes, J. E. Birth order as a selective factor among volunteer subjects. *Journal of Abnormal and Social Psychology*, 1962, **64**, 302.

Cochran, W. G., Mosteller, F., & Tukey, J. W. Statistical problems of the Kinsey report. *Journal of the American Statistical Association*, 1953, **48**, 673–716.

Coffin, T. E. Some conditions of suggestion and suggestibility. *Psychological Monographs*, 1941, **53** (4, Whole No. 241).

Crowne, D. P. The motive for approval: studies in the dynamics of influencibility and stereotypical self-acceptability. Unpublished manuscript, Ohio State University, 1961.

Dittes, J. E. Birth order and vulnerability to differences in acceptance. *American Psychologist*, 1961, **16**, 358. (Abstract.)

Edgerton, H. A., Britt, S. H., & Norman, R. D. Objective differences among various types of respondents to a mailed questionnaire. *American Sociological Review*, 1947, **4**, 435–444.

Foster, R. J. Acquiescent response set as a measure of acquiescence. *Journal of Abnormal and Social Psychology*, 1961, **63**, 155–160.

Frey, A. H., & Becker, W. C. Some personality correlates of subjects who fail to appear for experimental appointments. *Journal of Consulting Psychology*, 1958, **22**, 164.

Frye, R. L., & Adams, H. E. Effect of the volunteer variable on leaderless group discussion experiments. *Psychological Reports*, 1959, **5**, 184.

Greene, E. B. Abnormal adjustments to experimental situations. *Psychological Bulletin*, 1937, **34**, 747–748. (Abstract.)

Heilizer, F. An exploration of the relationship between hypnotizability and anxiety and/or neuroticism. *Journal of Consulting Psychology*, 1960, **24**, 432–436.

Himelstein, P. Taylor scale characteristics of volunteers and nonvolunteers for psychological experiments. *Journal of Abnormal and Social Psychology*, 1956, **52**, 138–139.

Howe, E. S. Quantitative motivational differences between volunteers and nonvolunteers for a psychological experiment. *Journal of Applied Psychology*, 1960, **44**, 115–120.

Hyman, H., & Sheatsley, P. B. The scientific method. In D. P. Geddes (Ed.), *An analysis of the Kinsey reports.* New York: New American Library, 1954. Pp. 93–118.

Lasagna, L., & von Felsinger, J. M. The volunteer subject in research. *Science*, 1954, **120**, 359–361.

Leipold, W. D., & James, R. L. Characteristics of shows and no-shows in a psychological experiment. *Psychological Reports*, 1962, **11**, 171–174.

Locke, H. J. Are volunteer interviewees representative? *Social Problems*, 1954, **1**, 143–146.

London, P. Subject characteristics in hypnosis research: Part I. A survey of experience, interest, and opinion. *International Journal of Clinical and Experimental Hypnosis*, 1961, **9**, 151–161.

London, P., Cooper, L. M., & Johnson, H. J. Subject characteristics in hypnosis research. II: Attitudes towards hypnosis, volunteer status, and personality measures. III: Some correlates of hypnotic susceptibility. Unpublished manuscript, University of Illinois, 1961.

Lubin, B., Levitt, E. E., & Zuckerman, M. Some personality differences between responders and nonresponders to a survey questionnaire. *Journal of Consulting Psychology*, 1962, **26**, 192.

McNemar, Q. Opinion-attitude methodology. *Psychological Bulletin*, 1946, **43**, 289–374.

Marlowe, D., & Crowne, D. P. Social desirability and response to perceived situational demands. *Journal of Consulting Psychology*, 1961, **25**, 109–115.

Martin, R. M., & Marcuse, F. L. Characteristics of volunteers and nonvolunteers for hypnosis. *Journal of Clinical and Experimental Hypnosis*, 1957, **5**, 176–180.

Martin, R. M., & Marcuse, F. L. Characteristics of volunteers and nonvolunteers in psychological experimentation. *Journal of Consulting Psychology*, 1958, **22**, 475–479.

Maslow, A. H. Self-esteem (dominance feelings) and sexuality in women. *Journal of Social Psychology*, 1942, **16**, 259–293.

Maslow, A. H., & Sakoda, J. M. Volunteer error in the Kinsey study. *Journal of Abnormal and Social Psychology*, 1952, **47**, 259–262.

Newman, M. Personality differences between volunteers and nonvolunteers for psychological investigation: self-actualization of volunteers and nonvolunteers for research in personality and perception. *Dissertation Abstracts*, 1957, **17**, 684. (Abstract.)

Norman, R. D. A review of some problems related to the mail questionnaire technique. *Educational and Psychological Measurement*, 1948, **8**, 235–247.

Perlin, S., Pollin, W., & Butler, R. N. The experimental subject: 1. The psychiatric evaluation and selection of a volunteer population. *American Medical Association Archives of Neurological Psychiatry*, 1958, **80**, 65–70.

Pollin, W., & Perlin, S. Psychiatric evaluation of "normal control" volunteers. *American Journal of Psychiatry*, 1958, **115**, 129–133.

Richards, T. W. Personality of subjects who volunteer for research on a drug (mescaline). *Journal of Projective Techniques*, 1960, **24**, 424–428.

Riecken, H. W. A program for research on experiments in social psychology. In N. Washburne (Ed.), *Decisions, values and groups*. Vol. II. New York: Pergamon Press, 1962. Pp. 25–41.

Riggs, Margaret M., & Kaess, W. Personality differences between volunteers and nonvolunteers. *Journal of Psychology*, 1955, **40**, 229–245.

Rosen, E. Differences between volunteers and nonvolunteers for psychological studies. *Journal of Applied Psychology*, 1951, **35**, 185–193.

Rosenbaum, M. E. The effect of stimulus background factors on the volunteering response. *Journal of Abnormal and Social Psychology*, 1956, **53**, 118–121.

Rosenbaum, M. E., & Blake, R. R. Volunteering as a function of field structure. *Journal of Abnormal and Social Psychology*, 1955, **50**, 193–196.

Schachter, S. *The psychology of affiliation*. Stanford, Calif.: Stanford University Press; London: Tavistock Publications, 1959.

Schachter, S., & Hall, R. Group-derived restraints and audience persuasion. *Human Relations*, 1952, **5**, 397–406.

Scheier, I. H. To be or not to be a guinea pig: preliminary data on anxiety and the volunteer for experiment. *Psychological Reports*, 1959, **5**, 239–240.

Schubert, D. S. P. Volunteering as arousal seeking. *American Psychologist*, 1960, **15**, 413. (Abstract.) Extended report available.

Siegman, A. Responses to a personality questionnaire by volunteers and nonvolunteers to a Kinsey interview. *Journal of Abnormal and Social Psychology*, 1956, **52**, 280–281.

Staples, F. R., & Walters, R. H. Anxiety, birth order and susceptibility to social influence. *Journal of Abnormal and Social Psychology*, 1961, **62**, 716–719.

Strickland, Bonnie R., & Crowne, D. P. Conformity under conditions of simulated group pressure as a function of the need for social approval. *Journal of Social Psychology*, 1962, **58**, 171–182.

Wallin, P. Volunteer subjects as a source of sampling bias. *American Journal of Sociology*, 1949, **54**, 539–544.

Weiss, J. M., Wolf, A., & Wiltsey, R. G. Birth order, recruitment conditions, and preferences for participation in group versus non-group experiments. *American Psychologist*, 1963, **18**, 356. (Abstract.)

16. On the Social Psychology of the Psychological Experiment: With Particular Reference to Demand Characteristics and their Implications[1]

Martin T. Orne[2]

In his provocative discussion of the psychological characteristics of the psychological experiment, Dr. Orne takes issue with the research model that assumes the subject to be no more than a passive responder to stimulation. He focuses on the very active role of the subject—his motivation, his perception of the research, and the unintended cues or demand characteristics that influence his reaction. Dr. Orne believes that we must take cognizance of the role of the subject as an active participant, and of the experiment as a unique kind of social relationship between subject and experimenter. The study of the demand characteristics and their control in the experimental situation is discussed, and the necessity of a more effective understanding of these factors for valid research in psychology is urged.

It is to the highest degree probable that the subject['s] *. . . general attitude of mind is that of ready complacency and cheerful willingness to assist the investigator in every possible way by reporting to him those very things which he is most eager to find, and that*

---

[1] Reprinted from the *American Psychologist*, 1962, **17**, 776–783. Copyright 1962 by the American Psychological Association, and reproduced by permission of the author and the publisher. This paper was presented at the Symposium, "On the Social Psychology of the Psychological Experiment," American Psychological Association Convention, New York, 1961.

The work reported here was supported in part by a Public Health Service Research Grant, M-3369, National Institute of Mental Health.

[2] I wish to thank my associates Ronald E. Shor, Donald N. O'Connell, Ulric Neisser, Karl E. Scheibe, and Emily F. Carota for their comments and criticisms in the preparation of this paper.

*the very questions of the experimenter . . . suggest the shade of reply expected . . . . Indeed
. . . it seems too often as if the subject were now regarded as a stupid automaton . . . .*

A. H. PIERCE, 1908[3]

Since the time of Galileo, scientists have employed the laboratory experiment as a method of understanding natural phenomena. Generically, the experimental method consists of abstracting relevant variables from complex situations in nature and reproducing in the laboratory segments of these situations, varying the parameters involved so as to determine the effect of the experimental variables. This procedure allows generalization from the information obtained in the laboratory situation back to the original situation as it occurs in nature. The physical sciences have made striking advances through the use of this method, but in the behavioral sciences it has often been difficult to meet two necessary requirements for meaningful experimentation: reproducibility and ecological validity.[4] It has long been recognized that certain differences will exist between the types of experiments conducted in the physical sciences and those in the behavioral sciences because the former investigates a universe of inanimate objects and forces, whereas the latter deals with animate organisms, often thinking, conscious subjects. However, recognition of this distinction has not always led to appropriate changes in the traditional experimental model of physics as employed in the behavioral sciences. Rather the experimental model has been so successful as employed in physics that there has been a tendency in the behavioral sciences to follow precisely a paradigm originated for the study of inanimate objects, i.e., one which proceeds by exposing the subject to various conditions and observing the differences in reaction of the subject under different conditions. However, the use of such a model with animal or human subjects leads to the problem that the subject of the experiment is assumed, at least implicitly, to be a *passive responder* to stimuli—an assumption difficult to justify. Further, in this type of model the experimental stimuli themselves are usually rigorously defined in terms of what *is done* to the subject. In contrast, the purpose of this paper will be to focus on what the human subject *does* in the laboratory: what motivation the subject is likely to have in the experimental situation, how he usually perceives behavioral research, what the nature of the cues is that the subject is likely to pick up, etc. Stated in other terms, what factors are apt to affect the subject's reaction to the well-defined stimuli in the situation? These factors comprise what will be referred to here as the "experimental setting."

Since any experimental manipulation of human subjects takes place within this larger framework or setting, we should propose that the above-mentioned factors must be further elaborated and the parameters of the experimental setting more carefully defined so that adequate controls can be designed to isolate the effects of the experimental setting from the effects of the experimental variables. Later in

---

[3] See reference list (Pierce, 1908).

[4] Ecological validity, in the sense that Brunswik (1947) has used the term: appropriate generalization from the laboratory to nonexperimental situations.

this paper we shall propose certain possible techniques of control which have been devised in the process of our research on the nature of hypnosis.

Our initial focus here will be on some of the qualities peculiar to psychological experiments. The experimental situation is one which takes place within the context of an explicit agreement of the subject to participate in a special form of social interaction known as "taking part in an experiment." Within the context of our culture the roles of subject and experimenter are well understood and carry with them well-defined mutual role expectations. A particularly striking aspect of the typical experimenter-subject relationship is the extent to which the subject will play his role and place himself under the control of the experimenter. Once a subject has agreed to participate in a psychological experiment, he implicitly agrees to perform a very wide range of actions on request without inquiring as to their purpose, and frequently without inquiring as to their duration.

Furthermore, the subject agrees to tolerate a considerable degree of discomfort, boredom, or actual pain, if required to do so by the experimenter. Just about any request which could conceivably be asked of the subject by a reputable investigator is legitimized by the quasi-magical phrase, "This is an experiment," and the shared assumption that a legitimate purpose will be served by the subject's behavior. A somewhat trivial example of this legitimization of requests is as follows:

A number of casual acquaintances were asked whether they would do the experimenter a favor; on their acquiescence, they were asked to perform five push-ups. Their response tended to be amazement, incredulity and the question "Why?" Another similar group of individuals were asked whether they would take part in an experiment of brief duration. When they agreed to do so, they too were asked to perform five push-ups. Their typical response was "Where?"

The striking degree of control inherent in the experimental situation can also be illustrated by a set of pilot experiments which were performed in the course of designing an experiment to test whether the degree of control inherent in the *hypnotic* relationship is greater than that in a waking relationship.[5] In order to test this question, we tried to develop a set of tasks which waking subjects would refuse to do, or would do only for a short period of time. The tasks were intended to be psychologically noxious, meaningless, or boring, rather than painful or fatiguing.

For example, one task was to perform serial additions of each adjacent two numbers on sheets filled with rows of random digits. In order to complete just one sheet, the subject would be required to perform 224 additions! A stack of some 2,000 sheets was presented to each subject—clearly an impossible task to complete. After the instructions were given, the subject was deprived of his watch and told, "Continue to work; I will return eventually." Five and one-half hours later, the *experimenter* gave up! In general, subjects tended to continue this type of task for several hours, usually with little decrement in performance. Since we were trying to find a task which would be discontinued spontaneously within a brief period, we tried to create a more frustrating situation as follows:

Subjects were asked to perform the same task described above but were also

---

[5] These pilot studies were performed by Thomas Menaker.

told that when finished the additions on each sheet, they should pick up a card from a large pile, which would instruct them on what to do next. However, every card in the pile read,

> You are to tear up the sheet of paper which you have just completed into a minimum of thirty-two pieces and go on to the next sheet of paper and continue working as you did before; when you have completed this piece of paper, pick up the next card which will instruct you further. Work as accurately and as rapidly as you can.

Our expectation was that subjects would discontinue the task as soon as they realized that the cards were worded identically, that each finished piece of work had to be destroyed, and that, in short, the task was completely meaningless.

Somewhat to our amazement, subjects tended to persist in the task for several hours with relatively little sign of overt hostility. Removal of the oneway screen did not tend to make much difference. The postexperimental inquiry helped to explain the subjects' behavior. When asked about the tasks, subjects would invariably attribute considerable meaning to their performance, viewing it as an endurance test or the like.

Thus far, we have been singularly unsuccessful in finding an experimental task which would be discontinued, or, indeed, refused by subjects in an experimental setting.[6,7] Not only do subjects continue to perform boring, unrewarding tasks, but they do so with few errors and little decrement in speed. It became apparent that it was extremely difficult to design an experiment to test the degree of social control in hypnosis, in view of the already *very high degree of control in the experimental situation itself.*

The quasi-experimental work reported here is highly informal and based on samples of three or four subjects in each group. It does, however, illustrate the remarkable compliance of the experimental subject. The only other situations where such a wide range of requests are carried out with little or no question are those of complete authority, such as some parent-child relationships or some doctor-patient relationships. This aspect of the experiment as a social situation will not become apparent unless one tests for it; it is, however, present in varying degrees in all experimental contexts. Not only are tasks carried out, but they are performed with care over considerable periods of time.

Our observation that subjects tend to carry out a remarkably wide range of instructions with a surprising degree of diligence reflects only one aspect of the motivation manifested by most subjects in an experimental situation. It is relevant to consider another aspect of motivation that is common to the subjects of most psychological experiments: high regard for the aims of science and experimentation.

A volunteer who participates in a psychological experiment may do so for a

---

[6] Tasks which would involve the use of actual severe physical pain or exhaustion were not considered.

[7] This observation is consistent with Frank's (1944) failure to obtain resistance to disagreeable or nonsensical tasks. He accounts for this "primarily by *S*'s unwillingness to break the tacit agreement he had made when he volunteered to take part in the experiment, namely, to do whatever the experiment required of him" (p. 24).

wide variety of reasons ranging from the need to fulfill a course requirement, to the need for money, to the unvoiced hope of altering his personal adjustment for the better, etc. Over and above these motives, however, college students tend to share (with the experimenter) the hope and expectation that the study in which they are participating will in some material way contribute to science and perhaps ultimately to human welfare in general. We should expect that many of the characteristics of the experimental situation derive from the peculiar role relationship which exists between subject and experimenter. Both subject and experimenter share the belief that whatever the experimental task is, it is important, and that as such no matter how much effort must be exerted or how much discomfort must be endured, it is justified by the ultimate purpose.

If we assume that much of the motivation of the subject to comply with any and all experimental instructions derives from an identification with the goals of science in general and the success of the experiment in particular,[8] it follows that the subject has a stake in the outcome of the study in which he is participating. For the volunteer subject to feel that he has made a useful contribution, it is necessary for him to assume that the experimenter is competent and that he himself is a "good subject."

The significance to the subject of successfully being a "good subject" is attested to by the frequent questions at the conclusion of an experiment, to the effect of, "Did I ruin the experiment?" What is most commonly meant by this is, "Did I perform well in my role as experimental subject?" or "Did my behavior demonstrate that which the experiment is designed to show?" Admittedly, subjects are concerned about their performance in terms of reinforcing their self-image; nonetheless, they seem even more concerned with the utility of their performances. We might well expect then that as far as the subject is able, he will behave in an experimental context in a manner designed to play the role of a "good subject" or, in other words, *to validate the experimental hypothesis*. Viewed in this way, the student volunteer is *not* merely a passive responder in an experimental situation but rather he has a very real stake in the successful outcome of the experiment. This problem is implicitly recognized in the large number of psychological studies which attempt to conceal the true purpose of the experiment from the subject in the hope of thereby obtaining more reliable data. This maneuver on the part of psychologists is so widely known in the college population that even if a psychologist is honest with the subject, more often than not he will be distrusted. As one subject pithily put it, "Psychologists always lie!" This bit of paranoia has some support in reality.

The subject's performance in an experiment might almost be conceptualized as problem-solving behavior; that is, at some level he sees it as his task to ascertain the true purpose of the experiment and respond in a manner which will support the hypotheses being tested. Viewed in this light, the totality of cues which convey an experimental hypothesis to the subject become significant determinants of subjects' behavior. We have labeled the sum total of such cues as the "*demand characteristics*

8 This hypothesis is subject to empirical test. We should predict that there would be measurable differences in motivation between subjects who perceive a particular experiment as "significant" and those who perceive the experiment as "unimportant."

of the experimental situation " (Orne, 1959*a*). These cues include the rumors or campus scuttlebutt about the research, the information conveyed during the original solicitation, the person of the experimenter, and the setting of the laboratory, as well as all explicit and implicit communications during the experiment proper. A frequently overlooked, but nonetheless very significant source of cues for the subject lies in the experimental procedure itself, viewed in the light of the subject's previous knowledge and experience. For example, if a test is given twice with some intervening treatment, even the dullest college student is aware that some change is expected, particularly if the test is in some obvious way related to the treatment.

The demand characteristics perceived in any particular experiment will vary with the sophistication, intelligence, and previous experience of each experimental subject. To the extent that the demand characteristics of the experiment are clear-cut, they will be perceived uniformly by most experimental subjects. It is entirely possible to have an experimental situation with clear-cut demand characteristics for psychology undergraduates which, however, does not have the same clear-cut demand characteristics for enlisted army personnel. It is, of course, those demand characteristics which are perceived by the subject that will influence his behavior.

We should like to propose the heuristic assumption that a subject's behavior in any experimental situation will be determined by two sets of variables: (*a*) those which are traditionally defined as experimental variables and (*b*) the perceived demand characteristics of the experimental situation. The extent to which the subject's behavior is related to the demand characteristics, rather than to the experimental variable, will in large measure determine both the extent to which the experiment can be replicated with minor modification (i.e., modified demand characteristics) and the extent to which generalizations can be drawn about the effect of the experimental variables in nonexperimental contexts [the problem of ecological validity (Brunswik, 1947)].

It becomes an empirical issue to study under what circumstances, in what kind of experimental contexts, and with what kind of subject populations, demand characteristics become significant in determining the behavior of subjects in experimental situations. It should be clear that demand characteristics cannot be eliminated from experiments; all experiments will have demand characteristics, and these will always have some effect. It does become possible, however, to study the effect of demand characteristics as opposed to the effect of experimental variables. However, techniques designed to study the effect of demand characteristics need to take into account that these effects result from the subject's *active* attempt to respond appropriately to the *totality* of the experimental situation.

It is perhaps best to think of the perceived demand characteristics as a contextual variable in the experimental situation. We should like to emphasize that, at this stage, little is known about this variable. In our first study which utilized the demand characteristics concept (Orne, 1959*b*), we found that a particular experimental effect was present only in records of those subjects who were able to verbalize the experimenter's hypothesis. Those subjects who were unable to do so did not show the predicted phenomenon. Indeed we found that whether or not a given subject perceived the experimenter's hypothesis was a more accurate predictor of the subject's actual performance than his statement about what he thought he had done on the experimental task. It became clear from extensive interviews with subjects that response to the demand characteristics is not merely conscious compliance. When we speak of "playing the role of a good experimental subject," we use the concept analogously to the way in which Sarbin (1950) describes role playing in hypnosis: namely, largely on a nonconscious level. The demand characteristics of the situation help define the role of "good experimental subject," and the responses of the subject are a function of the role that is created.

We have a suspicion that the demand characteristics most potent in determining subjects' behavior are those which convey the purpose of the experiment effectively but not obviously. If the purpose of the experiment is not clear, or is highly ambiguous, many different hypotheses may be formed by different subjects, and the demand characteristics will not lead to clear-cut results. If, on the other hand, the demand characteristics are so obvious that the subject becomes fully conscious of the expectations of the experimenter, there is a tendency to lean over backwards to be honest. We are encountering here the effect of another facet of the college student's attitude toward science. While the student wants studies to "work," he feels he must be honest in his report; otherwise, erroneous conclusions will be drawn. Therefore, if the subject becomes acutely aware of the experimenter's expectations, there may be a tendency for biasing in the opposite direction. (This is analogous to the often observed tendency to favor individuals whom we dislike in an effort to be fair.)[9]

Delineation of the situations where demand characteristics may produce an effect ascribed to experimental variables, or where they may obscure such an effect and actually lead to systematic data in the opposite direction, as well as those experimental contexts where they do not play a major role, is an issue for further work. Recognizing the contribution to experimental results which may be made by the demand characteristics of the situation, what are some experimental techniques for the study of demand characteristics?

As we have pointed out, it is futile to imagine an experiment that could be created without demand characteristics. One of the basic characteristics of the human being is that he will ascribe purpose and meaning even in the absence of purpose and meaning. In an experiment where he knows some purpose exists, it is inconceivable for him not to form some hypothesis as to the purpose, based on some cues, no matter how meager; this will then determine the demand characteristics which will be perceived by and operate for a particular subject. Rather than eliminating this variable then, it becomes necessary to take demand characteristics into account, study their effect, and manipulate them if necessary.

---

[9] Rosenthal (1961) in his recent work on experimenter bias, has reported a similar type of phenomenon. Biasing was maximized by ego involvement of the experimenters, but when an attempt was made to increase biasing by paying for "good results," there was a marked reduction of effect. This reversal may be ascribed to the experimenters' becoming too aware of their own wishes in the situation.

One procedure to determine the demand characteristics is the systematic study of each individual subject's perception of the experimental hypothesis. If one can determine what demand characteristics are perceived by each subject, it becomes possible to determine to what extent these, rather than the experimental variables, correlate with the observed behavior. If the subject's behavior correlates better with the demand characteristics than with the experimental variables, it is probable that the demand characteristics are the major determinants of the behavior.

The most obvious technique for determining what demand characteristics are perceived is the use of postexperimental inquiry. In this regard, it is well to point out that considerable self-discipline is necessary for the experimenter to obtain a valid inquiry. A great many experimenters at least implicitly make the demand that the subject not perceive what is really going on. The temptation for the experimenter, in, say, a replication of an Asch group pressure experiment, is to ask the subject afterwards, "You didn't realize that the other fellows were confederates, did you?" Having obtained the required, "No," the experimenter breathes a sigh of relief and neither subject nor experimenter pursues the issue further.[10] However, even if the experimenter makes an effort to elicit the subject's perception of the hypothesis of the experiment, he may have difficulty in obtaining a valid report because the subject as well as he himself has considerable interest in appearing naive.

Most subjects are cognizant that they are not supposed to know any more about an experiment than they have been told and that excessive knowledge will disqualify them from participating, or, in the case of a postexperimental inquiry, such knowledge will invalidate their performance. As we pointed out earlier, subjects have a real stake in viewing their performance as meaningful. For this reason, it is commonplace to find a pact of ignorance resulting from the intertwining motives of both experimenter and subject, neither wishing to create a situation where the particular subject's performance needs to be excluded from the study.

For these reasons, inquiry procedures are required to push the subject for information without, however, providing in themselves cues as to what is expected. The general question which needs to be explored is the subject's perception of the experimental purpose and the specific hypotheses of the experimenter. This can best be done by an open-ended procedure starting with the very general question of, "What do you think that the experiment is about?" and only much later asking specific questions. Responses of "I don't know" should be dealt with by encouraging the subject to guess, use his imagination, and in general, by refusing to accept this response. Under these circumstances, the overwhelming majority of students will turn out to have evolved very definite hypotheses. These hypotheses can then be judged, and a correlation between them and experimental performance can be drawn.

Two objections may be made against this type of inquiry: (*a*) that the subject's perception of the experimenter's hypotheses is based on his own experimental behavior, and therefore a correlation between these two variables may have little to

---

[10] Asch (1952) himself took great pains to avoid this pitfall.

do with the determinants of behavior, and (b) that the inquiry procedure itself is subject to demand characteristics.

A procedure which has been independently advocated by Riecken (1958) and Orne (1959a) is designed to deal with the first of these objections. This consists of an inquiry procedure which is conducted much as though the subject had actually been run in the experiment, without, however, permitting him to be given any experimental data. Instead, the precise procedure of the experiment is explained, the experimental material is shown to the subject, and he is told what he would be required to do; however, he is not permitted to make any responses. He is then given a postexperimental inquiry as though he had been a subject. Thus, one would say, "If I had asked you to do all these things, what do you think that the experiment would be about, what do you think I would be trying to prove, what would my hypothesis be?" etc. This technique, which we have termed the pre-experimental inquiry, can be extended very readily to the giving of pre-experimental tests, followed by the explanation of experimental conditions and tasks, and the administration of postexperimental tests. The subject is requested to behave on these tests as though he had been exposed to the experimental treatment that was described to him. This type of procedure is not open to the objection that the subject's own behavior has provided cues for him as to the purpose of the task. It presents him with a straight problem-solving situation and makes explicit what, for the true experimental subject, is implicit. It goes without saying that these subjects who are run on the pre-experimental inquiry conditions must be drawn from the same population as the experimental groups and may, of course, not be run subsequently in the experimental condition. This technique is one of approximation rather than of proof. However, if subjects describe behavior on the pre-inquiry conditions as similar to, or identical with, that actually given by subjects exposed to the experimental conditions, the hypothesis becomes plausible that demand characteristics may be responsible for the behavior.

It is clear that pre- and postexperimental inquiry techniques have their own demand characteristics. For these reasons, it is usually best to have the inquiry conducted by an experimenter who is not acquainted with the actual experimental behavior of the subjects. This will tend to minimize the effect of experimenter bias.

Another technique which we have utilized for approximating the effect of the demand characteristics is to attempt to hold the demand characteristics constant and eliminate the experimental variable. One way of accomplishing this purpose is through the use of simulating subjects. This is a group of subjects who are not exposed to the experimental variable to which the effect has been attributed, but who are instructed to act *as if* this were the case. In order to control for experimenter bias under these circumstances, it is advisable to utilize more than one experimenter and to have the experimenter who actually runs the subjects "blind" as to which group (simulating or real) any given individual belongs.

Our work in hypnosis (Damaser, Shor, & Orne, 1963; Orne, 1959b; Shor, 1959) is a good example of the use of simulating controls. Subjects unable to enter hypnosis are instructed to simulate entering hypnosis for another experimenter. The experimenter who runs the study sees both highly trained hypnotic subjects and simulators in random order and does not know to which group each subject belongs. Because the subjects are run "blind," the experimenter is more likely to treat the two groups of subjects identically. We have found that simulating subjects are able to perform with great effectiveness, deceiving even well-trained hypnotists. However, the simulating group is not exposed to the experimental condition (in this case, hypnosis) to which the given effect under investigation is often ascribed. Rather, it is a group faced with a problem-solving task: namely, to utilize whatever cues are made available by the experimental context and the experimenter's concrete behavior in order to behave as they think that hypnotized subjects might. Therefore, to the extent that simulating subjects are able to behave identically, it is possible that demand characteristics, rather than the altered state of consciousness, could account for the behavior of the experimental group.

The same type of technique can be utilized in other types of studies. For example, in contrast to the placebo control in a drug study, it is equally possible to instruct some subjects not to take the medication at all, but to act as if they had. It must be emphasized that this type of control is different from the placebo control. It represents an approximation. It maximally confronts the simulating subject with a problem-solving task and suggests how much of the total effect could be accounted for by the demand characteristics—assuming that the experimental group had taken full advantage of them, an assumption not necessarily correct.

All of the techniques proposed thus far share the quality that they depend upon the active cooperation of the control subjects, and in some way utilize his thinking process as an intrinsic factor. The subject does *not* just respond in these control situations but, rather, he is required *actively* to solve the problem.

The use of placebo experimental conditions is a way in which this problem can be dealt with in a more classic fashion. Psychopharmacology has used such techniques extensively, but here too they present problems. In the case of placebos and drugs, it is often the case that the physician is "blind" as to whether a drug is placebo or active, but the patient is not, despite precautions to the contrary; i.e., the patient is cognizant that he does not have the side effects which some of his fellow patients on the ward experience. By the same token, in psychological placebo treatments, it is equally important to ascertain whether the subject actually perceived the treatment to be experimental or control. Certainly the subject's perception of himself as a control subject may materially alter the situation.

A recent experiment[11] in our laboratory illustrates this type of investigation. We were interested in studying the demand characteristics of sensory deprivation experiments, independent of any actual sensory deprivation. We hypothesized that the overly cautious treatment of subjects, careful screening for mental or physical disorders, awesome release forms, and, above all, the presence of a "panic (release) button" might be more significant in producing the effects reported from sensory

[11] This experiment is described in a paper in preparation by M. T. Orne and K. E. Scheibe: The Contribution of Nondeprivation Factors in the Production of Sensory Deprivation Effects.

deprivation than the actual diminution of sensory input. A pilot study (Stare, Brown, & Orne, 1959), employing pre-inquiry techniques, supported this view. Recently, we designed an experiment to test more rigorously this hypothesis.

This experiment, which we called Meaning Deprivation, had all the *accoutrements* of sensory deprivation, including release forms and a red panic button. However, we carefully refrained from creating any sensory deprivation whatsoever. The experimental task consisted of sitting in a small experimental room which was well lighted, with two comfortable chairs, as well as ice water and a sandwich, and an optional task of adding numbers. The subject did not have a watch during this time, the room was reasonably quiet, but not soundproof, and the duration of the experiment (of which the subject was ignorant) was four hours. Before the subject was placed in the experimental room, 10 tests previously used in sensory deprivation research were administered. At the completion of the experiment, the same tasks were again administered. A microphone and a one-way screen were present in the room, and the subject was encouraged to verbalize freely.

The control group of 10 subjects was subjected to the identical treatment, except that they were told that they were control subjects for a sensory deprivation experiment. The panic button was eliminated for this group. The formal experimental treatment of these two groups of subjects was the same in terms of the objective stress—four hours of isolation. However, the demand characteristics had been purposively varied for the two groups to study the effect of demand characteristics as opposed to objective stress. Of the 14 measures which could be quantified, 13 were in the predicted direction, and 6 were significant at the selected 10% alpha level or better. A Mann-Whitney U test has been performed on the summation ranks of all measures as a convenient method for summarizing the overall differences. The one-tailed probability which emerges is $p = .001$, a clear demonstration of expected effects.

This study suggests that demand characteristics may in part account for some of the findings commonly attributed to sensory deprivation. We have found similar significant effects of demand characteristics in accounting for a great deal of the findings reported in hypnosis. It is highly probable that careful attention to this variable, or group of variables, may resolve some of the current controversies regarding a number of psychological phenomena in motivation, learning, and perception.

In summary, we have suggested that the subject must be recognized as an active participant in any experiment, and that it may be fruitful to view the psychological experiment as a very special form of social interaction. We have proposed that the subject's behavior in an experiment is a function of the totality of the situation, which includes the experimental variables being investigated and at least one other set of variables which we have subsumed under the heading, demand characteristics of the experimental situation. The study and control of demand characteristics are not simply matters of good experimental technique; rather, it is an empirical issue to determine under what circumstances demand characteristics significantly affect subjects' experimental behavior. Several empirical techniques have been proposed for this purpose. It has been suggested that control of these variables in particular may lead to greater reproducibility and ecological validity of psychological experiments. With an increasing understanding of these factors intrinsic to the experimental context, the experimental method in psychology may become a more effective tool in predicting behavior in nonexperimental contexts.

REFERENCES

Asch, S. E. *Social psychology.* New York: Prentice Hall, 1952.

Brunswik, E. *Systematic and representative design of psychological experiments with results in physical and social perception.* (Syllabus Series, No. 304) Berkeley: University of California Press, 1947.

Damaser, Esther C., Shor, R. E., & Orne, M. T. Physiological effects during hypnotically requested emotions. *Psychosomatic Medicine,* 1963, **25,** 334–343.

Frank, J. D. Experimental studies of personal pressure and resistance: I. Experimental production of resistance. *Journal of General Psychology,* 1944, **30,** 23–41.

Orne, M. T. The demand characteristics of an experimental design and their implications. Paper presented at the meeting of the American Psychological Association, Cincinnati, 1959*a.*

Orne, M. T. The nature of hypnosis: artifact and essence. *Journal of Abnormal and Social Psychology,* 1959*b,* **58,** 277–299.

Pierce, A. H. The subconscious again. *Journal of Philosophy, Psychology, and Scientific Methods,* 1908, **5,** 264–271.

Riecken, H. W. A program for research on experiments in social psychology. Paper presented at the Behavioral Sciences Conference, University of New Mexico, 1958.

Rosenthal, R. On the social psychology of the psychological experiment: with particular reference to experimenter bias. Paper presented at the meeting of the American Psychological Association, New York, 1961.

Sarbin, T. R. Contributions to role-taking theory: I. Hypnotic behavior. *Psychological Review,* 1950, **57,** 255–270.

Shor, R. E. Explorations in hypnosis: a theoretical and experimental study. Unpublished doctoral dissertation, Brandeis University, 1959.

Stare, F., Brown, J., & Orne, M. T. Demand characteristics in sensory deprivation studies. Unpublished seminar paper, Massachusetts Mental Health Center and Harvard University, 1959.

17. Covert Communication in the Psychological Experiment[1]

Robert Rosenthal

The focus of this paper is the unintended communication that takes place in the experimenter-subject dyad in psychological experiments. Taking the position that such communication is the norm in psychological research, Dr. Rosenthal discusses the resulting partial loss of control over the experimental inputs, and the influence on the subjects' response behavior. The nature and extent of such communication can be partly predicted by a knowledge of various experimenter characteristics, including sex, anxiety, and need for approval. Further, it is noted that this communication can be influenced by such factors as the experimenter's past laboratory experience, his perception of and relationship with the principal investigator of the research, the subjects' behavior, and the physical environment in which the research takes place.

Psychological laboratories and the psychological experiments conducted there are not the only scenes or means whereby we learn of human behavior. There is no doubt, however, that in our discipline as in others, the laboratory experiment is a preferred mode for the observation of nature. It is so preferred because of the greater control it gives us over the inputs to the experimental subject. Unlike the usual situation in the field or in the "real world," when we observe the behavior of the subject of a psychological experiment we are in a position to attribute his behavior to the antecedent conditions we have ourselves arranged.

In the paradigm psychological experiment, there is a subject whose behavior is to be observed and an experimenter whose functions include the control of inputs

[1] Reprinted from the *Psychological Bulletin*, 1967, **67**, 356–367. Copyright 1967 by the American Psychological Association, and reproduced by permission of the author and the publisher. The research described in this paper has been supported by research grants (G-17685, G-24826, GS-177, GS-714) from the Division of Social Sciences of the National Science Foundation. An earlier version of this paper was presented at the symposium "Ethical and Methodological Problems in Social Psychological Experiments," American Psychological Association, Chicago, September 1965.

to the subject. (The experimenter also often functions as a recorder of the subject's output, but this function of the experimenter is not important to the present discussion. It may be assumed for present purposes that the subject's response is recorded directly by an error-free automated system.) As part of the experimenter's function of controlling the subject's inputs, he engages in a variety of intended, programmed, overt communications with the subject. Such communications include the "instructions to subjects." Although the instructions are highly programmed, they, along with aspects of the physical scene (Riecken, 1962) and the overall design of the experiment as perceived by the subject, may unintentionally communicate to the subject something of what the experimenter is after. Such unintended information transmission has been discussed most fully by Orne (1962), who referred to such sources of cues as the *demand characteristics* of the experimental procedures. To the extent that these unintended cues tend to be systematic for a given experiment, and do not depend for their operation on *differential* communication to subjects by experimenters, they are not discussed here. Instead, the focus will be on variations in the covert and unintended communications that occur in the psychological experiment. Such variations are not random and are predictable to some extent from a knowledge of various characteristics of the experimenter and the subject.

One purpose of this paper is to illustrate the fact that unintended covert communications are the norm in psychological experiments. To the extent that the experimenter communicates unintentionally and differentially with his subjects he has lost some measure of control over the inputs. Since such control is a major reason for our reliance on the experimental method, there are serious implications. Serious as these implications may be for our interpretation of the results of experiments, it should not surprise us that different experimenters engage in different covert communication with different subjects. We should, in fact, be more surprised if such covert communication did not occur. Covert communications occur routinely in all other dyadic interactions; why then, should they not occur in the dyad composed of the experimenter and his subject?

The evidence for the experimenter's covert communication with his tacitly understanding subject comes from a program of experiments on experiments (Rosenthal, 1964). One purpose of this research program is primarily methodological. By taking account of the covert communication processes in the psychological experiment, techniques may be developed which will permit the drawing of more valid substantive conclusions about those experimental inputs about whose effects on the subject's behavior we want to learn. Another purpose of this research program is less methodological and more substantive. What we learn about the covert communication between experimenter and subject may teach us something about covert communication processes in other dyadic interactions as well. Laboratories need not simply be those places where we test, in simplified form, the hypotheses derived from the "real world." Laboratories, as Mills (1962) has pointed out, are just as "real" as the rest of the world.

THE EXPERIMENTER AS COVERT COMMUNICATOR

Covert communication between experimenter and subject could be demonstrated simply by showing that different experimenters behave differently toward their subjects in their conduct of a specific experiment and that these individual differences in behavior affect the subject's response. But it seems late in the history of psychology simply to demonstrate individual differences in behavior even when the people happen to be experimenters. It seems more useful, therefore, to concentrate on those cases of covert communication in which we can predict, more or less, just how he will communicate covertly with his subjects, before the experimenter even enters the laboratory.

Experimenter's Sex

There is a good deal of evidence that the sex of the experimenter can affect the responses of the experimental subject (Rosenthal, 1966; Sarason, 1965; Stevenson, 1965). What we have not known, however, is whether the effect of the sex of the experimenter was passive or active. By "passive effect" is meant that subjects respond differently to and for male and female experimenters simply because they are male or female. By "active effect" is meant that subjects respond differently to and for male and female experimenters because male and female experimenters treat the subjects differently. The best way to determine the extent to which any effects of the experimenter are active or passive is to make observations of the experimenter as he or she conducts an experiment.

In our research program we have employed two types of observers. One type of observer has been the subject himself. In several experiments, subjects have been asked to describe the behavior of their experimenter during the experimental transaction. An advantage of such observations by the subject himself is that there is no one closer to the experimenter during the experiment than the subject, and he is in a good position to see what the experimenter does. A disadvantage of such observations by the subjects themselves is that they may be contaminated by the responses subjects made during the experiment itself. Thus, if a subject has made conforming responses during an experiment in verbal conditioning, he may describe his experimenter as a more forceful, dominant person, not because the experimenter really was, but because that would justify to the subject and to others the subject's having conformed.

Another type of observer has been employed who was not a participant in the experiment itself. Instead, graduate and undergraduate students have observed sound motion pictures made of experimenters interacting with their subjects. Neither experimenters nor subjects knew that their interaction was being observed. The films were of five different samples of experimenters and subjects involving altogether 29 experimenters (5 of whom were females) and 86 subjects (of whom 21 were males). The details of the experiments which were filmed are given elsewhere (Rosenthal, Persinger, Mulry, Vikan-Kline, & Grothe, 1964a, 1964b). It is enough to know that in all the experiments filmed the task was the same. The experimenters presented to each of their subjects a series of 10 standardized photos of faces. Each face was to be judged as to how successful or unsuccessful the person appeared to be. All experimenters were to read the same instructions to their subjects and this reading lasted about a minute, on the average. Before reading the instructions, experimenters asked subjects for their name, age, major field, and marital status. This brief preinstructional period lasted on the average about half a minute.

Analysis of the films showed that even during this brief preinstructional period, male and female experimenters treated their subjects in a significantly different manner. Male experimenters interacting with either male or female subjects were a good deal more friendly in their interaction than were female experimenters ($r_{pb} = .47$; $p < .05$). Support for this finding comes from a different study employing the same experimental task. This time the observers of the experimenters' behavior were the subjects themselves. Suzanne Haley made the data available for this analysis. Her 86 female subjects judged their 12 male experimenters to be more friendly during the course of the experiment than their 2 female experimenters ($r_{pb} = .32$, $p < .005$). Regardless of whether we ask external observers or the subjects themselves, male experimenters are observed to behave differently than female experimenters. Such systematic differences in the treatment of subjects suggest that though experimenters may read the same instructions to their subjects, subjects contacted by male experimenters and subjects contacted by female experimenters are simply not in the same experiment. It should not surprise us, therefore, when male and female experimenters obtain different responses from their subjects. Whenever the warmth or friendliness of the experimenter can affect the subject's response, and that happens often (Gordon & Durea, 1948; Luft, 1953; Reece & Whitman, 1962), we may look also for the effect of the experimenter's sex.

The effect of the experimenter's sex is complicated by the effect of the subject's sex. Male and female subjects evoke different behavior from their experimenters. Neil Friedman (1964) made observations of the smiling behavior of the experimenters who had been filmed which were made available for this analysis. During the brief half-minute preceding the reading of the instructions, female subjects evoked more smiling behavior from their experimenters than did male subjects ($p < .05$). Only 12% of the experimenters smiled even a little at any male subject, but 70% of the experimenters smiled at least a little at their female subjects. From this evidence and from some more detailed analyses which suggest that female subjects may be more protectively treated by their experimenters (Rosenthal, 1966), it might be suggested that in the psychological experiment, chivalry is not dead. This news may be heartening socially, and it is interesting social psychologically, but it is very disconcerting methodologically. Sex differences are well established for many kinds of behavior. But a question must now be raised as to whether sex differences which emerge from psychological experiments are due to the subject's genes, morphology, enculturation, or simply to the fact that the experimenter treated his male and female subjects differently so that, in a sense, they were not really in the same experiment at all.

Male and female experimenters remember and respond to their subject's sex. They also remember their own sex. Female experimenters show a pattern of behavior which might be called "interested modesty" when interacting with their male subjects, while male experimenters show a pattern which might more simply be called "interested" when interacting with their female subjects. An indirect assessment of this interest comes from an analysis of the time spent in performing the preparations to show the subject the next stimulus photo. The timing of these portions was done by Richard Katz (1964), who made the data available for the present analysis. When male experimenters were contacting female subjects, it took them 16% longer to prepare to present the next stimulus than when they were contacting male subjects ($p < .01$). When female experimenters were contacting male subjects, it took them 13% longer to prepare the next stimulus for presentation than when they were contacting female subjects, though this difference was not significant statistically. Though the absolute amounts of time involved were measured in a few seconds, it appeared that among male experimenters especially, there was a tendency to stretch out the interaction with the opposite-sexed subject. This same finding of a prolongation of opposite sex experimental interactions has also been reported recently by Shapiro (1966) in an experiment on verbal conditioning.

Among our own female experimenters, evidence for their "modesty" in the motor channel of communication comes from observations of the degree to which experimenters leaned toward their subjects during the experimental transaction. (These observations were made by R. Katz, who made them available for this analysis.) Male and female experimenters leaned toward their female subjects to about the same degree. However, when the subjects were males, female experimenters did not lean as close as did their male colleagues ($p < .05$).

Further evidence for this relative modesty of female experimenters when contacting male subjects comes from a different, still preliminary sort of analysis. Observations of experimenters' friendliness were now made by two different groups of observers. One group watched the films but did not hear the sound track. Another group listened to the sound track but did not see the films. From this, a measure of motor or visual friendliness and an independent measure of verbal or auditory friendliness were available. (The correlation between ratings of friendliness obtained from these independent channels was only .29.) The results of this analysis are shown in Table 17-1. Among male experimenters, there was a tendency, not statistically significant, for their movements to show greater friendliness than their tone of voice, and to be somewhat unfriendly toward their male subjects in the auditory channel of communication. It was among the female experimenters that the more striking effects occurred. They were quite friendly toward their female subjects in the visual channel but not in the auditory channel. With male subjects, the situation was reversed significantly ($p < .05$). Though not friendly in the visual mode, female experimenters showed remarkable friendliness in the auditory channel when contacting male subjects.

TABLE 17-1

Experimenter Friendliness in Two Communication
Channels as a Function of Experimenter and Subject Sex

Experimenter sex	Subject sex	Communication channel		
		Visual	Auditory	Difference
Male	Male	3.00	−0.50	3.50
	Female	2.81	1.32	1.49
	Mean	2.90	0.41	
Female	Male	0.44	2.96	−2.52
	Female	1.75	0.25	1.50
	Mean	1.10	1.60	

The quantitative analysis of sound motion pictures is not yet far enough developed that we can say whether such channel discrepancy in the communication of friendliness is generally characteristic of women in our culture, or only of advanced women students in psychology, or only of female experimenters conducting experiments in person perception. Perhaps it would not be farfetched to attribute the obtained channel discrepancy to an ambivalence over how friendly they ought to be. Quite apart from considerations of processes of covert communication in the psychological experiment, such findings may have some relevance for a better understanding of communication processes in general.

Other Attributes

We have seen that the sex of the experimenter, a variable shown often to affect subjects' responses, is associated with different patterns of communication in the psychological experiment, patterns which may account in part for the effects on the subjects' responses. Further, we have seen that the sex of the subject affects the experimenters' behavior, so that it is hard to tell whether different responses obtained from male and female subjects are due to the subjects' difference in sex or to the differences in the behavior of their experimenters. There are many other characteristics of experimenters and of subjects which should be analogously investigated. Some beginnings have been made and some results have been reported (Rosenthal, 1966). Here we present brief examples of differences in the experimenter's behavior toward the subject of the experiment, differences which are predictable from a knowledge of various attributes of the experimenter. The examples are chosen from only those experimenter variables which have been shown by various investigators to affect the subjects' responses.

There is considerable evidence that the anxiety of the experimenter, as measured before he enters the laboratory, can be a significant determinant of his subjects' responses (e.g., Rosenthal, 1966; Sarason, 1965). But what does the more anxious experimenter do in the experiment that leads his subjects to respond differently? We might expect more anxious experimenters to be more fidgety, and that is just what they are. Experimenters scoring higher on the Taylor (1953) Manifest Anxiety scale are observed from their films to show a greater degree of general body activity ($r = .41$, $p = .09$) and in addition, to have a less dominant tone of voice ($r = -.43$, $p = .07$). What effects just such behavior on the part of the experimenter will have on the subjects' responses depends no doubt on the particular experiment being conducted and, very likely, on various characteristics of the subject as well. In any case, we must assume that a more anxious experimenter cannot conduct just the same experiment as a less anxious experimenter. It appears that in experiments which have been conducted by just one experimenter, the probability of successful replication by another investigator is likely to depend on the similarity of his personality to that of the original investigator.

Anxiety of the experimenter is just one of the experimenter variables affecting the subjects' responses in an unintended manner. Crowne and Marlowe (1964) have shown that subjects who score high on their scale of need for approval tend to behave in such a way as to gain the approval of the experimenter. Now there is evidence that suggests that experimenters who score high on this measure also behave in such a way as to gain approval from their subjects. Analysis of the filmed interactions showed that experimenters scoring higher on the Marlowe-Crowne scale spoke to their subjects in a more enthusiastic tone of voice ($r = .39$, $p < .10$) and in a more friendly tone of voice ($r = .47$, $p < .05$). In addition, they smiled more often at their subjects ($r = .44$, $p = .07$) and slanted their bodies more toward their subjects than did experimenters lower in the need for approval ($r = .39$, $p < .10$).

THE EXPERIMENTER AS
REACTIVE COMMUNICATOR

Experimenter's Experience

The kind of person the experimenter is *before* he enters his laboratory can in part determine the responses he obtains from his subjects. From the observation of experimenters' behavior during their interaction with their subjects there are some clues as to how this may come about. There is also evidence that the kind of person the experimenter becomes *after* he enters his laboratory may alter his behavior toward his subjects and lead him, therefore, to obtain different responses from his subjects.

In the folklore of psychologists who do experiments, there is the notion that sometimes, perhaps more often than we might expect, subjects contacted early in an experiment behave differently from subjects contacted later in an experiment. There may be something to this bit of lore even if we make sure that subjects seen earlier and later in an experiment come from the same population. The difference may be due to changes over the course of the experiment in the behavior of the experimenter. From what we know of performance curves we might, in fact, predict both a practice effect and a fatigue effect on the part of the experimenter. There is evidence for both. In the experiments which were filmed, experimenters became more accurate ($r = .25$, $p = .07$) and also faster ($r = .31$, $p = .03$) in the reading of their instructions to their later-contacted subjects. That seems simply to be a practice effect. In addition, experimenters became more bored or less interested over the course of the experiment as observed from their behavior in the experimental interaction ($r = .31$, $p = .02$). As we might also predict, experimenters became less tense with more experience ($r = -.26$, $p = .06$). The changes which occur in the experimenters' behavior during the course of their experiment affect their subjects' responses. In the experiments which were filmed, for example, subjects contacted by experimenters whose behavior changed as described rated the stimulus persons as less successful ($r = .31$, $p = .02$).

Subjects' Behavior

The experimenter-subject communication system is a complex of intertwining feedback loops. The experimenter's behavior, we have seen, can affect the subject's next reponse. But the subject's behavior can also affect the experimenter's behavior, which in turn affects the subject's behavior. In this way, the subject plays a part in the indirect determination of his own next response. The experimental details are given elsewhere (Rosenthal, 1966; Rosenthal, Kohn, Greenfield, & Carota, 1965). Briefly, in one experiment, half the experimenters had their experimental hypotheses confirmed by their first few subjects, who were actually accomplices. The remaining experimenters had their experimental hypotheses disconfirmed. This confirmation or disconfirmation of their hypotheses affected the experimenters' behavior sufficiently so that from their next subjects, who were bona fide and not accomplices, they obtained significantly different responses not only to the experimental task, but on standard tests of personality as well. These responses were predictable from a knowledge of the responses the experimenters had obtained from their earlier-contacted subjects.

There is an interesting footnote on the psychology of the accomplice which comes from the experiment alluded to. The accomplices had been trained to confirm or to disconfirm the experimenter's hypothesis by the nature of the responses they gave the experimenter. These accomplices did not, of course, know when they were confirming an experimenter's hypothesis or, indeed, that there were expectancies to be confirmed at all. In spite of the accomplices' training, they were significantly affected in the adequacy of their performance as accomplices by the expectancy the experimenter had of their performance, and by whether the experimenter's hypothesis was being confirmed or disconfirmed by the accomplices' responses. We can think of the accomplices as experimenters and the experimenters as their targets or "victims." It is interesting to know that experimental targets are not simply affected by experimental accomplices. The targets of our accomplices, like the subjects of our experimenters, are not simply passive responders. They "act back."

Experimental Scenes

One of the things that happens to the experimenter which may affect his behavior toward his subject, and thus the subject's response, is that he falls heir to a specific scene in which to conduct his experiment. Riecken (1962) has pointed out how much there is we do not know about the effects of the physical scene in which an experimental transaction takes place. We know little enough about how the scene affects the subject's behavior, we know even less about how the scene affects the experimenter's behavior.

The scene in which the experiment takes place may affect the subject's response in two ways. The effect of the scene may be direct, as when a subject judges others to be less happy when his judgments are made in an "ugly" laboratory (Mintz, 1957). The effect of the scene may also be indirect, as when the scene influences the experimenter to behave differently and this change in the experimenter's behavior leads to a change in the subject's response. The evidence that the physical scene may affect the experimenter's behavior comes from some data collected with Suzanne Haley. We had available eight laboratory rooms which were varied as to the "professionalness," the "orderliness," and the "comfortableness" of their appearance. The 14 experimenters of this study were randomly assigned to the eight laboratories. Experimenters took the experiment significantly more seriously if they had been assigned to a laboratory which was both more disordered and less comfortable ($R = .73$, $p = .02$). These experimenters were graduate students in the natural sciences or in law school. Perhaps they felt that scientifically serious business is carried on best in the cluttered and severely furnished laboratory which fits the stereotype of the scientist's ascetic pursuit of truth.

In this same experiment, subjects described the behavior of their experimenter during the course of the experiment. Experimenters who had been assigned to more professional appearing laboratories were described by their subjects as significantly more expressive-voiced ($r = .22$, $p = .05$), more expressive-faced ($r = .32$, $p = .005$), and as more given to the use of hand gestures ($r = .32$, $p = .005$). There were no films made of these experimenters interacting with their subjects, so we cannot be sure that their subjects' descriptions were accurate. There is a chance that the experimenters did not really behave as described but that subjects in different appearing laboratories perceive their experimenters differently because of the operation of context effects. The direct observation of experimenters' behavior in different physical contexts should clear up the matter to some extent.

Principal Investigators

More and more research is carried out in teams and groups so that the chances are increasing that any one experimenter will be collecting data not for himself alone.

More and more there is a chance that the data are being collected for a principal investigator to whom the experimenter is responsible. The basic data are presented elsewhere (Rosenthal, 1966), but here it can be said that the response a subject gives his experimenter may be determined in part by the kind of person the principal investigator is and by the nature of his interaction with the experimenter.

More specifically, personality differences among principal investigators, and whether the principal investigator has praised or reproved the experimenter for his performance of his data-collecting duties, affect the subjects' subsequent perception of the success of other people and also affect subjects' scores on standardized tests of personality (e.g., Taylor Manifest Anxiety scale).

In one experiment, there were 13 principal investigators and 26 experimenters. When the principal investigators collected their own data it was found that their anxiety level correlated positively with the ratings of the success of others (pictured in photographs) they obtained from their subjects ($r = .66$, $p = .03$). Each principal investigator was then to employ two research assistants. On the assumption that principal investigators select research assistants who are significantly like or significantly unlike themselves, the two research assistants were assigned to principal investigators at random. That was done so that research assistants' scores on the anxiety scale would not be correlated with their principal investigator's anxiety scores. The randomization was successful in that the principal investigators' anxiety correlated only .02 with the anxiety of their research assistants.

The research assistants then replicated the principal investigators' experiments. Remarkably, the principal investigators' level of anxiety also predicted the responses obtained by their research assistants from their new samples of subjects ($r = .40$, $p = .07$). The research assistants' own level of anxiety, while also positively correlated with their subjects' responses ($r = .24$, *ns*) was not as good a predictor of their own subjects' responses as was the anxiety level of their principal investigator. Something in the covert communication between the principal investigator and his research assistant altered the assistant's behavior when he subsequently contacted his subjects. We know the effect of the principal investigator was mediated in this indirect way to his assistant's subjects because the principal investigator had no contact of his own with those subjects.

Other experiments show that the data obtained by the experimenter depend in part on whether the principal investigator is male or female, whether the principal investigator makes the experimenter self-conscious about the experimental procedure, and whether the principal investigator leads the experimenter to believe he has himself performed well or poorly at the same task the experimenter is to administer to his own subjects. The evidence comes from studies in person perception, verbal conditioning, and motor skills (Rosenthal, 1966).

As we would expect, these effects of the principal investigator on his assistant's subjects are mediated by the effects on the assistant's behavior toward his subjects. Thus, experimenters who have been made more self-conscious by their principal investigator behave less courteously toward their subjects, as observed from films of their interactions with their subjects ($r = -.43$, $p = .07$). In a different experiment, involving this time a verbal conditioning task, experimenters who had been given more favorable evaluations by their principal investigator were described by their subsequently contacted subjects to be more casual ($r = .33$, $p < .01$), and more courteous ($r = .27$, $p < .05$). These same experimenters, probably by virtue of their altered behavior toward their subjects, obtained significantly more conditioning responses from their subjects. All 10 of the experimenters who had been more favorably evaluated by their principal investigator showed conditioning effects among their subjects ($p = .001$) but only 5 of the 9 experimenters who felt unfavorably evaluated obtained any conditioning ($p = 1.00$).

THE EXPERIMENTER AS HYPOTHESIS COMMUNICATOR

Ever since Pfungst's (1911) brilliant series of experiments with Clever Hans, we have known that the experimenter's hypothesis can be communicated quite unintentionally to his subject. Hans, it will be remembered, was that clever horse who could solve problems of mathematics and musical harmony with equal skill and grace, simply by tapping out the answers with his hoof. A committee of eminent experts testified that Hans, whose owner made no profit from his horse's talents, was receiving no cues from his questioners. Of course, Pfungst later showed that this was not so, that tiny head and eye movements were Hans's signals to begin and to end his tapping. When Hans was asked a question, the questioner looked at Hans's hoof, quite naturally so, for that was the way for him to determine whether Hans's answer was correct. Then, it was discovered that when Hans approached the correct number of taps, the questioner would inadvertently move his head or eyes upward—just enough that Hans could discriminate the cue, but not enough that even trained animal observers or psychologists could see it.

The "Clever Hans" phenomenon has also been demonstrated to occur in more ordinary and more recent experiments. The details are found elsewhere (Rosenthal, 1966). Briefly, the expectancy or hypothesis of the experimenter has been shown to be a significant determinant of the results of his research in studies of person perception, verbal conditioning, personality assessment, and animal learning. The basic paradigm for such studies has been to divide a sample of experimenters into two equivalent groups and to create in each an expectancy for the data they would obtain which was opposite in direction to the expectancy induced in the other group of experimenters. Thus in the animal learning studies, half the experimenters were told that their rats were from the special "Berkeley Stock" and were specially bred for maze brightness or "Skinner-box brightness." The remaining experimenters were told that their animals had been specially bred for maze or "Skinner-box dullness." The rats run by experimenters expecting good performance performed significantly better than did the rats run by experimenters expecting poor performance. This was equally true in maze learning and in operant learning experiments.

In the person perception studies, half the experimenters were told that their subjects (humans now) had been selected because they tended to see photos of people as reflecting a great deal of past success, while the remaining experimenters were told that their subjects had been selected for the perception of failure in other people's faces. Subjects were then randomly assigned to their experimenters who subtly communicated their expectancies to their subjects in such a way that subjects expected to be success perceivers became success perceivers while subjects expected to be failure perceivers became failure perceivers. We can safely say that the communication processes whereby subjects learned of experimenter expectations were subtle ones because for the last 5 years we have been analyzing films of such experiments and we have yet to find the specific cues that mediate the Clever Hans phenomenon to human subjects. This is not for want of careful observation. The films have been observed by dozens of psychologists, graduate students, and undergraduate students; and two doctoral dissertations were based on the analysis of these films (Friedman, 1964; Katz, 1964). We all wish Pfungst were here to help us now, though there is some experimental evidence that human subjects are not using the same sort of cues that Clever Hans employed.

What we do know of the communication to subjects of the experimenter's expectancy has been learned as much from experiments as from the analysis of films. The details of the research are available elsewhere (Rosenthal, 1966). To summarize briefly, we know that both visual and auditory cues are helpful to the subjects in their tacit understanding of the experimenter's covertly communicated messages. We know that the communication of expectancies can occur before the subject makes even his first response so that verbal or nonverbal reinforcements of desired responses will not do as an explanation. There are not yet sufficient data to be sure of this point, but there are indications that experimenters learn during the course of an experiment how better to communicate their expectancies to their subjects. Subjects contacted later in the experiment, therefore, tend to give responses more biased in the direction of their experimenter's hypothesis.[2]

Such a finding makes good sense. It may be asked, if the experimenter is learning to communicate unintentionally, who is the teacher? Most likely, the subject is the teacher. It seems to be rewarding to have one's expectations confirmed (Aronson, Carlsmith, & Darley, 1963; Carlsmith & Aronson, 1963; Harvey & Clapp, 1965; Sampson & Sibley, 1965). Therefore, whenever the subject responds in accordance with the experimenter's expectancy, the likelihood is increased that the experimenter will repeat any covert communicative behavior which may have preceded the subject's confirming response. Subjects, then, may quite unintentionally shape the experimenter's unintended communicative behavior. Not only does the experimenter influence his subjects to respond in the expected manner, but his subjects may well evoke just that unintended behavior which will lead subjects to respond as expected.

---

[2] For three experiments with a total of 54 experimenters, the combined *p* was less than .001, but it must be pointed out that in these studies we could not always be sure that there were no systematic subject differences which could have accounted for a greater effect of the experimenter's expectancy among later-contacted subjects.

As the work of Hefferline (1962) suggests, such communication may not fall under what we commonly call "conscious control."

When it was mentioned earlier that the observation of the films of experimenters interacting with their subjects had not solved the modern riddle of Clever Hans, it was not meant that the films had not been worthwhile. There has already been frequent reference to things learned about experiments and experimenters from these movies. There is a good deal more. One of the most exciting findings was that it was possible to predict whether an experimenter would subsequently influence his subjects to respond in accordance with his hypothesis from the experimenter's behavior during the first half-minute of his interaction with the subject. Experimenters who were more likeable, dominant, personal, relaxed, and important-acting during these initial seconds of the interaction and less given to leg movements, later obtained data significantly biased in the direction of their hypothesis (all the correlations exceeded .30 but were less than .43 and all p's were less than .05).

Observations were made of the sound films by one group of observers, of the silent films by another group, and of the sound track alone by a third group. Interestingly, during this phase of the experiment, it did not help the observers at all to have access to the sound track. None of the observations made by the group with access only to the sound track was predictive of subsequent effects of the experimenter's expectancy. The group of observers with access only to the silent films did just as well in predicting subsequent biasing as did the observers who had access to the sound films. During this brief preinstructional phase, then, tone of voice variables seemed to be of little consequence.

Observations of the experimenter's behavior during the instruction-reading period showed much the same pattern of variables to be predictive of subsequent biasing of the subject's responses. Only now there were a great many more predictor variables which reached significance, and the correlations became larger. (The largest of the newly significant predictors of subsequent biasing was the variable of professionalism of manner, $r = .45$, $p < .005$.) The details are presented elsewhere (Rosenthal, 1966), but one interesting phenomenon must be mentioned. During the instruction-reading period of the experiment, a number of tone of voice variables became significant predictors of the experimenter's subsequent unintended biasing effects. Very often, the direction of the predictive correlation with a variable judged from the sound track alone was in the opposite direction from the correlation with the same variable judged from the films without sound track. One example must do. Experimenters who later biased their subjects' responses more were *seen* as more honest ($r = .40$, $p < .01$) in the films but were *heard* as less honest ($r = -.30$, $p < .05$). Current work in the search for the cues mediating the Clever Hans phenomenon has turned to a closer examination of the implications for unintended communication processes of such channel discrepancy. Such an examination may have consequences for areas other than the social psychology of the psychological experiment. It is, for example, part of clinical lore, though the evidence is scanty (Ringuette & Kennedy, 1966), that such channel discrepancies may have important consequences for the development of psychopathology (Bateson, Jackson, Haley, & Weakland, 1956).

The clinical and social importance of a better understanding of discrepancies among communication channels has been recently implied in a study of the treatment of alcoholism. Tape recordings were made of nine physicians' voices as they talked about their experiences with alcoholic patients. There was no relationship between the amount of hostility judges perceived in the doctors' speech and the doctors' effectiveness in getting alcoholics to accept treatment. However, when the content was filtered out of the tape recordings, the degree of hostility found in the doctors' tone of voice alone was found to correlate significantly and negatively with his success in influencing alcoholics to accept treatment ($r = -.65, p = .06$; Milmoe, Rosenthal, Blane, Chafetz, & Wolf, 1967).

BEYOND THE EXPERIMENTER-SUBJECT DYAD

The particular patterns of covert communication which have been described as relevant to the experimenter's communication of his expectancy to his subject are no doubt specific to the type of experiment being performed. We are in no position to speak for the generality of any of these findings across different experiments, much less for their generality in the other "real world," that one outside the laboratory. But there are some conclusions to be drawn from the data presented here and from the program of research which has investigated the effects of the experimenter's expectancy.

Perhaps the most compelling and most general conclusion is that human beings can engage in highly effective and influential unprogrammed and unintended communication with one another. If such communication is responsible in the psychological experiment for the fulfillment of the experimenter's expectancy, it might also be responsible for the fulfillment of other expectancies held by humans outside the laboratory. If rats learn better when their experimenter thinks they will, then children may learn better if their teachers think they will.

The experiment, a longitudinal one, is not yet completed, but the results for the first year can be given (Rosenthal & Jacobson, 1966). The procedure was exactly as in the experiments on the effects of the experimenter's expectancy. All the children in an elementary school were given an intelligence test which was disguised as a test which would predict academic "blooming." There were 18 classes, 3 at each of six grade levels. By the use of a table of random numbers, about 20% of the children in each class were chosen for the experimental condition. The experimental treatment consisted of telling their teachers that they had scored on the predictive achievement test such that they would show unusual intellectual development within the next academic year. At the end of the academic year the children were retested with the same test of intelligence. For the 18 classes combined, children whose teachers expected them to gain in performance showed a significantly greater gain in IQ than did the control children, ($p < .02$), though the mean relative gain in

IQ was small (3.8 points). Teachers' expectancies, it turned out, made little difference in the upper grades. But at the lower levels the effects were dramatic. First graders purported to be bloomers gained 15.4 IQ points more than did the control children ($p = .002$), and the mean relative gain in one classroom was 25 points. In the second grade, the relative gain was 9.5 IQ points ($p < .02$), with one of the classes showing a mean gain of 18 points. These effects were especially surprising in view of the large gains in IQ made by the control group, which had to be surpassed by the experimental groups. Thus first graders in the control group gained 12 IQ points and second graders gained 7 IQ points, somewhat larger than might simply be ascribed to practice effects. More likely, the entire school was affected to some degree by being involved in an experiment with consequent good effects on the children's performance.[3]

Experimenters, teachers, probably psychotherapists, and probably "ordinary" people can affect the behavior of those with whom they interact by virtue of their expectations of what that behavior will be. Of course we must now try to learn how such communication takes place—how teachers communicate their expectations to their pupils. Considering the difficulties we have had in trying to answer that same question for the case of experimenters, whose inputs into the experimenter-subject interaction could be much more easily controlled and observed, we should not expect a quick or an easy solution. But there may be consolation drawn from the conviction that, at least, the problem is worth the effort.

REFERENCES

Aronson, E., Carlsmith, J. M., & Darley, J. M. The effects of expectancy on volunteering for an unpleasant experience. *Journal of Abnormal and Social Psychology*, 1963, **66**, 220–224.

Bateson, G., Jackson, D. D., Haley, J., & Weakland, J. H. Toward a theory of schizophrenia. *Behavioral Science*, 1956, **1**, 251–264.

Carlsmith, J. M., & Aronson, E. Some hedonic consequences of the confirmation and disconfirmation of expectancies. *Journal of Abnormal and Social Psychology*, 1963, **66**, 151–156.

Crowne, D. P., & Marlowe, D. *The approval motive.* New York: Wiley, 1964.

Friedman, N. The psychological experiment as a social interaction. Unpublished doctoral dissertation, Harvard University, 1964.

Gordon, L. V., & Durea, M. A. The effect of discouragement on the revised Stanford Binet Scale. *Journal of Genetic Psychology*, 1948, **73**, 201–207.

Harvey, O. J., & Clapp, W. F. Hope, expectancy, and reactions to the unexpected. *Journal of Personality and Social Psychology*, 1965, **2**, 45–52.

---

[3] These findings raise the question of what proportion of the effects of contemporary educational programs are due to the content of the programs rather than to the administrators' and teachers' expectancies. The social importance of these programs, to say nothing of the financial costs, make it appear important that program evaluations employ some form of "expectancy control group" (Rosenthal, 1966).

Hefferline, R. F. Learning theory and clinical psychology—an eventual symbiosis ? In A. J. Bachrach (Ed.), *Experimental foundations of clinical psychology*. New York: Basic Books, 1962. Pp. 97–138.

Katz, R. Body language: a study in unintentional communication. Unpublished doctoral dissertation, Harvard University, 1964.

Luft, J. Interaction and projection. *Journal of Projective Techniques*, 1953, **17**, 489–492.

Mills, T. M. A sleeper variable in small groups research: the experimenter. *Pacific Sociological Review*, 1962, **5**, 21–28.

Milmoe, S., Rosenthal, R., Blane, H. T., Chafetz, M. E., & Wolf, I. The doctor's voice: post-dictor of successful referral of alcoholic patients. *Journal of Abnormal Psychology*, 1967, **72**, 78–84.

Mintz, N. On the psychology of aesthetics and architecture. Unpublished manuscript, Brandeis University, 1957.

Orne, M. T. On the social psychology of the psychological experiment: with particular reference to demand characteristics and their implications. *American Psychologist*, 1962, **17**, 776–783.

Pfungst, O. *Clever Hans (the horse of Mr. von Osten): a contribution to experimental, animal, and human psychology*. Trans. C. L. Rahn. New York: Holt, 1911. Republished, 1965.

Reece, M. M., & Whitman, R.N. Expressive movements, warmth, and verbal reinforcements. *Journal of Abnormal and Social Psychology*, 1962, **64**, 234–236.

Riecken, H. W. A program for research on experiments in social psychology. In N. F. Washburne (Ed.), *Decisions, values and groups*. Vol. 2. New York: Pergamon Press, 1962. Pp. 25–41.

Ringuette, E. L., & Kennedy, T. An experimental study of the double bind hypothesis. *Journal of Abnormal Psychology*, 1966, **71**, 136–141.

Rosenthal, R. The effect of the experimenter on the results of psychological research. In B. A. Maher (Ed.), *Progress in experimental personality research*. Vol. 1. New York: Academic Press, 1964. Pp. 79–114.

Rosenthal, R. *Experimenter effects in behavioral research*. New York: Appleton-Century-Crofts, 1966.

Rosenthal, R., & Jacobson, L. Teachers' expectancies: determinants of pupils' IQ gains. *Psychological Reports*, 1966, **19**, 115–118.

Rosenthal, R., Kohn, P., Greenfield, P. M., & Carota, N. Experimenters' hypothesis-confirmation and mood as determinants of experimental results. *Perceptual and Motor Skills*, 1965, **20**, 1237–1252.

Rosenthal, R., Persinger, G. W., Mulry, R. C., Vikan-Kline, L., & Grothe, M. Changes in experimental hypotheses as determinants of experimental results. *Journal of Projective Techniques and Personality Assessment*, 1964a, **28**, 465–469.

Rosenthal, R., Persinger, G. W., Mulry, R. C., Vikan-Kline, L., & Grothe, M. Emphasis on experimental procedure, sex of subjects, and the biasing effects of experimental hypotheses. *Journal of Projective Techniques and Personality Assessment*, 1964b, **28**, 470–473.

Sampson, E. E., & Sibley, L. B. A further examination of the confirmation or non-confirmation of expectancies and desires. *Journal of Personality and Social Psychology*, 1965, **2**, 133–137.

Sarason, I. G. The human reinforcer in verbal behavior research. In L. Krasner &

L. P. Ullman (Eds.), *Research in behavior modifications: new developments and implications.* New York: Holt, Rinehart & Winston, 1965. Pp. 231–243.

Shapiro, J. L. The effects of sex, instructional set, and the problem of awareness in a verbal conditioning paradigm. Unpublished master's thesis, Northwestern University, 1966.

Stevenson, H. W. Social reinforcement of children's behavior. In L. P. Lipsitt & C. C. Spiker (Eds.), *Advances in child development and behavior.* Vol. 2. New York: Academic Press, 1965. Pp. 97–126.

Taylor, J. A. A personality scale of manifest anxiety. *Journal of Abnormal and Social Psychology*, 1953, **48**, 285–290.

18. Human Use of Human Subjects: The Problem of Deception in Social Psychological Experiments[1]

Herbert C. Kelman

Dr. Kelman discusses both the ethical and the methodological implications of a practice frequently used in certain types of psychological research: deception of the subject. This problem assumes serious proportions because of the many instances when an experiment requires the concealment of the true purpose and conditions, when false information is deliberately given the subject, or when he is exposed to embarrassing, painful, or humiliating consequences. Dr. Kelman cites examples of studies, the conduct of which is perhaps questionable from an ethical standpoint. A serious methodological implication of such deception is the increasing suspicion on the part of potential subjects of psychological researchers and their decreasing naiveté regarding techniques of psychological experimentation. Methods of dealing with this unfortunate and serious problem are suggested.

In 1954, in the pages of the *American Psychologist*, Edgar Vinacke raised a series of questions about experiments—particularly in the area of small groups—in which "the psychologist conceals the true purpose and conditions of the experiment, or positively misinforms the subjects, or exposes them to painful, embarrassing, or worse, experiences, without the subjects' knowledge of what is going on [p. 155]." He summed up his concerns by asking, "What . . . is the proper balance between the interests of science and the thoughtful treatment of the persons who, innocently,

[1] A portion of this article is also relevant to the section on "Ethical Problems in Research." Reprinted from the *Psychological Bulletin*, 1967, **67**, 1–11. Copyright 1967 by the American Psychological Association, and reproduced by permission of the author and the publisher. Paper read at the symposium on "Ethical and Methodological Problems in Social Psychological Experiments," held at the meetings of the American Psychological Association in Chicago, September 3, 1965. This paper is a product of a research program on social influence and behavior change supported by United States Public Health Service Research Grant MH-07280 from the National Institute of Mental Health.

supply the data? [p. 155]." Little effort has been made in the intervening years to seek answers to the questions he raised. During these same years, however, the problem of deception in social psychological experiments has taken on increasingly serious proportions.[2]

The problem is actually broader, extending beyond the walls of the laboratory. It arises, for example, in various field studies in which investigators enroll as members of a group that has special interest for them so that they can observe its operations from the inside. The pervasiveness of the problem becomes even more apparent when we consider that deception is built into most of our measurement devices, since it is important to keep the respondent unaware of the personality or attitude dimension that we wish to explore. For the present purposes, however, primarily the problem of deception in the context of the social psychological experiment will be discussed.

The use of deception has become more and more extensive, and it is now a commonplace and almost standard feature of social psychological experiments. Deception has been turned into a game, often played with great skill and virtuosity. A considerable amount of the creativity and ingenuity of social psychologists is invested in the development of increasingly elaborate deception situations. Within a single experiment, deception may be built upon deception in a delicately complex structure. The literature now contains a fair number of studies in which second- or even third-order deception was employed.

One well-known experiment (Festinger & Carlsmith, 1959), for example, involved a whole progression of deceptions. After the subjects had gone through an experimental task, the investigator made it clear—through word and gesture—that the experiment was over and that he would now "like to explain what this has been all about so you'll have some idea of why you were doing this [p. 205]." This explanation was false, however, and was designed to serve as a basis for the true experimental manipulation. The manipulation itself involved asking subjects to serve as the experimenter's accomplices. The task of the "accomplice" was to tell the next "subject" that the experiment in which he had just participated (which was in fact a rather boring experience) had been interesting and enjoyable. He was also asked to be on call for unspecified future occasions on which his services as accomplice might be needed because "the regular fellow couldn't make it, and we had a subject scheduled [p. 205]." These newly recruited "accomplices," of course, were the true subjects, while the "subjects" were the experimenter's true accomplices. For their presumed services as "accomplices," the true subjects were paid in advance—half of them receiving $1, and half $20. When they completed their service, however, the investigators added injury to insult by asking them to return their hard-earned cash. Thus, in this one study, in addition to receiving the

---

[2] In focusing on deception in *social* psychological experiments, I do not wish to give the impression that there is no serious problem elsewhere. Deception is widely used in most studies involving human subjects and gives rise to issues similar to those discussed in this paper. Some examples of the use of deception in other areas of psychological experimentation will be presented later in this paper.

usual misinformation about the purpose of the experiment, the subject was given feedback that was really an experimental manipulation, was asked to be an accomplice who was really a subject, and was given a $20 bill that was really a will-o'-the-wisp. One wonders how much further in this direction we can go. Where will it all end?

It is easy to view this problem with alarm, but it is much more difficult to formulate an unambiguous position on the problem. As a working experimental social psychologist, I cannot conceive the issue in absolutist terms. I am too well aware of the fact that there are good reasons for using deception in many experiments. There are many significant problems that probably cannot be investigated without the use of deception, at least not at the present level of development of our experimental methodology. Thus, we are always confronted with a conflict of values. If we regard the acquisition of scientific knowledge about human behavior as a positive value, and if an experiment using deception constitutes a significant contribution to such knowledge which could not very well be achieved by other means, then we cannot unequivocally rule out this experiment. The question for us is not simply whether it does or does not use deception, but whether the amount and type of deception are justified by the significance of the study and the unavailability of alternative (that is, deception-free) procedures.

I have expressed special concern about second-order deceptions, for example, the procedure of letting a person believe that he is acting as experimenter or as the experimenter's accomplice when he is in fact serving as the subject. Such a procedure undermines the relationship between experimenter and subject even further than simple misinformation about the purposes of the experiment; deception does not merely take place *within* the experiment, but encompasses the whole definition of the relationship between the parties involved. Deception that takes place while the person is within the role of subject for which he has contracted can, to some degree, be isolated, but deception about the very nature of the contract itself is more likely to suffuse the experimenter-subject relationship as a whole and to remove the possibility of mutual trust. Thus, I would be inclined to take a more absolutist stand with regard to such second-order deceptions—but even here the issue turns out to be more complicated. I am stopped short when I think, for example, of the ingenious studies on experimenter bias by Rosenthal and his associates (e.g., Rosenthal & Fode, 1963; Rosenthal, Persinger, Vikan-Kline, & Fode, 1963; Rosenthal, Persinger, Vikan-Kline, & Mulry, 1963). These experiments employed second-order deception in that subjects were led to believe that they were the experimenters. Since these were experiments about experiments, however, it is very hard to conceive of any alternative procedures that the investigators might have used. There is no question in my mind that these are significant studies; they provide fundamental inputs to present efforts at reexamining the social psychology of the experiment. These studies, then, help to underline even further the point that we are confronted with a conflict of values that cannot be resolved by fiat.

I hope it is clear from these remarks that my purpose in focusing on this problem is not to single out specific studies performed by some of my colleagues and to point a finger at them. Indeed, the finger points at me as well. I too have used deception, and have known the joys of applying my skills and ingenuity to the creation of elaborate experimental situations that the subjects would not be able to decode. I am now making active attempts to find alternatives to deception, but still I have not forsworn the use of deception under any and all circumstances. The questions I am raising, then, are addressed to myself as well as to my colleagues. They are questions with which all of us who are committed to social psychology must come to grips, lest we leave their resolution to others who have no under-standing of what we are trying to accomplish.

What concerns me most is not so much that deception is used, but precisely that it is used without question. It has now become standard operating procedure in the social psychologist's laboratory. I sometimes feel that we are training a generation of students who do not know that there is any other way of doing experiments in our field—who feel that deception is as much de rigueur as significance at the .05 level. Too often deception is used not as a last resort, but as a matter of course. Our attitude seems to be that if you can deceive, why tell the truth? It is this unquestioning acceptance, this routinization of deception, that really concerns me.

I would like to turn now to a review of the bases for my concern with the prob-lem of deception, and then suggest some possible approaches for dealing with it.

IMPLICATIONS OF THE USE OF DECEPTION IN SOCIAL PSYCHOLOGICAL EXPERIMENTS

My concern about the use of deception is based on three considerations: the ethical implications of such procedures, their methodological implications, and their implications for the future of social psychology.

1. *Ethical implications.* Ethical problems of a rather obvious nature arise in the experiments in which deception has potentially harmful consequences for the subject. Take, for example, the brilliant experiment by Mulder and Stemerding (1963) on the effects of threat on attraction to the group and need for strong leader-ship. In this study—one of the very rare examples of an experiment conducted in a natural setting—independent food merchants in a number of Dutch towns were brought together for group meetings, in the course of which they were informed that a large organization was planning to open up a series of supermarkets in the Netherlands. In the High Threat condition, subjects were told that there was a high probability that their town would be selected as a site for such markets, and the advent of these markets would cause a considerable drop in their business. On the advice of the executives of the shopkeepers' organizations, who had helped to arrange the group meetings, the investigators did not reveal the experimental manipulations to their subjects. I have been worried about these Dutch merchants ever since I heard about this study for the first time. Did some of them go out of business in anticipation of the heavy competition? Do some of them have an anxiety reaction every time they see a bulldozer? Chances are that they soon forgot about this threat (unless, of course, supermarkets actually did move into town) and that it

became just one of the many little moments of anxiety that must occur in every shopkeeper's life. Do we have a right, however, to add to life's little anxieties and to risk the possibility of more extensive anxiety purely for the purposes of our experiments, particularly since deception deprives the subject of the opportunity to choose whether or not he wishes to expose himself to the risks that might be entailed?

The studies by Bramel (1962, 1963) and Bergin (1962) provide examples of another type of potentially harmful effects arising from the use of deception. In the Bramel studies, male undergraduates were led to believe that they were homosexually aroused by photographs of men. In the Bergin study, subjects of both sexes were given discrepant information about their level of masculinity or femininity; in one experimental condition, this information was presumably based on an elaborate series of psychological tests in which the subjects had participated. In all of these studies, the deception was explained to the subject at the end of the experiment. One wonders, however, whether such explanation removes the possibility of harmful effects. For many persons in this age group, sexual identity is still a live and sensitive issue, and the self-doubts generated by the laboratory experience may take on a life of their own and linger on for some time to come.

Yet another illustration of potentially harmful effects of deception can be found in Milgram's (1963, 1965) studies of obedience. In these experiments, the subject was led to believe that he was participating in a learning study and was instructed to administer increasingly severe shocks to another person who after a while began to protest vehemently. In fact, of course, the victim was an accomplice of the experimenter and did not receive any shocks. Depending on the conditions, sizable proportions of the subjects obeyed the experimenter's instructions and continued to shock the other person up to the maximum level, which they believed to be extremely painful. Both obedient and defiant subjects exhibited a great deal of stress in this situation. The complexities of the issues surrounding the use of deception become quite apparent when one reads the exchange between Baumrind (1964) and Milgram (1964) about the ethical implications of the obedience research. There is clearly room for disagreement, among honorable people, about the evaluation of this research from an ethical point of view. Yet, there is good reason to believe that at least some of the obedient subjects came away from this experience with a lower self-esteem, having to live with the realization that they were willing to yield to destructive authority to the point of inflicting extreme pain on a fellow human being. The fact that this may have provided, in Milgram's (1964) words, "an opportunity to learn something of importance about themselves, and more generally, about the conditions of human action [p. 850]" is beside the point. If this were a lesson from life, it would indeed constitute an instructive confrontation and provide a valuable insight. But do we, for the purpose of experimentation, have the right to provide such potentially disturbing insights to subjects who do not know that this is what they are coming for? A similar question can be raised about the Asch (1951) experiments on group pressure, although the stressfulness of the situation and the implications for the person's self-concept were less intense in that context.

While the present paper is specifically focused on social psychological experiments, the problem of deception and its possibly harmful effects arises in other areas of psychological experimentation as well. Dramatic illustrations are provided by two studies in which subjects were exposed, for experimental purposes, to extremely stressful conditions. In an experiment designed to study the establishment of a conditioned response in a situation that is traumatic but not painful, Campbell, Sanderson, and Laverty (1964) induced—through the use of a drug—a temporary interruption of respiration in their subjects. "This has no permanently harmful physical consequences but is nonetheless a severe stress which is not in itself painful . . . [p. 628]." The subjects' reports confirmed that this was a "horrific" experience for them. "All the subjects in the standard series said that they thought they were dying [p. 631]." Of course the subjects, "male alcoholic patients who volunteered for the experiment when they were told that it was connected with a possible therapy for alcoholism [p. 629]," were not warned in advance about the effect of the drug, since this information would have reduced the traumatic impact of the experience.[3] In a series of studies on the effects of psychological stress, Berkun, Bialek, Kern, and Yagi (1962) devised a number of ingenious experimental situations designed to convince the subject that his life was actually in danger. In one situation, the subjects, a group of Army recruits, were actually "passengers aboard an apparently stricken plane which was being forced to 'ditch' or crash-land [p. 4]." In another experiment, an isolated subject in a desolate area learned that a sudden emergency had arisen (accidental nuclear radiation in the area, or a sudden forest fire, or misdirected artillery shells—depending on the experimental condition) and that he could be rescued only if he reported his position over his radio transmitter, "which has quite suddenly failed [p. 7]." In yet another situation, the subject was led to believe that he was responsible for an explosion that seriously injured another soldier. As the authors pointed out, reactions in these situations are more likely to approximate reactions to combat experiences or to naturally occurring disasters than are reactions to various laboratory stresses, but is the experimenter justified in exposing his subjects to such extreme threats?

So far, I have been speaking of experiments in which deception has potentially harmful consequences. I am equally concerned, however, about the less obvious cases, in which there is little danger of harmful effects, at least in the conventional sense of the term. Serious ethical issues are raised by deception per se and the kind of use of human beings that it implies. In our other interhuman relationships, most of us would never think of doing the kinds of things that we do to our subjects—exposing others to lies and tricks, deliberately misleading them about the purposes of the interaction or withholding pertinent information, making promises or giving assurances that we intend to disregard. We would view such behavior as a violation

---

[3] The authors reported, however, that some of their other subjects were physicians familiar with the drug; "they did not suppose they were dying but, even though they knew in a general way what to expect, they too said that the experience was extremely harrowing [p. 632]." Thus, conceivably, the purposes of the experiment might have been achieved even if the subjects had been told to expect the temporary interruption of breathing.

of the respect to which all fellow humans are entitled and of the whole basis of our relationship with them. Yet we seem to forget that the experimenter-subject relationship—whatever else it is—is a *real* interhuman relationship, in which we have responsibility toward the subject as another human being whose dignity we must preserve. The discontinuity between the experimenter's behavior in everyday life and his behavior in the laboratory is so marked that one wonders why there has been so little concern with this problem, and what mechanisms have allowed us to ignore it to such an extent. I am reminded, in this connection, of the intriguing phenomenon of the "holiness of sin," which characterizes certain messianic movements as well as other movements of the true-believer variety. Behavior that would normally be unacceptable actually takes on an aura of virtue in such movements through a redefinition of the situation in which the behavior takes place and thus of the context for evaluating it. A similar mechanism seems to be involved in our attitude toward the psychological experiment. We tend to regard it as a situation that is not quite real, that can be isolated from the rest of life like a play performed on stage, and to which, therefore, the usual criteria for ethical interpersonal conduct become irrelevant. Behavior is judged entirely in the context of the experiment's scientific contribution and, in this context, deception—which is normally unacceptable—can indeed be seen as a positive good.

The broader ethical problem brought into play by the very use of deception becomes even more important when we view it in the light of present historical forces. We are living in an age of mass societies in which the transformation of man into an object to be manipulated at will occurs "on a mass scale, in a systematic way, and under the aegis of specialized institutions deliberately assigned to this task [Kelman, 1965]." In institutionalizing the use of deception in psychological experiments, we are, then, contributing to a historical trend that threatens values most of us cherish.

2. *Methodological implications.* A second source of my concern about the use of deception is my increasing doubt about its adequacy as a methodology for social psychology.

A basic assumption in the use of deception is that a subject's awareness of the conditions that we are trying to create and of the phenomena that we wish to study would affect his behavior in such a way that we could not draw valid conclusions from it. For example, if we are interested in studying the effects of failure on conformity, we must create a situation in which the subjects actually feel that they have failed, and in which they can be kept unaware of our interest in observing conformity. In short, it is important to keep our subjects naïve about the purposes of the experiment so that they can respond to the experimental inductions spontaneously.

How long, however, will it be possible for us to find naïve subjects? Among college students, it is already very difficult. They may not know the exact purpose of the particular experiment in which they are participating, but at least they know, typically, that it is *not* what the experimenter says it is. Orne (1962) pointed out that the use of deception "on the part of psychologists is so widely known in the college population that even if a psychologist is honest with the subject, more often than not he will be distrusted." As one subject pithily put it, "'Psychologists always lie!'" Orne added that "This bit of paranoia has some support in reality [pp. 778–779]." There are, of course, other sources of human subjects that have not been tapped, and we could turn to them in our quest for naïveté. But even there it is only a matter of time. As word about psychological experiments gets around in whatever network we happen to be using, sophistication is bound to increase. I wonder, therefore, whether there is any future in the use of deception.

If the subject in a deception experiment knows what the experimenter is trying to conceal from him and what he is really after in the study, the value of the deception is obviously nullified. Generally, however, even the relatively sophisticated subject does not know the exact purpose of the experiment; he only has suspicions, which may approximate the true purpose of the experiment to a greater or lesser degree. Whether or not he knows the *true* purpose of the experiment, he is likely to make an effort to figure out its purpose, since he does not believe what the experimenter tells him, and therefore he is likely to operate in the situation in terms of his own hypothesis of what is involved. This may, in line with Orne's (1962) analysis, lead him to do what he thinks the experimenter wants him to do. Conversely, if he resents the experimenter's attempt to deceive him, he may try to throw a monkey wrench into the works; I would not be surprised if this kind of Schweikian game among subjects became a fairly well-established part of the culture of sophisticated campuses. Whichever course the subject uses, however, he is operating in terms of his own conception of the nature of the situation, rather than in terms of the conception that the experimenter is trying to induce. In short, the experimenter can no longer assume that the conditions that he is trying to create are the ones that actually define the situation for the subject. Thus, the use of deception, while it is designed to give the experimenter control over the subject's perceptions and motivations, may actually produce an unspecifiable mixture of intended and unintended stimuli that make it difficult to know just what the subject is responding to.

The tendency for subjects to react to unintended cues—to features of the situation that are not part of the experimenter's design—is by no means restricted to experiments that involve deception. This problem has concerned students of the interview situation for some time, and more recently it has been analyzed in detail in the writings and research of Riecken, Rosenthal, Orne, and Mills. Subjects enter the experiment with their own aims, including attainment of certain rewards, divination of the experimenter's true purposes, and favorable self-presentation (Riecken, 1962). They are therefore responsive to demand characteristics of the situation (Orne, 1962), to unintended communications of the experimenter's expectations (Rosenthal, 1963), and to the role of the experimenter within the social system that experimenter and subject jointly constitute (Mills, 1962). In any experiment, then, the subject goes beyond the description of the situation and the experimental manipulation introduced by the investigator, makes his own interpretation of the situation, and acts accordingly.

For several reasons, however, the use of deception especially encourages the subject to dismiss the stated purposes of the experiment and to search for alternative interpretations of his own. First, the continued use of deception establishes the reputation of psychologists as people who cannot be believed. Thus, the desire "to penetrate the experimenter's inscrutability and discover the rationale of the experiment [Riecken, 1962, p. 34]" becomes especially strong. Generally, these efforts are motivated by the subject's desire to meet the expectations of the experimenter and of the situation. They may also be motivated, however, as I have already mentioned, by a desire to outwit the experimenter and to beat him at his own game, in a spirit of genuine hostility or playful one-upmanship. Second, a situation involving the use of deception is inevitably highly ambiguous since a great deal of information relevant to understanding the structure of the situation must be withheld from the subject. Thus, the subject is especially motivated to try to figure things out and likely to develop idiosyncratic interpretations. Third, the use of deception, by its very nature, causes the experimenter to transmit contradictory messages to the subject. In his verbal instructions and explanations he says one thing about the purposes of the experiment; but in the experimental situation that he has created, in the manipulations that he has introduced, and probably in covert cues that he emits, he says another thing. This again makes it imperative for the subject to seek his own interpretation of the situation.

I would argue, then, that deception increases the subject's tendency to operate in terms of his private definition of the situation, differing (in random or systematic fashion) from the definition that the experimenter is trying to impose; moreover, it makes it more difficult to evaluate or minimize the effects of this tendency. Whether or not I am right in this judgment, it can, at the very least, be said that the use of deception does not resolve or reduce the unintended effects of the experiment as a social situation in which the subject pursues his private aims. Since the assumptions that the subject is naïve and that he sees the situation as the experimenter wishes him to see it are unwarranted, the use of deception no longer has any special obvious advantages over other experimental approaches. I am not suggesting that there may not be occasions when deception may still be the most effective procedure to use from a methodological point of view. But since it raises at least as many methodological problems as any other type of procedure does, we have every reason to explore alternative approaches and to extend our methodological inquiries to the question of the effects of using deception.

3. *Implications for the future of social psychology.* My third concern about the use of deception is based on its long-run implications for our discipline and combines both the ethical and methodological considerations that I have already raised. There is something disturbing about the idea of relying on massive deception as the basis for developing a field of inquiry. Can one really build a discipline on a foundation of such research?

From a long-range point of view, there is obviously something self-defeating about the use of deception. As we continue to carry out research of this kind, our potential subjects become more and more sophisticated, and we become less and less able to meet the conditions that our experimental procedures require. Moreover, as we continue to carry out research of this kind, our potential subjects become increasingly distrustful of us, and our future relations with them are likely to be undermined. Thus, we are confronted with the anomalous circumstance that the more research we do, the more difficult and questionable it becomes.

The use of deception also involves a contradiction between our experimental procedures and our long-range aims as scientists and teachers. In order to be able to carry out our experiments, we are concerned with maintaining the naïveté of the population from which we hope to draw our subjects. We are all familiar with the experimenter's anxious concern that the introductory course might cover the auto-kinetic phenomenon, need achievement, or the Asch situation before he has had a chance to complete his experimental runs. This perfectly understandable desire to keep procedures secret goes counter to the traditional desire of the scientist and teacher to inform and enlighten the public. To be sure, experimenters are interested only in temporary secrecy, but it is not inconceivable that at some time in the future they might be using certain procedures on a regular basis with large segments of the population and thus prefer to keep the public permanently naïve. It is perhaps not too fanciful to imagine, for the long run, the possible emergence of a special class, in possession of secret knowledge—a possibility that is clearly antagonistic to the principle of open communication to which we, as scientists and intellectuals, are so fervently committed.

DEALING WITH THE PROBLEM OF DECEPTION IN SOCIAL PSYCHOLOGICAL EXPERIMENTS

If my concerns about the use of deception are justified, what are some of the ways in which we, as experimental social psychologists, can deal with them? I would like to suggest three steps that we can take: increase our active awareness of the problem, explore ways of counteracting and minimizing the negative effects of deception, and give careful attention to the development of new experimental techniques that dispense with the use of deception.

1. *Active awareness of the problem.* I have already stressed that I would not propose the complete elimination of deception under all circumstances, in view of the genuine conflict of values with which the experimenter is confronted. What is crucial, however, is that we always ask ourselves the question whether deception, in the given case, is necessary and justified. How we answer the question is less important than the fact that we ask it. What we must be wary of is the tendency to dismiss the question as irrelevant and to accept deception as a matter of course. Active awareness of the problem is thus in itself part of the solution, for it makes the use of deception a matter for discussion, deliberation, investigation, and choice. Active awareness means that, in any given case, we will try to balance the value of an experiment that uses deception against its questionable or potentially harmful effects. If we engage in this process honestly, we are likely to find that there are many occasions when we or our students can forego the use of deception—either

because deception is not necessary (that is, alternative procedures that are equally good or better are available), because the importance of the study does not warrant the use of an ethically questionable procedure, or because the type of deception involved is too extreme (in terms of the possibility of harmful effects or of seriously undermining the experimenter-subject relationship).

2. *Counteracting and minimizing the negative effects of deception.* If we do use deception, it is essential that we find ways of counteracting and minimizing its negative effects. Sensitizing the apprentice researcher to this necessity is at least as fundamental as any other part of research training.

In those experiments in which deception carries the potential of harmful effects (in the more usual sense of the term), there is an obvious requirement to build protections into every phase of the process. Subjects must be selected in a way that will exclude individuals who are especially vulnerable; the potentially harmful manipulation (such as the induction of stress) must be kept at a moderate level of intensity; the experimenter must be sensitive to danger signals in the reactions of his subjects and be prepared to deal with crises when they arise; and, at the conclusion of the session, the experimenter must take time not only to reassure the subject, but also to help him work through his feelings about the experience to whatever degree may be required. In general, the principle that a subject ought not to leave the laboratory with greater anxiety or lower self-esteem than he came with is a good one to follow. I would go beyond it to argue that the subject should in some positive way be enriched by the experience, that is, he should come away from it with the feeling that he has learned something, understood something, or grown in some way. This, of course, adds special importance to the kind of feedback that is given to the subject at the end of the experimental session.

Postexperimental feedback is, of course, the primary way of counteracting negative effects in those experiments in which the issue is deception as such, rather than possible threats to the subject's well-being. If we do deceive the subject, then it is our obligation to give him a full and detailed explanation of what we have done and of our reasons for using this type of procedure. I do not want to be absolutist about this, but I would suggest this as a good rule of thumb to follow: Think very carefully before undertaking an experiment whose purposes you feel unable to reveal to the subjects even after they have completed the experimental session. It is, of course, not enough to give the subject a perfunctory feedback, just to do one's duty. Postexperimental explanations should be worked out with as much detail as other aspects of the procedure and, in general, some thought ought to be given to ways of making them meaningful and instructive for the subject and helpful for rebuilding his relationship with the experimenter. I feel very strongly that to accomplish these purposes, we must keep the feedback itself inviolate and under no circumstance give the subject false feedback or pretend to be giving him feedback while we are in fact introducing another experimental manipulation. If we hope to maintain any kind of trust in our relationship with potential subjects, there must be no ambiguity that the statement "The experiment is over and I shall explain to you what it was all about" means precisely that and nothing else. If subjects have reason to suspect even that statement, then we have lost the whole basis for a decent human relationship with our subjects and all hope for future cooperation from them.

3. *Development of new experimental techniques.* My third and final suggestion is that we invest some of the creativity and ingenuity, now devoted to the construction of elaborate deceptions, in the search for alternative experimental techniques that do not rely on the use of deception. The kind of techniques that I have in mind would be based on the principle of eliciting the subject's positive motivations to contribute to the experimental enterprise. They would draw on the subject's active participation and involvement in the proceedings and encourage him to cooperate in making the experiment a success—not by giving the results he thinks the experimenter wants, but by conscientiously taking the roles and carrying out the tasks that the experimenter assigns to him. In short, the kind of techniques I have in mind would be designed to involve the subject as an active participant in a joint effort with the experimenter.

Perhaps the most promising source of alternative experimental approaches are procedures using some sort of role playing. I have been impressed, for example, with the role playing that I have observed in the context of the Inter-Nation Simulation (Guetzkow, Alger, Brody, Noel, & Snyder, 1963), a laboratory procedure involving a simulated world in which the subjects take the roles of decision-makers of various nations. This situation seems to create a high level of emotional involvement and to elicit motivations that have a real-life quality to them. Moreover, within this situation—which is highly complex and generally permits only gross experimental manipulations—it is possible to test specific theoretical hypotheses by using data based on repeated measurements as interaction between the simulated nations develops. Thus, a study carried out at the Western Behavioral Sciences Institute provided, as an extra, some interesting opportunities for testing hypotheses derived from balance theory, by the use of mutual ratings made by decision-makers of Nations A, B, and C, before and after A shifted from an alliance with B to an alliance with C.

A completely different type of role playing was used effectively by Rosenberg and Abelson (1960) in their studies of cognitive dilemmas. In my own research program, we have been exploring different kinds of role-playing procedures with varying degrees of success. In one study, the major manipulation consisted in informing subjects that the experiment to which they had just committed themselves would require them (depending on the condition) either to receive shocks from a fellow subject, or to administer shocks to a fellow subject. We used a regular deception procedure, but with a difference: We told the subjects before the session started that what was to follow was make-believe, but that we wanted them to react as if they really found themselves in this situation. I might mention that some subjects, not surprisingly, did not accept as true the information that this was all make-believe and wanted to know when they should show up for the shock experiment to which they had committed themselves. I have some question about the effectiveness of this particular procedure. It did not do enough to create a high level of involvement, and it turned out to be very complex since it asked subjects to role-play subjects, not people. In this sense, it might have given us the worst of both worlds, but I still think it is worth some further exploration. In another experiment, we were interested in creating differently structured attitudes about an organization by feeding different kinds of information to two groups of subjects. These groups were then asked to take specific actions in support of the organization, and we measured attitude changes resulting from these actions. In the first part of the experiment, the subjects were clearly informed that the organization and the information that we were feeding to them were fictitious, and that we were simply trying to simulate the conditions under which attitudes about new organizations are typically formed. In the second part of the experiment, the subjects were told that we were interested in studying the effects of action in support of an organization on attitudes toward it, and they were asked (in groups of five) to role-play a strategy meeting of leaders of the fictitious organization. The results of this study were very encouraging. While there is obviously a great deal that we need to know about the meaning of this situation to the subjects, they did react differentially to the experimental manipulations and these reactions followed an orderly pattern, despite the fact that they knew it was all make-believe.

There are other types of procedures, in addition to role playing, that are worth exploring. For example, one might design field experiments in which, with the full cooperation of the subjects, specific experimental variations are introduced. The advantages of dealing with motivations at a real-life level of intensity might well outweigh the disadvantages of subjects' knowing the general purpose of the experiment. At the other extreme of ambitiousness, one might explore the effects of modifying standard experimental procedures slightly by informing the subject at the beginning of the experiment that he will not be receiving full information about what is going on, but asking him to suspend judgment until the experiment is over.

Whatever alternative approach we try, there is no doubt that it will have its own problems and complexities. Procedures effective for some purposes may be quite ineffective for others, and it may well turn out that for certain kinds of problems there is no adequate substitute for the use of deception. But there *are* alternative procedures that, for many purposes, may be as effective or even more effective than procedures built on deception. These approaches often involve a radically different set of assumptions about the role of the subject in the experiment: They require us to *use* the subject's motivation to cooperate rather than to bypass it; they may even call for increasing the sophistication of potential subjects, rather than maintaining their naïveté. My only plea is that we devote some of our energies to active exploration of these alternative approaches.

REFERENCES

Asch, S. E. Effects of group pressure upon the modification and distortion of judgments. In H. Guetzkow (Ed.), *Groups, leadership, and men.* Pittsburgh: Carnegie Press, 1951. Pp. 177–190.

Baumrind, D. Some thoughts on ethics of research: after reading Milgram's "Behavioral Study of Obedience." *American Psychologist*, 1964, **19**, 421–423.

Bergin, A. E. The effect of dissonant persuasive communications upon changes in a self-referring attitude. *Journal of Personality*, 1962, **30**, 423–438.

Berkun, M. M., Bialek, H. M., Kern, R. P., & Yagi, K. Experimental studies of psychological stress in man. *Psychological Monographs*, 1962, **76**(15, Whole No. 534).

Bramel, D. A dissonance theory approach to defensive projection. *Journal of Abnormal and Social Psychology*, 1962, **64**, 121–129.

Bramel, D. Selection of a target for defensive projection. *Journal of Abnormal and Social Psychology*, 1963, **66**, 318–324.

Campbell, D., Sanderson, R. E., & Laverty, S. G. Characteristics of a conditioned response in human subjects during extinction trials following a single traumatic conditioning trial. *Journal of Abnormal and Social Psychology*, 1964, **68**, 627–639.

Festinger, L., & Carlsmith, J. M. Cognitive consequences of forced compliance. *Journal of Abnormal and Social Psychology*, 1959, **58**, 203–210.

Guetzkow, H., Alger, C. F., Brody, R. A., Noel, R. C., & Snyder, R. C. *Simulation in international relations*. Englewood Cliffs, N. J.: Prentice-Hall, 1963.

Kelman, H. C. Manipulation of human behavior: an ethical dilemma for the social scientist. *Journal of Social Issues*, 1965, **21**(2), 31–46.

Milgram, S. Behavioral study of obedience. *Journal of Abnormal and Social Psychology*, 1963, **67**, 371–378.

Milgram, S. Issues in the study of obedience: a reply to Baumrind. *American Psychologist*, 1964, **19**, 848–852.

Milgram, S. Some conditions of obedience and disobedience to authority. *Human Relations*, 1965, **18**, 57–76.

Mills, T. M. A sleeper variable in small groups research: the experimenter. *Pacific Sociological Review*, 1962, **5**, 21–28.

Mulder, M., & Stemerding, A. Threat, attraction to group, and need for strong leadership. *Human Relations*, 1963, **16**, 317–334.

Orne, M. T. On the social psychology of the psychological experiment: with particular reference to demand characteristics and their implications. *American Psychologist*, 1962, **17**, 776–783.

Riecken, H. W. A program for research on experiments in social psychology. In N. F. Washburne (Ed.), *Decisions, values and groups*. Vol. 2. New York: Pergamon Press, 1962. Pp. 25–41.

Rosenberg, M. J., & Abelson, R. P. An analysis of cognitive balancing. In M. J. Rosenberg et al., *Attitude organization and change*. New Haven: Yale University Press, 1960. Pp. 112–163.

Rosenthal, R. On the social psychology of the psychological experiment: the experimenter's hypothesis as unintended determinant of experimental results. *American Scientist*, 1963, **51**, 268–283.

Rosenthal, R., & Fode, K. L. Psychology of the scientist: V. Three experiments in experimenter bias. *Psychological Reports*, 1963, **12**, 491–511. (Monogr. Suppl. 3-V12).

Rosenthal, R., Persinger, G. W., Vikan-Kline, L., & Fode, K. L. The effect of early data returns on data subsequently obtained by outcome-biased experimenters. *Sociometry*, 1963, **26**, 487–498.

Rosenthal, R., Persinger, G. W., Vikan-Kline, L., & Mulry, R. C. The role of the research assistant in the mediation of experimenter bias. *Journal of Personality*, 1963, **31**, 313–335.

Vinacke, W. E. Deceiving experimental subjects. *American Psychologist*, 1954, **9**, 155.

RESEARCH WITH
ANIMAL SUBJECTS

The use of animal subjects, particularly the rat, in psychological research, is a legitimate and long-standing area of study in psychology. Due to some physiological and behavioral similarities between animals and humans, it is possible to generalize, cautiously, from the results of animal experiments to human behavior. Also, the conditions and dangers of certain kinds of experiments preclude the use of human subjects and these experiments could not be performed without the availability of animal subjects. Another advantage of using animal subjects is that their pre-experiment experiences, as well as genetic factors, can be controlled with a degree of precision not permissible with human beings.

There are, however, some weaknesses and limitations in research with animal subjects as discussed in the following articles. It is perhaps instructive (but at least amusing) to note that "there is very little wrong with the rat that cannot be overcome by the education of the experimenters."[1]

---

[1] H. F. Harlow, "Mice, Monkeys, Men, and Motives," *Psychological Review*, Vol. 60 (1953), p. 31.

19. The Snark Was a Boojum[1]

Frank A. Beach

In tracing the development and decline of comparative psychology in the United States, Dr. Beach notes that psychologists have studied the Norway rat more than any other animal. Surely this is not a true comparative psychology, he suggests, if "50 per cent of the experiments analyzed here have been conducted on one one-thousandth of one per cent of the known species." An equally clear restriction is found in the kinds of behavior studied by animal psychologists: conditioning and learning have been the major focus. Such exclusive subject and behavior concentration has both advantages and disadvantages. If, however, more psychologists adopted a comparative approach and broadened the base and scope of animal psychology, then psychology's claim to be a science of behavior would be more legitimate.

Those of you who are familiar with the writings of Lewis Carroll will have recognized the title of this address as a quotation from his poem "The Hunting of the Snark." Anyone who has never read that masterpiece of whimsy must now be informed that the hunting party includes a Bellman, a Banker, a Beaver, a Baker and several other equally improbable characters. While they are sailing toward the habitat of their prey the Bellman tells his companions how they can recognize the quarry. The outstanding characters of the genus *Snark* are said to be its taste which is described as "meager but hollow," its habit of getting up late, its very poor sense of humor and its overweening ambition. There are several species of Snarks. Some relatively harmless varieties have feathers and bite, and others have whiskers and scratch. But, the Bellman adds, there are a few Snarks that are Boojums.

When the Baker hears the word, Boojum, he faints dead away, and after his companions have revived him he explains his weakness by recalling for their benefit the parting words of his Uncle.

[1] Reprinted from the *American Psychologist*, 1950, **5**, 115–124. Copyright 1950 by the American Psychological Association, and reproduced by permission of the author and the publisher. Presidential address delivered before the Division of Experimental Psychology of the American Psychological Association, September 7, 1949.

If your Snark be a Snark, that is right:
Fetch it home by all means—you may serve it
   with greens
And it's handy for striking a light.

****

But oh, beamish nephew, beware of the day,
If your Snark be a Boojum! For then,
You will softly and suddenly vanish away,
And never be met with again!

Much later in the story they finally discover a Snark, and it is the Baker who first sights the beast. But by great misfortune that particular Snark turns out to be a Boojum and so of course the Baker softly and suddenly vanishes away.

Thirty years ago in this country a small group of scientists went Snark hunting. It is convenient to personify them collectively in one imaginary individual who shall be called the Comparative Psychologist. The Comparative Psychologist was hunting a Snark known as Animal Behavior. His techniques were different from those used by the Baker, but he came to the same unhappy end, for his Snark also proved to be a Boojum. Instead of animals in the generic sense he found one animal, the albino rat, and thereupon the Comparative Psychologist suddenly and softly vanished away. I must admit that this description is somewhat overgeneralized. A few American psychologists have done or are doing behavioral research that is broadly comparative. All honor to that tiny band of hardy souls who are herewith excepted from the general indictment that follows.

It is my aim, first, to trace the initial development and subsequent decline of Comparative Psychology in the United States. Secondly, I intend to propose certain explanations for the attitude of American psychologists toward this branch of the discipline. And finally I will outline some of the potential benefits that may be expected to follow a more vigorous and widespread study of animal behavior.

Instead of beginning with the uncritical assumption of a mutual understanding, let me define the basic terms that will be used. Comparative psychology is based upon comparisons of behavior shown by different species of animals including human beings. Comparisons between *Homo sapiens* and other animals are legitimate contributions to comparative psychology, but comparisons between two or more non-human species are equally admissible. Like any other responsible scientist the Comparative Psychologist is concerned with the understanding of his own species and with its welfare; but his primary aim is the exposition of general laws of behavior regardless of their immediate applicability to the problems of human existence. Now this means that he will not be content with discovering the similarities and differences between two or three species. Comparisons between rats and men, for example, do not in and of themselves constitute a comparative psychology although they may well represent an important contribution toward the establishment of such a field. A much broader sort of approach is necessary and it is the failure to recognize this fact that has prevented development of a genuine comparative psychology in this country.

PAST AND CURRENT TRENDS

The history of comparative behavior studies in America is reflected in the contents of our journals that are expressly devoted to articles in this field. They have been the *Journal of Animal Behavior* and its successor, the *Journal of Comparative and Physiological Psychology*. Animal studies have, of course, been reported in other publications but the ones mentioned here adequately and accurately represent the general interests and attitudes of Americans toward the behavior of non-human animals. I have analyzed a large sample of the volumes of these journals, starting with Volume I and including all odd-numbered volumes through 1948. I have classified the contents of these volumes in two ways—first in terms of the species of animal used, and second in terms of the type of behavior studied. Only research reports have been classified; summaries of the literature and theoretical articles have been excluded from this analysis.

Types of animals studied. Figure 19-1 shows the number of articles published and the total number of species dealt with in these articles. The number of articles

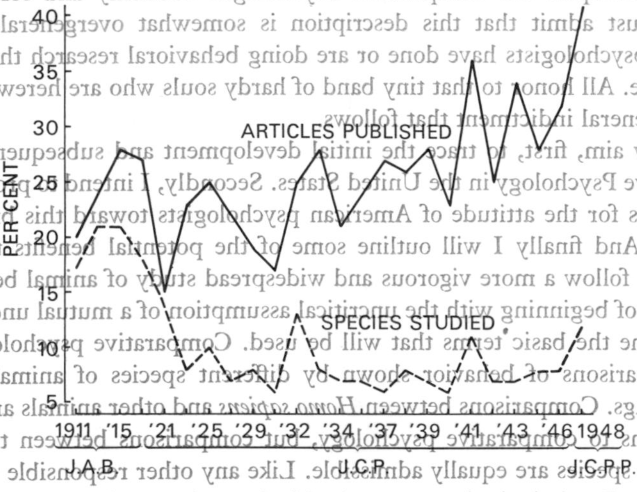

FIGURE 19-1. Number of articles published and variety of species used as subjects.

has tended to increase, particularly in the last decade; but the variety of animals studied began to decrease about 30 years ago and has remained low ever since. In other words, contributors to these journals have been inclined to do more and more experiments on fewer and fewer species.

Data represented in Figure 19-2 further emphasize the progressive reduction in the number of species studied. Here we see that the *Journal of Animal Behavior*

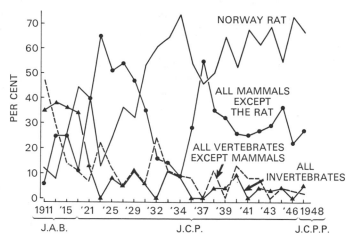

FIGURE 19-2. Per cent of all articles devoted to various phyla, classes or species.

contained nearly as many articles dealing with invertebrates as with vertebrates; but interest in invertebrate behavior fell off sharply after World War I and, as far as this type of analysis is capable of indicating, it never rose appreciably thereafter. The attention paid to behavior of invertebrates during the second decade of this century is also reflected in the policy of publishing annual surveys of recent research. Each volume of the *Journal of Animal Behavior* contains one systematic review devoted to lower invertebrates, another dealing with spiders and insects with the exception of ants, a third summarizing work on ants and a single section covering all studies of vertebrates.

Figure 19-2 shows that in the early years of animal experimentation submammalian vertebrates, which include all fishes, amphibians, reptiles, and birds, were used as experimental subjects more often than mammals. But a few mammalian species rapidly gained popularity and by approximately 1920, more work was being done on mammals than on all other classes combined. Now there are approximately 3,500 extant species of mammals, but taken together they make up less than onehalf of one per cent of all animal species now living. A psychology based primarily upon studies of mammals can, therefore, be regarded as comparative only in a very restricted sense. Moreover the focus of interest has actually been even more narrow than this description implies because only a few kinds of mammals have been used in psychological investigations. The Norway rat has been the prime favorite of psychologists working with animals, and from 1930 until the present more than half of the articles in nearly every volume of the journal are devoted to this one species.

During the entire period covered by this survey the odd-numbered volumes of the journals examined includes 613 experimental articles. Nine per cent of the total deal with invertebrates; 10 per cent with vertebrates other than mammals; 31 per cent with mammals other than the rat; and 50 per cent are based exclusively upon the Norway rat. There is no reason why psychologists should not use rats as subjects in some of their experiments, but this excessive concentration upon a single species has precluded the development of a comparative psychology worthy of the name. Of the known species of animals more than 96 per cent are invertebrates. Vertebrates below the mammals make up 3.2 per cent of the total; and the Norway rat represents .001 per cent of the types of living creatures that might be studied. I do not propose that the number of species found in a particular phyletic class determines the importance of the group as far as psychology is concerned; but it is definitely disturbing to discover that 50 per cent of the experiments analyzed here have been conducted on one one-thousandth of one per cent of the known species.

Some studies of animal behavior are reported in journals other than the ones I have examined but the number of different animals used in experiments published elsewhere is even fewer. The six issues of the *Journal of Experimental Psychology* published in 1948 contain 67 reports of original research. Fifty of these articles deal with human subjects and this is in accord with the stated editorial policy of favoring studies of human behavior above investigations of other species. However, 15 of the 17 reports describing work on non-human organisms are devoted to the Norway rat.

During the current meetings of the APA, 47 experimental reports are being given under the auspices of the Division of Experimental Psychology. The published abstracts show that in half of these studies human subjects were employed while nearly one-third of the investigations were based on the rat.

Is the Experimental Psychologist going to softly and suddenly vanish away in the same fashion as his one-time brother, the Comparative Psychologist? If you permit me to change the literary allusion from the poetry of Lewis Carroll to that of Robert Browning, I will venture a prediction. You will recall that the Pied Piper rid Hamelin Town of a plague of rats by luring the pests into the river with the music of his magic flute. Now the tables are turned. The rat plays the tune and a large group of human beings follow. . . . Unless they escape the spell that *Rattus norvegicus* is casting over them, Experimentalists are in danger of extinction.[2]

Types of behavior studied. I trust that you will forgive me for having demonstrated what to many of you must have been obvious from the beginning—namely, that we have been extremely narrow in our selection of types of animals to be studied.

[2] (Editor's footnote.) Ten years after the appearance of Beach's paper, M. E. Bitterman (Toward a comparative psychology of learning; *American Psychologist,* 1960, **15,** 704-712) noted that: "If we make the computations required to bring these curves up to date, we find no significant change in the state of affairs decried by Beach. . . . If we . . . look at a broader sample of journals, the effect becomes even more striking. *About 90% of our work on animal learning has been done with the rat*" (p. 704) (editor's italics).

Now let us turn our attention to the types of behavior with which psychologists have concerned themselves.

Articles appearing in our sample of volumes of the journals can be classified under seven general headings: (1) conditioning and learning; (2) sensory capacities, including psychophysical measurements, effects of drugs on thresholds, etc.; (3) general habits and life histories; (4) reproductive behavior, including courtship, mating, migration, and parental responses; (5) feeding behavior, including diet selection and reactions to living prey; (6) emotional behavior, as reflected in savageness and wildness, timidity and aggressive reactions; and (7) social behavior, which involves studies of dominance and submission, social hierarchies, and interspecies symbiotic relations.

In classifying articles according to type of behavior studied I have disregarded the techniques employed by the investigator. It is often necessary for an animal to learn to respond differentially to two stimuli before its sensory capacities can be measured; but in such a case the article was listed as dealing with sensory capacity rather than learning. The aim has been to indicate as accurately as possible the kind of behavior in which the experimenter was interested rather than his methods of studying it.

It proved possible to categorize 587 of the 613 articles. Of this total, 8.6 per cent dealt with reproductive behavior, 3.7 per cent with emotional reactions, 3.2 per cent with social behavior, 3.0 per cent with feeding, and 2.8 per cent with general habits. The three most commonly-treated types of behavior were (1) reflexes and simple reaction patterns, (2) sensory capacities, and (3) learning and conditioning. Figure 19-3 shows the proportion of all articles devoted to each of these three major categories.

The figure makes it clear that conditioning and learning have always been of considerable interest to authors whose work appears in the journals I have examined. As a matter of fact slightly more than 50 per cent of all articles categorized in this analysis deal with this type of behavior. The popularity of the subject has increased appreciably during the last 15 years, and only once since 1927 has any other kind of behavior been accorded as many articles per volume. This occurred in 1942 when the number of studies dealing with reflexes and simple reaction patterns was unusually large. The temporary shift in relative emphasis was due almost entirely to a burst of interest in so-called "neurotic behavior" or "audiogenic seizures."

Combining the findings incorporated in Figures 19-2 and 19-3, one cannot escape the conclusion that psychologists publishing in these journals have tended to concentrate upon one animal species and one type of behavior in that species. Perhaps it would be appropriate to change the title of our journal to read "The Journal of Rat Learning," but there are many who would object to this procedure because they appear to believe that in studying the rat they are studying all or nearly all that is important in behavior. At least I suspect that this is the case. How else can one explain the fact that Professor Tolman's book, "Purposive Behavior in Animals and Men," deals primarily with learning and is dedicated to the white rat,

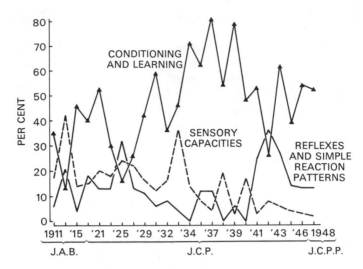

FIGURE 19-3. Per cent of all articles concerned
with various psychological functions.

"where, perhaps, most of all, the final credit or discredit belongs." And how else
are we to interpret Professor Skinner's 457-page opus which is based exclusively
upon the performance of rats in bar-pressing situations but is entitled simply "The
Behavior of Organisms"?

INTERPRETATION OF TRENDS

In seeking an interpretation of the demonstrated tendency on the part of so
many experimentalists to restrict their attention to a small number of species and a
small number of behavior patterns, one comes to the conclusion that the current
state of affairs is in large measure a product of tradition. From its inception,
American psychology has been strongly anthropocentric. Human behavior has been
accepted as the primary object of study and the reactions of other animals have been
of interest only insofar as they seemed to throw light upon the psychology of our
own species. There has been no concerted effort to establish a genuine comparative
psychology in this country for the simple reason that with few exceptions American
psychologists have no interest in animal behavior *per se*.

Someone, I believe it was W. S. Small at Clark University in 1899, happened
to use white rats in a semi-experimental study. The species "caught on," so to speak,
as a laboratory subject, and gradually displaced other organisms that were then being
examined. Psychologists soon discovered that rats are hardy, cheap, easy to rear,

and well adapted to a laboratory existence. Because of certain resemblances between the associative learning of rats and human beings, *Rattus norvegicus* soon came to be accepted as a substitute for *Homo sapiens* in many psychological investigations. Lack of acquaintance with the behavioral potentialities of other animal species and rapid increase in the body of data derived from rat studies combined to progressively reduce the amount of attention paid to other mammals, to sub-mammalian vertebrates and to invertebrate organisms. Today the trend has reached a point where the average graduate student who intends to do a thesis problem with animals turns automatically to the white rat as his experimental subject; and all too often his professor is unable to suggest any alternative.

To sum up, I suggest that the current popularity of rats as experimental subjects is in large measure the consequence of historical accident. Certainly it is not the result of systematic examination of the available species with subsequent selection of this particular animal as the one best suited to the problems under study.

Concentration of experimental work upon learning seems to stem almost exclusively from the anthropocentric orientation of American psychology. Learning was very early accepted as embodying the most important problems of human behavior; and accordingly the majority of animal investigations have been concerned with this type of activity.

ADVANTAGES AND DISADVANTAGES OF CONCENTRATION

I have no wish to discount the desirable aspects of the course which experimental psychology has been pursuing. There are many important advantages to be gained when many independent research workers attack similar problems using the same kinds of organisms. We see this to be true in connection with various biological sciences. Hundreds of geneticists have worked with the fruitfly, *Drosophila*. And by comparing, combining, and correlating the results of their investigations, it has been possible to check the accuracy of the findings, to accelerate the acquisition of new data, and to formulate more valid and general conclusions than could have been derived if each worker dealt with a different species. Something of the same kind is happening in psychology as a result of the fact that many investigators are studying learning in the rat, and I repeat that this is a highly desirable objective.

Another valuable result achieved by the methods currently employed in experimental psychology is the massing of information and techniques pertaining to rat behavior to a point which permits use of this animal as a pedagogical tool. A recent article in the *American Psychologist* reveals that each student in the first course in psychology at Columbia University is given one or two white rats which he will study throughout the semester. This, it seems to me, is an excellent procedure. The beginning student in physiology carries out his first laboratory exercises with the common frog. The first course in anatomy often uses the dogfish or the cat as a sample organism. And college undergraduates learn about genetics by breeding fruitflies. But the usefulness of the rat as a standardized animal for undergraduate instruction, and the preoccupation of mature research workers with the same, single species are two quite different things.

Advanced research in physiology is not restricted to studies of the frog and although many geneticists may confine their personal investigations to *Drosophila*, an even larger number deals with other animal species or with plants. As a matter of fact, the benefits that students can derive from studying one kind of animal as a sample species must always stand in direct proportion to the amount of information research workers have gathered in connection with other species. The rat's value as a teaching aid in psychology depends in part upon the certainty with which the student can generalize from the behavior he observes in this one animal; and this in turn is a function of available knowledge concerning other species.

There is another obvious argument in favor of concentrating our efforts on the study of a single animal species. It is well expressed in Professor Skinner's book, "The Behavior of Organisms."

In the broadest sense a science of behavior should be concerned with all kinds of organisms, but it is reasonable to limit oneself, at least in the beginning, to a single representative species.

I cannot imagine that anyone would quarrel with Skinner on this point and I am convinced that many of the psychologists currently using rats in their investigational programs would agree with him in his implicit assumption that the Norway rat *is* a "representative species." But in what ways is it "representative," and how has this "representativeness" been demonstrated? These questions lead at once to a consideration of the disadvantages of overspecialization in terms of animals used and types of behavior studied.

To put the question bluntly: Are we building a general science of behavior or merely a science of rat learning? The answer is not obvious to me. Admittedly there are many similarities between the associative learning of lower animals and what is often referred to as rôte learning in man. But the variety of organisms which have been studied, and the number of techniques which have been employed are so limited, it is difficult to believe that we can be approaching a comprehensive understanding of the basic phenomena of learning. It may be that much remains to be discovered by watching rats in mazes and problem boxes, but it is time to ask an important question. How close are we getting to that well-known point of diminishing returns? Would we not be wise to turn our attention to other organisms and to devise new methods of testing behavior before we proceed to formulate elaborate theories of learning which may or may not apply to other species and other situations.

Another very important disadvantage of the present method in animal studies is that because of their preoccupation with a few species and a few types of behavior, psychologists are led to neglect many complex patterns of response that stand in urgent need of systematic analysis. The best example of this tendency is seen in the current attitude toward so-called "instinctive" behavior.

The growing emphasis upon learning has produced a complementary reduction in the amount of study devoted to what is generally referred to as "unlearned behavior." Any pattern of response that does not fit into the category of learned behavior as currently defined is usually classified as "unlearned" even though it has not been analyzed directly. Please note that the classification is made in strictly negative terms *in spite of the fact that the positive side of the implied dichotomy is very poorly defined*. Specialists in learning are not in accord as to the nature of the processes involved, nor can they agree concerning the number and kinds of learning that may occur. But in spite of this uncertainty most "learning psychologists" confidently identify a number of complex behavior patterns as "unlearned." Now the obvious question arises: Unless we know what learning is—unless we can recognize it in all of its manifestations—how in the name of common sense can we identify any reaction as "unlearned"?

The fact of the matter is that none of the responses generally classified as "instinctive" have been studied as extensively or intensively as maze learning or problem-solving behavior. Data relevant to all but a few "unlearned" reactions are too scanty to permit any definite conclusion concerning the role of experience in the shaping of the response. And those few cases in which an exhaustive analysis has been attempted show that the development of the behavior under scrutiny is usually more complicated than a superficial examination could possibly indicate.

For example, there is a moth which always lays its eggs on hackberry leaves. Females of each new generation select hackberry as an oviposition site and ignore other potential host plants. However, the eggs can be transferred to apple leaves, and when this is done the larvae develop normally. Then when adult females that have spent their larval stages on apple leaves are given a choice of materials upon which to deposit their eggs, a high proportion of them select apple leaves in preference to hackberry. This control of adult behavior by the larval environment does not fit into the conventional pigeon-hole labeled "instinct," and neither can it be placed in the category of "learning." Perhaps we need more categories. Certainly we need more data on more species and more kinds of behavior.

Primiparous female rats that have been reared in isolation usually display biologically effective maternal behavior when their first litter is born. The young ones are cleaned of fetal membranes, retrieved to the nest, and suckled regularly. However, females that have been reared under conditions in which it was impossible for them to groom their own bodies often fail to clean and care for their newborn offspring. Observations of this nature cannot be disposed of by saying that the maternal reactions are "learned" rather than "instinctive." The situation is not so simple as that. In some way the early experience of the animal prepares her for effective maternal performance even though none of the specifically maternal responses are practiced before parturition.

It seems highly probable that when sufficient attention is paid to the so-called "instinctive" patterns, we will find that their development involves processes of which current theories take no account. What these processes may be we shall not discover by continuing to concentrate on learning as we are now studying it. And yet it is difficult to see how a valid theory of learning can be formulated without a better understanding of the behavior that learning theorists are presently categorizing as "unlearned."

POTENTIAL RETURNS FROM THE COMPARATIVE APPROACH

If more experimental psychologists would adopt a broadly comparative approach, several important goals might be achieved. Some of the returns are fairly specific and can be described in concrete terms. Others are more general though no less important.

Specific advantages. I have time to list only a few of the specific advantages which can legitimately be expected to result from the application of comparative methods in experimental psychology. In general, it can safely be predicted that some of the most pressing questions that we are now attempting to answer by studying a few species and by employing only a few experimental methods would be answered more rapidly and adequately if the approach were broadened.

Let us consider learning as one example. Comparative psychology offers many opportunities for examination of the question as to whether there are one or many kinds of learning and for understanding the rôle of learning in the natural lives of different species. Tinbergen (1942) has reported evidence indicating the occurrence of one-trial learning in the behavior of hunting wasps. He surrounded the opening of the insect's burrow with small objects arranged in a particular pattern. When she emerged, the wasp circled above the nest opening for a few seconds in the usual fashion and then departed on a hunting foray. Returning after more than an hour, the insect oriented directly to the pattern stimulus to which she had been exposed only once. If the pattern was moved during the female's absence she was able to recognize it immediately in its new location.

Lorenz's concept of "imprinting" offers the learning psychologist material for new and rewarding study. Lorenz (1935) has observed that young birds of species that are both precocial and social quickly become attached to adults of their own kind and tend to follow them constantly. Newly-hatched birds that are reared by parents of a foreign species often form associations with others of the foster species and never seek the company of their own kind. A series of experiments with incubator-reared birds convinced Lorenz that the processes underlying this sort of behavior must occur very early in life, perhaps during the first day or two after hatching, and that they are irreversible, or, to phrase it in other terms, that they are not extinguished by removal of reinforcement.

J. P. Scott's studies (1945) of domestic sheep reveal the importance of early learning in the formation of gregarious habits. Conventional learning theories appear adequate to account for the phenomena, but it is instructive to observe the manner in which the typical species pattern of social behavior is built up as a result of reinforcement afforded by maternal attentions during the nursing period.

The general importance of drives in any sort of learning is widely emphasized. Therefore it would seem worth while to study the kinds of drives that appear to motivate different kinds of animals. In unpublished observations upon the ferret, Walter Miles found that hunger was not sufficient to produce maze learning. Despite prolonged periods of food deprivation, animals of this species continue to explore every blind alley on the way to the goal box.

Additional evidence in the same direction is found in the studies of Gordon (1943) who reports that non-hungry chipmunks will solve mazes and problem boxes when rewarded with peanuts which the animals store in their burrows but do not eat immediately. Does this represent a "primary" drive to hoard food or an "acquired" one based upon learning?

Many experimentalists are concerned with problems of sensation and perception; and here too there is much to be gained from the comparative approach. Frings' studies (1948) of chemical sensitivity in caterpillars, rabbits and men promise to increase our understanding of the physiological basis for gustatory sensations. In all three species there appears to be a constant relationship between the ionic characteristics of the stimulus material and its effectiveness in evoking a sensory discharge. The investigations of Miles and Beck (1949) on reception of chemical stimuli by honey bees and cockroaches provides a test for the theory of these workers concerning the human sense of smell.

The physical basis for vision and the role of experience in visual perception have been studied in a few species but eventually it must be investigated on a broader comparative basis if we are to arrive at any general understanding of the basic principles involved. Lashley and Russell (1934) found that rats reared in darkness give evidence of distance perception without practice; and Hebb (1937) added the fact that figure-ground relationships are perceived by visually-naive animals of this species. Riesen's (1947) report of functional blindness in apes reared in darkness with gradual acquisition of visually-directed habits argues for a marked difference between rodents and anthropoids; and Senden's (1932) descriptions of the limited visual capacities of human patients after removal of congenital cataract appear to support the findings on apes. But the difference, if it proves to be a real one, is not purely a function of evolutionary status of the species involved. Breder and Rasquin (1947) noted that fish with normal eyes but without any visual experience are unable to respond to food particles on the basis of vision.

I have already mentioned the necessity for more extensive examination of those patterns of behavior that are currently classified as "instinctive." There is only one way to approach this particular problem and that is through comparative psychology. The work that has been done thus far on sexual and parental behavior testifies, I believe, to the potential returns that can be expected if a more vigorous attack is launched on a broader front.

We are just beginning to appreciate the usefulness of a comparative study of social behavior. The findings of Scott which I mentioned earlier point to the potential advantages of using a variety of animal species in our investigation of interaction between members of a social group. Carpenter's (1942) admirable descriptions of group behavior in free-living monkeys point the way to a better understanding of dominance, submission, and leadership.

One more fairly specific advantage of exploring the comparative method in psychology lies in the possibility that by this means the experimentalist can often discover a particular animal species that is specially suited to the problem with which he is concerned. For example, in recent years a considerable amount of work has been done on hoarding behavior in the laboratory rat. The results are interesting, but they indicate that some rats must learn to hoard and some never do so. Now this is not surprising since Norway rats rarely hoard food under natural conditions. Would it not seem reasonable to begin the work with an animal that is a natural hoarder? Chipmunks, squirrels, mice of the genus *Peromyscus,* or any one of several other experimental subjects would seem to be much more appropriate.

And now, as a final word, I want to mention briefly a few of the more general facts that indicate the importance of developing comparative psychology.

General advantages. For some time it has·been obvious that psychology in this country is a rapidly expanding discipline. Examination of the membership roles of the several Divisions of this Association shows two things. First, that the number of psychologists is increasing at a prodigious rate; and second that the growth is asymmetrical in the sense that the vast majority of new workers are turning to various applied areas such as industrial and clinical psychology.

It is generally recognized that the applied workers in any science are bound to rely heavily upon "pure" or "fundamental" research for basic theories, for general methodology and for new points of view. I do not suggest that we, as experimentalists, should concern ourselves with a comparative approach to practical problems of applied psychology. But I do mean to imply that if we intend to maintain our status as indispensable contributors to the science of behavior, we will have to broaden our attack upon the basic problems of the discipline. This will sometimes mean sacrificing some of the niceties of laboratory research in order to deal with human beings under less artificial conditions. It may also mean expanding the number of non-human species studied and the variety of behavior patterns investigated.

Only by encouraging and supporting a larger number of comparative investigations can psychology justify its claim to being a true science of behavior. European students in this field have justly condemned Americans for the failure to study behavior in a sufficiently large number of representative species. And non-psychologists in this country are so well aware of our failure to develop the field that they think of animal behavior as a province of general zoology rather than psychology. Top-rank professional positions that might have been filled by psychologically trained investigators are today occupied by biologists. Several large research foundations are presently supporting extensive programs of investigation into the behavior of sub-human animals, and only in one instance is the program directed by a psychologist.

CONCLUSION

If we as experimental psychologists are missing an opportunity to make significant contributions to natural science—if we are failing to assume leadership in an area of behavior investigation where we might be useful and effective—if these things are true, and I believe that they are, then we have no one but ourselves to blame. We insist that our students become well versed in experimental design. We drill them in objective and quantitative methods. We do everything we can to make them into first rate experimentalists. And then we give them so narrow a view of the field of behavior that they are satisfied to work on the same kinds of problems and to employ the same methods that have been used for the past quarter of a century. It would be much better if some of our well-trained experimentalists were encouraged to do a little pioneering. We have a great deal to offer in the way of professional preparation that the average biologist lacks. And the field of animal behavior offers rich returns to the psychologist who will devote himself to its exploration.

I do not anticipate that the advanced research worker whose main experimental program is already mapped out will be tempted by any argument to shift to an entirely new field. But those of us who have regular contact with graduate students can do them a service by pointing out the possibilities of making a real contribution to the science of psychology through the medium of comparative studies. And even in the absence of professorial guidance the alert beginner who is looking for unexplored areas in which he can find new problems and develop new methods of attacking unsettled issues would be wise to give serious consideration to comparative psychology as a field of professional specialization.

REFERENCES

Breder, C. M., & Rasquin, P. Comparative studies in the light sensitivity of blind characins from a series of Mexican caves. *Bulletin of the American Museum of Natural History*, 1947, **89**, Article 5, 325–351.

Carpenter, C. R. Characteristics of social behavior in nonhuman primates. *Transactions of the New York Academy of Sciences*, 1942, Ser. 2, **4**, No. 8, 248.

Frings, H. A contribution to the comparative physiology of contact chemoreception. *Journal of Comparative and Physiological Psychology*, 1948, **41**, 25–35.

Gordon, K. The natural history and behavior of the western chipmunk and the mantled ground squirrel. *Oregon State Monograph Studies in Zoology*, 1943, No. 5, 7–104.

Hebb, D. O. The innate organization of visual activity. I. Perception of figures by rats reared in total darkness. *Journal of General Psychology*, 1937, **51**, 101–126.

Lashley, K. S., & Russell, J. T. The mechanism of vision. XI. A preliminary test of innate organization. *Journal of Genetic Psychology*, 1934, **45**, 136–144.

Lorenz, K. Der Kumpan in der Umwelt des Vogels. *J. f. Ornith.*, 1935, **83**, 137–213.

Miles, W. R., & Beck, L. H. Infrared absorption in field studies of olfaction in honeybees. *Proceedings of the National Academy of Sciences*, 1949, **35**(6), 292–310.

Riesen, A. H. The development of visual perception in man and chimpanzee. *Science*, 1947, **106**, 107–108.

Scott, J. P. Social behavior, organization and leadership in a small flock of domestic sheep. *Comparative Psychology Monographs*, 1945, **18**(4), 1–29.

Senden, M. v. *Raum- und Gestaltauffassung bei operierten Blindgeborenen vor und nach der Operation*. Leipzig: Barth, 1932.

Tinbergen, N. An objectivistic study of the innate behaviour of animals. *Biblio. Biotheoret.*, 1942, **1**, Pt. 2, 39–98.

20. Experimental Naïveté and Experiential Naïveté[1]

Richard Christie

There is a large body of literature that indicates the importance of early experience on later behavior. Taking this as a starting point, Dr. Christie inquires into the failure of animal experimenters to consider their subjects' pre-experiment experiences as a possible source of influence in the experimental situation. He notes that journal articles provide very little information on the pre-experimental life of the animal subjects. Yet, these same articles rarely fail to describe their subjects as experimentally naïve. He suggests that great variability exists in the treatment of animals in different laboratories and cites evidence that these pre-experiment variations in treatment could markedly affect experimental task behavior. It is also noted that the use of cage-reared rats may unduly restrict both the scope and generalizability of behavioral data.

It may seem to be a truism to assert that early experience in the life of any complex organism leaves an experiential residue which affects later behavior. Students of personality have amassed a considerable amount of evidence relating to the effects of early experience upon adult behavior in homo sapiens (Miller & Hutt, 1949). In view of this impressive array of evidence indicating the importance of early experience upon subsequent behavior, few animal experimenters would deny that pre-experimental experience is important in the study of human behavior. With few exceptions, however, they have tended to overlook the possible effects of early experience upon the behavior of animals. They do not specifically deny that such a problem exists; they seem rather to be either unaware of it or to neglect it. It might well be argued that they hold an implicit double standard in their disregard of such factors in the study of animal behavior.

Beach (1950) points out that 50 per cent of the reports on animal experiments in

[1] Reprinted from the *Psychological Bulletin*, 1951, **48**, 327–339. Copyright 1951 by the American Psychological Association, and reproduced by permission of the author and the publisher. The author is indebted to Charlotte E. Christie for surveying the recent literature and abstracting information pertinent to the pre-experimental care of animals.

the *Journal of Comparative Psychology* and its successor, the *Journal of Comparative and Physiological Psychology*, since 1930 have been made on the Norway rat, although the latter accounts for only .001 per cent of all species available for study. Since the behavior of the rat has been most intensively studied and forms the basis for the most extensive contemporary learning theories, it seems well to focus attention on the area of rat experimentation. A casual perusal of the literature will soon demonstrate that the description of the subjects follows an invariant pattern: "the subjects were N experimentally naïve rats of such and such a strain." What, then, is the essence of experimental naïveté? Explicit is the fact that the animals have never been used in an experiment. Implicit in such a description are alternate premises: either that the animals' previous experience is of no importance whatsoever, or, that it is so uniform that every *experimentally naïve* rat is a standardized little mechanism subject to exactly the same pre-experimental influences in laboratories at California, Iowa, or elsewhere.

Results of recent research suggest that it might be well to scrutinize more closely the implicit assumptions made by experimentalists who utilize rats as subjects. As yet there is not enough evidence to specify precisely what sorts of pre-experimental experiences might affect the experimental performance of rats. There is enough evidence, however, to make it worth while to examine the provocative data. The present paper is therefore addressed to the practical and theoretical suggestions posed by these findings. It will be centered around two queries: (1) Is it legitimate to assume that all *experimentally naïve* rats will display similar behavior as adults? and (2) Does the use of *experimentally naïve* rats unduly limit the findings of experimenters?

THE COMPARABILITY OF EXPERIMENTALLY NAÏVE RATS

The bulk of studies published on animal experimentation in the journals of the American Psychological Association is carried in the *Journal of Experimental Psychology* and the *Journal of Comparative and Physiological Psychology*. In 1949 the former contained 18 articles describing experiments utilizing rats as subjects, the latter 38, making a total of 56 articles in this area. While scrutinizing these articles to determine the pre-experimental history of the animals used as subjects, certain interesting facts come to light.

Source. In 26 (47.2 per cent) of the 56 experiments scrutinized, *no mention was made of the source* from which the subjects were obtained. In some instances the assumption might be made that the animals were from the colonies maintained in the universities in which the studies were carried out. That this assumption need not necessarily be true is evident from the fact that in some studies in which the source was mentioned, the rats used were obtained from both the university colony and from animal supply houses as well as from other sources.

Nineteen (33.9 per cent) of the articles report that the animals were obtained from the colonies maintained by departments of psychology. In five (8.9 per cent) cases the animals were obtained from animal supply houses. Two (3.6 per cent) experiments report the use of rats obtained from nonpsychological colonies, viz., the Department of Agricultural Chemistry and the Home Economics Department. Two (3.6 per cent) other experiments utilized subjects who were partially from university colonies and in part from other sources—these in one case being procured from a local dealer, and in the other, they were wild rats from the Rodent Control Office of the City of Baltimore and the United States Public Health Service. Two (3.6 per cent) other experiments report the use of unselected stock from local dealers.

Aside from the wide variability of strains (which may or may not be reported) from such diverse sources, the factors of differential maintenance schedules, caging, and handling must be considered. When rats from nonlocal colonies are used, there is also the effect of transportation to be weighed. At the University of California the author used in experiments 130 rats from the colony maintained by the Department of Psychology. These animals were obtained when they were four weeks of age and kept until they were about four months old. During this period only one rat died. More recently the author obtained 60 animals three and a half weeks of age from an animal supply house. Three of these animals died in transit, and two more died immediately afterward. Deprivation severe enough to kill 1 of 12 animals during transportation contrasts with the much lower rate found in animals from a local colony. It seems quite plausible that such a difference in amount of deprivation or hardship might have persisting effects upon the survivors.

Maintenance schedule. Information relating to pre-experimental maintenance schedules was extremely sketchy, being mentioned in only one series of experiments. In the absence of fuller information it is necessary to rely upon personal observation. In most laboratories a constant supply of water is available during the pre-experimental life of the rat. Feeding tends to be more varied. In some laboratories the animals always have a constant supply of food available; in others they are fed once a day. The type of food varies considerably among laboratories. In some cases rats are reared upon dry mash, some on wet mash, some on kibbled biscuit, while others have a basic diet to which greens are added. It is impossible in almost all cases to determine from the data given in articles anything about the pre-experimental deprivation schedule of the animals involved, the only safe assumption being that there is considerable variability.

There is one further factor in regard to maintenance schedules which may be of importance. The responsibility for taking care of laboratory animals varies quite widely. In some instances faculty members are responsible for the care and maintenance of the animals, sometimes graduate students have the responsibility, and in other instances nonacademic employees are in charge. It is somewhat dubious to suppose that all of the aforementioned would be equally concerned to see that the animals never suffered deprivation. Within the relatively limited knowledge of the author, there are several instances in which the individual in charge of the animals neglected to feed them on schedule, with resultant deprivation. There is also the factor of accidental blockage of water bottles, resulting in unscheduled thirst for the subjects. Since there is never a mention of such factors in experimental reports, it is impossible to determine the frequency with which they occur.

Caging. Again we suffer from an almost complete lack of information. Laboratories visited by the author vary in having from one to twelve rats per cage. There is no standard cage design so that the size of the cage as well as the number of animals per cage is an uncontrolled variable. The only safe assumption is, unless the description specifically says otherwise, that the animals were reared in cages of some sort.

Handling. Once again there is no comparable information upon which comparisons of pre-experimental life might be based. In many cases when rats are obtained immediately prior to the experiment, the experimenters themselves do not know the previous history of the handling of the subjects. Aside from deliberate handling of the animals to insure greater docility, which is sometimes reported, the nature of the cages used is, in many cases, a determinant of the amount of handling received by the animals. Some cages are constructed so that droppings fall through a mesh floor and it is consequently possible to rear animals without touching them. In other cases bottomless cages rest in pans filled with shavings so that it is necessary to transfer rats to other cages while cleaning the home cages. In this fashion the animals receive a good deal of unpremeditated handling.

Aside from the quantitative amount of handling, there are not inconsiderable differences in qualitative aspects. Some experimenters dislike rats and handle them most gingerly in a nervous fashion. Others are quite at ease with animals and allow them to crawl over their shoulders, nibble their ears, and are otherwise quite permissive in their handling. In uncontrolled observations the author as well as other experimenters have often been able to tell which experimenter has handled which rats by the differences in the quality of the rats' behavior when picked up, as well as the amount of freezing, defecation, and other indices of nervousness when the animals were placed in a maze.

THE EQUATING OF EXPERIMENTAL NAÏVETÉ WITH EXPERIENTIAL NAÏVETÉ

If anyone wished to maintain that all rats have similar pre-experimental experiences, the indicated paucity of relevant information certainly leaves the burden of proof upon the protagonist of this viewpoint. To judge from the superficial amount of information available, the range of variability in pre-experimental care is considerable.

The crucial question in this regard is whether the variation in the pre-experimental life of the normal laboratory rat has any effect upon subsequent behavior in experimental situations. If not, the preceding observations are only of cursory interest; if so, they have an important bearing on the interpretations of experimental findings. Once again we are faced with a paucity of relevant information. There is, however, enough evidence regarding the effects of pre-experimental variables to suggest that the problem is a valid one.

The failure to specify the source of the subjects used in rat experiments may in certain instances conceal the fact that animals of different strains are being used. Pigmented rats have better vision than albinos and would be expected to do better in experiments in which visual cues are important. Some strains have been bred for specific sorts of abilities and will perform differently in various situations. Tryon's maze-bright and maze-dull rats were bred for performance in a tunnel maze. Krechevsky (1933) found that they were responding to different types of cues. He argued that the maze-bright rats were relying upon spatial rather than visual hypotheses in problem solution.

Another unknown factor would be differential breeding in different laboratories of animals originally obtained from a common strain. How comparable are contemporary rats whose remote ancestors were of the Wistar strain? Obtaining animals from different sources also means that the previously cited variables of caging, maintenance schedules, and handling are often unknown to the experimenters themselves.

Hunt (1941) gave rats experience in food deprivation when they were quite young. These rats were found to hoard significantly more pellets as adults than were nondeprived control rats and animals which had experienced an equivalent amount of deprivation later in life. This suggests that experiments involving hunger as motivation might be affected by early deprivation.

An experiment by Christie (to be published) indicates that early deprivation is important in an experimental test of latent learning under reversed motivation. In a modification of Kendler's (1947) variation on the Spence and Lippitt (1946) experiment, it was found that pre-experimental deprivation training had marked effects upon adult performance. The basic design of the experiment involved a single choice point maze with food in the right-hand goal box and water in the left goal box. Animals were trained under hunger motivation while satiated for water. They received an equal number of experiences in both sides of the maze by the application of free and forced choices. In two experiments[2] by the author with subjects which had experienced a "normal" rearing in cages with food and water constantly present, it was found that their behavior conformed to that reported by Kendler. On test trials the animals would continue to the previously rewarding right-hand side whether motivated by hunger or thirst. Two groups of rats which had been subjected to systematic pre-experimental deprivation of food and water extending between the thirtieth and ninetieth days of life displayed significantly different behavior when trained and tested under the same conditions. These animals tended to prefer the left-hand goal box containing the water bottle even though they had never been rewarded at that point.

These experiments indicate that extensive deprivation in pre-experimental life

---

[2] The role of drive discrimination in learning under irrelevant motivation, *Journal of Experimental Psychology*, 1951, **42**, 13–19; A further examination of the non-reinforcement position in learning under irrelevant motivation (in preparation).

will have effects upon adult behavior in certain sorts of experiments. The amount of deprivation necessary to produce an effect and the sort of experimental situation in which such early deprivation might be of importance are as yet unknown. The possible effects of accidental deprivation or different forms of maintenance schedules cannot be specified, although they may be important uncontrolled variables.

As far as the author knows, there is no direct evidence bearing upon the possible effects of different sorts of caging upon the behavior of rats, with the exception of one experiment by Patrick and Laughlin (1934), who reared rats in two different sorts of cages. A control group was reared in mesh-walled cages of the sort which are generally used. An experimental group was reared in special cages with glass walls and without any shadow-producing matter in the cages. When tested for wall-seeking behavior as adults, the experimental rats showed significantly more exploratory behavior in open places. Whether rats reared in large cages would learn different things from rats reared in small cages is a moot question. Ligon (1929) has shown that a cage mate is effective as an incentive in maze learning. Maltzman (1950) mentions a number of as yet unpublished studies conducted in Spence's laboratory utilizing a social cage, i.e., one with cage mates, as an incentive. Possible socialization effects resulting from different numbers of rats being reared together would seem to be worthy of investigation.

The evidence on the effect of handling is, fortunately, experimentally documented. Karn and Porter (1946) compared a number of pretraining experiences: (1) habituation to handling, (2) familiarity with the maze, (3) familiarity with the maze and goal orientation, and (4) habituation to being detained in an enclosure similar to the starting compartment in the maze. It was found that all of these conditions led to more rapid learning in subsequent experimentation. The first mentioned is most pertinent to the present discussion, since it has been already pointed out that differential amounts of handling might occur both deliberately and accidentally.

Although the amount of evidence is scanty, it does indicate that perhaps one of the reasons for the frequent inability of experimenters to obtain comparable results in similar experiments might be the unequal sorts of pre-experimental influences resulting from differences in source, maintenance schedules, caging, and handling. Animals from a wide variety of backgrounds are all *experimentally naïve*; this does not automatically make them *experientially naïve*, nor should it imply that their pre-experimental histories are equivalent.

To assist in the evaluation of experimental results, it is suggested that the following data relevant to pre-experimental variables be included in experimental reports of rat experiments:

1. The strain, source, and age at weaning of the animals.
2. The pre-experimental maintenance schedule.
3. The type of caging utilized.
4. The amount of handling received by the animals prior to the experiments.
5. Any accidental deprivation or other possible traumatic experience.

If these data are included in all reports, it might be possible to clarify the reasons underlying some of the differences in results reported in similar experiments. It has long been a source of wry amusement that Iowa and California rats often perform quite differently in comparable experiments. In this context differences in the pre-experimental treatment of rats are interesting. California rats are of the Tryon strain, are reared in cages from which the animals have to be removed approximately once a week while the cages are being cleaned, and are reared on dry mash. According to Professor Kenneth W. Spence (personal communication) Iowa rats are of Hall's nonemotional stock, are reared in cages which can be cleaned without handling of the rats, and are reared on pellets. In both laboratories the usual number of rats per cage is four, so one variable appears to be controlled. Whether these differences in pre-experimental life are related to differing performance as adults is a moot question. Karn and Porter (1946) found that only one transfer from the living cage to another one and back once a day for six days prior to experimentation was sufficient to increase the "latent" learning ability of rats. The California rats are normally handled a dozen times or so prior to the commencement of experimental training, in contrast to two or three handling experiences of the Iowa rats. Both groups would, of course, normally receive handling the week prior to actual experimentation in order to increase docility. It is questionable whether this would suffice to equalize the effects of differential amounts of prior handling.

The author does not wish to espouse a rat phenomenology. It is suggested, however, that experimenters consider the extremes of the range of restriction of stimuli present in the pre-experimental life of the rat and reflect upon the relatively great importance which variation in these might have upon the rat's life. The more standardized the pre-experimental influences, the more valid the comparison of results obtained from different laboratories. If differing results are still found, the search for the responsible variables can be legitimately delimited to those present in the experimental situation itself.

POSSIBLE LIMITATIONS ARISING FROM THE STUDY OF EXPERIENTIALLY NAÏVE RATS

If, as the preceding discussion suggests, unintended variations in the pre-experimental life of the laboratory rat may be enough to create important differences in experimental behavior, an important question may be raised. What would be the effect of deliberately introducing drastic differences in the pre-experimental world of the rat?

The pertinence of this query arises from the fact that the average laboratory rat is reared under unique circumstances. He is confined to a relatively small area in which he has to engage in simple operations in order to satisfy his needs. The range of potential stimuli to which he is exposed is arbitrarily limited. The activities which, under more varied environmental conditions, might be learned as means of relieving physiological tensions are not developed. His world is relatively static and is not conducive to the full development of the rat's potential behavioral repertoire.

Comparable restriction of experience on the human level is extremely rare. The findings of the retardation of the children in Colvin Hollow (Sherman & Henry, 1933) where they experienced a good deal more freedom than the average laboratory rat, illustrates the effect of relatively meager environmental stimulation. Feral man has not proved adaptive to the man-made mazes of civilization. If the patients of Freud had spent their infancy and adolescence in cages, it is interesting to speculate as to the sorts of personality mechanisms he might have uncovered. As it is, he has been criticized for drawing upon maladjusted, bourgeois Viennese for principles which were generalized to all mankind. If this criticism has any legitimate basis, it is difficult to justify the study of cage-reared rats in an effort to understand the behavior of rats reared in a much richer environment.

The hard-bitten rat-runner might agree with the foregoing comments, but could point out that the simple pre-experimental life of the average laboratory rat eliminates many extraneous variables and leaves the basic ones open for investigation. This is a perfectly legitimate position, although the preceding section indicates that it may be a dubious assumption in view of the uncontrolled variability that does exist. In the initial stages of theory-building simple beginnings are undoubtedly best, but it is the responsibility of the theorist to demonstrate that the principles uncovered in the study of rats with a restricted background are applicable to the behavior of rats reared under more varied environmental conditions. In the opinion of the author, this should be done before application of the principles is made to human behavior.

There is experimental evidence relative to the subsequent behavior of rats subjected to varying degrees of pre-experimental richness of environmental experience which indicates that it differs from that of rats reared under "normal," i.e., cage conditions. The experiments are few in number, but their implications cannot be neglected. In discussing them, reference will be made to quantitative and qualitative differences in learning ability. By *quantitative differences*, we mean that the behavior of the rats with richer experience differs from that of experimentally naïve rats, but only in degree. Thus, although faster or slower learning might be manifested, it would not invalidate the principles governing the behavior of the usual laboratory rat. "Qualitative differences in learning . . ." means that the behavior displayed is interpreted as involving additional principles necessary to explain the differences in performance between the two groups.

Hebb (1949) reports two exploratory studies which are relevant. In the first he contrasted the behavior of two groups of rats, one subjected to "normal" cage conditions, the other to an even more restricted pre-experimental life. The latter group was blinded in infancy, but otherwise was reared under conditions identical to the first group. The animals reared under "normal" conditions were blinded at the age of three months. When both groups were five months of age they were tested in a series of experiments. It was found that rote learning tasks did not differentiate the two groups. In a task involving a change of response given at eight months of age, it was found, however, that every late-blinded animal did better than every early-blinded animal. Hebb interpreted this as indicating the permanent effect of early experience upon problem-solving ability at maturity.

The finding that animals subjected to meager early experiences did more poorly than animals subjected to "normal" rearing suggested a further exploratory study. What would happen if "normal" rats were contrasted with a group of rats who had richer early environmental experience? Hebb took seven animals home and reared them as pets. During this period of time they experienced a good deal of time outside their cages, running about the house. When these pets were compared with cage-reared rats in a total of 21 test situations, it was found that the pets all scored in the top third of the total distribution for cage-reared and pets (25 cage-reared animals were used). Inasmuch as Hebb does not describe the testing situations, it is impossible to determine whether there were qualitative as well as quantitative differences in their problem-solving behavior.

An experiment by Christie (to be published) indicates that qualitative differences do appear, at least in certain experimental situations. In a modification of Kendler's (1947) experiment previously mentioned, a group of rats which had been given extra-maze exploratory experience was tested. The exploration training was given under satiation on an elevated runway and an open table top. Food and water were present on the table, and the animals received 20 exploratory experiences of 24 hours' duration between the ages of one and three months. When these animals were tested under conditions identical to those previously alluded to, it was found that they displayed behavior significantly different from that of cage-reared animals which also had never experienced deprivation. The early explorers did go to the water bottle and drink when thirsty, as contrasted with cage-reared rats which continued going to the goal box containing food where they had been previously reinforced. Richer early experience in this case quite definitely led to qualitatively different behavior.

These findings led to another series of experiments (not yet prepared for publication) designed to determine what effects early exploration would have upon the behavior of rats in place-learning experiments. Rats which were given extensive experience upon changing configurations of tables connected with runways were tested, as were cage-reared controls. Food and water were always present on one of the tables and in the cages. The exploratory training extended through the second and third months of the rats' lives.

The first experiment required the animals to travel from a starting point fixed in space to a goal which was also fixed in space. The route between was a multiple T-maze with nine choice points. The maze was shifted on every trial so that the animals never traversed the same path from the starting point to the goal. Under these conditions it was found that both groups of animals displayed indications of place learning but that the early explorers learned more rapidly, so the differences were quantitative rather than qualitative.

In a second experiment the location of the goal was fixed, but the starting point was shifted in space. The route to the goal also varied from trial to trial in this experiment. After a training series the animals were placed upon a new starting point and had an option of choosing from a number of radiating paths, one of which led directly to the goal. The cage-reared animals made chance responses to the correct path, whereas the early explorers chose the correct path at a significant level. In this situation we find qualitatively different behavior differentiating the animals on the basis of their early experience.

In a third, still more complex situation, neither group gave significant evidence of having learned the problem. Thus, in situations of varying difficulty, it was found that in the simplest the early explorers displayed a quantitative superiority, in a more complex situation a qualitative superiority, and in a very difficult situation no difference in performance was demonstrable.

Interesting differences in the rats' behavior during all the testing were observed, these differences bearing no known relationship to learning criteria. At the inception of the experiments, all rats were given four practice trials on running down runways to food. The early explorers were undisturbed by this training. The cage-reared animals behaved as might be expected. They were quite excited, and there was a high incidence of freezing and defecation. They would not voluntarily advance down the elevated runway but had to be coaxed.

For all three experiments the median time per trial was plotted against the number of trials. Both groups show a typical performance curve in running-time for all three experiments—starting slowly and then reaching a plateau. This plateau was reached after an equivalent number of trials for both groups. Of special interest is the fact that the running-speed of the early explorers was consistently twice as fast as that of the cage-reared animals during all three experiments. At the completion of the last experiment the cage-reared animals had had a month's daily experience on elevated mazes; yet the difference in running time was still significantly faster for the early explorers. Quite extensive adult experience on elevated mazes on the part of the cage-reared rats was not sufficient to compensate for the early exploratory experiences received by the experimental group.

This difference in gross behavior of the two groups was so great that observers who had never seen rats run a maze could readily differentiate between the two groups on the basis of the manner in which they ran the maze. The early explorers were not only much faster but ran the maze in what might be described as a "slap-dash" manner. When approaching choice points (all of which were new to them on every trial), they displayed little hesitancy and would often make a choice without slowing down. An indication of this abandon is illustrated by their behavior when they chose blinds. They would occasionally be running so rapidly that they would be unable to stop at the end of the blind alley and would skid over the end of the maze and slide half-way down the support to the floor before they could stop. They would then climb back up to the maze and start running again, with no observable effects on their subsequent behavior. The cage-reared rats never displayed such behavior. No cage-reared rat ever ran off the end of a maze. Cage-reared rats also displayed different behavior at choice points, since they tended to be much more hesitant with a good deal of freezing and "VTEing."

If further experimental work confirms the initial finding—namely, qualitatively superior behavior in problem-solving situations when rats with a wide degree of pre-experimental experience are used as subjects—certain implications follow. A greater range of observed behavior leads to a broader empirical basis for theoretical conceptualization. Just as the factor analyst is limited in his findings by a narrow range of behavioral correlations, so is an animal theorist limited by the narrow range of behavior exhibited by cage-reared rats.

A further area which could profitably be investigated would be that of various genetic hypotheses in which rats are used as experimental subjects. A good deal of the emphasis in personality theory has been on developmental aspects of learning. These have been, as Gibson (1950) points out, relatively neglected in the area of animal experimentation, Hebb (1949) being a refreshing exception. Many possible permutations of early deprivation and types of exploration and learning are possible which would be of considerable potential value in clarifying various relationships of early experience to later behavior.

The continued equating of *experimental naïveté* with *experiential naïveté* means quite bluntly, in the author's opinion, that animal experimenters are not studying the principles of behavior, nor the principles of rat behavior, but the behavior of cage-reared rats. For many purposes this is quite adequate; for a more generalized theory of behavior it seems to fall short of asking what seems to be an extremely important question: What are the effects of earlier experience upon subsequent behavior?

SUMMARY

A survey of recent articles on rat experiments reveals that very meager information is available on the pre-experimental life of the *experimentally naïve* subjects. As far as can be determined, a considerable amount of variability in treatment occurs in various laboratories. Experiments were cited which indicate that these variations might have an appreciable effect upon the behavior of adult rats and might underlie some of the contradictory findings reported in the literature. Suggestions for additional data on the pre-experimental care of rats were made so that comparisons between experiments might be more validly made.

It was further argued that the exclusive use of cage-reared rats might unduly limit the body of behavioral data, thus having a restrictive influence upon the theoretical inferences made from analyses of the data. Recent experiments were reviewed which indicate that rats with early exploratory training exhibit as adults qualitatively different behavior from that of rats without this early training. Further research designed to ascertain the effects of differential pre-experimental training is needed.

REFERENCES

Beach, F. A. The Snark was a Boojum. *American Psychologist*, 1950, **5**, 115–124.
Christie, R. The effect of some early experiences in the latent learning of adult rats. (To be published.)

Gibson, J. J. The implications of learning theory for social psychology. In J. G. Miller (Ed.), *Experiments in social process.* New York: McGraw-Hill, 1950.

Hebb, D. O. *Organization of behavior.* New York: Wiley, 1949.

Hunt, J. McV. The effects of infant feeding frustration upon adult hoarding. *Journal of Abnormal and Social Psychology*, 1941, **36**, 338–360.

Karn, H. W., & Porter, J. M., Jr. The effects of certain pre-training procedures upon maze performance and their significance for the concept of latent learning. *Journal of Experimental Psychology*, 1946, **36**, 461–469.

Kendler, H. H. An investigation of latent learning in a T-maze. *Journal of Comparative and Physiological Psychology*, 1947, **40**, 265–270.

Krechevsky, I. Hereditary nature of "hypotheses." *Journal of Comparative Psychology*, 1933, **16**, 99–116.

Ligon, E. M. A comparative study of certain incentives in the learning of the white rat. *Comparative Psychology Monographs*, 1929, **6**, 1–95.

Maltzman, I. M. An interpretation of learning under an irrelevant need. *Psychological Review*, 1950, **57**, 181–187.

Miller, D. R., & Hutt, M. L. Value interiorization and personality development. *Journal of Social Issues*, 1949, **5**(4), 2–30.

Patrick, J. R., & Laughlin, R. M. Is the wall-seeking tendency in the white rat an instinct? *Journal of Genetic Psychology*, 1934, **44**, 378–389.

Sherman, M., & Henry, T. R. *Hollow folk.* New York: Crowell, 1933.

Spence, K. W., & Lippitt, R. An experimental test of the sign-gestalt theory of trial and error learning. *Journal of Experimental Psychology*, 1946, **36**, 491–502.

21. Behavior: Confinement, Adaptation, and Compulsory Regimes in Laboratory Studies[1]

J. Lee Kavanau

The thesis of this article is that much of the characteristic adaptive response behavior of domestic animals is lost because they are inbred and many generations removed from their natural environments. The behavior demonstrated in the laboratory is limited and does not display the "full range and vigor of responses" available to the species in its wild state. Dr. Kavanau further suggests that because the sterile cage environments restrict natural activity outlets, the animal, when given the means to modify its environment in an experiment, will repeatedly do so. As a result, the behavior of such animals cannot be interpreted on the basis of the stimulus and response alone.

A few generalizations emerging from ethologically oriented laboratory studies of wild rodents have important bearings on the rationale and design of experiments on learning and reinforcement. Depriving animals of natural outlets for activity by confining them in small and barren enclosures greatly influences their behavior. Thus, when given the means to modify their environment in ways that do not subject them to great stress, captive rodents exercise this control repeatedly.[2] These animals find it rewarding to attain and to exercise a high degree of control over their environment, perhaps in partial substitution for the freedom of action enjoyed in the wild but denied by confinement. Accordingly, rodents repeatedly turn on and off (or otherwise modify) any suitable variable placed under their

[1] Reprinted from *Science*, 31 January 1964, **143**, 490, with the permission of the author and the American Association for the Advancement of Science. Copyright 1964 by the American Association for the Advancement of Science. Supported by grants from the National Institute of Mental Health and the National Science Foundation.

[2] J. L. Kavanau, *Behaviour*, Vol. 20 (1963), 251; "Automatic Monitoring of the Activities of Small Mammals," in K. E. F. Watt (Ed.), *Systems Analysis in Ecology* (New York, Academic Press, 1966), pp. 99–146; *Science*, Vol. 155 (1967), 1623–1639. Also J. L. Kavanau, *Ecology*, Vol. 43 (1962), 161; Vol. 44 (1963), 95; *Animal Behaviour*, Vol. 11 (1963), 263.

control, whether it is intracranial stimulation, a motor-driven activity wheel, lights or sound, or whether it is merely the ability to visit a nest, run a wheel, jump on and off a platform, patrol an enclosure, traverse mazes, or gnaw wood into fine fibers.

The initial responses of rodents in laboratory enclosures do not reflect the preferences or behavior of animals adapted to the experimental situation, but rather those of animals forced to endure unnatural and completely arbitrary conditions and schedules of confinement and experimentation. The time required for animals to adapt to the "insults" of laboratory experimentation is measured not in minutes or hours but in days or weeks.[3] Thus, even in experiments for which the design and analysis do not penetrate beyond regarding the animal as a convenient experimental machine or black box, the responses to daily short experimental sessions generally give information only about the initial, and often rebellious, reactions of the "machine" to abnormal and enforced working conditions. Only studies over long periods permit the delineation of adaptational from adapted behavior.

When a confined animal is exposed to arbitrary or unexpected changes in environment or regime, but is provided with the means for counteracting these changes, it typically does so. For example, if the experimenter turns on a motor-driven activity wheel in which an animal is forced to run, but which the animal can turn off, the animal immediately and invariably turns the motor off.[4] Conversely, if an animal is running a motor-driven activity wheel that it has turned on itself, and the experimenter turns the motor off, it immediately turns the motor back on. Similarly, if a light is periodically turned on by the experimenter and the animal can operate a stepping switch which steps it off by degrees, the animal generally steps it fully off.[5] If, instead, the experimenter periodically turns the light off, the animal, even though nocturnal, often steps the light fully on. Only after weeks of this full opposition to arbitrarily imposed conditions does the animal adapt to the regime and adjust the changed light intensity to a characteristically preferred low level, rather than merely to the opposite extreme of the imposed condition.

Thus, taken alone, the nature of a specific stimulus (or activity) is an unreliable guide for interpreting the behavior of small mammals given control over its initiation or cessation, or both, or forcefully exposed to it. Stimuli which are rewarding or punishing in certain circumstances have the opposite effect under other conditions.[6] The seemingly enigmatic findings on self- and non-self-initiated intracranial stimulation and on the effects of shock on learning and avoidance[7] no longer are paradoxical

---

[3] *Ibid.*

[4] J. L. Kavanau, *Behaviour*, Vol. 20 (1963), 251; "Automatic Monitoring of the Activities of Small Mammals," in K. E. F. Watt (Ed.), *Systems Analysis in Ecology* (New York, Academic Press, 1966), pp. 99–146; *Science*, Vol. 155 (1967), 1623–1639.

[5] *Ibid.*

[6] *Ibid.* Also J. L. Kavanau, *Ecology*, Vol. 43 (1962), 161; Vol. 44 (1963), 95; *Animal Behaviour*, Vol. 11 (1963), 263.

[7] K. F. Muenzinger, *Journal of Comparative Psychology*, Vol. 17 (1934), 267; N. E. Miller, *Science*, Vol. 126 (1957), 1271; W. W. Roberts, *Journal of Comparative and Physiological Psychology*, Vol. 51 (1958), 391, 400.

when the effects of subjecting experimental animals to compulsory regimes and of greatly limiting their control over their environment are taken into account.

Using such atypical species representatives as domestic rats and mice for laboratory studies of behavior narrows the animal response spectrum to a point where its significance for adaptation, survival, and evolution becomes highly questionable. These selectively inbred animals are hundreds of generations removed from the wild. Their bland behavior tells us mainly how animals react to experimental regimes after many of the characteristic adaptive responses of the species have been largely or completely lost. Domestic animals remain convenient vegetalized strains for physiological studies, but only wild animals provide the full range and vigor of responses upon which solutions to the central problems of behavior must be based.

Important advantages to the use of wild rodents stem from their extraordinary capacities to learn complex contingencies and to gain detailed familiarity with a vast laboratory "habitat." Mice of the genus *Peromyscus* have mastered programs in which seven different manipulanda involving four different functions were in use concurrently.[8] These animals also learn their way through burrow-simulating mazes of unprecedented complexity—containing hundreds of blind alleys—without extrinsic reward.[9] There is no reason to believe that these remarkable feats even approach the limits of the learning capacity of the wild animal, although they far exceed the performances of domestic rodents. The animals readily learn to distinguish the functions of several identical manipulanda. Accordingly, identical levers can be used both to initiate and terminate environmental and activity changes, and they can be located at many positions and their functions interchanged and rotated, bringing this variable under close experimental control.

[8] J. L. Kavanau, *Ecology*, Vol. 43 (1962), 161; Vol. 44 (1963), 95; *Animal Behaviour*, Vol. 11 (1963), 263.

[9] D. H. Brant & J. L. Kavanau, *Ecology*, Vol. 46 (1965), 452; *Nature*, Vol. 204 (1964), 267.

ANALYSIS AND REPORTING
OF RESEARCH RESULTS

Once data from psychological research have been collected they must be summarized and interpreted, and for the bulk of research today this is done by means of statistical analysis. A variety of statistical tools are available and most graduate and undergraduate training includes the technical aspects of how and when to use different statistical tests, though not always the theoretical bases of the development and application of such tools. Several of the following articles deal with the sometimes incorrect and inappropriate use of statistics.

Once data are analyzed and interpreted they must then be communicated to fellow professionals, usually through the psychological journals. Several authors discuss the effects of statistical analyses on the biasing of selection policies in the journals which may result in a loss of much important information. That the journals may also be insufferably dull, as some have alleged, is an interesting point to ponder (in a burst of apathy inspired monthly by the new journal arrivals).

22. At Random: Sense and Nonsense[1]

Quinn McNemar

In this discussion, Dr. McNemar focuses on "the statistical weapons that have, during the last 30 years, threatened to conquer psychology." Covering the major parametric and nonparametric techniques, he points to their frequent inappropriate, as well as incorrect, use and concludes that the relationship between statistics and psychology is not of a utopian nature. Turning to the research results published in the journals, Dr. McNemar questions the confidence that can be placed in reported levels of significance. Selective factors operate such that negative or non-hypothesis-supporting data are less likely to be published. Hence, those results that are published "are more likely to involve false rejection of null hypotheses than indicated by the stated levels of significance." The use of mathematical models is also analyzed.

Thirty years ago Murchison's *Foundations of Experimental Psychology* led a reviewer to a gloomy conclusion. To appreciate this, some of you will need to be reminded that said *Foundations* was far more inclusive of psychology than the 1934 and the 1951 *Handbooks of Experimental Psychology*. Our reviewer, after noting that 9 of the 23 authors of *Foundations* were not psychologists, said that the problem of learning seemed to be the only one that a psychologist could call his own. He went on to point out that learning was too much concerned with statistical interpretation of empirical data. Then he concluded that "psychology as a science is now bankrupt" and should be turned over to two groups of receivers: the biologists (broadly defined) and the statisticians.

This conclusion of 30 years ago was not greeted with universal gloom. Your speaker knows of at least one budding graduate student who, at the time, was delighted to hear that a statistician could look forward to employment.

Now all of us who are assembled here know that psychology did not go bankrupt. In fact, some of us strongly believe that our state of solvency is such that we are the

[1] Reprinted from the *American Psychologist*, 1960, **15**, 295–300. Copyright 1960 by the American Psychological Association, and reproduced by permission of the author and the publisher. Presidential Address to the Western Psychological Association, San Diego, California, April 1959. The rationale for the title required 1000 words of nonsense, given to the listener but spared the reader!

logical receivers for other disciplines. We regard ourselves as both the foundation stone and the pinnacle of all behavioral sciences and are even willing to take over a large segment of medicine.

What has happened during the last 30 years that saved psychology from the biologists and the statisticians? One quick answer is that the biologists and the statisticians were appalled at the risks involved in becoming the receivers.

A second quick hypothesis is that psychologists saved psychology by making great discoveries. Do any of you know of any evidence that might support this hypothesis?

A third hypothesis easily comes to mind: great inspiring leaders emerged. Whom would you nominate? Boring in his 1929 *History of Experimental Psychology* lamented the lack of a great man. We fear that history is repeating itself.

A nonsensical null hypothesis is that there are no psychologists today—that those who call themselves psychologists know no psychology. None of us will wish to accept such a distasteful null hypothesis; so each of us will immediately find evidence, in his own mind, mind you, that refutes this null hypothesis. Since there are 374 people in this room, all convinced that the country is well supplied with knowledgeable psychologists, we can readily calculate the statistical significance of our combined result: one-half to the 374th power. This proves beyond a shadow of binomial doubt that psychologists exist today.

But we should hurry on to some specific hypotheses. Strictly speaking, with no theory we should not use the term hypothesis, so we will merely ask questions to which we will seek answers.

Question A. To what extent have the biologically oriented *wormed* their way into American psychology? A sample of 100 APA members, drawn at random, indicates in terms of expressed interests that only 1% can be characterized as fifth columnists for biology. This figure receives support from a random sample of 100 titles in the 1958 *Psychological Abstracts*, for which 4% have a biological slant. Thus we have conclusive evidence that psychology has not risen to the level of biology.

Question B. To what extent have the statisticians taken over? For the samples just mentioned, 1% of APA members call themselves statisticians, and 3% of the abstracts deal primarily with statistics. We would seem to be safe from an invidious invasion by the statisticians; but, before we crow too much about this, we should consider possible inadequacies of our data: maybe the statisticians who get into the APA are hesitant when it comes to listing their interest as stat, and maybe the articles back of the 100 abstracts were shot full of good, or bad, statistics. The answer to this question involves so many complications that we postpone further discussion until later in this paper.

Question C. Having rejected the great discoveries and the great men hypotheses, we next raise the question as to whether the survival of psychology can be attributed to a lot of little discoveries barely significant statistically and scientifically, and to a number of little men who are fairly significant to insignificant others. In answering the first part of this, we are looking for events that do not smell of biology or smack of statistics and that were not anticipated in the 1930 extrapolation by the reviewer of the *Foundations of Experimental Psychology*.

The only randomness involved in this part of our investigation can be described briefly as the random observations of a vagrant and skeptical mind. I invite each of you to consider your own random thoughts as to discoveries, inventions, and concepts of the last 30 years, involving only simple stat and no biology, that have provided activity outlets for those who call themselves psychologists. Now to my list.

Psychologists discovered, but did not invent, the Rorschach. A psychologist invented, without discovery, the MMPI. The availability of these two instruments has kept a sizable number of psychologists busy at the technician level and has also inspired a lot of research activity. Whether knowledge of psychology has increased as a result of our increasing knowledge of these two instruments is debatable. There are among us some well-informed cynics who would not mourn if the Rorschach were banished to the domain of anthropology and the MMPI were given back to the land of lakes.

No doubt most of us would agree that the development of a science depends in large part upon the invention of measuring instruments. Psychologists have come up with an appalling number of tests during the past 30 years, but only a few of these have led to research activity. Most of us will recall the spurt of interest in attitude research following the development of the Thurstone and the Likert scaling techniques. Those in the clinical area will readily agree that a lot of articles have been inspired by the Wechsler-Bellevue, and no one can doubt that the TAT has sparked many investigations. But it does not require much imagination to predict that other instruments will lead to more and more unimaginative research. It is so easy to say: For your dissertation, why don't you apply the ZANY to such and such groups?

A couple of side remarks slipped into my paper here. First, the number of tests produced during the last 30 years far outstrips the number of good ideas as to what to test. Second, too many test builders think that the best way to repel the statisticians is to ignore the statistical and psychometric theory of test construction. The attitude seems to be: what was good enough for Woodworth and Cady is good enough for me.

Perhaps the most significant discovery of the last 30 years by psychologists was the existence of psychoanalytic theory, that inexhaustible source of hypotheses, concepts, jargons, and explanations, and the breeding ground for all sorts of therapies. How could clinical psychology survive if forced to develop a nonpsychoanalytic ego of its own? How could we talk about personality and personality development if we did not have the psychoanalytic vocabulary?

The reviewer of *Foundations* would be pleased at the upsurge of research in learning, but likely distressed by the fact that so much learning research is now being done on that friend of the biologist, the white rat, and by an even greater infiltration of statistics. Not only do we have statistical analysis and statistical interpretation of learning data, but also statistical theories of learning. This is a sad state of affairs for those with an antistatistical bias who happen to regard learning as the only real psychology.

Other discoveries or concepts that have helped to preserve psychology as a discipline include level of aspiration, frustration-aggression, need systems (instincts stink), concept formation, reinforcement, semantic differential, Q sorts of all sorts, dissonance, critical incidents, scaling techniques galore, the new look perception, etc., etc.

Well, having, I hope, made the point that psychology has not been taken over by the biologists, I must go on to consider the inroads of the statisticians; and here I will feel more at home. It is difficult to understand why the reviewer of *Foundations* became so alarmed about the role of statistics. Perhaps his attempts to understand T. L. Kelley's chapters on statistics in *Foundations* gave rise to that affliction, common among psychologists, known as number anxiety. He should have taken comfort from those chapters because Kelley's writing was not easy to understand, hence not apt to promote the use of statistical methods.

Actually, at that time statisticians had little to offer beyond simple (several measures), partial, and multiple correlation, plus a garden variety of significance test known as the critical ratio. But there is no denying that in the '20s an otherwise drab dissertation could be made to look impressive by the use of multiple correlation.

Let us take a look at the arsenal of statistics. What are the statistical weapons that have, during the last 30 years, threatened to conquer psychology?

Aside from goodness of fit, the extensive applications of chi square did not percolate into psychology until the 1930's. Its use has not enslaved psychologists, but its frequent misuse has contributed some astoundingly fallacious significance levels. Perhaps the all-time high in misuse occurred recently when a well-known social-perception psychologist inflated his sample size 36-fold: that is, he had 36 observations on each of 25 cases, leading to 900 observations which were then treated as independent for the chi square analysis. This is one way of getting high statistical significance with little prospect that similar results will be found by those who replicate the study.

The analysis of variance technique did not invade psychology until the late 1930's, and the proponents wrote as though this would be the technique that would rescue psychology from its research doldrums. For a time the statistical power figure in one midwestern department insisted that all dissertations involve analysis of variance. And there are those who seem to think that the more complex the design the better, even though the introduced complexity also introduces bewildering complexity of interpretation. Furthermore, too many users of the analysis of variance seem to regard the reaching of a mediocre level of significance as more important than any descriptive specification of the underlying averages. It can be argued that tests of significance are necessary but not sufficient conditions for the development of a science. Sooner or later we should begin the task of nailing down some descriptive parameters.

It has often been said that psychologists are captivated by the magic of words. One bit of evidence for this is their reaction to R. A. Fisher's book entitled *The Design of Experiments*. The word "design" became epidemic just as though psychologists had never previously planned an experiment. This term is now as much overused and misused as that vague word "pattern." We eagerly borrowed the word design, but apparently very few ever read enough of this Fisher book to get an appreciation of what could be, in my opinion, the most useful of all statistical methods, namely, the covariance adjustment technique. It is a "natural" for the many situations where experimental control of variables is either not feasible or impossible. If the restrained use of analysis of variance has been a boon to certain laboratory experimentation, as I believe it has, the covariance method can be a real godsend to those in social, child, clinical, and educational psychology where frequent use must be made of intact groups.

As most of you know, an invention of the early '30s was factor analysis, a technique usually associated with statistics but which is not at all statistical in the inference sense. Despite glib talk about using factor analysis to test hypotheses, practically no users of factor analysis ever test hypotheses for the simple and compelling reason that it is impossible to test hypotheses with variable data without having an appropriate measure of random error. Then there is the complication that different factoring techniques lead to different results, a fact which seems to be all too frequently forgotten by devoted disciples of a particular technique.

For example, the conclusion is being drawn from factor studies that MMPI scales taken singly do not tap a common trait, that is, that the items within a scale do not involve a general factor. Now this may be so, but it is not proven by using a factor technique which practically precludes a general factor. Indeed, it can be validly argued that for this type of situation one should, in fairness to test authors, use a factor method that lets a possible general factor emerge.

A commonly given defense of factor analysis is that the results thereof, though not conclusive of anything, provide clues and hypotheses for further work. Nobly said; but the follow-up rarely goes beyond more factoring, with results nearly as inconclusive as the first analysis.

The tendency of some psychologists to try to keep up with the Joneses is illustrated by the fervor with which they advocate nonparametric methods as the answer to all statistical prayers. It seems not to matter that the mathematical statisticians have not yet provided adequate criteria for choosing from among competing nonparametric techniques. It seems not to matter that these methods are inefficient or wasteful of data. It seems not to matter whether a nonparametric test will provide an answer to a logical scientific question. What does matter is that we have a set of new toys plus an urge to be up-to-date, so we look around for an excuse for using the new instead of the tried and true. This shows our progressivism, gets us out of the old fogey camp, possibly a manifestation of rebellion against parental authority.

One entirely fallacious argument in favor of most nonparametric tests is that old-fashioned tests presume an interval or equal-unit scale of measurement. We did not need to have a symposium at a recent APA meeting to settle this little controversy. We need to know only that, given a population of measures which are normal or moderately or even considerably skewed in distribution, successive samplings will unfailingly lead to ratios, such as ts or Fs, that will follow very closely their respective theoretical distributions despite the metric or nonmetric character of the starting scores.

In a recent textbook from the Oxford University Press the author carefully nurtures the myth that an interval scale is requisite for the use of means, standard deviations, and product-moment correlation coefficients, then proceeds to use the product-moment r with log transformed scores which most certainly will not be on an equal-unit scale. This absurdity is matched by those who would overcome the lack of interval scales by using Spearman's rho. Now the argument against the product-moment r is that the required processes of addition are not justified unless we have an equal-unit scale. By the same token we cannot use Spearman's rho since it *is* a product-moment r between two sets of ranks and since no one has yet, or ever will, demonstrate that ranks follow an interval scale. If we followed these misguided purists, we would quit computing correlations.

Let me hasten on to say that quite a few psychologists have already found another way to talk about the relationship between variables without ever resorting to a correlation coefficient or an equation representing a relationship. All of you are familiar with the procedure. Scores on one variable are available or easily obtainable for a sizable number of individuals. The top and bottom, say, 10% of cases are then measured on a second variable, and the two means are computed. If the difference is significant at the 5% level by a t test, it is concluded that the two variables are related. A simple design with simple statistical treatment, all leading to a simple conclusion. What could be simpler? And why not such a simple approach? Well, let us take a simple-minded look at this extreme groups method.

Suppose each extreme group represents 10% of a possible supply of 170 cases—that is, 17 high and 17 lows—and that the two-tailed t test yields significance at the 5% level. Now it can be shown that the obtained difference between means corresponds to a correlation of only .20. Let us take another example: 10% of a supply of 440 permits 44 cases for each of the extreme groups; a one-tailed critical ratio test indicates significance at the .05 level. This time the exultation over a significant difference actually pertains to a piddling underlying correlation of .10. Of course, there are those who shout when an actually computed r of .10 reaches the .05 level, but others can see the trivial basis for the shouting. By the extreme groups method everybody is kept in a state of blissful ignorance. Furthermore, the extreme groups design is particularly fallacious in case the underlying relationship happens, unbeknownst, to be nonlinear.

Oh, yes, I hear some of you thinking that the use of extreme groups is economical for preliminary work. True, but so much of what should be regarded as preliminary gets published, then quoted as the last word, which it usually is because the investigator is too willing to rest on the laurels that come from finding a significant difference. Why should he worry about the *degree* of relationship or its possible lack of linearity?

Well, from the foregoing not entirely random observations regarding the role of statistics in psychology during the past 30 years, two rather obvious conclusions can be drawn. First, that psychology, but not every psychologist, has successfully resisted the domination of statistics. Second, that McNemar, being forever a worry-wart about statistical usage, is not yet convinced that the relationship between psychology and statistics is utopian. Whether or not an optimal balance between the two can be attained leads me to a few speculations about the future.

Since World War II, the population of mathematical statisticians has grown by leaps and bounds. This should be a blessing, but there are certain dangers. In the first place, the mathematical statisticians admit that they can no longer keep up with each other, so what is the hope for the rest of us? Secondly, as the statistics departments become stronger and stronger, they will continue (with increasing likelihood of success) their efforts to take over all statistics teaching, and the teaching of statistics at a level comprehensible to most psychology students will nearly vanish.

At this point I would like to digress to consider very briefly the training of psychology students in statistics, a problem with which I have struggled for a quarter of a century. Needless to say, I strongly believe that psychologists should have a sound understanding of all commonly used techniques. This they need for intelligent and critical reading of research literature; this they need in order to plan their own research so as to have an efficient design which will permit adequate statistical analysis. The teaching task is, in part, that of maintaining enthusiasm sufficient to sell but not oversell statistics. I do not want a student of mine to trudge off weighted down with a box full of statistical tools in search of a research problem that permits him to display skill with his tools. The research problem should come first; then at the designing stage the available tools should be scrutinized, but with the ever present thought that there is merit in simplicity.

Let us return to our future mathematical statistician who, aside from *his* teaching, will insist on a few things, among which will be an expurgation of correlation coefficients in favor of regression analysis. Now I have personally been battered around a bit in attempting to defend the psychologist's use of correlation coefficients, and, so far, I have come out on top by the simple device of pinpointing the ignorance of statisticians concerning the problems faced by psychologists.

Another thing that the statistician will insist on has to do with the problem of sampling, and his requirements will be of two sorts: he will make it mandatory that representativeness be guaranteed by appropriate sampling methods, and he will make the not unreasonable demand that psychologists start sampling the universe of people instead of the universe of college sophomores or of Psychology 1 students. His justifiable insistence on the latter point will have two effects: some psychologists will broaden their base of operations, with a consequent derivation of generalizations that will have some generality; while others will scurry to the rat lab with the argument that a rat is a rat is a rat.

A further look in my crystal ball revealed Dr. Statistician and Dr. Psychologist in earnest conversation. No, Dr. Stat was not on a therapeutic couch; rather he was questioning the meaningfulness of the level of significance as used by Dr. Psych. Dr. Psych's first thought, no doubt prompted by guilt feelings, was that he was about to be criticized for using the rather lenient 5% level for judging significance. Dr. Stat said no, that was not his worry. So Dr. Psych said: "Surely, you do not believe that I fail to understand the simple fact that my chosen 5% level indicates the probability of making the Type 1 error." "Oh no, not that," said Dr. Stat. Then he went on to say that maybe Dr. Psych did not quite appreciate some selective factors that disrupt the meaning of the significance levels for results being published in the journals. Dr. Psych bristled at the implication that psychologists had not eliminated the old bogey of selective factors. Did Dr. Stat not know that psychologists know how to design experiments in such a way as to preclude questioning of the results because of selective factors? "Oh yes, I will grant that," said Dr. Stat, "but let us calm down and take a look."

Dr. Stat then made the following points, all of which you will agree have, because of selective factors, a bearing on the confidence to be placed in the levels of significance reported in journals.

First, journal editors may and do tend to reject manuscripts because of so-called negative findings—that is, failure to have statistically significant results.

Second, papers lacking in positive findings may not be submitted by a potential author because of the fear of rejection or fear that readers, if the piece is published, will think he is unable to prove the obvious statistically.

Third, when writing his paper an author may, partly to save space and partly because negative results are of little interest, report from among a sizable number of computed comparisons only those that are significant. The reader is not told about this selection.

Fourth, most psychologists without intentional eavesdropping know that occasionally their theory oriented colleagues simply discard all data of an experiment as bad data if not in agreement with the theory, and start over. The theory is, of course, always good. Keep trying, and good data will be found. Reported ESP results are often criticized on this point.

Thus, we have at least four factors that operate in such a way that negative instances or data that do not support hypotheses and/or theory are less apt to be published. It follows that published results are more likely to involve false rejection of null hypotheses than indicated by the stated levels of significance. Perhaps this is one reason why replications by others so often fail to agree with so-called initial experiments.

At the present time, a new would-be conqueror of psychology is occasionally making forays into our midst. He does not take prisoners, but he does frequently capture minds, with a consequent defection to his camp. His battle cry is that he really has the one and only approach and solution to all, or nearly all, psychological problems. This tends to lure those among us who have a low tolerance for the ambiguity that flourishes in psychology.

By now, some of you must have guessed that this chap is none other than the fellow with his hands full of mathematical models. He will write a model for anything except psychoanalysis, which of course means that psychoanalysis is not science by his standards. In one sense, this model business is nothing more than a new name for old hat stuff. Years ago we had rational learning curves and some use of differential equations in psychology. But these earlier efforts involving mathematics seem to spring from a researcher looking for a tool; currently, someone who knows some mathematics seems to be looking for a place to apply his mathematics. This is on a par with the statistician in search of an application for *his* techniques.

Among things that worry me about model builders is the apparent ease by which a student who has had only freshman college mathematics can build models. One suspects that such building rests on a foundation of mathematical quicksand and psychological bog. Now I would not go on record as opposed to all attempts at model construction in psychology. Indeed, models in the scaling and measurement area have been useful, and the area of learning has derived benefit from mathematical thinking. And, of course, there is nearly always some gain to psychology from the enthusiasm with which the latest wrinkle is pursued, if it is pursued to include data gathering. Data frequently survive the reason for their collection.

This question of the usefulness of mathematical models and, to a certain extent, the value of high powered statistical techniques is debatable. One might turn to the physicists with the expectation that their experience with mathematics would serve as a guide; but, since mathematics in physics is a part of their heritage, contemporary physicists have not experienced the trials and tribulations encountered in the early stages of the mathematizing of their science.

About three years ago, Terman showed me a longhand letter written by E.B. Wilson. Perhaps some of you would like a little biographical information about Wilson. He was made, at the tender age of 32, Professor of Mathematical Physics and Chairman of the Department of Physics at the Massachusetts Institute of Technology and, by the age of 33, had published a fat and awesome textbook on advanced calculus. A member of the National Academy of Sciences, he has been President of the American Statistical Association and of the American Academy of Arts and Sciences and of the Social Science Research Council.

Well, Wilson had been reading a book on mathematical models in learning, which he characterized as beautiful mathematics but questioned as to how much psychology it contained. From this longhand letter to Terman, I excerpted two sentences which struck me as containing wisdom on a par with that found in the Great Books. It is fitting that I close my remarks by quoting these two unpublished sentences from the pen of a scholarly mathematician-scientist. Wilson wrote:

We have to beware of mathematicians; they are indispensable but dangerous to science and scientists. Their indispensability comes in cleaning up a science when it is already pretty well known and their danger is in prematurely involving us in too complicated methods based on premature postulating of insufficiently established "laws."

23. The Difference Between Statistical Hypotheses and Scientific Hypotheses[1]

Robert C. Bolles

What is the difference between the hypotheses of the statistician and those of the scientist? In answering this question, Dr. Bolles states that the scientist attempts to understand some natural phenomenon, while the statistician concerns himself with the mathematical properties of a particular set of numbers. He suggests that when a statistician rejects the null hypothesis he can be fairly certain that his alternative hypothesis is correct. This is not the case with the scientist who must, in the same circumstances, consider whether the statistical model chosen was really appropriate, and whether alternative hypotheses are plausible. Discussing several research examples, Dr. Bolles demonstrates the difficulty for the scientist whose confidence in his hypothesis is ultimately a function of his ability to reject alternative hypotheses, rather than of statistical significance levels.

When a professional statistician runs a statistical test he is usually concerned only with the mathematical properties of certain sets of numbers, but when a scientist runs a statistical test he is usually trying to understand some natural phenomenon. The hypotheses the statistician tests exist in a world of black and white, where the alternatives are clear, simple, and few in number, whereas the scientist works in a vast gray area in which the alternative hypotheses are often confusing, complex, and limited in number only by the scientist's ingenuity.

The present paper is concerned with just one feature of this distinction, namely, that when a statistician rejects the null hypothesis at a certain level of confidence, say .05, he may then be fairly well assured ($p = .95$) that the alternative statistical hypothesis is correct. However, when a scientist runs the same test, using the same

[1] Reprinted from *Psychological Reports*, 1962, **11**, 639–645, with the permission of the author and the publisher.

numbers, rejecting the same null hypothesis, he cannot in general conclude with $p = .95$ that his scientific hypothesis is correct.

In assessing the probability of his hypothesis he is also obliged to consider the probability that the *statistical model* he assumed for purposes of the test is really applicable. The statistician can say "*if* the distribution is normal," or "*if* we assume the parent population is distributed exponentially." These ifs cost the statistician nothing, but they can prove to be quite a burden on the poor E whose numbers represent controlled observations not just symbols written on paper.

The scientist also has the burden of judging whether his hypothesis has a greater probability of being correct than other hypotheses that could also explain his data. The statistician is confronted with just two hypotheses, and the decision which he makes is only between these two. Suppose he has two samples and is concerned with whether the two means differ. The observed difference can be attributed either to random variation (the null hypothesis) or to the alternative hypothesis that the samples have been drawn from two populations with different means. Ordinarily these two alternatives exhaust the statistician's universe. The scientist, on the other hand, being ultimately concerned with the nature of natural phenomena, has only started his work when he rejects the null hypothesis. An example may help to illustrate these two points.

Consider the following situation. Two groups of rats are tested for water consumption after one, the experimental group, has been subjected to a particular treatment. Suppose the collected data should appear as shown in Table 23-1.[2]

TABLE 23-1

Number of Animals in Each Group Drinking a
Given Amount of Water

N	0 cc.	1 cc.	2 cc.	3 cc.	4 cc.	...	12 cc.
Control Ss	15	3	2	0	0	...	0
Experimental Ss	12	3	0	0	4	...	1

After the data are collected, E can pretend he is a statistician for a while and say to himself, "Let's assume the populations are normal and try a t test." The t statistic is encouragingly large but not large enough (which is just as well because of the difficulty that would arise in attempting to justify the assumption of normality). Several transformations of the data are tried, but they don't help. Our E recognizes that he needs another statistical model. Perhaps a non–parametric test would work, one which is not sensitive to the great skewness of the data, and one which makes no assumption about the underlying distribution. A Mann-Whitney

---

[2] The problem, the data, and the claim of significance are those of Siegel and Siegel (1949); what follows is my construction.

test is discouraging. A chi-square test (tried even though the expected frequencies in the important cells at the tails of the distribution are really too small) does not even approach a significant value.

By this time E, weary of being an amateur statistician, consults a professional one who tells him that, *if* we can assume the populations have exponential distributions, then we can use Festinger's test (1943). This works ($F = 4.83$). In due time E publishes a report in which a highly significant ($p < .01$) increase in water consumption is attributed to the experimental treatment.

Inspection of the table, however, should lead to some skepticism. If our E has actually discovered anything about nature, he has found that (1) most animals under these test conditions don't drink more than 2 cc., and (2) his experimental treatment may make a *few* animals drink a good deal more than normal. 4 cc. or more.

It is necessary to digress a moment in order to notice that throughout this whole scientific episode our E's behavior has been above reproach. Even when he was acting like a statistician he wasn't *just* hunting for a test that would work; he was also searching for a test and a model, that would fit his particular problem. The t test will not work, not just because it is inappropriate from a statistical point of view, but also because it tests the wrong thing. The t test tests whether the means are different. The Mann-Whitney test, for another example, is appropriate in the statistical sense, but it too is primarily sensitive to differences in means, and so is likely to pick up only the first phenomenon our E has discovered (that most Ss drink very little) and not the second (that some Ss respond to treatment). E should use a test which is sensitive to his special problem such as the Kolmogorov-Smirnov test which is highly sensitive to differences in the *shapes* of distributions, or a test specifically for the difference in *skewness* between the two distributions.[3]

Enough statistical digression. The point about which our E, as a scientist, should be concerned is the discrepancy between the high level of statistical significance obtained ($p < .01$) and the lingering doubts he must have whether there may be some explanation for his data other than the experimental treatment (subjective $p = ?$). There are two very good but often ignored reasons for the discrepancy, as I suggested above. One source of doubt is that the probability of correctness of the scientist's hypothesis depends not only upon the probability of rejecting the null hypothesis, but also upon the probability that the statistical model is appropriate. Now, with the non-parametric tests there is little problem here, and in fact, that is their great virtue.[4]

[3] Or he may replicate the study to get a larger n so that other tests will have more power. This is probably the best approach, especially if he varies the experimental conditions in order to find out how to get better control over the rare event.

[4] The power of the Mann-Whitney, for example, is usually cited as approaching .95 that of the t test, in those conditions where the latter is appropriate. Considering that there is usually at least a .05 chance that any given set of data does not come from a normal population, the Mann-Whitney emerges as perhaps the more powerful test for testing scientific (as against statistical) hypotheses. Moreover, its loss of statistical power with small samples may be more than offset by the scientist's gain in assurance that the underlying model is appropriate.

Our *E* with the thirsty rats wisely eschewed the *t* test, and he probably would have even if it had yielded significance, not because it was "wrong," but because it would not have given him any assurance that his scientific hypothesis had been confirmed. But what, we may ask, is the probability that the populations which his two groups represent are actually distributed exponentially? I must say they don't look exponential. The samples are much too small to give us any assurance that the model might be appropriate. Let us be generous and say that the model has a .50 chance of being applicable. What becomes of *E*'s claimed high significance level?

Poor *E* has a more serious matter to worry about, a more vexing source of doubt. His whole case hinges on the performance of one animal, the one that drank 12 cc. The remaining 39 *S*s don't give him a thing, with any test. Now suppose that the true state of affairs is this: The experimental treatment really has no appreciable effect upon water consumption. But let us suppose, however, that there occurs, every once in a while, a bubble in the animal's homecage drinking tube, which prevents normal drinking. If this were the case, and if bubbles occur, say, $2\frac{1}{2}\%$ of the time, then about 50% of the time a bubble *S* will appear in the experimental group, so *E* will get just the results he got about 50% of the time.[5] Moreover, if he continues to use the Festinger test, we can expect him half the time to get highly significant differences in support of his hypothesis, whatever his hypothesis may be!

The problem here, basically, is that statistical rejection of the null hypothesis tells the scientist only what he was already quite sure of—the animals are not behaving randomly. The fact the null hypothesis can be rejected with a *p* of .99 does not give *E* an assurance of .99 that his particular hypothesis is true, but only that *some* alternative to the null hypothesis is true. He may not like the bubble hypothesis because it is *ad hoc*. But that is quite irrelevant. What is crucial is that the bubble hypothesis, or some other hypothesis, may be more probable than his own. The final confidence he can have in his scientific hypothesis is not dependent upon statistical significance levels; it is ultimately determined by his ability to reject alternatives.

Consider another illustration. Suppose we are interested in whether a certain stimulus will have reinforcing power for a certain group of 20 animals. After pre-training on a straightaway, we run them 15 trials in a T-maze which has the stimulus in question on one side and not on the other. We collect our data and graph them in the hope of seeing a typical learning curve. But what we find is Fig. 23-1. All is not lost, though, apparently, because it is still possible to conclude from the data that the stimulus *did* have a reinforcing effect, and that the associated *p* value is less than .002![6]

---

[5] The other half of the time the experiment will be disastrous for *E*'s hypothesis, however. He had better just do the study once; that way he has at least a .50 chance of getting high significance in the favorable direction, and no more than a .50 chance of discovering that the real world is full of bubbles.

[6] The problem, the data, and the conclusions are D'Amato's (1955). Note that performance on the first trial was at 50%. This was prearranged by putting the reinforcer on both sides for half the *S*s and on neither side for the other half.

The first thing to look for is whether there is a rising trend in the points of Fig. 23-1. It turns out that the best fit line *does* rise, but that an *F* test for the significance of the trend shows it to be less than would be expected on the basis of the day-to-day variation. To find a significant difference anywhere here, we have to ignore the data of Fig. 23-1 and turn our attention to the number of responses

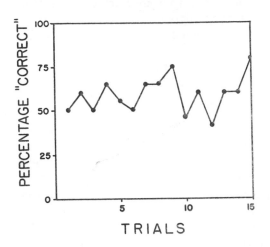

FIGURE 23-1. The performance of rats alleged
to have learned to go to one side of a T-maze.

made by each *S* to the "reinforced" side, during its 15 trials. The 20 such scores have a mean of 8.8 which proves to be highly significantly different from the expected value of 7.5 ($p = .002$). (The learning curve, correspondingly, runs along at about 59% instead of 50%.) What this significance test tells us is that the animals probably weren't running randomly.[7] But it is a long way from that to the inference that learning has occurred because of the special stimulus.

One hypothesis with a high *a priori* probability is that most of the animals gave scores that lay quite close to 7.5 but that one or two animals, with strong unlearned position habits, continued going to the side to which they had gone on the first trial. The probability that in the sampling process, just those one or two animals with strong positions habits should be placed under the same condition, and under the particular condition that the "reinforcer" was on their preferred side, is fairly small, but still a great deal larger than the reported significance level. This hypothesis can be ruled out, however, but by certain features of the data and not on grounds of its *a priori* probability. We can deduce from the small *SD* (1.47) that few of the animals could have had position habits of appreciable strength. In fact, we can deduce (with a little effort) from the size of the *SD* that no more than

---

[7] No one who has ever run animals would seriously consider that they might run randomly. What the null hypothesis implies in empirical terms is that the different animals were doing different things at different times so that the total set of *scores* looks as if it were random.

one *S* could have had extreme position habit, and that even this was not actually the case, since one *S* could not have moved the mean from 7.5 to 8.8. Hence, we must conclude that the distribution represents a tightly bunched set of scores, whose mean is indeed significantly larger than 7.5.

But this suggests another hypothesis, which does account for the data, and which also has a high *a priori* probability. The hypothesis is simply that most animals have slight position habits. According to this hypothesis, any particular animal could be expected to go to one side 8 or 9 or 10 times out of 15. (We have already noted the high significance level indicating how consistent this is.) The setting of the performance level at 50% on the first trial is a red herring; it does not set the expected percentage correct at 50%—that would be true in any case before it was known which was the preferred side for a given animal. Now that the data are in, we can see (according to this hypothesis) that the preferred side happened to be predominantly on the same side for which *S* was "reinforced." To assess the probability that a significantly high proportion of the animals had the "reinforcement" on their preferred side (which would be good evidence that the reinforcement was effective), we must go back to the data of Fig. 23-1. Performance over the last 14 trials was at 59%, while the performance on Trial 1 was 50%. The question is whether *E*'s performance on Trial 1, when he was selecting the side to put the critical stimulus, is significantly different from the 59% baseline for the animal's performance?[8] The answer is that it is well within the trial by trial variation. There was that much or more variation from the mean on 6 of the trials.

So, what it comes down to is that the animals did show slight but consistent preferences for one side or the other; the *p* figure of .002 shows this. The important question is whether these slight and consistent preferences are due to a slight but consistent effect of the experimental treatment, or whether they would have occurred without the treatment and *E* was just a little unlucky in trying to counterbalance them. Which is the more probable?

The point of this message is not that it is futile to do experiments (although it might be wise to be cautious of some of the statistician's favorite designs). Rather, the emphasis should be upon the distinction between why scientists run statistical tests and why statisticians do it. The former run tests for the same reason they run experiments, in the attempt to understand natural physical phenomena. The latter do it in the attempt to understand mathematical phenomena. The scientist gains his understanding through the rejection or confirmation of scientific hypotheses, but this depends upon much more than merely rejecting or failing to reject the null hypothesis. It depends partly upon the confirmation from other investigators (e.g., Amsel & Maltzman, 1950; Wike & Casey, 1954), particularly as the experimental conditions are varied (e.g., Siegel & Brantley, 1951; Amsel & Cole, 1953). Confirmation of scientific hypotheses also depends in part upon whether they can be incorporated into a larger theoretical framework (e.g., Hull, 1943). Final confirma-

---

[8] Or put another way, what is the probability that 20 animals, all with slight position habits, will distribute themselves on one particular trial so that the group will depart 9 percentage points from its mean value.

tion of scientific hypotheses and the larger theories they support depends upon whether they can stand the test of time.

These processes have to move slowly. As Bakan (1953) has observed, the development of a scientific idea is gradual, like learning itself; its probability of being correct increases gradually from one experimental verification to the next, as response probability increases from one trial to the next. The effect of any single experimental verification is not to confirm a scientific hypothesis but only to make its *a posteriori* probability a little higher than its *a priori* probability. Our present day over-reliance upon statistical hypothesis testing is apt to obscure this feature of the scientific enterprise. We have almost come to believe that an assertion about the nature of the empirical world can be validated (at least with a probability level such as .95 or .99) in one stroke if the data demonstrate statistical significance. Is it any wonder then that our use of statistical hypothesis testing is rapidly passing from routine to ritual?

SUMMARY

One of the chief differences between the hypotheses of the statistician and those of the scientist is that, when the statistician has rejected the null hypothesis, his job is virtually finished. The scientist, however, has only just begun his task. He must also be able to show that the statistical model underlying the test is applicable to his empirical situation because whatever significance level he obtained for the test, his confidence in his scientific hypothesis must be reduced below that by any lack of confidence in the model. Furthermore, confidence in his scientific hypothesis is reduced by the plausibility of alternative hypotheses. Hence the scientist's ultimate confidence in his hypothesis may be far lower than the significance level he can report.

REFERENCES

Amsel, A., & Cole, K. F. Generalization of fear motivated interference with water intake. *Journal of Experimental Psychology*, 1953, **46**, 243–247.

Amsel, A., & Maltzman, I. The effect upon generalized drive strength of emotionality as inferred from the level of consummatory response. *Journal of Experimental Psychology*, 1950, **40**, 563–569.

Bakan, D. Learning and the principle of inverse probability. *Psychological Review*, 1953, **60**, 360–370.

D'Amato, M. R. Transfer of secondary reinforcement across the hunger and thirst drives. *Journal of Experimental Psychology*, 1955, **49**, 352–356.

Festinger, L. An exact test of significance for means of samples drawn from populations with an exponential frequency distribution. *Psychometrika*, 1943, **8**, 153–160.

Hull, C. L. *Principles of behavior*. New York: Appleton-Century, 1943.

Siegel, P. S., & Brantley, J. J. The relationship of emotionality to the consummatory response of eating. *Journal of Experimental Psychology*, 1951, **42**, 304–306.

Siegel, P. S., & Siegel, H. S. The effect of emotionality on the water intake of the rat. *Journal of Comparative and Physiological Psychology*, 1949, **42**, 12–16.

Wike, E. L., & Casey, A. The secondary reinforcing value of food for thirsty animals. *Journal of Comparative and Physiological Psychology*, 1954, **47**, 240–243.

24. The Test of Significance in Psychological Research[1]

David Bakan

The statistical test of significance is used in most psychological research today. In this critical evaluation, Dr. Bakan reviews the basic logic associated with the use of the test of significance and argues that it fails to provide "the information concerning psychological phenomena characteristically attributed to it." He notes some of the difficulties associated with the null hypothesis: it will probably be false anyway, there being no good reason to expect it to be true in any population; and the publication practices of journals encourage the reporting of small effects thereby increasing the possibility of Type I error. Dr. Bakan also discusses various misinterpretations of the nature of the test of significance such as taking p as a "measure" of significance, and confusing the aggregate with the general, and suggests some alternatives.

The vast majority of investigations which pass for research in the field of psychology today entail the use of statistical tests of significance. Most characteristically, when a psychologist finds a problem he wishes to investigate he converts his intuitions and hypotheses into procedures which will yield a test of significance, and will characteristically allow the result of the test of significance to bear the essential responsibility for the conclusions he will draw.

I will attempt to show that the test of significance does not provide the information concerning psychological phenomena characteristically attributed to it; and that, furthermore, a great deal of mischief has been associated with its use. If the test of significance does not yield the expected information concerning the psychological phenomena under investigation, we may well speak of a crisis; for then a good deal of the research of the last several decades must be questioned. What will be said in this paper is hardly original. It is, in a certain sense, what "everybody knows." To say it "out loud" is, as it were, to assume the role of the

[1] Reprinted from D. Bakan, *On Method: Toward a Reconstruction of Psychological Investigation* (San Francisco, Jossey-Bass, 1967), Chapter 1, Pp. 1–29, with the permission of the author and the publisher.

child who pointed out that the emperor really had no clothes on. Little of what is contained in this paper is not already available in the literature, and the literature will be cited.

Lest what is being said here be misunderstood, some clarification needs to be made at the outset. It is not a blanket criticism of statistics, of mathematics, or, for that matter, even of the test of significance when it can be appropriately used, as in certain decision situations. The argument is rather that the test of significance has been carrying too much of the burden of scientific inference. It may well be the case that wise and ingenious investigators can find their way to reasonable conclusions from data because and in spite of their procedures. Too often, however, even wise and ingenious investigators, for varieties of reasons not the least of which are the editorial policies of our major psychological journals, which we will discuss below, tend to credit the test of significance with properties it does not have.

The test of significance has as its aim obtaining information concerning a characteristic of a *population* which is itself not directly observable, whether for practical or more intrinsic reasons. What is observable is the *sample*. The work assigned to the test of significance is that of aiding in making inferences from the observed sample to the unobserved population.

The critical assumption involved in testing significance is that, if the experiment is conducted properly, the characteristics of the population have a designably determinative influence on samples drawn from it; that, for example, the mean of a population has a determinative influence on the mean of a sample drawn from it. Thus, if P, the population characteristic, has a determinative influence on S, the sample characteristic, then there is some license for making inferences from S to P.

If the determinative influence of P on S could be put in the form of simple logical implication, that P implies S, the problem would be quite simple. For, then we would have the simple situation: if P implies S, and if S is false, P is false. There are some limited instances in which this logic applies directly in sampling. For example, if the range of values in the population is between 3 and 9 (P), then the range of values in any sample must be between 3 and 9 (S). Should we find a value in a sample of, say, 10, it would mean that S is false; and we could assert that P is false.

It is clear from this, however, that, strictly speaking, one can only go from the denial of S to the denial of P; and not from the assertion of S to the assertion of P. It is within this context of simple logical implication that the Fisher school of statisticians have made important contributions—and it is extremely important to recognize this as the context.

In contrast, approaches based on the theorem of Bayes (Edwards, Lindman, & Savage, 1963; Keynes, 1948; Savage, 1954; Schlaifer, 1959) would allow inferences to P from S even when S is not denied, as S adding something to the credibility of P when S is found to be the case. One of the most viable alternatives to the use of the test of significance involves the theorem of Bayes; and the paper by Edwards et al. (1963) is particularly directed to the attention of psychologists for use in psychological research.

The notion of the null hypothesis[2] promoted by Fisher (1947) constituted an advance within this context of simple logical implication. It allowed experimenters to set up a null hypothesis complementary to the hypothesis that the investigator was interested in, and provided him with a way of positively confirming his hypothesis. Thus, for example, the investigator might have the hypothesis that, say, normals differ from schizophrenics. He would then set up the null hypothesis that the means in the population of all normals and all schizophrenics were equal. Thus, the rejection of the null hypothesis constituted a way of asserting that the means of the populations of normals and schizophrenics were different, a seemingly reasonable device whereby to affirm a logical antecedent.

The model of simple logical implication for making inferences from S to P has another difficulty which the Fisher approach sought to overcome. This is that it is rarely meaningful to set up any simple "P implies S" model for parameters that we are interested in. In the case of the mean, for example, it is rather that P has a determinative influence on the frequency of any specific S. But one experiment does not provide many values of S to allow the study of their frequencies. It gives us only one value of S. The sampling distribution is conceived which specifies the relative frequencies of all possible values of S. Then, with the help of an adopted level of significance, we could, in effect, say that S was false; that is, any S which fell in a region whose relative theoretical frequency under the null hypothesis was, say, 5 per cent would be considered false. If such an S actually occurred, we would be in a position to declare P to be false, still within the model of simple logical implication.

It is important to recognize that one of the essential features of the Fisher approach is what may be called the "once-ness" of the experiment; the inference model takes as critical that the experiment has been conducted once. If an S which has a low probability under the null hypothesis actually occurs, it is taken that the null hypothesis is false. As Fisher (1947) put it, why should the theoretically rare event under the null hypothesis actually occur to "us"? If it does occur, we take it that the null hypothesis is false. Basic is the idea that "the theoretically unusual does not happen to me."[3] It should be noted that the referent for all probability

---

[2] There is some confusion in the literature concerning the meaning of the term "null hypothesis." Fisher used the term to designate any exact hypothesis that we might be interested in disproving, and "null" was used in the sense of that which is to be nullified (see, for example, Berkson, 1942). It has, however, also been used to indicate a parameter of zero (see, for example, Lindquist, 1940): the difference between the population means is zero, or the correlation coefficient in the population is zero, the difference in proportions in the population is zero, etc. Since both meanings are usually intended in psychological research, it causes little difficulty.

[3] I playfully once conducted the following "experiment": Suppose, I said, that every coin has associated with it a "spirit"; and suppose, furthermore, that if the spirit is implored properly, the coin will veer head or tail as one requests of the spirit. I thus invoked the spirit to make the coin fall head. I threw it once; it came up head. I did it again; it came up head again. I did this six times, and got six heads. Under the null hypothesis the probability of occurrence of six heads is $(1/2)^6 = .016$, significant at the 2 per cent level of significance. I have never repeated the experiment. But, then, the logic of the inference model does not really demand that I do! It may be objected that the coin, or my tossing, or even my observation was biased. But I submit that such things were in all likelihood not as involved in the result as corresponding things in most psychological research.

considerations is neither in the population itself nor the subjective confidence of the investigator. It is rather in a hypothetical population of experiments all conducted in the same manner, but only one of which is actually conducted. Thus, of course, the probability of falsely rejecting the null hypothesis if it were true is exactly that value which has been taken as the level of significance. Replication of the experiment vitiates the validity of the inference model, unless the replication itself is taken into account in the model and the probabilities of the model modified accordingly (as is done in various designs which entail replication, where, however, the total experiment, including the replications, is again considered as *one* experiment). According to Fisher (1947), "it is an essential characteristic of experimentation that it is carried out with limited resources." In the Fisher approach, the "limited resources" is not only a making of the best out of a limited situation, but is rather an integral feature of the inference model itself. Lest he be done a complete injustice, it should be pointed out that he did say, "In relation to the test of significance, we may say that a phenomenon is experimentally demonstrable when we know how to conduct an experiment which will rarely fail to give us statistically significant results." However, although Fisher "himself" believes this, it is not built into the inference model.[4]

As already indicated, research workers in the field of psychology place a heavy burden on the test of significance. Let us consider some of the difficulties associated with the null hypothesis.

1. *The a priori reasons for believing that the null hypothesis is generally false anyway.* One of the common experiences of research workers is the very high frequency with which significant results are obtained with large samples. Some years ago, the author had occasion to run a number of tests of significance on a battery of tests collected on about 60,000 subjects from all over the United States. Every test came out significant. Dividing the cards by such arbitrary criteria as east versus west of the Mississippi River, Maine versus the rest of the country, North versus South, etc., all produced significant differences in means. In some instances, the differences in the sample means were quite small, but nonetheless, the *p* values were all very low. Nunnally (1960) has reported a similar experience involving correlation coefficients on 700 subjects. Joseph Berkson (1938) made the observation almost 30 years ago in connection with chi-square:

I believe that an observant statistician who has had any considerable experience with applying the chi-square test repeatedly will agree with my statement that, as a matter of observation, when the numbers in the data are quite large, the *P*'s tend to come out small. Having observed this, and on reflection, I make the following dogmatic statement, referring for illustration to the normal curve: "If the normal curve is fitted to a body of data representing any real observations whatever of quantities in

---

[4] Possibly not even this criterion is sound. It may be that a number of statistically significant results which are borderline "speak for the null hypothesis rather than against it" (Edwards et al., 1963). If the null hypothesis were really false, then with an increase in the number of instances in which it can be rejected, there should be some substantial proportion of more dramatic rejections rather than borderline rejections.

the physical world, then if the number of observations is extremely large—for instance, on an order of 200,000—the chi-square P will be small beyond any usual limit of significance.

This dogmatic statement is made on the basis of an extrapolation of the observation referred to and can also be defended as a prediction from *a priori* considerations. For we may assume that it is practically certain that any series of real observations does not actually follow a normal curve *with absolute exactitude* in all respects, and no matter how small the discrepancy between the normal curve and the true curve of observations, the chi-square P will be small if the sample has a sufficiently large number of observations in it.

If this be so, then we have something here that is apt to trouble the conscience of a reflective statistician using the chi-square test. For I suppose it would be agreed by statisticians that a large sample is always better than a small sample. If, then, we know in advance the P that will result from an application of a chi-square test to a large sample, there would seem to be no use in doing it on a smaller one. But since the result of the former test is known, it is no test at all [pp. 526–527].

As one group of authors has put it, "in typical applications . . . the null hypothesis . . . is known by all concerned to be false from the outset" (Edwards, Lindman, and Savage, 1963). The fact of the matter is that there is really no good reason to expect the null hypothesis to be true in any population. Why should the mean, say, of all scores east of the Mississippi be identical to all scores west of the Mississippi? Why should any correlation coefficient be exactly .00 in the population? Why should we expect the ratio of males to females to be exactly 50:50 in any population? Or why should different drugs have exactly the same effect on any population parameter (Smith, 1960)? A glance at any set of statistics on total populations will quickly confirm the rarity of the null hypothesis in nature.

The reason the null hypothesis is characteristically rejected with large samples was made patent by the theoretical work of Neyman and Pearson (1933). The probability of rejecting the null hypothesis is a function of five factors: whether the test is one- or two-tailed, the level of significance, the standard deviation, the amount of deviation from the null hypothesis, and the number of observations. The choice of a one- or two-tailed test is the investigator's; the level of significance is also based on the choice of the investigator; the standard deviation is a given of the situation and is characteristically reasonably well estimated; the deviation from the null hypothesis is what is unknown; and the choice of the number of cases in psychological work is characteristically arbitrary or expediential. Should there be any deviation from the null hypothesis in the population, no matter how small—and we have little doubt but that such a deviation usually exists—a sufficiently large number of observations will lead to the rejection of the null hypothesis. As Nunnally (1960) put it,

if the null hypothesis is not rejected, it is usually because the N is too small. If enough data are gathered, the hypothesis will generally be rejected. If rejection of the null hypothesis were the real intention in psychological experiments, there usually would be no need to gather data [p. 643].

2. *Type I error and publication practices.* The Type I error is the error of rejecting the null hypothesis when it is indeed true, and its probability is the level of significance. Later in this paper we will discuss the distinction between sharp and loose null hypotheses. The sharp null hypothesis, which we have been discussing, is an exact value for the null hypothesis as, for example, the difference between population means being precisely zero. A loose null hypothesis is one in which it is conceived of as being "around" null. Sharp null hypotheses, as we have indicated, rarely exist in nature. Assuming that loose null hypotheses are not rare, and that their testing may make sense under some circumstances, let us consider the role of the publication practices of our journals in their connection.

It is the practice of editors of our psychological journals, receiving many more papers than they can possibly publish, to use the magnitude of the p values reported as one criterion for acceptance or rejection of a study. For example, consider the following statement made by Arthur W. Melton (1962) on completing twelve years as editor of the *Journal of Experimental Psychology*, certainly one of the most prestigious and scientifically meticulous psychological journals. In listing the criteria by which articles were evaluated, he said:

The next step in the assessment of an article involved a judgment with respect to the confidence to be placed in the findings—confidence that the results of the experiment would be repeatable under the conditions described. In editing the *Journal* there has been a strong reluctance to accept and publish results related to the principal concern of the research when those results were significant at the .05 level, whether by one- or two-tailed test. This has not implied a slavish worship of the .01 level, as some critics may have implied. Rather, it reflects a belief that it is the responsibility of the investigator in a science to reveal his effect in such a way that no reasonable man would be in a position to discredit the results by saying that they were the product of the way the ball bounces [pp. 553–554].

His clearly expressed opinion that nonsignificant results should not take up the space of the journals is shared by most editors of psychological journals. It is important to point out that I am not advocating a change in policy in this connection. In the total research enterprise where so much of the load for making inferences concerning the nature of phenomena is carried by the test of significance, the editors can do little else. The point is rather that the situation in regard to publication makes manifest the difficulties in connection with the overemphasis on the test of significance as a principal basis for making inferences.

McNemar (1960) has rightly pointed out that not only do journal editors reject papers in which the results are not significant, but that papers in which significance has not been obtained are not submitted, that investigators select out their significant findings for inclusion in their reports, and that theory-oriented research workers tend to discard data which do not work to confirm their theories. The result of all of this is that "published results are more likely to involve false rejection of null hypotheses than indicated by the stated levels of significance," that is, published results which are significant may well have Type I errors in them far in excess of, say, the 5 per cent which we may allow ourselves.

The suspicion that the Type I error may well be plaguing our literature is given confirmation in an analysis of articles published in the *Journal of Abnormal and Social Psychology* for one complete year (Cohen, 1962). Analyzing seventy studies in which significant results were obtained with respect to the power of the statistical tests used, Cohen found that power, the probability of rejecting the null hypothesis when the null hypothesis was false, was characteristically meager. Theoretically, with such tests, one should not often expect significant results even when the null hypothesis was false. Yet, there they were! Even if deviations from null existed in the relevant populations, the investigations were characteristically not powerful enough to have detected them. This strongly suggests that there is something additional associated with these rejections of the null hypotheses in question. It strongly points to the possibility that the manner in which studies get published is associated with the findings; that the very publication practices themselves are part and parcel of the probabilistic processes on which we base our conclusions concerning the nature of psychological phenomena. Our total research enterprise is, at least in part, a kind of scientific roulette, in which the "lucky," or constant player, "wins," that is, gets his paper or papers published. And certainly, going from 5 per cent to 1 per cent does not eliminate the possibility that it is "the way the ball bounces," to use Melton's phrase. It changes the odds in this roulette, but it does not make it less a game of roulette.

The damage to the scientific enterprise is compounded by the fact that the publication of "significant" results tends to stop further investigation. If the publication of papers containing Type I errors tended to foster further investigation so that the psychological phenomena with which we are concerned would be further probed by others, it would not be too bad. But it does not. Quite the contrary. As Lindquist (1940) has correctly pointed out, the danger to science of the Type I error is much more serious than the Type II error—for when a Type I error is committed, it has the effect of stopping investigation. A highly significant result appears definitive, as Melton's comments indicate. In the twelve years that he edited the *Journal of Experimental Psychology*, he sought to select papers which were worthy of being placed in the "archives," as he put it. Even the strict repetition of an experiment and not getting significance in the same way does not speak against the result already reported in the literature. For failing to get significance, speaking strictly within the inference model, only means that that experiment is inconclusive; whereas the study already reported in the literature, with a low p value, is regarded as conclusive. Thus we tend to place in the archives studies with a relatively high number of Type I errors, or, at any rate, studies which reflect small deviations from null in the respective populations; and we act in such a fashion as to reduce the likelihood of their correction. From time to time the suggestion has arisen that journals should open their pages for "negative results," so called. What is characteristically meant is that the null hypothesis has not been rejected at a conventional level of significance. This is hardly a solution to the problem simply because a failure to reject the null hypothesis is not a "negative result." It is only an instance in which the experiment is inconclusive.

To make this point clearer let us consider the odd case in which the null hypothesis may actually be true; say, the difference between means of a given measure of two identifiable groups in the population is precisely zero. Let us imagine that over the world there are one hundred experimenters who have independently embarked on testing this particular null hypothesis. By the theory under which the whole test of significance is conceived, approximately ninety-five of these experimenters would wind up by not being able to reject the null hypothesis, that is, their results would not be significant. It is not likely that they would write up their experiments and submit them to any journals. However, approximately five of these experimenters would find that their observed difference in means is significant at the 5 per cent level of significance. It is likely that they would write up their experiments and submit them for publication. Indeed, one might imagine interesting quarrels arising among them concerning priority of discovery, if the differences came out in the same direction, and controversy, if the differences came out in different directions. In the former instance, the psychological community might even take it as evidence of "replicability" of the phenomenon, in the latter instance as evidence that the scientific method is "self-corrective." The other ninety-five experimenters would wonder what they did wrong. And this is in the odd instance in which the true difference between means in the population is precisely zero!

The psychological literature is filled with misinterpretations of the nature of the test of significance. One may be tempted to attribute this to such things as lack of proper education, the simple fact that humans may err, and the prevailing tendency to take a cookbook approach in which the mathematical and philosophical framework out of which the tests of significance emerge are ignored; that, in other words, these misinterpretations are somehow the result of simple intellectual inadequacy on the part of psychologists. However, such an explanation is hardly tenable. Graduate schools are adamant with respect to statistical education. Any number of psychologists have taken out substantial amounts of time to equip themselves mathematically and philosophically. Psychologists as a group do a great deal of mutual criticism. Editorial reviews prior to publication are carried out with eminent conscientiousness. There is even a substantial literature devoted to various kinds of "misuse" of statistical procedures, to which not a little attention has been paid.

It is rather that the test of significance is profoundly interwoven with other strands of the psychological research enterprise in such a way that it constitutes a critical part of the total cultural-scientific tapestry. To pull out the strand of the test of significance would seem to make the whole tapestry fall apart. In the face of the intrinsic difficulties that the test of significance provides, we rather attempt to make an "adjustment" by attributing to the test of significance characteristics which it does not have, and overlook characteristics that it does have. The difficulty is that the test of significance can, especially when not considered too carefully, do *some* work; for, after all, the results of the test of significance *are* related to the phenomena in which we are interested. One may well ask whether we do not have here, perhaps, an instance of the phenomenon that learning under partial reinforcement is very highly resistant to extinction. Some of these misinterpretations are as follows:

1. *Taking the p value as a "measure" of significance.* A common misinterpretation of the test of significance is to regard it as a "measure" of significance. It is interpreted as the answer to the question "How significant is it?" A *p* value of .05 is thought of as less significant than a *p* value of .01, and so on. The characteristic practice on the part of psychologists is to compute, say, a *t*, and then "look up" the significance in the table, taking the *p* value as a function of *t*, and thereby a "measure" of significance. Indeed, since the *p* value is inversely related to the magnitude of, say, the difference between means in the sample, it can function as a kind of "standard score" measure for a variety of different experiments. Mathematically, the *t* is actually very similar to a "standard score," entailing a deviation in the numerator, and a function of the variation in the denominator; and the *p* value is a "function" of *t*. If this use were explicit, it would perhaps not be too bad. But it must be remembered that this is using the *p* value as a statistic descriptive of the sample alone, and does not automatically give an inference to the population. There is even the practice of using tests of significance in studies of total populations, in which the observations cannot by any stretch of the imagination be thought of as having been randomly selected from any designable population.[5] Using the *p* value in this way, in which the statistical inference model is even hinted at, is completely indefensible; for the single function of the statistical inference model is making inferences to populations from samples.

The practice of "looking up" the *p* value for the *t*, which has even been advocated in some of our statistical handbooks (e.g., Lacey, 1953; Underwood et al., 1954), rather than looking up the *t* for a given *p* value, violates the inference model. The inference model is based on the presumption that one initially adopts a level of significance as the specification of that probability which is too low to occur to "us," as Fisher has put it, in this one instance, and under the null hypothesis. A purist might speak of the "delicate problem . . . of fudging with a posteriori alpha values [levels of significance]" (Kaiser, 1960), as though the levels of significance were initially decided upon, but rarely do psychological research workers or editors take the level of significance as other than a "measure."

But taken as a "measure," it is only a measure of the sample. Psychologists often erroneously believe that the *p* value is "the probability that the results are due to chance," as Wilson (1961) has pointed out; that a *p* value of .05 means that the chances are .95 that the scientific hypothesis is correct, as Bolles (1962) has pointed out; that it is a measure of the power to "predict" the behavior of a population (Underwood et al., 1954); and that it is a measure of the "confidence that the results of the experiment would be repeatable under the conditions described," as Melton (1962) put it. Unfortunately, none of these interpretations are within the inference model of the test of significance. Some of our statistical handbooks have "allowed" misinterpretation. For example, in discussing the erroneous rhetoric associated with talking of the "probability" of a population parameter (in the inference model there is no probability associated with something which is either true or false), Lindquist

---

[5] It was decided not to cite any specific studies to exemplify points such as this one. The reader will undoubtedly be able to supply them for himself.

(1940) said, "For most practical purposes, the end result is the same as if the 'level of confidence' type of interpretation is employed." Ferguson (1959) wrote, "The .05 and .01 probability levels are descriptive of our degree of confidence." There is little question but that sizable differences, correlations, etc., in samples, especially samples of reasonable size, speak more strongly of sizable differences, correlations, etc., in the population; and there is little question but that if there is real and strong effect in the population, it will continue to manifest itself in further sampling. However, these are inferences which *we* may make. They are outside the inference model associated with the test of significance. The p value within the inference model is only the value which we take to be as how improbable an event could be under the null hypothesis, which we judge will not take place to "us," in this one experiment. It is not a "measure" of the goodness of the other inferences which we might make. It is an a priori condition that we set up whereby we decide whether or not we will reject the null hypothesis, not a measure of significance.

There is a study in the literature (Rosenthal and Gaito, 1963) which points up sharply the lack of understanding on the part of psychologists of the meaning of the test of significance. The subjects were nine members of the psychology department faculty, all holding doctoral degrees, and ten graduate students, at the University of North Dakota; and there is little reason to believe that this group of psychologists was more or less sophisticated than any other. They were asked to rate their degree of belief or confidence in results of hypothetical studies for a variety of p values, and for N's of 10 and 100. That there should be a relationship between the average rated confidence or belief and p value, as they found, is to be expected. What is shocking is that these psychologists indicated substantially greater confidence or belief in results associated with the larger sample size for the same p values. According to the theory, especially as this has been amplified by Neyman and Pearson (1933), the probability of rejecting the null hypothesis for any given deviation from null and p value increases as a function of the number of observations. The rejection of the null hypothesis when the number of cases is small speaks for a more dramatic effect in the population; and if the p value is the same, the probability of committing a Type I error remains the same. Thus one can be more confident with a small N than a large N. The question is, how could a group of psychologists be so wrong? I believe that this wrongness is based on the commonly held belief that the p value is a "measure" of degree of confidence. Thus, the reasoning behind such a wrong set of answers by these psychologists may well have been something like this: the p value is a measure of confidence; but a larger number of cases also increases confidence; therefore, for any given p value, the degree of confidence should be higher for the larger N. The wrong conclusion arises from the erroneous character of the first premise, and from the failure to recognize that the p value is a function of sample size for any given deviation from null in the population. The author knows of instances in which editors of very reputable psychological journals have rejected papers in which the p values and N's were small on the grounds that there were not enough observations, clearly demonstrating that the same mode of thought is operating in them. Indeed, rejecting the null hypothesis with a small N is indicative of a strong deviation from null in the population, the mathematics of the test of significance having already taken into account the smallness of the sample. Increasing the N increases the probability of rejecting the null hypothesis; and in these studies rejected for small sample size, that task has already been accomplished. These editors are, of course, in some sense the ultimate "teachers" of the profession; and they have been teaching something which is patently wrong.

2. *Automaticity of inference.* What may be considered to be a dream, fantasy, or ideal in the culture of psychology is that of achieving complete automaticity of inference. The making of inductive generalizations is always somewhat risky. In Fisher's *The Design of Experiments* (1947), he made the claim that the methods of induction could be made rigorous, exemplified by the procedures which he was setting forth. This is indeed quite correct in the sense indicated earlier. In a later paper (Fisher, 1955), he made explicit what was strongly hinted at in his earlier writing, that the methods which he proposed constituted a relatively complete specification of the process of induction:

That such a process of induction existed and was possible to normal minds, has been understood for centuries; it is only with the recent development of statistical science that an analytic account can now be given, about as satisfying and complete, at least, as that given traditionally of the deductive processes [p. 74].

Psychologists certainly took the procedures associated with the t test, F test, and so on, in this manner. Instead of having to engage in inference themselves, they had but to "run the tests" for the purpose of making inferences, since, as it appeared, the statistical tests were analytic analogues of inductive inference. The "operationist" orientation among psychologists, which recognized the contingency of knowledge on the knowledge-getting operations and advocated their specification, could, it would seem, "operationalize" the inferential processes simply by reporting the details of the statistical analysis. It thus removed the burden of responsibility, the chance of being wrong, the necessity for making inductive inferences, from the shoulders of the investigator and placed them on the tests of significance. The contingency of the conclusion upon the experimenter's decision of the level of significance was managed in two ways. The first, by resting on a kind of social agreement that 5 per cent was good, and 1 per cent better. The second in the manner which has already been discussed, by not making a decision of the level of significance, but only reporting the p value as a "result" and a presumably objective "measure" of degree of confidence. But that the probability of getting significance is also contingent upon the number of observations has been handled largely by ignoring it.

A crisis was experienced among psychologists when the matter of the one-versus the two-tailed test came into prominence; for here the contingency of the result of a test of significance on a decision of the investigator was simply too conspicuous to be ignored. An investigator, say, was interested in the difference between two groups on some measure. He collected his data, found that Mean A was greater than Mean B in the sample, and ran the ordinary two-tailed t test; and, let us say, it was not significant. Then he bethought himself. The two-tailed test tested against *two* alternatives, that the population Mean A was greater than population Mean B and vice versa. But then, he really wanted to know whether Mean A was greater than Mean B. Thus, he could run a one-tailed test. He did this and found, since the one-tailed test is more powerful, that his difference was now significant.

Now here there was a difficulty. The test of significance is not nearly so automatic an inference process as had been thought. It is manifestly contingent on the decision of the investigator as to whether to run a one- or a two-tailed test. And, somehow, making the decision *after* the data were collected and the means computed seemed like "cheating." How should this be handled? Should there be some central registry in which one registers one's decision to run a one- or two-tailed test before collecting the data? Should one, as one eminent psychologist once suggested to me, send oneself a letter so that the postmark would prove that one had predecided to run a one-tailed test? The literature on ways of handling this difficulty has grown quite a bit in the strain to overcome somehow this particular clear contingency of the results of a test of significance on the decision of the investigator. The author will not attempt here to review this literature, except to cite one very competent paper which points up the intrinsic difficulty associated with this problem, the *reductio ad absurdum* to which one comes. Kaiser (1960), early in his paper, distinguished between the logic associated with the test of significance and other forms of inference, a distinction which, incidentally, Fisher would hardly have allowed: "The arguments developed in this paper are based on logical considerations in statistical inference. (We do not, of course, suggest that statistical inference is the only basis for scientific inference.)" But then, having taken the position that he is going to follow the logic of statistical inference relentlessly, he said (Kaiser's italics): "*we cannot logically make a directional statistical decision or statement when the null hypothesis is rejected on the basis of the direction of the difference in the observed sample means.*" One really needs to strike oneself in the head! If Sample Mean A is greater than Sample Mean B, and there is reason to reject the null hypothesis, in what other direction can it reasonably be? What kind of logic is it that leads one to believe that it could be otherwise than that Population Mean A is greater than Population Mean B? We do not know whether Kaiser intended his paper as a *reductio ad absurdum*, but it certainly turned out that way.

The issue of the one- versus the two-tailed test genuinely challenges the presumptive "objectivity" characteristically attributed to the test of significance. On the one hand, it makes patent what was the case under any circumstances (at the least in the choice of level of significance, and the choice of the number of cases in the sample), that the conclusion is contingent upon the decision of the investigator. An astute investigator, who foresaw the results, and who therefore predecided to use a one-tailed test, will get one p value. The less astute but honorable investigator, who did not foresee the results, would feel obliged to use a two-tailed test, and would get another p value. On the other hand, if one decides to be relentlessly logical within the logic of statistical inference, one winds up with the kind of absurdity which we have cited above.

3. *The confusion of induction to the aggregate with induction to the general.* Consider a not atypical investigation of the following sort: A group of, say, twenty normals and a group of, say, twenty schizophrenics are given a test. The tests are scored, and a *t* test is run, and it is found that the means differ significantly at some level of significance, say 1 per cent. What inference can be drawn? As we have already indicated, the investigator could have insured this result by choosing a sufficiently large number of cases. Suppose we overlook this objection, which we can to some extent, by saying that the difference between the means in the population must have been large enough to have manifested itself with only forty cases. But still, what do we know from this? The only inference which this allows is that the mean of all normals is different from the mean of all schizophrenics in the populations from which the samples have presumably been drawn at random. (Rarely is the criterion of randomness satisfied. But let us overlook this objection too.)

The common rhetoric in which such results are discussed is in the form "Schizophrenics differ from normals in such and such ways." The sense that both the reader and the writer have of this rhetoric is that it has been justified by the finding of significance. Yet clearly it does not mean *all* schizophrenics and *all* normals. All that the test of significance justifies is that measures of central tendency of the aggregates differ in the populations. The test of significance has *not* addressed itself to anything about the schizophrenia or normality which characterizes *each* member of the respective populations. Now it is certainly possible for an investigator to develop a hypothesis about the nature of schizophrenia from which he may infer that there should be differences between the means in the populations; and his finding of a significant difference in the means of his sample would add to the credibility of the former. However, that 1 per cent which he obtained in his study bears only on the means of the populations and is not a "measure" of the confidence that he may have in his hypothesis concerning the nature of schizophrenia. There are two inferences that he must make. One is that of the sample to the population, for which the test of significance is of some use. The other is from his inference concerning the population to his hypothesis concerning the nature of schizophrenia. The *p* value does not bear on this second inference. The psychological literature is filled with assertions which confound these two inferential processes.

Or consider another hardly atypical style of research. Say an experimenter divides forty subjects at random into two groups of twenty subjects each. One group is assigned to one condition and the other to another condition, perhaps, say, massing and distribution of trials. The subjects are given a learning task, one group under massed conditions, the other under distributed conditions. The experimenter runs a *t* test on the learning measure and again, say, finds that the difference is significant at the 1 per cent level of significance. He may then say in his report, being more careful than the psychologist who was studying the difference between normals and schizophrenics (being more "scientific" than his clinically interested colleague), that "the mean in the population of learning under massed conditions is lower than the mean in the population of learning under distributed conditions," feeling that he can say this with a good deal of certainty because of his test of significance.

But here too (like his clinical colleague) he has made two inferences, and not one, and the 1 per cent bears on the one but not the other. The statistical inference model certainly allows him to make his statement for the population, but only for *that* learning task, and the p value is appropriate only to that. But the generalization to "massed conditions" and "distributed conditions" beyond that particular learning task is a second inference with respect to which the p value is not relevant. The psychological literature is plagued with any number of instances in which the rhetoric indicates that the p value does bear on this second inference.

Part of the blame for this confusion can be ascribed to Fisher who, in *The Design of Experiments* (1947), suggested that the mathematical methods which he proposed were exhaustive of scientific induction, and that the principles he was advancing were "common to all experimentation." What he failed to see and to say was that after an inference was made concerning a population parameter, one still needed to engage in induction to obtain meaningful scientific propositions.

To regard the methods of statistical inference as exhaustive of the inductive inferences called for in experimentation is completely confounding. When the test of significance has been run, the necessity for induction has hardly been completely satisfied. However, the research worker knows this, in some sense, and proceeds, as he should, to make further inductive inferences. He is, however, still ensnarled in his test of significance and the presumption that it is the whole of his inductive activity, and thus mistakenly takes a low p value for the measure of the validity of his other inductions.

The seriousness of this confusion may be seen by again referring back to the Rosenthal and Gaito study and the remark by Berkson which indicate that research workers believe that a large sample is better than a small sample. We need to refine the rhetoric somewhat. Induction consists in making inferences from the particular to the general. It is certainly the case that, as confirming particulars are added, the credibility of the general is increased. However, the addition of observations to a sample is, in the context of statistical inference, not the addition of particulars but the modification of what is one particular in the inference model, the sample aggregate. In the context of statistical inference, it is not necessarily true that "a large sample is better than a small sample." For, as has been already indicated, obtaining a significant result with a small sample suggests a larger deviation from null in the population, and may be considerably more meaningful. Thus more particulars are better than fewer particulars in the making of an inductive inference; but not necessarily a larger sample.

In the marriage of psychological research and statistical inference, psychology brought its own reasons for accepting this confusion, reasons which inhere in the history of psychology. Measurement psychology arises out of two radically different traditions, as has been pointed out by Guilford (1936) and Cronbach (1957), and the matter of putting them together raised certain difficulties. The one tradition seeks to find propositions concerning the nature of man in general—propositions of a general nature, with each individual a particular in which the general is manifest. This is the kind of psychology associated with the traditional experimental psychology of Fechner, Ebbinghaus, Wundt, and Titchener. It seeks to find the laws which characterize the "generalized, normal, human, adult mind" (Boring, 1950). The research strategy associated with this kind of psychology is straightforwardly inductive. It seeks inductive generalizations which will apply to every member of a designated class. A single particular in which a generalization fails forces a rejection of the generalization, calling for either a redefinition of the class to which it applies or a modification of the generalization. The other tradition is the psychology of individual differences, which has its roots more in England and the United States than on the Continent. We may recall that when the young American, James McKeen Cattell, who invented the term "mental test," came to Wundt with his own problem of individual differences, it was regarded by Wundt as *ganz Amerikanisch* (Boring, 1950).

The basic datum for an individual-differences approach is not anything that characterizes each of two subjects, but the difference between them. For this latter tradition, it is the aggregate which is of interest, and not the general. One of the most unfortunate characteristics of many studies in psychology, especially in experimental psychology, is that the data are treated as aggregates while the experimenter is trying to infer general propositions. There is hardly an issue of most of the major psychological journals reporting experimentation in which this confusion does not appear several times, and in which the test of significance, which has some value in connection with the study of aggregates, is not interpreted as a measure of the credibility of the general proposition in which the investigator is interested. Roberts and Wist examined sixty articles from psychological literature from the point of view of the aggregate-general distinction. In twenty-five of the articles it was unambiguous that the authors had drawn general-type conclusions from aggregate-type data.

Thus, what took place historically in psychology is that instead of attempting to synthesize the two traditional approaches to psychological phenomena, which is both possible and desirable, a syncretic combination took place of the methods appropriate to the study of aggregates with the aims of a psychology which sought for general propositions. One of the most overworked terms, which added not a little to the essential confusion, was "error," which was a kind of umbrella term for (at the least) variation among scores from different individuals, variation among measurements for the same individual, and variation among samples.

Let us add another historical note. In 1936, Guilford published his well-known *Psychometric Methods*. In this book, which became a kind of "bible" for many psychologists, he made a noble effort at a "Rapprochement of Psychophysical and Test Methods." He observed, quite properly, that mathematical developments in each of the two fields might be of value in the other, that "Both psychophysics and mental testing have rested upon the same fundamental statistical devices." There is no question of the truth of this. However, what he failed to emphasize sufficiently was that mathematics is so abstract that the same mathematics is applicable to rather different fields of investigation without there being any necessary further identity between them. (One would not, for example, argue that business and genetics are essentially the same because the same arithmetic is applicable to market research and in the investigation of the facts of heredity.) A critical point of contact between the two traditions was in connection with scaling, in which Cattell's principle that "equally often noticed differences are equal unless always or never noticed" (Guilford, 1936) was adopted as a fundamental assumption. The "equally often noticed differences" is, of course, based on aggregates. By means of this assumption, one could collapse the distinction between the two areas of investigation. Indeed, this is not really too bad if one is alert to the fact that it is an assumption, one which even has considerable pragmatic value. As a set of techniques whereby data could be analyzed, that is, as a set of techniques whereby one could describe one's findings, and then make inductions about the nature of the psychological phenomena, what Guilford put together in his book was eminently valuable. However, around this time the work of Fisher and his school was coming to the attention of psychologists. It was attractive for several reasons. It offered advice for handling "small samples." It offered a number of eminently ingenious new ways of organizing and extracting information from data. It offered ways by which several variables could be analyzed simultaneously, away from the old notion that one had to keep everything constant and vary only one variable at a time. It showed how the effect of the "interaction" of variables could be assessed. But it also claimed to have mathematized induction! The Fisher approach was thus "bought," and psychologists got a theory of induction in the bargain, a theory which seemed to exhaust the inductive processes. Whereas the question of the "reliability" of statistics had been a matter of concern for some time before (although frequently very garbled), it had not carried the burden of induction to the degree that it did with the Fisher approach. With the acceptance of the Fisher approach the psychological research worker also accepted, and then overused, the test of significance, employing it as the measure of the significance, in the largest sense of the word, of his research efforts.

Earlier, a distinction was made between sharp and loose null hypotheses. One of the major difficulties associated with the Fisher approach is the problem presented by sharp null hypotheses; for, as we have already seen, there is reason to believe that the existence of sharp null hypotheses is characteristically unlikely. There have been some efforts to correct for this difficulty by proposing the use of loose null hypotheses; in place of a single point, a region being considered null. Hodges and Lehmann (1954) have proposed a distinction between "statistical significance," which entails the sharp hypothesis, and "material significance," in which one tests the hypothesis of a deviation of a stated amount from the null point instead of the null point itself. Edwards (1950) has suggested the notion of "practical significance" in which one takes into account the meaning, in some practical sense, of the magnitude of the deviation from null together with the number of observations which have been involved in getting statistical significance. Binder (1963) has equally argued that a subset of parameters be equated with the null hypothesis. Essentially what has been suggested is that the investigator make some kind of a decision concerning "How much, say, of a difference makes a difference?" The difficulty with this solution, which is certainly a sound one technically, is that in psychological research we do not often have very good grounds for answering this question. This is partly due to the inadequacies of psychological measurement, but mostly due to the fact that the answer to the question of "How much of a difference makes a difference?" is not forthcoming outside of some particular practical context. The question calls forth another question, "How much of a difference makes a difference *for what*?"

This brings us to one of the major issues within the field of statistics itself. The problems of the research psychologist do not generally lie within practical contexts. He is rather interested in making assertions concerning psychological functions which have a reasonable amount of credibility associated with them. He is more concerned with "What is the case?" than with "What is wise to do?" (see Rozeboom, 1960).

It is here that the decision-theory approach of Neyman, Pearson, and Wald (Neyman, 1937, 1957; Neyman & Pearson, 1933; Wald, 1939, 1950, 1955) becomes relevant. The decision-theory school, still basing itself on some basic notions of the Fisher approach, deviated from it in several respects:

1. In Fisher's inference model, the two alternatives between which one chose on the basis of an experiment were "reject" and "inconclusive." As he said in *The Design of Experiments* (1947), "the null hypothesis is never proved or established, but is possibly disproved, in the course of experimentation." In the decision-theory approach, the two alternatives are rather "reject" and "accept."

2. Whereas in the Fisher approach the interpretation of the test of significance critically depends on having one sample from a hypothetical population of experiments, the decision-theory approach conceives of, is applicable to, and is sensible with respect to numerous repetitions of the experiment.

3. The decision-theory approach added the notions of the Type II error (which can be made only if the null hypothesis is accepted) and power as significant features of their model.

4. The decision-theory model gave a significant place to the matter of what is concretely lost if an error is made in the practical context, on the presumption that "accept" entailed one concrete action, and "reject" another. It is in these actions and their consequences that there is a basis for deciding on a level of confidence. The Fisher approach has little to say about the consequences.

As it has turned out, the field of application par excellence for the decision-theory approach has been the sampling inspection of mass-produced items. In sampling inspection, the acceptable deviation from null can be specified; both "accept" and "reject" are appropriate categories; the alternative courses of action can be clearly specified; there is a definite measure of loss for each possible action; and the choice can be regarded as one of a series of such choices, so that one can minimize the over-all loss (see Barnard, 1954). Where the aim is only the acquisition of knowledge without regard to a specific practical context, these conditions do not often prevail. Many psychologists who learned about analysis of variance from books such as those by Snedecor (1946) found the examples involving hog weights, etc., somewhat annoying. The decision-theory school makes it clear that such practical contexts are not only "examples" given for pedagogical purposes, but actually are essential features of the methods themselves.

The contributions of the decision-theory school essentially revealed the intrinsic nature of the test of significance beyond that seen by Fisher and his colleagues. They demonstrated that the methods associated with the test of significance constitute not an assertion, or an induction, or a conclusion calculus, but a decision- or risk-evaluation calculus. Fisher (1955) has reacted to the decision-theory approach in polemic style, suggesting that its advocates were like "Russians [who] are made familiar with the ideal that research in pure science can and should be geared to technological performance, in the comprehensive organized effort of a five-year plan for the nation." He also suggested an American "ideological" orientation: "In the U.S. also the great importance of organized technology has I think made it easy to confuse the process appropriate for drawing correct conclusions, with those aimed rather at, let us say, speeding production, or saving money."[6] But perhaps a more reasonable way of looking at this is to regard the decision-theory school to have explicated what was already implicit in the work of the Fisher school.

What then is our alternative, if the test of significance is really of such limited appropriateness ? At the very least it would appear that we would be much better off if we were to attempt to estimate the magnitude of the parameters in the populations; and recognize that we then need to make other inferences concerning the psychological phenomena which may be manifesting themselves in these magnitudes. In terms of a statistical approach which is an alternative, the various methods associated with the theorem of Bayes, referred to earlier, may be appropriate; and the paper by Edwards, Lindman, and Savage (1963) and the book by Schlaifer (1959) are good starting points. However, what is expressed in the theorem of Bayes alludes to the more general process of inducing propositions concerning the nonmanifest (which is what the population is a special instance of) and ascertaining the way in which what is manifest (of which the sample is a special instance) bears on it. This is what the scientific method has been about for centuries. However, if the reader who might be sympathetic to the considerations set forth in this paper quickly goes out and reads some of the material on the Bayesian approach with the hope that thereby he will find a new basis for automatic inference, this paper will have misfired, and he will be disappointed.

What we have indicated in this paper in connection with the test of significance in psychological research may be taken as an instance of a kind of essential mindlessness in the conduct of research which may be related to the presumption of the nonexistence of mind in the subjects of psychological research. Karl Pearson once indicated that higher statistics was only common sense reduced to numerical appreciation. However, that base in common sense must be maintained with vigilance. When we reach a point where our statistical procedures are substitutes instead of aids to thought, and we are led to absurdities, then we must return to common sense. Tukey (1962) has very properly pointed out that statistical pro-

---

[6] For a reply to Fisher, see Pearson (1955).

cedures may take our attention away from the data, which constitute the ultimate base for any inferences which we might make. Schlaifer (1959) has dubbed the error of the misapplication of statistical procedures the "error of the third kind," the most serious error which can be made. Berkson has suggested the use of "the interocular traumatic test, you know what the data mean when the conclusion hits you between the eyes" (Edwards et al., 1963). We must overcome the myth that if our treatment of our subject matter is mathematical it is therefore precise and valid. We need to overcome the handicap associated with limited competence in mathematics, a competence that makes it possible for us to run tests of significance while it intimidates us with a vision of greater mathematical competence if only one could reach up to it. Mathematics can serve to obscure as well as reveal.

Most important, we need to get on with the business of generating psychological hypotheses and proceed to do investigations and make inferences which bear on them, instead of, as so much of our literature would attest, testing the statistical null hypothesis in any number of contexts in which we have every reason to suppose that it is false in the first place.

REFERENCES

Barnard, G. A. Sampling inspection and statistical decisions. *Journal of the Royal Statistical Society* (B), 1954, **16**, 151–165.

Berkson, J. Some difficulties of interpretation encountered in the application of the chi-square test. *Journal of the American Statistical Association*, 1938, **33**, 526–542.

Berkson, J. Tests of significance considered as evidence. *Journal of the American Statistical Association*, 1942, **37**, 325–335.

Binder, A. Further considerations on testing the null hypothesis and the strategy and tactics of investigating theoretical models. *Psychological Review*, 1963, **70**, 101–109.

Bolles, R. C. The difference between statistical hypotheses and scientific hypotheses. *Psychological Reports*, 1962, **11**, 639–645.

Boring, E. G. *A history of experimental psychology.* (2nd ed.) New York: Appleton-Century-Crofts, 1950.

Cohen, J. The statistical power of abnormal-social psychological research: a review. *Journal of Abnormal and Social Psychology*, 1962, **65**, 145–153.

Cronbach, L. J. The two disciplines of scientific psychology. *American Psychologist*, 1957, **12**, 671–684.

Edwards, A. L. *Experimental design in psychological research.* New York: Rinehart, 1950.

Edwards, W., Lindman, H., & Savage, L. J. Bayesian statistical inference for psychological research. *Psychological Review*, 1963, **70**, 193–242.

Ferguson, L. *Statistical analysis in psychology and education.* New York: McGraw-Hill, 1959.

Fisher, R. A. *The design of experiments.* (4th ed.) Edinburgh: Oliver & Boyd, 1947.

Fisher, R. A. Statistical methods and scientific induction. *Journal of the Royal Statistical Society* (B), 1955, **17**, 69–78.

Guilford, J. P. *Psychometric methods.* New York: McGraw-Hill, 1936.

Hodges, J. L., & Lehman, E. L. Testing the approximate validity of statistical hypotheses. *Journal of the Royal Statistical Society* (B), 1954, **16**, 261–268.

Kaiser, H. F. Directional statistical decision. *Psychological Review,* 1960, **67**, 160–167.

Keynes, J. M. *A treatise on probability.* London: Macmillan, 1948.

Lacey, O. L. *Statistical methods in experimentation.* New York: Macmillan, 1953.

Lindquist, E. F. *Statistical analysis in educational research.* Boston: Houghton Mifflin, 1940.

McNemar, Q. At random: sense and nonsense. *American Psychologist,* 1960, **15**, 295–300.

Melton, A. W. Editorial. *Journal of Experimental Psychology,* 1962, **64**, 553–557.

Neyman, J. Outline of a theory of statistical estimation based on the classical theory of probability. *Philosophical Transactions of the Royal Society* (A), 1937, **236**, 333–380.

Neyman, J. "Inductive behavior" as a basic concept of philosophy of science. *Review of the Mathematical Statistics Institute,* 1957, **25**, 7–22.

Neyman, J., & Pearson, E. S. On the problem of the most efficient tests of statistical hypotheses. *Philosophical Transactions of the Royal Society* (A), 1933, **231**, 289–337.

Nunnally, J. The place of statistics in psychology. *Education and Psychological Measurement,* 1960, **20**, 641–650.

Pearson, E. S. Statistical concepts in their relation to reality. *Journal of the Royal Statistical Society* (B), 1955, **17**, 204–207.

Roberts, C. L., & Wist, E. An empirical sidelight on the aggregate-general distinction. (Unpublished manuscript.)

Rosenthal, R., & Gaito, J. The interpretation of levels of significance by psychological researchers. *Journal of Psychology,* 1963, **55**, 33–38.

Rozeboom, W. W. The fallacy of the null-hypothesis significance test. *Psychological Bulletin,* 1960, **57**, 416–428.

Savage, L. J. *The foundations of statistics.* New York: Wiley, 1954.

Schlaifer, R. *Probability and statistics for business decisions.* New York: McGraw-Hill, 1959.

Smith, C. A. B. Review of N. T. J. Bailey, *Statistical methods in biology. Applied Statistics,* 1960, **9**, 64–66.

Snedecor, G. W. *Statistical methods.* (4th ed.) Ames: Iowa State College Press, 1946.

Tukey, J. W. The future of data analysis. *Annals of Mathematical Statistics,* 1962, **33**, 1–67.

Underwood, B. J., Duncan, C. P., Taylor, J. A., & Cotton, J. W. *Elementary statistics.* New York: Appleton-Century-Crofts, 1954.

Wald, A. Contributions to the theory of statistical estimation and testing hypotheses. *Annals of Mathematical Statistics,* 1939, **10**, 299–326.

Wald, A. *Statistical decision functions.* New York: Wiley, 1950.

Wald, A. *Selected papers in statistics and probability.* New York: McGraw-Hill, 1955.

Wilson, K. V. Subjectivist statistics for the current crisis. *Contemporary Psychology,* 1961, **6**, 229–231.

25. The Concept of Statistical Significance and the Controversy about One-Tailed Tests[1]

H. J. Eysenck

The discussion by Dr. Eysenck begins by noting the common misunderstanding and perhaps misuse of the term "significance" which serves as a restatement of the probability values. These values have a more precise meaning than the labels "significant" and "nonsignificant." It is suggested that surplus meaning has been attributed to the word "significant," "and it has become a shibboleth which divides the successful from the unsuccessful research." Such subjective meaning has no place in the interpretation of results; it is argued that results should be reported objectively in terms of the probability of disproof of the null hypothesis by means of the two-tailed test. The point is also made that a "*statement of one-tail probability is not a statement of fact, but of opinion, and should not be offered instead of, but only in addition to, the factual two-tailed probability . . .*".

Several controversial papers regarding the uses and abuses of the one-tailed test of significance have recently appeared (Burke 1953, 1954; Goldfried 1959; Hick 1952; Jones 1952, 1954; Marks 1951, 1953). As Goldfried (1959) points out, "the important question debated is not *if* it should be used, but rather *when* it should be used." It is suggested here that most of the disagreements emerging from this controversy stem from a misunderstanding of the term "significance," and it is further suggested that the same misunderstanding runs through many discussions of two-tailed tests as well. It will be suggested that in the sense in which Goldfried's statement is meant, it has been the wrong question which has been debated; neither

[1] Reprinted from the *Psychological Review*, 1960, **67**, 269–271. Copyright 1960 by the American Psychological Association, and reproduced by permission of the author and the publisher.

one-tailed nor two-tailed tests should be used at all in the sense envisaged by most of the writers quoted.

The outcome of the statistical examination of experimental results is always stated in terms of the probability of disconfirmation of the null hypothesis; the set of values which these p values can take is continuous in the interval from 0 to 1. It is customary to take arbitrary p values, such as .05 and .01, and use them to dichotomize this continuum into a *significant* and an *insignificant* portion. This habit has no obvious advantage, if what is intended is merely a restatement of the probability values; these are already given in any case and are far more precise than a simple dichotomous statement. Indeed, gross absurdities result from taking these verbal statements too seriously; the difference between a C.R. of 1.90 and another of 2.00 is quite negligible, yet one falls on one side of the dichotomy, the other on the other side. This has led to such summary statements as: "almost significant," or "significant at the 10% level." If the verbal dichotomous scale is not satisfactory—as it clearly is not—the answer surely is to keep to the continuous p scale, rather than subdivide the verbal scale.

However, surplus meaning has accrued to the word "significant," and it has become a shibboleth which divides the successful from the unsuccessful research. It is frequently interpreted as almost guaranteeing reproducibility of results, while failure to reach significance is interpreted as disconfirmation. Hence the urgent desire to achieve respectability and significance by one-tailed tests, if need be, and the argument regarding when the cachet of "significance" can be bestowed upon a research result. Yet the argument, and the achievement or nonachievement of significance, do not alter the facts of the case, which are contained in the statement of the p value of the results. Anything beyond these facts depends upon interpretation, and is subjective; it does not alter the facts of the case in the slightest.

As an example of the necessity of interpretation, consider the a priori probability of the conclusion. Suppose that an experiment on ESP were carried out with all the precautions which human ingenuity can devise, so that even the most sceptical had to agree that no fault could be found with the experimental design. *Suppose* also that a p value of .05 were achieved. Would this be considered "significant," in the sense of guaranteeing reproducibility? Critics would point out quite rightly that where the a priori probability is very low, as in this case, much higher p values would be required to carry significance. Logicians are agreed that interpretation of experimental results must call on all available knowledge about the subject in question; a priori probability is a kind of summary statement of much of this knowledge. It cannot be overlooked in arriving at a conclusion regarding "significance" when the term carries the surplus meaning indicated.

That interpretation comes into the problem very much is clear when we look at such conditions as those suggested by Kimmel (1957) as criteria for the use of one-tailed tests. He suggests, for instance, that they may be used if results in the opposite direction would be psychologically meaningless or could not be deduced from any psychological theory. These are obviously not objective criteria, but depend on what the author (or reader) considers psychologically meaningless, or the kind of theory he may hold. Opinions will differ, and consequently some readers will agree to the use of the one-tailed test in a particular case, others will not. Thus to some readers the results will appear *significant*, to others *insignificant*.

The whole argument seems to be about *words*, not about *facts*: Is the word "significant" to be used in a given situation, or is it not? This would only matter if the word carried some objective meaning not contained in the probability figures; we have argued that it does carry surplus meaning, but that this is not of an objective kind. Consequently, nothing important is changed by omitting the term altogether in the report, leaving interpretation to the reader. After all, the only true proof of reproducibility is reproduction! Verbal assertions of "significance" have no more meaning than the *droit du pour* at the court of Louis XIV.

The solution is to separate quite clearly and decisively the *objective statement of the probability of disproof* of the *null hypothesis* (by means of a two-tailed test), and the *subjective evaluation and interpretation of the results*. The reader would be able to accept the first statement as a statement of fact and would then be able to judge for himself the arguments presented by the author regarding the *meaning* of these facts. These arguments might be based on results of previous experiments, predictions made on the basis of more or less widely accepted theories, number of cases involved, a priori lack of acceptability of the conclusions, and other similar grounds; an explicit statement of the arguments would enable the reader to decide for himself the acceptability of the conclusions in a manner precluded by the simple statement of one-tailed probability. *A statement of one-tail probability is not a statement of fact, but of opinion, and should not be offered instead of, but only in addition to, the factual two-tailed probability*; if it is offered at all, it should be accompanied by a full statement of the arguments in favor of its facilitating a more meaningful interpretation of the data. In the writer's opinion, it would be better to drop such statements of one-tailed probability altogether and rely entirely on appropriate argumentation to establish the meaning of the observed (two-tailed) probabilities.

Implicit in this recommendation is the corollary that the mechanical evaluation of experimental results in terms of "significant" and "not significant" be dropped outright. Interpretation is implicit in the statement of one-tailed probabilities, but it is also implicit in the statement of two-tailed probabilities if these are *automatically* interpreted as being significant or not significant, with all the surplus meaning carried by these terms. The experimenter should give his (two-tailed) p values and then proceed to argue regarding the acceptability of the conclusions on the basis already indicated. There have appeared in the literature solemn discussions about the possible causes for discrepancies between two experiments, one of which gave significant, the other insignificant results; yet the respective t values were almost identical, one lying just on the one side, the other just on the other side, of the arbitrary 5% line. Such arguments are unrealistic and would be avoided if p values were compared, rather than verbal statements. Two experiments giving p values of .048 and .056 are in excellent agreement, although one is significant, while the other is not.

To summarize the main point of this note briefly, we would say that verbal statements regarding "significance" are at best supererogatory restatements in an inconvenient dichotomous form of results already properly stated in terms of a continuous system of p values; at worst they carry unjustified surplus meaning of an entirely subjective kind under the guise of an objective and mathematically meaningful statement. Subjective judgments of reproducibility cannot reasonably be based on the mechanical application of a rule of thumb whose only usefulness lies in the elementary instruction of undergraduates lacking in mathematical background; if they are to be made at all they demand complex consideration of a priori probabilities. It is suggested that the accurate and factual statement of probabilities (two-tailed) should be mandatory and that all subjective considerations, arguments, and judgments should be clearly separated from such factual statements. It is implied that judgments of "significance" belong with the subjective side, and it is also implied that the calculation of p values on the basis of one-tailed tests has no place in psychology.

REFERENCES

Burke, C. J. A brief note on one-tailed tests. *Psychological Bulletin*, 1953, **50**, 384–387.

Burke, C. J. Further remarks on one-tailed tests. *Psychological Bulletin*, 1954, **51**, 587–590.

Goldfried, M. R. One tailed tests and "unexpected" results. *Psychological Review*, 1959, **66**, 79–80.

Hick, W. E. A note on one-tailed and two-tailed tests. *Psychological Review*, 1952, **59**, 316–318.

Jones, L. V. Tests of hypotheses: one-sided and two-sided alternatives. *Psychological Bulletin*, 1952, **49**, 43–46.

Jones, L. V. A rejoinder on one-tailed tests. *Psychological Bulletin*, 1954, **51**, 585–586.

Kimmel, H. D. Three criteria for the use of one-tailed tests. *Psychological Bulletin*, 1957, **54**, 351–353.

Marks, M. R. Two kinds of experiment distinguished in terms of statistical operations. *Psychological Bulletin*, 1951, **58**, 179–184.

Marks, M. R. One- and two-tailed tests. *Psychological Review*, 1953, **60**, 203–208.

26. The Importance of Negative Results in Psychological Research[1]

Reginald Smart

Reviewing two years of each of four popular journals, Dr. Smart found that the frequency of reported negative results was quite low. Data from unpublished sources revealed a higher frequency of negative results. It was concluded that for several reasons, particularly author and journal editor selection, negative results are much less likely to be published than positive results. Discussing the implications of this finding, he suggested that much important information is being lost since researchers are made aware of only those studies supporting a particular hypothesis and not those failing to support it. Other practical, statistical, and heuristic implications of unreported negative results are noted and the publication of brief abstracts of studies yielding negative results is called for.

A common saying among graduate students in the days before analysis of variance was "c.r.'s of three or no Ph.D." Despite the doubtful validity of this jibe at graduate school policy on negative results the reader of modern psychological journals cannot fail to be impressed with the large number of positive results reported. In article after article one notes that the author has formulated and tested hypotheses and almost invariably found statistical support for them. Despite the importance of negative results in any science, their absence in psychological journals has rarely been noted or commented upon.

The only data on the proportions of negative results reported have been assembled by Sterling (1959) who reviewed research in four commonly read psychological journals.[2] He found that only 8 out of 294 research papers failed to confirm the experimental hypotheses. This would be less than 3 per cent whereas about 5 per cent would be expected in view of the commonly used .05 level of probability for conferring "significance." The 5 per cent which Sterling anticipated would be valid

[1] Reprinted from the *Canadian Psychologist*, 1964, **5a**, 225–232, by permission of the author and the Canadian Psychological Association.

[2] The Journals of: Experimental Psychology, Clinical Psychology, and Social Psychology for 1955, and the Journal of Comparative and Physiological Psychology for 1956.

expectation only if it were assumed that psychologists are always working with "true" experimental hypotheses, and that reported studies accurately reflect the total scientific effort with regard to the fate of experimental hypotheses.

The purposes of this study are to determine whether the low proportion of reported negative results persists and whether there is some selection in the papers printed such that negative results are unlikely to be published. Attempts will also be made to indicate the potential importance of negative results, to examine the reasons for the biased reporting of results, and to suggest some methods of bringing negative results into the psychological literature.

Data relating to the actual proportion of negative outcomes among all statistical tests made (both published and unpublished) are extremely difficult to assemble. For this reason, the only reported study of negative results (Sterling, 1959) was confined exclusively to published papers and it showed that 3 per cent contained negative results. In order to determine whether negative findings are still infrequent, the same journals which Sterling used in 1955 and 1956 were examined for 1961 or 1962. The results are shown in Table 26-1 and it can be seen that the percentage

TABLE 26-1

The Proportion of Negative and Positive Results in
Psychological Research Journals

(Journals of)	Percentages are shown in brackets		
	Number of Papers Using Statistical Tests	Number with Positive Results	Number with Negative Results
Experimental Psychology (1962, Vol. 63)	90	83 (92.3)	7 (7.7)
Comparative and Physiological (1962, Nos. 1, 2, 3)	66	61 (92.4)	5 (7.6)
Clinical Psychology (1961)	88	81 (91.4)	7 (8.6)
Social Psychology (1962)	65	57 (87.7)	8 (12.3)
APA Annual Meeting (1962)	83	66 (79.5)	17 (20.5)
Dissertation Abstracts (1962)	86	60 (69.8)	26 (30.2)

of negative results range from 7.6 to 12.3. Sterling did not indicate that his findings of 3 per cent negative results does not differ significantly from the 5 per cent expectation (chi square equals 3.20, P. > .05 < .10) assuming all null hypotheses tested are, in fact, false. It should also be noted from Table 26-1 that all of the journals examined had, in 1961 or 1962, percentages of negative results greater than 5 per cent.[3] Since psychologists are probably *not* always working with false null hypotheses an important question is how well does the percentage reported correspond with the negative results actually obtained by psychologists—including both published and unpublished results ? Some provisional answers are offered here by showing that certain large but unpublished collections of psychological studies contain a higher proportion of negative results than do psychological journals, and that Ph.D. theses with negative results are less likely to be published than are those with positive results.

It was felt that samples of unpublished papers such as those presented at psychological meetings would contain many papers with negative results. In order to examine this possibility a random sample of 100 papers given at the 1962 APA meeting was drawn from the reported abstracts of these papers (American Psychological Association, 1962). Each abstract was classified as being characterized by negative or positive results; papers which did not test a hypothesis, or were clinical histories or theoretical studies were counted separately. It can be seen from data in Table 26-1 that 20.5% of these papers contained negative results as compared with the 7.6 to 12.3 per cent average in published papers. The difference between the APA abstracts and published papers in terms of number of negative results is significant for all journals examined (P. < .02) except the Journal of Social Psychology. This result tends to suggest some selection in the papers which are published since many papers given at the APA meeting are eventually reported in the journals examined above. If the 1962 APA meeting is representative of most psychological meetings then there is a considerable body of psychological experimentation which is characterized by negative results, but remains unpublished. Abstracts of papers for the APA meeting are prepared and published but they are not indexed by subject; they rarely appear in the Psychological Abstracts, so that, essentially, they are lost if they are not published in some journal. The loss entailed by the non-reporting of negative results is even greater considering the large number of psychological meetings for which no abstracts are ever published.

A further search for negative results was made in the Dissertation Abstracts—another depository for unpublished research reports. From the six issues for 1962 three were randomly selected (nos. 1, 4, and 5) and all of the Ph.D. theses in Psychology listed were categorized according to whether they contain positive or negative results in the manner described above. It can be seen from Table 26-1 that 30.2 per cent of these theses were characterized by negative results as opposed to the 9.1 per cent for the journals. It would be difficult to argue that the Dissertation Abstracts represents current psychological experimentation, containing as it

[3] The reason for the discrepancy may be due to a difference in the classification of results as "negative." Sterling used several complex procedures for classifying papers with multi-variate designs. He tried to determine the most important hypothesis and if it was rejected then the paper was listed as "negative." If the most important hypothesis could not be identified he classed a paper as negative if at least half of the null hypotheses were not rejected. The author found it impossible to identify the "most important hypotheses" and merely categorized a paper as negative if at least half of the null hypotheses were not rejected.

does only a non-random sample of certain Ph.D. theses. In order to expand the data for the present argument a random selection of Ph.D. theses from 1956 was made (from Dissertation Abstracts, Vol. 16, 1, pp. 152-167). Each of 37 theses was categorized as positive or negative and an attempt was made to see whether theses with positive results were more often published than those with negative results. All issues of the Psychological Abstracts from 1955 to 1963 were searched for papers based on these theses. It was found that 12 of the 23 positive theses were published but only 2 of the 14 negative ones were ($\chi^2 = 5.31$, P. $< .03$). This indicates that the type of outcome in a thesis is associated with the probability of publication; negative theses are rarely published. If this dependence of publication on outcome holds for all psychological research then our journals are not nearly representative of the total research effort.

The finding that a particular mountain contains no gold fails to move prospectors and speculators whereas news of a strike quickens all of their pulses. In scientific undertakings, however, the failure to find the gold of positive results has important implications. Unless the scientist is aware of *all* experimental tests performed for a certain hypothesis then a rational decision as to warrantability of the hypothesis cannot be reached. If the reader becomes aware only of studies supporting the hypothesis and others failing to support it are unavailable to him then his decision as to its validity will often be wrong. Sterling (1959) has pointed out the statistical questions raised by lack of reported negative results and the difficulty which ensues for statistical inference if the type of outcome determines whether a paper is published. As Sterling (1959) has stated, this problem is especially important in psychology, where replications are rarely performed and even more rarely reported in the journals [4] (Sterling, 1959; Lubin, 1957).

The importance of negative results does not rest solely on their necessity for statistical decisions, particularly in view of the finding that their reported frequency is not significantly lower than expected on statistical bases. It can be argued that they serve several equally essential functions. Negative results are not "negative" in any absolute sense where statistical tests are made, and for every negative result there is a probability that the null hypothesis was wrongly accepted. It may also be that more is learned from an experiment with negative results than from one with positive results. For example, a negative result with P. $< .98$ allows us to accept the null hypotheses with greater confidence than the .05 level commonly used for rejecting null hypotheses.

Negative results are also not completely "negative" in the sense that they give no information. At the very least, they indicate that if an experiment is performed in a particular way then we learn nothing positive about the variables under consideration. In many such studies slight procedural variations, a different population, or varied statistical analyses might have led to more positive results. Cohen (1962), for example, has examined a series of articles in the abnormal-social area of psychology and determined the power to detect small, medium, and large effects of each

---

[4] For example, Sterling found that none of the 294 studies he examined was a replication of any earlier study.

statistical test used. He found that very few such tests, given the sample sizes used, could reject a null hypothesis when the effect was small, and only 50% could reject it when the effect was moderate. Only when a large effect existed could most (80%) of the studies reject the null hypothesis. This suggests that the sample sizes used in this type of research are far too small and that "much research is resulting in spuriously negative results" (Cohen, 1962, p. 153). Cohen has further suggested that "a generation of researchers could be profitably employed in repeating interesting studies which originally used inadequate sample sizes." As shown above, it is precisely those studies which are unpublished because of their negative results which probably would justify repetition. However, these are the studies least likely to be replicated because of being lost to the scientific community.

Results which favour the null hypothesis also have several further roles in science. Ostensibly, the purpose of any science is to describe functional laws relating the variables within its purview. But this also implies that something is known of the variables which are unimportant and of the instances in which a particular law does *not* hold. If this information exists but is not generally known because unpublished then our knowledge about that law is still circumscribed.

The reporting of negative results, provided they are based on well designed experiments with adequate sample sizes, can also serve as a warning to researchers that a particular area or approach is unfruitful. If such reports are unavailable then the possibility of further negative results is established. Without an awareness of the negative results in his area, the researcher is unable, except by accident, to make any improvements which might lead to positive results. As has been stated, one can retard science only by *not* reporting findings or "by otherwise obstructing the publication of scientific results. Erroneous statements, so long as they are openly published, do not indefinitely impede the progress of science, for they are ultimately corrected by new observations and interpretations" (AAAS Committee on Science in the Promotion of Human Welfare, 1963). This argument provides a further basis for the belief that withholding negative results from publication has a retrogressive effect on scientific development.

Two main explanations stand out as possible reasons for the neglect of negative results. It may be that such results are not submitted for publication or that they are submitted but turned down by journal editors. So far, it has not been possible to determine the relative proportions of negative and positive results in the total number of papers submitted for publication but it would be interesting to do so. Oblique references to unpublished negative results are not difficult to find in the literature[5] and perhaps researchers make some conscious or unconscious censorship in what is submitted for publication. Author selection seems unlikely to completely explain this suppression in view of the relatively large proportion of negative results reported at the APA meetings and in Ph.D. theses.

Many papers with negative results probably fail to appear because of editorial

[5] See, for example, Miller's paper (1956), in which negative results in replications of Conger's (1951), and Masserman and Yum's (1946) work on the effects of alcohol on conflict, are mentioned but not published.

policies which reject these papers outright, or subject them to more critical scrutiny than papers characterized by positive findings. Unambiguous statements of editorial policy on negative results are difficult to find. However, Smith (1956) during his editorship of the Journal of Abnormal and Social Psychology stated that:

Too often the failure to obtain anticipated results occurs in a context in which the procedures employed are of questionable adequacy and the measures of uncertain relevance or reliability. In such instances, interpretation is inherently so ambiguous that the report is properly judged to fall below the threshold of acceptable significance . . . The case is different with studies that obtain negative findings in the course of replicating previously published work in which positive findings have been reported. Provided that replication is exact in relevant particulars—or that the methods as described are ones demonstrated to be relevant and reliable for the purpose—failure to confirm an anticipated relationship can represent a contribution of major importance, reopening questions that had been prematurely closed. Since positive findings in agreement with prior hypotheses tend, other things equal, to support the validity of the procedures employed, it is appropriate that the technical adequacy of studies that come out negatively be more searchingly scrutinized.

This policy clearly states that studies without the anticipated results are more carefully examined unless they are replications of earlier studies with positive results. As shown above, replications of any kind are rarely published, and negative results are important even if they are not in replications of previously published work. Their loss because of special editorial criticism is deplorable in view of their importance for statistical inference and their possible heuristic value.

The argument that studies with positive results tend, more than those with negative ones, to support the validity of the procedures employed is a specious one, predicated on the assumption that only false null hypotheses are being tested. It must frequently occur that valid procedures are employed in studies which obtain negative results simply because the variables chosen are weak, or irrelevant to the measurements made. Another consideration is that positive results, far from supporting the validity of the procedure employed, might merely confirm the experimenter's expectations about the outcome. As Rosenthal has argued (1964), experimenters are usually deeply involved in the outcomes of their studies and the most common preference seems to be for confirmation of one's hypotheses. Rosenthal's studies of experimenter bias (1963a, 1963b) have shown that experimenters usually obtain the data they expect or want to obtain from their subjects, and that even the experimenter's research assistants can obtain these expected results if they have only minimal knowledge of the experimenter's biases. Questions arise, then, as to how many studies with positive results represent more than the experimenter's self-fulfilling prophecies and as to how many could be replicated by an unbiased experimenter. Perhaps special credence should be placed in studies obtaining negative results in the face of the experimenter's expectations of positive results.

Given the importance of negative results and their special neglect so far, the manner in which they might be brought into the literature is an important but perplexing question. At a time when scientific papers are being produced at an approximate rate of 3.8 articles per minute[6] caution must attend any effort to further increase their volume. This paper presents no brief for publishing any results not based on solidly designed and well executed studies, however, the scientist should publish every statistical test made under such conditions—regardless of the fate of the null hypothesis. In order to make a paper eligible for publication the author should merely be convinced that a study with negative results has a rationale for its existence and that it gives the variables under investigation a reasonable chance to show their effectiveness. Once these questions are decided in the affirmative the study becomes valuable as a piece of scientific communication. It is difficult to estimate the increment to the scientific literature which might result from publishing negative results based on well designed studies. If the 9.1 per cent average in the journals now is compared with the 20 per cent found in the APA meeting abstracts then the increment appears no greater than 10 per cent.

It would probably not be economical to publish a "journal of negative results" and the recent scarcity of journal space makes it unlikely that most editors would publish many papers with negative results. Nevertheless, each journal could publish the abstracts of such papers or even their titles with the authors' names and the source from which full reports could be obtained. Some such righting of the ratio of negative to positive results would provide a needed addition to the psychological literature, even if it did show our occasional fallibility in choosing variables for study.

REFERENCES

American Association for the Advancement of Science Committee on Science in the Promotion of Human Welfare. Science and the race problem. *Science*, 1963, **142**, 558–563.

American Psychological Association. Program of the seventieth annual convention. *American Psychologist*, 1962, **16**(6).

Bourne, C. P. *The world's technical journal literature: an estimate of volume origin, language, field, indexing and abstracting.* Menlo Park: Stanford Research Institute, 1961.

Cohen, J. The statistical power of abnormal-social psychological research: a review. *Journal of Abnormal and Social Psychology*, 1962, **65**, 145–153.

Conger, J. J. The effects of alcohol on conflict behaviour in the albino rat. *Quarterly Journal of Studies on Alcohol*, 1951, **12**, 1–29.

Lubin, A. Replicability as a publication criterion. *American Psychologist*, 1957, **8**, 519–520.

Masserman, J. H., & Yum, K. S. An analysis of the influence of alcohol on experimental neuroses in cats. *Psychosomatic Medicine*, 1946, **101**, 36–52.

Miller, N. E. Effect of drugs on motivation. *Annals of the New York Academy of Sciences*, 1956, **65**, 318–333.

[6] This sobering figure is based on Bourne's estimate (1961) of 2×10^6 scientific articles being published per year.

Rosenthal, R. Experimenter outcome-orientation and the results of the psychological experiment. *Psychological Bulletin*, 1964, **61**, 405–412.

Rosenthal, R., & Fode, K. L. The psychology of the scientist: three experiments in experimenter bias. *Psychological Reports*, 1963*a*, **12**, 491–511.

Rosenthal, R., Persinger, G. W., Vikan-Kline, L., & Mulry, R. C. The role of the research assistant in the mediation of experimenter bias. *Journal of Personality*, 1963*b*, **31**, 313–335.

Smith, M. B. Editorial. *Journal of Abnormal and Social Psychology*, 1956, **52**, 1–4.

Sterling, T. D. Publication decisions and their possible effects on inferences drawn from tests of significance—or vice versa. *Journal of the American Statistical Association*, 1959, **54**, 30–34.

27. On the Futility of Aggregating Individual Learning Curves[1]

Nicholas Baloff & Selwyn W. Becker

The traditional use of mean learning curves to summarize the data of a number of subjects is criticized. It is argued that such curves tend to eliminate from view individual differences in learning. Often the aggregate learning curve describes only a few, and sometimes none, of the individual curves from which it was derived. It is also asserted that the aggregate curves may yield meaningless information about the underlying process being investigated. Examples are cited that vividly demonstrate these problems and the advantages of studying individual differences are discussed.

For several decades the development and interpretation of "mean learning curves," curves based on data aggregated over several Ss, has been a traditional methodology in experiments on human and animal learning. In this paper we will argue that such aggregate learning curves can yield either meaningless or spurious information about the underlying learning process and also obscure important individual differences in learning. Although portions of our argument are based on statements which have appeared in the literature over the last two decades, continued reliance on the mean learning curve necessitates a comprehensive restatement and elaboration of the issues involved.[2]

One of the major problems associated with mean learning curves is the impossibility of deducing the characteristics of the component individual learning curves by merely examining the functional form of the aggregate curve. All too often

[1] Reprinted from *Psychological Reports*, 1967, **20**, 183–191, with the permission of the authors and the publisher.

[2] Use of mean learning curves to describe data intended to illuminate both the effects of different treatments as well as the underlying learning process is so widespread as to be almost "traditional." For a few recent examples see: Bogartz and Carterette (1963), Cohen and Hut (1963), Duncan (1960), Ebenholtz (1963), Horowitz, Lippman, Norman, and McConkie (1964), Jeffrey and Cohen (1964), Lipsitt and LoLordo (1963), Mandler, Cowan, and Gold (1964), Miller and Lasko (1964), and Petre (1964).

the mean learning curve will describe the functional form of few, if any, of the individual learning curves from which it was developed. In these cases, it is clearly impossible to deduce the form of the individual curves from the aggregate curve. A particularly vivid illustration of this situation can be encountered when *S*s' learning is of an insightful nature and the resulting individual curves are step functions. If all *S*s do not achieve their insight on the same trial, averaging such a group of functions can yield a continuous, negatively accelerated group curve that does not describe any of the individual functions in the group. A hypothetical illustration of this situation was provided by Hayes (1953) when he demonstrated how the combination of step functions could yield aggregate curves of sigmoid or exponential form.

That Hayes' demonstration is not limited to hypothetical situations became evident to us when we attempted to test an hypothesis about the functional form of group learning curves. In that attempt we used a task described by McCurdy and Lambert (1952). Since their task resembles others that have been used in a variety of human learning experiments, it will be useful to describe our experience in some detail.

McCurdy and Lambert's task provided an *S* or a number of *S*s with 2-position rotary switches. *S*s were instructed to light a signal lamp whenever it was dark by turning one of the switches. They were further instructed to learn how to do this without making a single unnecessary movement. If the switches were numbered, say for example from 1 to 10, then a *fixed series* like 3, 1, 5, 3, 6, 1, 4, 1, would determine which switch would light the signal lamp. "The experimenter (who controls which switch is the correct one on every trial) follows his pattern without telltale breaks until the subject makes one errorless run through the series" (McCurdy & Lambert, 1952, p. 480). The significant feature of this task is that the correct switches occur in a fixed recurring pattern. If and when *S* discovers the sequence, his errors drop sharply. McCurdy and Lambert write: "The subject must realize that the switch changes occur . . . in a regularly recurrent series, . . . the realization must come as an outright discovery by the subject" (McCurdy & Lambert, 1952, p. 481). We used this task with 11 groups of 5 *S*s. Each of the 5 *S*s, seated around a table, had before him 2 switches. In the center of the table was a signal lamp. *S*s were told to light the lamp whenever it went dark by activating one of the switches. They were instructed to do this as quickly and with as few ineffective switch movements as possible. Our recurring series was 1, 8, 3, 6, 9. The switches were so numbered and arranged that each *S* had one correct switch every 5 trials. A trial was defined as the time it took *S*s to light the signal lamp after *E* extinguished it. The number of switch movements per trial was automatically recorded. The data are presented following the procedure outlined by McCurdy and Lambert. The number of errors per run (once through the recurring series, in our case, 5 trials) are presented for each group in Fig. 27-1. The aggregate curve, based on the 11 individual curves, is shown in Fig. 27-2. The marked differences between the aggregate curve and nearly all of the 11 from which it arose are apparent. The aggregate curve in this instance is not only meaningless, it actually yields

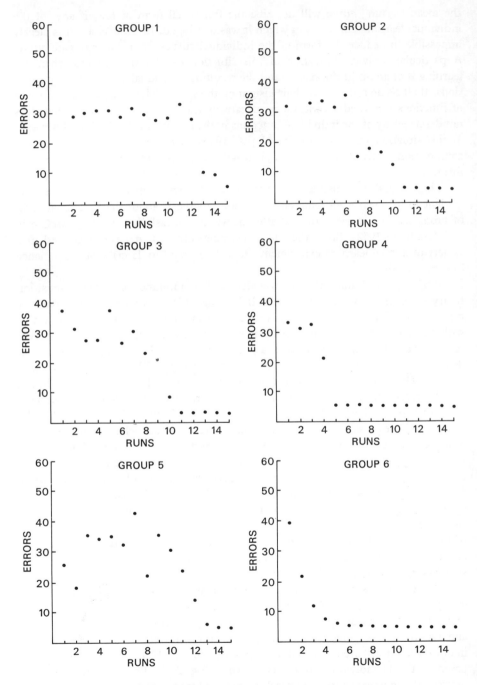

FIGURE 27-1. Reduction in number of errors
per run (block of 5 trials) for each of 11 groups.

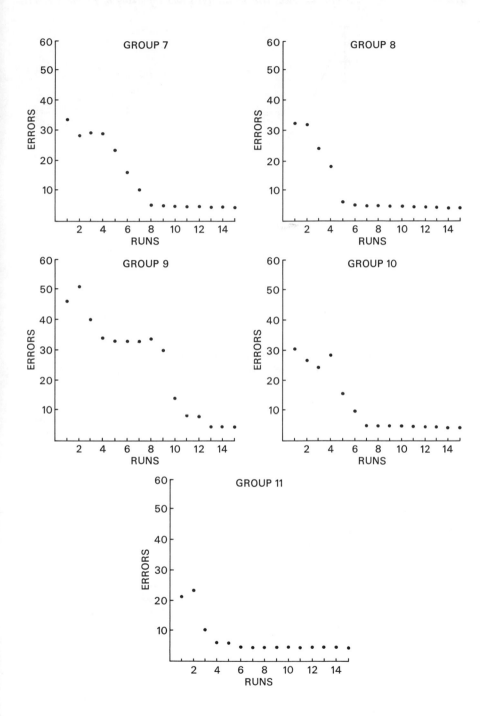

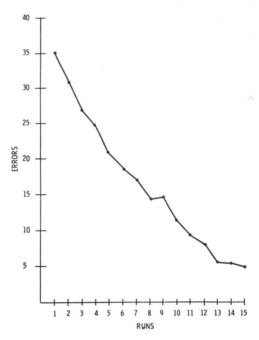

FIGURE 27-2. Reduction in number of errors per run (block of 5 trials) aggregated over 11 groups.

misinformation about the individuals it was meant to describe on the "average."[3]

As we have already indicated, there is reason to believe that the problem of aggregating step functions is not confined to this single instance. From a partial review of the recent learning literature, we suggest that a number of research designs may have characteristics similar to those of our example (Adams, 1954; Paul & Noble, 1964; Farese & Noble, 1960; Noble, Alcock, & Farese, 1958; Noble, 1957a, 1957b). In each of these studies, Ss were required to respond to a repetitive fixed series of stimuli. Only aggregate learning curves are reported, and all conclusions and generalizations are based on these aggregate curves. In all but the first study cited the authors fitted a familiarly-shaped "growth function" to their aggregate learning curves. Since individual learning curves are not presented or discussed, it is not possible to judge whether these aggregate curves represent a combination of growth functions or *misrepresent* a combination of step functions resulting from insightful learning. However, since the characteristics of the tasks in these studies are similar to those of McCurdy and Lambert's task, we question the utility and meaning of these aggregate results.

The problem of developing an aggregate curve whose functional form is different

[3] The experiment we described involved group learning, and the unit of analysis is the group, hence aggregating the curves for 11 groups into one curve is analogous to aggregating the curves for a number of individuals into a single curve.

from any of the individual curves is not restricted to insightful learning character-ized by step functions. Hayes (1953) also demonstrated that aggregating hypothetical *convex* functions can result in a *concave* exponential function and that aggregating *exponential* functions can yield a *sigmoidal* function. Similarly, Sidman (1952), has shown that aggregating *linear* learning curves with different learning rate parameters can hypothetically yield an *exponential* function.

The foregoing arguments are based on hypothetical examples or empirical cases. Looking at the aggregation problem from a mathematical point of view, it can be demonstrated that in many cases the aggregation of individual learning curves of the same functional form will yield an aggregate learning curve of a *different* functional form—except in the unlikely case that the model or equation parameters are equal for each of the individual curves. Most of the exponential, sigmoidal or "growth" and power functions—functional forms of greatest interest in research on learning—are subject to this aggregation problem.[4] Since the aggregate curve cannot be of the same form as the individual curves, except under the equal-parameter assumption, it is obvious that the aggregate curve cannot serve to specify uniquely the form of the individual curves in these cases. We have yet to find an author who has cared to assume equal parameters for all *S*s.

In an attempt to preserve the respectability of the aggregate learning curves, Estes (1956) has shown that aggregating individual curves of certain functional forms does result in a mean curve of the same type. Unfortunately, the functions that exhibit this property have not been of particular interest in the past. Estes also argues that aggregate curves can, under special conditions, be used to test the hypothesis that the mean curve is not *inconsistent* with one or another postulated form of the individual curves. This procedure in no way assures us that some form or forms other than that postulated actually underlie the aggregate curve. Although Estes' test yields little information, it perhaps is better than no test at all. However, we are not aware of any published report in which it was used as a means of examin-ing the consistency between the observed functional form of the aggregate curve and the assumed form of the individual curves.

To this point we have cited hypothetical examples and presented empirical evidence that combining similar individual learning curves *can* yield an aggregate curve of an entirely different form. We also have cited mathematical proofs that combining certain individual learning curves (except under particular and im-probable conditions) *must* yield an aggregate curve of a form different from the individual ones. In summary, then, we can state that mean learning curves typically give us no basis for inference about the individual learning functions they purport to summarize. Further, models of learning developed from aggregated curves can prove to be a source of considerable confusion and spurious conclusions.

The inadvisability of using aggregate learning curves can be generalized beyond the case where one is primarily interested in the functional form of the learning curve or the correspondence between individual and aggregate curves. Comparing

---

[4] For an explicit statement of when this condition exists, see Estes (1956), Sidman (1952), and Bakan (1954).

the effects of different treatments on the learning process through the use of mean curves can also be fraught with difficulties. Estes recognized this in passing when he stated that "... the uncritical use of mean curves even for such purposes as determining the effect of an experimental treatment upon rate of learning ... is attended by considerable risk" (Estes, 1956, p. 134). He did not, however, make clear what these risks might be.

We can illustrate the risk of using aggregate curves for this purpose by assuming that individual Ss have roughly linear learning curves on a cognitive task. Assume further that small quantities of phenobarbital are administered as the treatment and that this acts as a depressant on some people and as an energizer on others. The result could be that the rate of learning is increased in certain Ss and reduced in others. Alternately, the treatment could conceivably change the actual forms of the individual's learning functions, yielding concave and convex forms depending on the effect of the treatment. In either case, the differential effects could cancel nicely, giving an essentially linear aggregate curve in which the rate of learning is the same as that of a control group. If the aggregate curves are accepted at face value without reference to the behavior of the individual learning phenomena, the conclusion could be made that phenobarbital has no effect on the rate of learning of the "average individual," a conclusion that might be false for every individual in the group. The point is clear: since we cannot infer the shape and behavior of the underlying individual learning processes from aggregate curves, the indiscriminant use of such curves as a means of summarizing treatment effects is a dubious procedure.

The above example also illustrates how the use of aggregate data can obscure a wealth of data on individual differences. Tryon (1934) made this point three decades ago when he noted that:

The intensive study of the average behavior of a species ... generally leads the ... psychologist to ignore the more interesting differences between individuals from whom the "average individual" is abstracted. The "average individual" is, in fact, a man-made fiction, and the behavior of a species can be properly understood only by considering variations in behavior of all (or a random sample) the individuals who are classed in it (p. 409).

Hovland (1951), almost two decades later still felt it necessary to write:

Much of the literature on human learning is presented in terms of the broadest types of generalization possible. But every worker in the field is struck by the wide variability from individual to individual in even the simplest types of learning. Greatly needed are systematic investigations of the source of variability (p. 632).

The degree to which these exhortations have been ignored is evident from an examination of human learning literature since 1951. "Average" human learning, as represented by aggregate learning curves, continues to be the focus of interest with little investigation of individual differences. Eckstrand summarized the situation succinctly by noting that, "In no other area of behavior study has the topic of individual differences been more neglected" (Eckstrand, 1962, p. 405).

The advantages that could derive from a thorough study of individual differences in human learning are apparent. To begin with, it would be possible to determine whether individual learning curves can be efficiently described by a single functional relationship. That is, it would be possible to *test* the concept of a species learning curve for given tasks, rather than implicitly or explicitly assuming that one exists. If it is possible to demonstrate the existence of a species learning curve—a single function that adequately describes the learning curves of different individuals within a species—then it would be meaningful to investigate individual differences in the parameters of the function, as well as effects on the parameters of different treatments or conditions.

Whether a researcher is interested in the general shape of a species learning curve or in the individual differences summarized by variations in parameter values is, of course, a matter of personal preference. However, a strong reason for interest in individual differences was given by Eckstrand when he urged, ". . . taking advantage of individual differences and tailoring the learning environment to each learner . . . to produce efficiency which is higher than can be achieved by ignoring individual differences and optimizing the learning environment for the average learner" (Eckstrand, 1962, p. 409).

The implications of our arguments to this point seem clear. If one is interested in a species learning curve, the form of the curve for a particular task, or the average effects of different treatments on the parameters of a group learning curve, we suggest that much greater emphasis be placed on studying the learning behavior of the individual. Only a systematic examination of individual learning curves can resolve the grave questions that have been raised about the meaning of the aggregate curves reported in the past several decades. Further, this change in focus holds promise of yielding information on individual differences that is crucial to a proper understanding of human learning.

The suggested focus on individual learning behavior is likely to encounter claims that individual learning phenomena are too irregular or too poorly behaved to be studied and described mathematically. This allegation is not a new one. It has been used as a rationale for the development of aggregate curves for several decades. However, we doubt that individual learning behavior is, or need be, this difficult to analyze. Some evidence for this position can be found in a few reports where individual learning curves were successfully examined (Reed & Zinszer, 1943; DuBois & Bunch, 1949; Murdoch, 1960). In addition, extreme variability of data may at times be a result of experimental design factors rather than an inherent property of the individual. Finally, in cases where variability is evident and unavoidable, means of reducing this variability, other than aggregating across individuals, might be applied. For example, in some cases, it may be possible to eliminate a significant amount of variation by averaging the values of the dependent variable over two or more trials. This type of "smoothing" will often reduce the variability of individual observations while still maintaining the integrity of any underlying regularity in the data.

REFERENCES

Adams, J. A. Multiple versus single problem training in human problem solving. *Journal of Experimental Psychology*, 1954, **45**, 15–18.

Bakan, D. A generalization of Sidman's results on group and individual functions and a criterion. *Psychological Bulletin*, 1954, **51**, 63–64.

Bogartz, R. S., & Carterette, E. C. Free recall of redundant strings of symbols by children. *Journal of Experimental Psychology*, 1963, **66**, 399–408.

Cohen, B. H., & Hut, P. A. Learning of responses to stimulus classes and to specific stimuli. *Journal of Experimental Psychology*, 1963, **66**, 274–280.

DuBois, P. H., & Bunch, M. E. A new technique for studying group learning. *American Journal of Psychology*, 1949, **62**, 272–278.

Duncan, C. P. Description of learning to learn in human subjects. *American Journal of Psychology*, 1960, **73**, 108–114.

Ebenholtz, S. M. Serial learning: position learning and sequential associations. *Journal of Experimental Psychology*, 1963, **66**, 353–362.

Eckstrand, G. A. Individuality in the learning process: some issues and implications. *Psychological Record*, 1962, **12**, 405–416.

Estes, W. K. The problem of inference from curves based on group data. *Psychological Bulletin*, 1956, **53**, 134–140.

Farese, F. J., & Noble, C. E. Trial and error versus mixed-selective learning in man. *Perceptual and Motor Skills*, 1960, **10**, 115–122.

Hayes, K. J. The backward curve: a method for the study of learning. *Psychological Review*, 1953, **60**, 269–275.

Horowitz, L. M., Lippman, L. G., Norman, S. A., & McConkie, G. W. Compound stimuli in paired-associate learning. *Journal of Experimental Psychology*, 1964, **67**, 132–141.

Hovland, C. I. Human learning and retention. In S. S. Stevens (Ed.), *Handbook of experimental psychology*. New York: Wiley, 1951. Pp. 613–689.

Jeffrey, W. E., & Cohen, L. B. Effect of spatial separation of stimulus, response and reinforcement on selective learning in children. *Journal of Experimental Psychology*, 1964, **67**, 577–580.

Lipsitt, L. P., & LoLordo, V. M. Interactive effect of stress and stimulus generalization on childrens' oddity learning. *Journal of Experimental Psychology*, 1963, **66**, 210–214.

Mandler, G., Cowan, P. A., & Gold, C. Concept learning and probability matching. *Journal of Experimental Psychology*, 1964, **67**, 514–522.

McCurdy, H. G., & Lambert, W. E. The efficiency of small human groups in the solution of problems requiring genuine cooperation. *Journal of Personality*, 1952, **20**, 478–494.

Miller, M. E., & Lasko, V. Effect of constant versus varied pairing of simultaneous intentional- and incidental-learning materials with different rates and numbers of exposures. *Journal of Experimental Psychology*, 1964, **67**, 256–262.

Murdoch, B. B. The immediate retention of unrelated words. *Journal of Experimental Psychology*, 1960, **60**, 222–234.

Noble, C. E. Human trial-and-error learning. *Psychological Reports*, 1957a, **3**, 377–398.

Noble, C. E. The length-difficulty relationship in compound trial-and-error learning. *Journal of Experimental Psychology*, 1957*b*, **54**, 246–252.

Noble, C. E., Alcock, W. T., & Farese, F. J. Habit reversal under differential instructions in compound trial-and-error learning. *Journal of Psychology*, 1958, **46**, 253–264.

Paul, N. T., & Noble, C. E. Influence of successive habit reversals on human learning and transfer. *Journal of Experimental Psychology*, 1964, **68**, 37–43.

Petre, R. D. Concept acquisition as a function of stimulus-equivalence pretraining with identical and dissimilar stimuli. *Journal of Experimental Psychology*, 1964, **67**, 360–364.

Reed, H. B., & Zinszer, H. A. The occurrence of plateaus in telegraphy. *Journal of Experimental Psychology*, 1943, **33**, 130–135.

Sidman, M. A note on functional relations obtained from group data. *Psychological Bulletin*, 1952, **49**, 263–269.

Tryon, R. C. Individual differences. In F. A. Moss (Ed.), *Comparative psychology*. Englewood Cliffs: Prentice-Hall, 1934.

ETHICAL PROBLEMS IN RESEARCH

There are serious ethical considerations in at least certain types of psychological research involving human subjects that force the investigator to balance his responsibility to his science and to those who, willingly or unwillingly, enter his laboratory to serve as subjects. The American Psychological Association is aware of and sensitive to this problem and has issued the "Ethical Standards of Psychologists"[1] which reads, in part:

a. Only when a problem is of scientific significance and it is not practicable to investigate it in any other way is the psychologist justified in exposing research subjects . . . to physical or emotional stress as part of an investigation.
b. When a reasonable possibility of injurious after-effects exists, research is conducted only when the subjects or their responsible agents are fully informed of this possibility and agree to participate nevertheless.
c. The psychologist seriously considers the possibility of harmful after-effects and avoids them, or removes them as soon as permitted by the design of the experiment (pp. 59–60).

That these standards are sometimes "stretched" if not violated is the subject of the following two articles. These articles also present guidelines for the protection of subjects. Reflecting the increasing concern over the problem, the United States Public Health Service, a large research grant-supporting agency, issued in 1966 a policy designed to encourage appropriate ethical considerations on the part of those receiving grants from them. The article by Dr. Kelman (pp. 212–226), including a discussion of the ethical considerations of deception as practiced in psychological research, is also relevant here.

[1] American Psychological Association, "Ethical Standards of Psychologists," *American Psychologist*, Vol. 18 (1963), pp. 56–60.

28. Ethical Issues in Research with Human Subjects[1]

Wolf Wolfensberger

Reflecting the growing concern in professional and lay circles about ethical issues in research, Dr. Wolfensberger discusses the problem of recruitment of subjects for medical, social, and behavioral science research. Dealing with the types of consent and the contents of consent agreements, he notes five "rights" that the subject may yield to the experimenter. Further, the different types of risks involved in various kinds of research are discussed and a set of ten guidelines for the ethical conduct of research are formulated for the purpose of protecting the subject from emotional and physical harm and exploitation.

A number of disciplines engaging in clinical practice with humans have been concerned with questions of ethics for some time, and their considerable experience provides a basis for the evolution of widely accepted codes of professional conduct. Ethics in research, however, is still rather virgin territory. What little there is in the way of codification is very inadequate. Cranberg[2] pointed out that the 1953 code of ethics of the American Psychological Association[3] was apparently the only one existent in 1963 that had been officially adopted by a scientific organization. Another code, applicable mainly to medical research with human subjects but not (as far as I know) officially embraced by any professional or scientific group, was promulgated at the Nuremberg war-crime trials.[4] More recently, the World Medical Association[5] in 1964 passed a statement on human experimentation known as the

[1] Reprinted from *Science*, 6 January 1967, **155**, 47–51, with the permission of the author and the American Association for the Advancement of Science. Copyright 1967 by the American Association for the Advancement of Science. Supported by PHS grant HD 00370. I thank George Ebling of Plymouth State Home and Training School, Northville, Mich., R. A. Kurtz of Notre Dame Univ., and Charles Fishell for suggestions and criticism.

[2] L. Cranberg, *Science*, Vol. 141 (1963), 1242.

[3] American Psychological Association, Washington, D. C., 1953; see also *American Psychologist*, Vol. 18 (1963), 56.

[4] H. A. Stevens, in J. Oster (Ed.), *Intern. Copenhagen Congr. Sci. Study of Mental Retardation* (Copenhagen, Berlingske Bogtrykkeri, 1964), Vol. 1, p. 37.

[5] World Medical Association, *British Medical Journal*, Vol. 2 (1964), 177.

Declaration of Helsinki. Britain's Medical Research Council, also in 1964, published a "Statement . . . intended to serve as a guide . . ." on "Responsibility in investigation on human subjects."[6] Other organizations also have taken steps toward codification of ethics in research but no code, statement, guide, or other set of widely adopted principles yet has the degree of clarity and adequacy that appears feasible and necessary to guide researchers through certain problem areas.

In the past, when lack or inadequacy of rules in research had not been perceived as a major problem, researchers muddled along in the belief or hope that procedures and conventions either in common use or approved by their peers were proper and ethical. At times it was even assumed that a novel procedure entailing unknown degrees of risk, or a procedure requiring definite risks, could be made respectable by having the experimenter share the risk with the subject, or by using volunteers. We have now arrived at a point in the evolution of science at which both scientists and the intelligent lay public consider universality of procedure, approval by peers, sharing of risks, and even use of volunteers questionable or even unacceptable and unethical in some research situations.

A number of recent events have thrust the question of ethics in research into sharp focus. The censuring by the regents of the University of the State of New York[7] of a respected hospital and of respected physicians will probably constitute a landmark in the development of codification of ethics in research. This decision censured research procedures that are believed by many scientists in the field to be rather conventional. Then there were the uproar over Project Camelot;[8] the widespread concern with the psychological test movement, culminating in the recent congressional hearings;[9] and even the battle over animal-research legislation, and the wave of recent publicity regarding instances of cruelty to research dogs. Indeed, the concern with research practices is probably only one expression of broader-current reexamination and formulation of the rights of the individual. Related expressions may be widespread interest in draft laws, civil rights, the rights of an accused, the right to privacy, compensation to victims of crime, and the concern expressed by both the public and various professional and scientific bodies about the need to update or establish professional codes of ethics in general.[10]

The degree to which concern about conduct of research has grown among the intelligent lay public is of interest. Controversial news items about recent conduct of research were carried in many and diverse news media: The *Wall Street Journal*

    [6] British Medical Research Council, *ibid.*, p. 178.

    [7] E. Langer, *Science*, Vol. 151 (1966), 663.

    [8] Much of an entire issue of *American Psychologist* (21 May 1966) is devoted to the Camelot affair.

    [9] See the entire November 1965 issue of *American Psychologist*, as well as parts of the May 1966 issue.

    [10] *Time* reported (19 August 1966) that the American Bar Association is studying modernization of its 60-year-old canon of ethics; and (15 July 1966) a government suit to prescribe revision of the code of ethics of the College of American Pathologists. The supradisciplinary American Association on Mental Deficiency [*American Journal of Mental Deficiency*, Vol. 71 (1966), 340] appears to be moving toward establishment of a standing committee on ethics and practices.

ran several articles on problems of ethics in research,[11] and the *Saturday Review*[12] devoted 10 pages to the subject, covering some aspects of the New York decision in even greater detail than did *Science*. It is also of note that no one discipline has been singled out by public criticism. Thus medical researchers were most affected by the New York regents' decision; social scientists, by the Camelot affair; and behavioral scientists, by the "anti-test" movement.[13]

There is a danger that, if scientists do not respond to the public's concern about research conduct, research rules will be imposed on science from without. Such rules may be formulated in an emotional atmosphere; may be selective, inconsistent, and inadequate; and may be enacted into law in such a fashion as to be unnecessarily burdensome, restrictive, and rigid—or even absurd, as in the spoof example conjured up by Burnham.[14] Again, we have a recent illustration of how awkward regulations may develop. Presumably the New York regents' decision is now binding on medical researchers under their jurisdiction, yet it falls far short of providing adequate guidance. It contains ambivalent-appearing statements such as the following:

No consent is valid unless it is made by a person with legal and mental capacity to make it, and is based on a disclosure of all material facts. . . . We do not say that it is necessary in all cases of human experimentation to obtain consents from relatives. . . .".[15]

How close some scientists are to being governed by outrightly unserviceable research rules was also revealed in a nationwide survey conducted by myself and colleagues.[16] One object of this survey was to ascertain the limits that superintendents of state institutions for the mentally retarded would place on behavioral research, and to identify in turn what limits and administrative obstacles behavioral researchers in retardation had encountered or anticipated encountering.

Both groups of respondents expressed strong concern for the need to safeguard the rights and integrity of retarded subjects of research and of their families. However, we were surprised to find that, when "experiment" was mentioned in connection with a handicapped individual, responses from both groups were not only strong and emotional but at times absolutely irrational. Consistently with such irrationality, some institutions reported working under sets of rules that were meaningless or which, if they were applied literally, would exclude virtually all activity identified as research. The irrationality of this situation is underlined by the fact that one of the major arguments advanced in favor of the continued existence of large institutions for the retarded is their potential contribution to research.

Another "semanticism," which is somewhat of an argument-stopper, has to do

[11] For example: *Wall Street Journal*, 31 August 1964, 21 January 1966.

[12] *Saturday Review*, 5 February 1966.

[13] In early 1966 PHS notified its research grantees that in future each grantee agency must establish a formal review procedure aimed at safeguarding the rights and welfare of research subjects. This step almost certainly resulted from recent events.

[14] P. J. Burnham, *Science*, Vol. 152 (1966), 448.

[15] E. Langer, *op. cit.*

[16] W. Wolfensberger *et al.*, *Mental Retardation*, Vol. 3(6) (1965), 7.

with the sacredness or inviolability of the individual. The argument that research must not violate a person's integrity is very powerful and tends to elicit whole-hearted agreement. However, the fact is that society constantly encroaches upon individual lives and freedoms for the sake of the community or mankind as a whole. We do not give driving licenses to 12-year-olds—no matter how competently an individual youngster may drive. Traffic and labor laws, the draft for the armed forces, and many other conventions, designed and tolerated for what is believed to be the welfare of society, may detrimentally affect an individual. In some instances we may infringe the rights of an individual not in order to benefit or punish him, prevent him from harming others, or keep him from harming himself, but to benefit others— as when we levy taxes (without individual consent) or ask a man to risk his life (perhaps with his consent) to save women and children during a shipwreck. The crucial point is not that conventions be fair and just in each instance, but that they be administered in a fashion characterized as constituting "due process."

The controversy regarding conduct of research has served to increase the tension between the long-range interests of society, science, and progress, on the one hand, and the rights of the individual, on the other. It is important that this tension should be a creative one resulting in a higher order of problem-solving that safeguards both interests, rather than a solution that gravely impedes the progress of science. Society must preserve the delicate balance between these interests, realizing that the cost of excessive restriction of research can come very dear.

If a code of due process or research ethics is ever to be formulated, it must be based on clearly stated principles. In order to identify these principles, the issues must be sharply defined and disentangled from the irrationalities and clichés in which they are currently enmeshed. I shall now attempt such disentanglement and sharpening, and refinement of principle.[17]

TYPES OF CONSENT

The cornerstone of all considerations of the welfare and protection of subjects appears to be what has been called informed consent. This term refers to a person's ability to consent freely to serve in an experiment in which he adequately under-stands both what is required of him and the "cost" or risk to him.

What ethical guidelines now exist have usually been promulgated primarily relative to adult subjects of adequate mentality and communication skills. Ethical problems can greatly increase in complexity when a human subject's ability to absorb information or to consent is inadequate. One or both inadequacies may exist in the mentally retarded, the emotionally disturbed, children, those suffering from impairment of consciousness by disease or age, or those who perceive themselves

---

[17] A similar attempt was recently undertaken by O. M. Ruebhausen and O. G. Brim, Jr., who addressed themselves most thoughtfully to the specific topic of privacy and behavioral research; see *American Psychologist*, Vol. 21 (1966), 423.

under threat or duress if they refuse to participate—such as prisoners or college students. Obviously, the capacity to become informed or to consent freely is a continuous and not a categorical variable.

One problem has been disagreement as to the extent of information required to make a consent valid. Some individuals have taken a very narrow view, insisting that even the most minute aspect of an experiment[18] should be disclosed to the subject; such interpretation of the term "informed" would negate the conduct of many important projects for which it is mandatory that the subject be ignorant of certain aspects of the research. For instance, a recent psychosocial research project, having potential implications for the very survival of our democratic way of life,[19] could not have been conducted with fully informed subjects.

I propose that consent be considered "informed" when all essential aspects are understood by the subject. Essential aspects consist primarily of information regarding the "rights" (see following section) yielded to an experimenter by a subject; the types and degrees of risk involved; and the detrimental or beneficial consequences, if any, that may directly affect the subject. Explanation of the purpose of a study should probably be considered a desirable but not essential element unless the results could affect the subject directly. Some experiments are so technical as to be unintelligible even to scientific peers from outside a speciality area; they could not be meaningfully explained to many or any lay subjects. It is particularly important that the potentially endless detailing of minutiae of an experiment, per se, does not come to be considered the only adequate method of informing.

CONTENTS OF THE CONSENT AGREEMENT

Surprisingly, it appears that no clear distinctions have yet been drawn regarding the type of content of consent agreements. Such distinctions, however, appear to be very helpful in sharpening the issues.

Generally it appears that in the consent agreement the subject may yield one or more of five "rights" to the experimenter: (i) Invasion of privacy; (ii) donation or sacrifice of personal resources such as time, attention, dignity, and physical, mental, or emotional energy; (iii) surrender of autonomy, as in hypnotic, drug, or brain-stimulation studies, or in studies entailing restriction of movement and action; (iv) exposure to procedures entailing mental or physical pain or discomfort, but no risk of injury or lasting harm; and (v) exposure to procedures that may entail risk of physical or emotional injury.

Although the experimenter is asking in each instance that the subject surrender what is ordinarily considered to be a legal or moral right, it becomes apparent that

[18] For instance, at recent Congressional hearings [*American Psychologist*, Vol. 21 (1966), 404] some lines of questioning and testimony implied that a parent should be permitted to inspect every question his child might be asked during the course of a school-related research project.

[19] S. Milgram, *Journal of Abnormal Psychology*, Vol. 67 (1963), 371; *Human Relations*, Vol. 18 (1965), 57.

the rigor of requirements for consent may conceivably be permitted to vary, and that codes of research conduct should perhaps take into account what is being asked of a subject. Ordinarily, it would appear to be much more objectionable to risk infliction of bodily injury without a valid consent than to inflict a 5-minute loss of time upon a person. The criteria for invasion of privacy appear especially apt to vary: For instance, it is conceivable that a researcher is working in a setting that invades privacy as part of routine and sanctioned operation; a marriage-guidance clinic is a good example. In such situations privacy during research is protected by preservation of confidentiality or anonymity, or of both, rather than by non-use of the already available highly personal information.

In some situations, such as with infants or with institutionalized lower-functioning retardates, there may be very little for which a researcher can ask in a request for consent because whatever a subject ordinarily has to give has never been possessed, or has already been given—or taken. Such a subject may have little if any autonomy and privacy, his threshold for pain or unpleasantness may be very high, and his consciousness may be so impaired that emotional trauma is unlikely to occur. Some personal resources, such as time, he may still possess, but such a resource may not be deemed valuable to him because he has large and unutilized amounts of it. Unpleasant as it sounds and is, the one thing that such a person usually still has that a researcher may want is part of his bodily functioning.

TYPES OF RESEARCH

Since the very question of experimental risk, especially for handicapped subjects, appears so apt to arouse emotions that can becloud reason, conceptualization of the relation between certain types of research and experimental risks may be helpful. I propose that there are roughly three levels of research, and even though there is an underlying continuum most experiments with human subjects can probably be assigned to one of these levels.

In level-1 research, experimental activities and procedures are employed but are not consciously recognized or formally labeled as research. A considerable amount of the clinical management of human beings falls into this category. Many techniques of diagnosis and treatment, widely practiced in medicine, psychiatry, clinical psychology, social work, education, rehabilitation, and other human-management professions, lack adequate empirical validation and must be considered tentative and experimental. Indeed, innumerable human-management and administrative practices are no more than ill-controlled experiments. Examples are the current fad of introducing crawling exercises in some schools in order to accelerate progress in reading, use of drugs in medical practice on an intuitive basis, and manipulation of the social milieus of institutions or hospital wards. In the field of mental retardation, such ordinary events as a mixed dance, a trial-and-error work assignment, or even a trip to the toilet can become an experimental act.

There appear to be three reasons why such activities are not recognized or labeled as research: (i) a certain hyperclinical type of practitioner finds it difficult to think of himself as being a researcher, and may even attach negative values to research activities; (ii) some experimentation loses its research identification because of its sloppiness; and (iii) some experimental and ultimately nonvalidated procedures have been adopted so universally that they have lost their research identification.

There is no doubt that level-1 research can be risky to the subject. An invalidated medical treatment, like bloodletting as practiced in the 18th century, can be worse than no treatment at all. Is it really so inconceivable that some widely current but insufficiently validated human-management practices (psychotherapy, for example) may constitute the bloodletting of the 20th century?

Research at level 1 may also consist of the utilization of impersonal and grouped data collected in the course of routine and accepted operations of agencies. Thus school-enrollment, traffic-accident, and armed forces selection and rejection studies use information pertaining to individuals, group such information, and make it the substance of research. Such data are often collected without the knowledge or consent of the subjects and may or may not affect them.

Research at level 2 is clearly identified and conceptualized as research. Usually, but not necessarily, a distinct manipulation of subjects, individually or in groups, is entailed; at times it may be identified as research more by its "unnaturalness" than by anything else. A situation in which for several hours a subject has to push a button whenever a light appears on a screen (in a vigilance experiment, for instance) is perceived quite differently from assignment to a dishwashing task as perhaps in a study of vocational-training practices. Regardless of the oddity of the task, a crucial characteristic of level-2 research is that it stays close to the mainstream of knowledge; the procedures employed are well tried, tend to be familiar at least to specialists, and are known to be harmless; the new knowledge sought is usually modest; and possible outcomes of the research can be fairly well described in advance. Most importantly, risk to the subject is very small, perhaps even smaller than in the often poorly conceptualized and planned and chaotically conducted level-1 research.

It is research at level 3 that tends to give rise to most of the ethical concern. Level-3 research is risky to the subject; either previous work has shown it to be risky or the procedures are novel and untried, and outcomes are less predictable. The fact that this kind of research may occasionally promise more substantial increments in knowledge is likely to lead to dilemmas.

TYPES OF RISK

Risk to the subject may exist at any level of research, but there is a very useful distinction between risk that is *intrinsic* to the experimental task and risk *extrinsic* to it. Intrinsic risk arises from the very nature of the task. For instance, a drug may trigger convulsions or allergic reactions; a spinal tap carries a low but definite risk of damage to the central nervous system; and sensory deprivation can result in disturbed behavior.

Extrinsic risk might be viewed as being little or not at all under the control of the experimenter, and not being ordinarily foreseeable; it might be subdivided into types *a* and *b*. Thus type-*a* extrinsic risk may refer to consequences for which the experimenter or his agency is legally liable, even though they comply most meticulously with ethical demands. For example, a subject may slip on the waxed floor of the experimental room, break his leg, and sue for compensation. Type-*b* extrinsic risk may refer to consequences for which the experimenter or his agency is not legally liable: a subject may be struck by a car as he leaves home on his way to the experiment.

Some extrinsic risks are difficult to classify, especially those arising from psychic processes within the subject, of which the experimenter has little or no knowledge. For instance, even the most innocuous research task may seem threatening to some subject; such a perceived threat can cause psychological stress, which in turn can result in physical harm. It is unlikely but conceivable that the mere request to serve as a subject in an "experiment" might lead to heart failure. I have in fact witnessed a breakdown in functioning in a mildly retarded teenager who was asked to leave class and spend a few minutes on an undemanding, simple, and utterly harmless task; it appeared that a "friend" had told him something to the effect that the psychologist was going to cut his head open.

Except in instances in which research involves only record data, the researcher can never state with certainty that a subject will not experience some kind of trauma. At best, he can estimate the level of probability of trauma if intrinsic research risks exist, or state that, if trauma occurs, it will occur because of the extrinsic risks.

The distinction I have drawn may appear labored, but it becomes more meaningful when applied to factual problem situations. For example, several respondents in the obstacles survey cited [20] proclaimed strong opposition to inclusion of mentally retarded subjects in any experiment entailing even the slightest risk. Unless the distinction between intrinsic and extrinsic risks were clearly conceptualized, such a rule, if consequentially applied, would prohibit *all* research with retarded subjects except analysis of case-file data.

GUIDELINES

Guidelines for ethical conduct of research should be based on clearly identifiable and internally consistent principles. It is important that issues be stated with maximum clarity, so that problems for which no specific solutions have been previously formulated can be handled in the light of the broader principles. I shall state some principles and guidelines that can be derived, at least in part, from the considerations discussed above.

1. The more deleterious an experimental effect may be to a subject, the more precautions the researcher should take.

[20] W. Wolfensberger *et al.*, *op. cit.*

2. "Risk-sharing" between experimenter and subject in no way releases the experimenter from any obligation toward his subject.

3. The more serious or extensive the right that the researcher wants a subject to surrender, the more consideration and effort should be devoted to the problem of consent or release.

4. No consent for level-1 research should be required at this time to use a procedure which, although it may be experimental and nonvalidated in nature, is used primarily for treating a person therapeutically, *if* (i) the procedure is considered justifiable and appropriate by qualified peers, and (ii) a consent (to treatment) appropriate to the occasion and to the risk inherent in the procedure has been obtained.

5. No consent appears necessary if the right needed by the experimenter is already possessed by him or by the legal body that he represents; then consent by that legal body, rather than by the subject, must be obtained. For example, a member of the armed forces loses certain rights of autonomy, which in turn might be delegated by the proper authorities to an experimenter without the subject's consent or knowledge. However, it would appear to be desirable to obtain the personal consent of each subject if this is at all feasible; furthermore, if there is uncertainty as to whether the legal body in question possesses the rights required by the experimenter, then, in proportion to the extent of the rights involved, the experimenter should exert efforts to obtain opinions on this question from a group of impartial referees who could be considered qualified to judge.

6. I propose that except under extraordinary circumstances no consent is required where (level-1) research is conducted on record-file data if (i) such data are grouped, or their anonymity is otherwise assured, so that no subject is identified and no definite statement can be made about any specific subject; and (ii) the manipulation of the research data does not lead to consequences detrimental to a subject.

7. Where level-2 research is involved (that is, risks are extrinsic), and where only modest and reasonable amounts of rights i and ii (privacy and personal resources) are concerned, consent may be obtained by means of a routine release form. Thus agencies such as institutions, public clinics, and university hospitals might explain to their clients, during the intake process, the research orientation of the agency and the type of research that might be typically involved, and ask for the clients' cooperation and signature. Much would depend on the manner in which this approach was handled. My personal experience is that it may be best to inform the subject or his agents as early as possible, both orally and in writing, of four things: (i) there is little likelihood that the research will benefit the subject; (ii) the subject's participation may benefit many others like him in the future, and research is the only way to improve certain services, conditions, and treatments; (iii) the research will entail no undue (that is, considered unreasonable by most people) discomfort, consumption of time, or loss of privacy; and there is no direct risk; and (iv) participation is voluntary.

Such a routine release may not be legal in all states, but it can be very important in certain agencies, such as institutions for the retarded. If a broad release were not obtained, even the most harmless and minor participation in research would require a specific release. In some research-oriented institutions, a resident may be called upon several times a year to serve as a subject, and obtaining a specific release each time would be prohibitively cumbersome. Moreover, after placing residents many parents are no longer accessible, do not visit or answer mail, and may live many hundreds of miles distant. In short, unless either the superintendent were the guardian—and the trend is away from this practice—or a general release were obtained upon admission, little or no research on mental retardation could be conducted in such institutions. The implications of such a situation would be vast and horrendous.

Hyman[21] makes the point that an issue must be drawn on the question of when an experimenter may use a person as a subject. However, I believe that the type of risk involved, though a separate issue, affects the drawing of the first issue since it bears upon the type of consent required. I must point out that my proposal may not be entirely consistent with the Medical Research Council statement,[22] which can be interpreted to advocate that a specific rather than general consent should be obtained when a research procedure is not intended directly to benefit a subject.

8. When level-2 research calls for right iv, a borderline case exists. Then a decision to obtain a specific release may be based on the degree of discomfort or pain involved and on purely psychosocial considerations such as a subject's familiarity with the procedures and the public emotion that the research could generate.

9. A specific and relatively detailed release for research either on level 3 or entailing right iii appears to be mandatory.

10. The more reason there is to question a subject's ability to give a free, informed consent, the more care should be taken to assure that consent is free and informed, or that the responsible agent's release is appropriate; here the advice of the Medical Research Council[23] appears sound: one should obtain consent not only in written form but also in the presence of witnesses who can provide consensual agreement regarding the subject's understanding and freedom of choice.

It is not sufficient for the researcher to exercise restraint in eliciting consent; he must also ascertain to a reasonable degree that a subject, even a volunteer, does not *perceive* himself coerced when he is not. For instance, no matter what a prisoner is told, he is likely to believe that by not volunteering to serve in a cancer-cell-injection experiment he may delay his parole; thus he may be under a subtle form of coercion. College students are particularly apt to believe that refusal to volunteer as subjects in an instructor's experiment will jeopardize their progress—and they are often right. The researcher should go out of his way to create an atmosphere and structure that permit a truly free choice.

Finally, not ethics but wisdom dictates that, when emotionally charged situations and issues are involved (such as research with "live cancer," and handicapped

21 W. A. Hyman, *Science*, Vol. 152 (1966), 865.
22 British Medical Research Council, *op. cit.*
23 *Ibid.*

children), the researcher should consider raising his safeguards to a level above that required by ethical considerations alone.

Let us reflect for a moment how the above guidelines and considerations would have applied to the researchers censured by the New York regents. Within the framework that I propose, one crucial question would have hinged on whether the injection of live cancer cells was definitely known to be harmless (risk thus being extrinsic) or was merely likely to be so (risk being small but definite and intrinsic). If it were clearly established that the risk was extrinsic,[24] we would ascertain that the researchers were not asking for surrender of privacy, autonomy, or health, but only for very modest amounts of rights ii and iv: that is, a little time and bother and a little discomfort. With subjects of sound mind, a routine research release obtained on the subject's admission to hospital should then have sufficed, but, with aged individuals with questionable clarity of mind, the situation would appear to be borderline between choice of a routine or of a specific release. The choice would definitely be tipped in favor of a specific release by the presence of an emotionally charged element such as use of "live cancer cells."

CONCLUSION

It is obvious that many disciplines confront ethical problems in research in which situational details may vary, but in which the same ethical principles may prevail. I write not in order to propose a definitive set of rules but to demonstrate how situations posing ethical problems can be reduced and more readily resolved by rational analysis of underlying issues and principles; I hope to stimulate further analysis and dialogue. It might be particularly helpful if researchers in a wide range of disciplines contributed experiences permitting a sharpening of guidelines. Finally, it is conceivable that a code of ethics might eventually be promulgated by a supradisciplinary body such as the AAAS, and that such a code could then be adapted and adopted by other scientific bodies and professional organizations— even by specific agencies such as research institutes, clinics, institutions, and schools.

---

[24] Apparently, this point was not sufficiently established in this case; for example, see W. A. Hyman, *op. cit.* If, however, injection of live cancer cells were definitely known to be harmless, their injection, aside from the emotional element involved, should have required no more stringent considerations regarding consent than would be involved in the injection of, say, saline solution.

29. Privacy and Behavioral Research[1]

Panel on Privacy and Behavioral Research

Because of the mounting concern over the possibility of invasion of privacy in behavioral research, the President's Office of Science and Technology appointed a panel, in 1966, to investigate the problem and propose research guidelines. The panel's study revealed a limited number of cases where the investigating scientists had not taken sufficient care to protect the rights of their subjects. It is pointed out that the scientist has a definite obligation to respect the privacy of his subjects and protect them from permanent physical or emotional harm. Further, it is urged that subject participation be on a voluntary and informed consent basis in so far as this is compatible with the objectives of the research. Five recommendations are proposed for those engaged in the support, administration, and performance of behavioral research.

In recent years there have been growing threats to the privacy of individuals. Wiretapping, electronic eavesdropping, the use of personality tests in employment, the use of the lie detector in security or criminal investigations, and the detailed scrutiny of the private lives of people receiving public welfare funds all involve invasions of privacy. Although the social purpose is usually clear, the impact on the persons involved may be damaging. Our society has become more and more sensitive to the need to avoid such damage.

This concern has led to extensive discussion about the propriety of certain procedures in behavioral research, by the Congress, by officials in the various agencies of the government, by university officials, by the scientific community generally, and by leaders in professional societies in the behavioral sciences. The Office of Science and Technology appointed a panel,[2] in January 1966, to examine

---

[1] Reprinted from *Science*, 3 February 1967, **155**, 535–538, with the permission of the American Association for the Advancement of Science. Copyright 1967 by the American Association for the Advancement of Science.

[2] The Panel on Privacy and Behavioral Research was appointed by the President's Office of Science and Technology. The members of the panel are as follows: Kenneth E. Clark (chairman), dean, College of Arts and Sciences, University of Rochester, Rochester, New York; Bernard Berelson, vice president, Population Council, Inc., New York, N.Y.; Edward J. Bloustein, president, Bennington College, Bennington, Vermont; George E. Pake,

these issues and to propose guidelines for those who are engaged in behavioral research or associated with its support and management.

The panel has restricted its attention to issues of privacy arising in connection with programs of data collection and study which are intimately associated with behavioral research. For example, it has not reviewed a number of the programs for data collection which are sponsored by the federal government, such as the various censuses, health and welfare statistics, and financial information secured from business and industry. These programs may also encroach upon the privacy of individuals, either through the burden of disclosure which they impose on respondents or through their availability for unintended purposes.

It is our opinion that the principles described in this report for protection of privacy in behavioral research should apply equally to such inquiries. When response is mandatory, as in the case of information that must be furnished to the government, there is an even greater burden on the sponsoring agency to protect the individual against disclosure unless disclosure is specifically sanctioned by statute.

The panel has not reviewed in detail the wide variety of mechanical or electronic devices which make it possible to intrude into private lives. We have become acquainted with a few of the problems in that field, however, and are dismayed to observe the disregard for human values indicated by the advocacy or actual practice of eavesdropping, the use of lie detection without clear justification, and the frequent willingness to institute surveillance procedures to handle the problems of a small proportion of our population at the risk of eroding the rights and the quality of life for the majority.

Likewise, the panel has not reviewed in detail the propriety of procedures involved in employment or social welfare activities. Enough examples have been brought to our attention, however, to make us feel that examination of procedures in these spheres is needed also.

The attitudes of various segments of our society about proper procedures for the protection of privacy and the right to self-determination have been explored by the panel. It has reviewed relevant research in the behavioral sciences and the administrative practices of universities and government agencies. It has also consulted with the scientific community through its professional organizations.

---

provost, Washington University, St. Louis, Missouri; Colin S. Pittendrigh, dean, Graduate School, Princeton University, Princeton, New Jersey; Oscar M. Ruebhausen, Debevoise, Plimpton, Lyons & Gates, New York, N.Y.; Walter S. Salant, Economics Studies Division, Brookings Institution, Washington, D.C.; Robert Sears, dean, School of Humanities and Sciences, Stanford University, Palo Alto, California; Benson R. Snyder, psychiatrist-in-chief, Medical Department, Massachusetts Institute of Technology, Cambridge; Frederick P. Thieme, vice president, University of Washington, Seattle; Lawrence N. Bloomberg, assistant chief, Office of Standards, Bureau of the Budget, Washington, D.C.; and Colin M. MacLeod, deputy director, Office of Science and Technology (now vice president for medical affairs, The Commonwealth Fund, New York, N.Y.). Consultant to the panel is Richard M. Michaels, technical assistant, Office of Science and Technology, Washington, D.C. The full text of the report will be available about 1 March 1967 from the Superintendent of Documents, Government Printing Office, Washington, D.C. 20402.

THREATS TO PRIVACY

The right to privacy is the right of the individual to decide for himself how much he will share with others his thoughts, his feelings, and the facts of his personal life. It is a right that is essential to insure dignity and freedom of self-determination. In recent years there has been a severe erosion of this right by the widespread and often callous use of various devices for eavesdropping, lie detection, and secret observation in politics, in business, and in law enforcement. Indeed, modern electronic instruments for wiretapping and bugging have opened any human activity to the threat of illicit invasion of privacy. This unwholesome state of affairs has led to wide public concern over the methods of inquiry used by agencies of public employment, social welfare, and law enforcement.

Behavioral research, devoted as it is to the discovery of facts and principles underlying human activity of all types, comes naturally under scrutiny in any examination of possible threats to privacy. All of the social sciences, including economics, political science, anthropology, sociology, and psychology, take as a major object of study the behavior of individuals, communities, or other groups. In one context or another, investigators in all of these disciplines frequently need to seek information that is private to the men, women, and children who are the subjects of their study. In most instances this information is freely given by those who consent to cooperate in the scientific process. But the very nature of behavioral research is such that there is a risk of invasion of privacy if unusual care is not taken to secure the consent of research subjects, or if the data obtained are not given full confidentiality.

While the privacy problem in scientific research is small in comparison to that which exists in employment interviewing, social welfare screening, and law enforcement investigations, the opportunity for improper invasion is not negligible. About 35,000 behavioral scientists are engaged in research in the United States, 2100 new Ph.D.'s are graduated each year, and the total number of students enrolled for advanced degrees in the behavioral sciences exceeds 40,000 at the present time.

It is probable that relatively few of the studies undertaken by these scientists raise serious questions of propriety in relation to privacy and human dignity. From a survey of articles published in professional journals and of research grant applications submitted to government agencies, we have concluded that most scientists who conduct research in privacy-sensitive areas are aware of the ethical implications of their experimental designs and arrange to secure the consent of subjects and to protect the confidentiality of the data obtained from them.

It cannot be denied, however, that, in a limited number of instances, behavioral scientists have not followed appropriate procedures to protect the rights of their subjects, and that in other cases recognition of the importance of privacy–invading considerations has not been as sophisticated, or the considerations as affirmatively implemented, as good practice demands. Because of this failure there has been pressure from some quarters, both within the government and outside of it, to place arbitrary limits on the research methods which may be used. Behavioral scientists as a group do not question the importance of the right to privacy and are understandably concerned when suggestions are made that the detailed processes of science should be subjected to control by legislation or arbitrary administrative ruling. All scientists are opposed to restrictions which may curtail important research. At the same time they have an obligation to insure that all possible steps are taken to assure respect for the privacy and dignity of their subjects.

CONFLICTING RIGHTS

It is clear that there exists an important conflict between two values, both of which are strongly held in American society.

The individual has an inalienable right to dignity, self-respect, and freedom to determine his own thoughts and actions within the broad limits set by the requirements of society. The essential element in privacy and self-determination is the privilege of making one's own decision as to the extent to which one will reveal thoughts, feelings, and actions. When a person consents freely and fully to share himself with others—with a scientist, an employer, or a credit investigator—there is no invasion of privacy, regardless of the quality or nature of the information revealed.

Behavioral science is representative of another value vigorously championed by most American citizens, the right to know anything that may be known or discovered about any part of the universe. Man is part of this universe, and the extent of the federal government's financial support of human behavioral research (on the order of $300 million in 1966) testifies to the importance placed on the study of human behavior by the American people. In the past there have been conflicts between theological beliefs and the theoretical analyses of the physical sciences. These conflicts have largely subsided, but the behavioral sciences seem to have inherited the basic conflict that arises when strongly held beliefs or moral attitudes —whether theologically, economically, or politically based—are subjected to the free-ranging process of scientific inquiry. If society is to exercise its right to know, it must free its behavioral scientists as much as possible from unnecessary restraints. Behavioral scientists in turn must accept the constructive restraints that society imposes in order to establish that level of dignity, freedom, and personal fulfillment that men treasure virtually above all else in life.

The root of the conflict between the individual's right to privacy and society's right of discovery is the research process. Behavioral science seeks to assess and to measure many qualities of men's minds, feelings, and actions. In the absence of informed consent on the part of the subject, these measurements represent invasion of privacy. The scientist must therefore obtain the consent of his subject.

To obtain truly informed consent is often difficult. In the first place, the nature of the inquiry sometimes cannot be explained adequately because it involves complex variables that the nonscientist does not understand. Examples are the personality variables measured by questionnaires, and the qualities of cognitive processes measured by creativity tests. Secondly, the validity of an experiment is sometimes destroyed if the subject knows all the details of its conduct. Examples include drug-testing, in which the effect of suggestion (placebo effect) must be avoided, and studies of persuasability, in which the subjects remain ignorant of the influences that are being presented experimentally. Clearly, then, if behavioral research is to be effective, some modification of the traditional concept of informed consent is needed.

Such a change in no sense voids the more general proposition that the performance of human behavioral research is the product of a partnership between the scientist and his subject. Consent to participate in a study must be the norm before any subject embarks on the enterprise. Since consent must sometimes be given despite an admittedly inadequate understanding of the scientific purposes of the research procedures, the right to discontinue participation at any point must be stipulated in clear terms. In the meantime, when full information is not available to the subject and when no alternative procedures to minimize the privacy problem are available, the relationship between the subject and the scientist (and between the subject and the institution sponsoring the scientist) must be based upon trust. This places the scientist and the sponsoring institution under a fiduciary obligation to protect the privacy and dignity of the subject who entrusts himself to them. The scientist must agree to treat the subject fairly and with dignity, to cause him no inconvenience or discomfort unless the extent of the inconvenience and discomfort has been accepted by the subject in advance, to inform the subject as fully as possible of the purposes of the inquiry or experiment, and to put into effect all procedures which will assure the confidentiality of whatever information is obtained.

Occasionally, even this degree of consent cannot be obtained. Naturalistic observations of group behavior must sometimes be made unbeknownst to the subjects. In such cases, as well as in all others, the scientist has the obligation to insure full confidentiality of the research records. Only by doing so, and by making certain that published reports contain no identifying reference to a given subject, can the invasion of privacy be minimized.

Basically, then, the protection of privacy in research is assured first by securing the informed consent of the subject. When the subject cannot be completely informed, the consent must be based on trust in the scientist and in the institution sponsoring him. In any case the scientist and his sponsoring institution must insure privacy by the maintenance of confidentiality.

In the end, the fact must be accepted that human behavioral research will at times produce discomfort to some subjects, and will entail a partial invasion of their privacy. Neither the principle of privacy nor the need to discover new knowledge can supervene universally. As with other conflicting values in our society, there must be constant adjustment and compromise, with the decision as to which value is to govern in a given instance to be determined by a weighing of the costs and the gains —the cost in privacy, the gain in knowledge. The decision cannot be made by the investigator alone, because he has a vested interest in his own research program, but must be a positive concern of his scientific peers and the institution which sponsors his work. Our society has grown strong on the principle of minimizing costs and maximizing gains, and, when warmly held values are in conflict, there must be a thoughtful evaluation of the specific case. In particular we do not believe that detailed governmental controls of research methods or instruments can substitute for the more effective procedures which are available and carry less risk of damage to the scientific enterprise.

ETHICAL ASPECTS OF HUMAN RESEARCH

Greater attention must be given to the ethical aspects of human research. The increase in scientists and in volume of research provides more chance for carelessness or recklessness and, in the hurried search for useful findings, can lead to abuses. Furthermore, if standards are not carefully maintained, there could develop an atmosphere of disregard for privacy that would be altogether alien to the spirit of American society. The increased potentials for damage and for fruitful outcomes from new knowledge are in no small part results of increased federal support of behavioral science. While no one would suggest that ethical standards should be different for scientists supported by public funds and for those supported by private funds, the government has an especially strong obligation to support research only under conditions that give fullest protection to individual human dignity. Government must avow and maintain the highest standards for the guidance of all.

To summarize, three parties—the investigator, his institution, and the sponsoring agency—have the responsibility for maintaining proper ethical standards with respect to government-sponsored research. The investigator designs the research and is in the best position to evaluate the propriety of his procedures. He has, therefore, the ultimate responsibility for insuring that his research is both effective and ethical.

The formalization of our ethics concerning privacy in connection with research is too recent, and perhaps too incomplete, to permit the assumption that all investigators have a full understanding of the proper methods for protecting the rights of subjects. Furthermore, the investigator is first and foremost a scientist in search of new knowledge, and it would not be in accord with our understanding of human motivation to expect him always to be as vigilant for his subject's welfare as he is for the productiveness of his own research.

We conclude, therefore, that responsibility must also be borne by the institution which employs the investigator. The employing institution is often a university or a government laboratory in which there are other scientists capable of reviewing the research plan. Such persons, drawn in part from disciplines other than the behavioral sciences, can present views that are colored neither by self-interest nor by the blind spots that may characterize the specific discipline of the investigator.

Finally, the sponsoring agency is obligated to make certain that both the investigator and his institution are fully aware of the importance of the ethical aspects of the research and that they have taken the necessary steps to discharge their responsibility to the human subjects involved. We believe that, in the majority of instances, it is neither necessary nor desirable for an agency to exceed this level of responsibility.

CONCLUSIONS

From our examination of the relation of behavioral science research to the right to privacy, we have been led to the following conclusions.

1. While most current practices in the field pose no significant threat to the privacy of research subjects, a sufficient number of exceptions have been noted to warrant a sharp increase in attention to procedures that will assure protection of this right. The increasing scale of behavioral research is itself an additional reason for focusing attention in this area.

2. Participation by subjects must be voluntary and based on informed consent to the extent that this is consistent with the objectives of the research. It is fully consistent with the protection of privacy that, in the absence of full information, consent be based on trust in the qualified investigator and the integrity of his institution.

3. The scientist has an obligation to insure that no permanent physical or psychological harm will ensue from the research procedures, and that temporary discomfort or loss of privacy will be remedied in an appropriate way during the course of the research or at its completion. To merit trust, the scientist must design his research with a view to protecting, to the fullest extent possible, the privacy of the subjects. If intrusion on privacy proves essential to the research, he should not proceed with his proposed experiment until he and his colleagues have considered all of the relevant facts and he has determined, with support from them, that the benefits outweigh the costs.

4. The scientist has the same responsibility to protect the privacy of the individual in published reports and in research records that he has in the conduct of the research itself.

5. The primary responsibility for the use of ethical procedures must rest with the individual investigator, but government agencies that support behavioral research should satisfy themselves that the institution which employs the investigator has effectively accepted its responsibility to require that he meet proper ethical standards.

6. Legislation to assure appropriate recognition of the rights of human subjects is neither necessary nor desirable if the scientists and sponsoring institutions fully discharge their responsibilities in accommodating to the claim of privacy. Because of its relative inflexibility, legislation cannot meet the challenge of the subtle and sensitive conflict of values under consideration, nor can it aid in the wise decision making by individuals which is required to assure optimum protection of subjects, together with the fullest effectiveness of research.

RECOMMENDATIONS

These conclusions lead us to make the following recommendations.

1. That government agencies supporting research in their own laboratories or in outside institutions require those institutions to agree to accept responsibility for the ethical propriety of human research performed with the aid of government funds.

2. That the methods used for institutional review be determined by the institutions themselves. The greatest possible flexibility of methods should be encouraged in order to build effective support for the principle of institutional responsibility within universities or other organizations. Institutions differ in their internal structures and operating procedures, and no single rigid formula will work for all.

3. That investigators and institutions be notified of the importance of consent and confidentiality as ethical requirements in research design, and that when either condition cannot be met, an explanation of the reasons be made in the application for funds.

4. That when research is undertaken directly by, or purchased on specification by, a government agency, responsibility for protection of privacy lies with the agency. When independent research is funded by the government, however, responsibility lies primarily with the scientist and his institution, and research instruments or design should not be subject to detailed review by government agencies with respect to protection of privacy.

5. That universities and professional associations be encouraged to emphasize the ethical aspects of behavioral research. When a training grant is made, a university should be requested to indicate its understanding that support of education on the ethics of research is one of the purposes of the grant.

RELEVANCE

A criticism frequently leveled against contemporary scientific psychology is that it lacks meaning for the problems faced by man. The critics say that many studies conducted on behavior, while ingeniously planned and painstakingly executed, have little relevance to human problems. Highly minute aspects of behavior are studied *ad nauseam* under well-controlled laboratory conditions and articles and books are written on the learning of nonsense syllables, but *where*, the critics ask, *is man*?

Psychologists are told that because of the nature of their subject matter they have an obligation to mankind. Yet when mankind, in the form of professionals in other disciplines, comes to psychology for help, "they are disappointed and, indeed, often aggrieved. What they begin to read with enthusiasm they put down with depression. What seemed promising turns out to be sterile, palpably trivial, or false and, in any case, a waste of time."[1]

Is such harsh criticism justified by psychology's past and present record? Do we have a deeper understanding of man today than before the emergence of scientific psychology? And, regardless of the answers to these questions, is the question of relevance relevant to any science?

The following articles explore some of these problems and deal with the applicability of laboratory research findings to practical situations and the meaningfulness of the topics chosen for study.

[1] R. A. Littman, "Psychology: The Socially Indifferent Science," *American Psychologist* Vol. 16 (1961), p. 232.

30. Problem-Centering vs. Means-Centering in Science[1]

Abraham H. Maslow

One reason for a possible lack of relevance in a science such as psychology is that the practitioners may focus more on method and technique than on the meaningfulness and significance of the problem. Research problems may be chosen on the basis of how well they fit existing methodology and not how worthwhile they may be to mankind or the advance of science. Dr. Maslow speaks of this situation as one which confuses the means of science with its ends. He notes that "It is only the goals or ends of science that dignify and validate its methods." The discussion focuses on a number of consequences for science and scientists of the emphasis on means, one of which is the publication of much trivial or inconsequential (though technically correct) research.

Through the last decade or two, more and more attention has been given to the shortcomings and sins of "official" science. Discussion of the sources of these failings has, however, been neglected. This paper attempts to show that many of the weaknesses of orthodox science are consequences of a means or technique-centered approach to the defining of science.

By means-centering, I refer to the tendency to consider that the essence of science lies in its instruments, techniques, procedures, apparatus and its methods rather than in its problems, questions, functions or goals. In its unsophisticated form, means-centering confuses scientists with engineers, physicians, dentists, laboratory technicians, glass blowers, urinanalysts, machine tenders, etc. Means-centering at the highest intellectual levels most usually takes the form of making synonyms of "science" and "scientific method."[2]

[1] Reprinted from *Philosophy of Science*, 1946, **13**, 326–331, with the permission of the author and the publisher. Copyright © 1946, The Williams & Wilkins Company, Baltimore, Md. 21202, U.S.A.

[2] The writer concedes that "method" is defined by some in a very broad and very sophisticated manner in order to avoid foreseen dangers. I consider even this to be a mistake if only because undesirable conclusions are drawn by less wise individuals no matter how they are forewarned.

1. *Inevitable stress on elegance, polish, "technique," and apparatus, has as a frequent consequence a playing down of meaningfulness, vitality, and significance of the problem and of creativeness in general.* Almost any candidate for the Ph.D. in science will understand what this means in practice. A methodologically satisfactory experiment, whether trivial or not, is rarely criticized. A bold, groundbreaking problem, because it often involves crudeness in conception and prosecution, and also because it may be a "failure," is too often criticized to death before it is ever begun. Indeed, the word "criticism" in the scientific literature seems usually to mean only criticism of method, technique, logic, etc. I do not recall seeing, in the literature with which I am familiar, any paper which criticized another paper for being unimportant, trivial or inconsequential.

The tendency is growing therefore to say that the dissertation problem itself doesn't matter—only so it be well done. In a word, it need no longer be a "contribution to knowledge." The Ph.D. candidate is required to know the techniques of his field and the already accumulated data in it. It is not usually stressed that good research ideas are also desirable. As a consequence it is possible for completely and obviously uncreative people to become "scientists" in spite of the fact that an "uncreative scientist" is as self-contradictory as a mute orator.

At a lower level—in the teaching of science in the high school and college— similar results can be seen. The student is encouraged to identify science with directed manipulations of apparatus, and with rote procedures learned out of a cook book,—in a word, following other people's leads and repeating what other people have already discovered. Nowhere is he taught that a scientist is different from a technician or a historian of science.

It is easy to misunderstand the point of these contentions. I do not wish to underplay method; I wish only to point out that even in science, means may easily be confused with ends. It is only the goals or ends of science that dignify and validate its methods. The working scientist must, of course, be concerned with his techniques, but only because they can help him achieve his proper ends. Once he forgets this, he becomes like the man spoken of by Freud who spent all his time polishing his glasses instead of putting them on and seeing with them.

2. *Means-centering tends to push into a commanding position in science the technicians, and the "apparatus men," rather than the "question-askers" and the problem-solvers.* Without wishing to create an extreme and unreal dichotomy, it is still possible to point out a difference between those who know only *how* to do and those who also know *what* to do. These former individuals, of whom there are always a large number, tend inevitably to become a class of priests in science, authorities on protocol, on procedure, and, so to speak, on ritual and ceremonial. While such people have been no more than a nuisance in the past, now that science becomes a matter of national and international policy, they may become an active danger.

3. *Means-centering tends strongly to over-value quantification indiscriminately and as an end in itself.* This must be true because of the greater stress of means-centered science on *how* statements are made rather than on what is said. Elegance and

precision are then counterposed to pertinence and breadth of implication. This mistake has often been criticized but its origins have less often been discussed.

4. *Means-centered scientists tend, in spite of themselves, to fit their problems to their techniques rather than the contrary.* Their beginning question tends to be "Which problems can I attack with the techniques and equipment I now possess?" rather than what it should more often be, "Which are the most pressing, the most crucial problems I could spend my time on?" How else explain the fact that most run-of-the-mill scientists spend their lifetimes in a small area whose boundaries are defined, not by a basic question about the world, but by the limits of a piece of apparatus or of a technique? In psychology, few people see any humor in the concept of an "animal psychologist" or a "statistical psychologist," i.e., individuals who don't mind working with *any* problem so long as they can use, respectively, their animals or their statistics.

5. *Means-centering tends strongly to create a hierarchy of sciences, in which, quite perniciously, physics is considered to be more "scientific" than biology, biology than psychology, and psychology than sociology.* Such an assumption of hierarchy is possible only on the basis of elegance, success, and precision of technique. From the point of view of a problem-centered science, such a hierarchy would never be suggested, for who could maintain that questions about unemployment, or race prejudice, or love are, in any intrinsic way, less important than questions about stars, or sodium or kidney function.

6. *Means-centering tends to compartmentalize the sciences too strongly, to build walls between them that divide them into separate territories.* Jacques Loeb, when asked whether he was a neurologist, or a chemist, or a physicist, a psychologist or a philosopher, answered only, "I solve problems." Certainly this ought to be a more usual answer. And it would be well for science if it had more men like Loeb. But these desiderata are clearly discouraged by the philosophy which makes the scientist into a technician rather than a venturesome truth-seeker.

If scientists looked upon themselves as problem-solvers rather than specialized technicians, there would now be something of a rush to the newest scientific frontier, to the psychological and social problems about which we know least and should know most. Why is it that there is so little traffic across these departmental borders? How does it happen that a thousand scientists prosecute physical or chemical research for every dozen who pursue the psychological problems? Which would be better for mankind, to put a thousand fine minds to producing better bombs (or even better penicillin) or to set them to work on the problems of nationalism or psychotherapy or exploitation?

7. *Means-centering in science creates too great a cleavage between scientists and other truth-seekers, and between their various methods of searching after truth and understanding.* If we define science as a search for truth, insight and understanding, we must be hard put to it to differentiate between the scientists on the one hand, and the poets, artists and philosophers on the other hand. Their avowed problems may be the same. Ultimately, of course, a semantically honest differentiation could be made, and it must be admitted that it would have to be mostly on the basis of

difference in method and in techniques of guarding against mistakes. And yet it would clearly be better for science if this gap between the scientist and the poet and the philosopher were less abysmal than it is today. Means-centering simply puts them into different realms; problem-centering would conceive of them as mutually helpful collaborators. The biographies of most of the great scientists show that the latter is more nearly true than the former. Many of the greatest scientists have themselves been also artists and philosophers, and have often derived as much sustenance from philosophers as from their scientific colleagues.

8. *Means-centering tends inevitably to bring into being a scientific "orthodoxy," which in turn creates a heterodoxy.* Questions and problems in science can rarely be formulated, classified or put into a filing system. The questions of the past are no longer questions, but answers. The questions of the future have not yet come into existence. But it *is* possible to formulate and classify the methods and techniques of the past. These then are termed the "laws of scientific method." Canonized, crusted about with tradition and history, they tend to become binding upon the present day (rather than merely suggestive or helpful). In the hands of the less creative, the timid, the conventional, these "laws" become virtually a demand that we solve our present problems *only* as our forefathers solved theirs.

Such an attitude is especially dangerous for the psychological and social sciences. Here the injunction to be "truly" scientific is usually translated as "Use the techniques of the physical and life sciences." Hence we have the tendency among many psychologists and social scientists to imitate old techniques rather than to create and invent the new ones made necessary by the fact that their problems and their data are intrinsically different from those of the physical sciences.

8a. *One main danger of scientific orthodoxy is that it tends to block the development of new techniques.* If the "laws of scientific method" have already been formulated, it remains only to apply them. New methods, new ways of doing things, must inevitably be suspect, and have usually been greeted with hostility, e.g., psychoanalysis, gestalt psychology, Rorschach testing. The expectation of such hostility probably is partly to blame for the fact that there have not yet been invented the relational logics and mathematics demanded by the new psychological and social sciences.

Ordinarily, the advance of science is a collaborative product. How else could limited individuals make important, even great, discoveries? When there is no collaboration, the advance is apt to stop dead until there shows up some giant who needs no help. Orthodoxy means the denial of help to the heterodox. Since few, (of the heterodox, as well as of the orthodox), are geniuses, this implies continuous, smooth advance only for orthodox science. We may expect heterodox ideas to be held up for long periods of weary neglect or opposition, to "break through" rather suddenly (if they are correct), and then to become in turn orthodox.

8b. *Another, probably more important, danger of the orthodoxy fostered by means-centering, is that it tends to limit more and more the jurisdiction of science.* Not only does it block the development of new techniques; it also tends to block the asking of many questions, on grounds that the reader might well expect by now, that such questions cannot be answered by currently available techniques, e.g., questions about the subjective, questions about values, questions about religion. It is only such foolish grounds that make possible that unnecessary confession of defeat, that contradiction in terms, the concept of the "unscientific problem," as if there were *any* question that we dared not ask. Surely, anyone who had read and understood the history of science would not dare to speak of an *unsolvable* problem; he would speak only of problems which have not yet been solved. Phrased in this latter way, we have a clear incentive to action, to further exercise of ingenuity and inventiveness. Phrased in terms of current scientific orthodoxy, i.e., "What can we do with scientific method (as we know it)?", we are encouraged to the opposite, i.e., to voluntarily imposed self-limitations, to abdication from huge areas of human interest. This tendency can go to the most incredible and dangerous extremes. It has even happened in recent discussions of congressional efforts to set up a national research foundation, that many physicists suggested the exclusion from its benefits of all the psychological and social sciences on the grounds that they weren't "scientific" enough. On what possible basis could this statement have been made if not an exclusive respect for polished and successful techniques, and a complete lack of awareness of the question-asking nature of science and its rooting in human values? How shall I as a psychologist translate this and other similar jibes from my physicist friends? Ought I to use their techniques? But these are useless for my problems. Ought I then to give up my problems to deal only with physical problems? But how would that get the psychological problems solved? Ought they not to be solved? Or ought scientists to abdicate from the field completely and give it back to the theologians? Or is there perhaps implied an *ad hominem* sneer? Is it implied that the psychologists are stupid and the physicists intelligent? But on what grounds can such an inherently improbable statement be made? Impressions? Then I must report *my* impression that there are as many fools in any one scientific group as in any other. Which impression is more valid? No! I can see no other translation possible except one that by concealed implication gives the primary place to technique—perhaps the only place.

8c. *Means-centered orthodoxy encourages scientists to be "safe" rather than bold and daring.* It makes the normal business of the scientist seem to be moving ahead inch by inch on the well laid out roads rather than cutting new paths through the unknown. It forces conservative rather than radical approaches to the not-yet-known. It tends to make him into a settler rather than a pioneer.

The proper place for the scientist—once in a while at least—is in the midst of the unknown, the chaotic, the dimly seen, the unmanageable, the mysterious, the not-yet-well-phrased. This is where a problem-oriented science would have him be as often as necessary. And this is just where he is discouraged from going by a means-stressing approach to science.

9. *Over-stress on methods and techniques encourages scientists to think (a) that they are more objective and less subjective than they actually are and that (b) they need not concern themselves with values.* Methods are ethically neutral; problems and questions may not be, for sooner or later, they involve all the knotty arguments about

values. One way of avoiding the problem of values is to stress the techniques of science rather than the goals of science. Indeed, it seems very probable that one of the main roots of the means-centered orientation in science is the strenuous effort to be as objective (non-valued) as possible.

But science was not, is not and cannot be completely objective, which is to say, independent of human values. Furthermore, it is highly debatable whether it ought even to *try* to be (that is, *completely* objective rather than as-objective-as-it-is-possible-for-human-beings-to-be). All the mistakes listed in this paper attest to the dangers of attempting to neglect the shortcomings of human nature. Not only is it impossible to divorce reason from human emotions and motivations, but it is highly undesirable even to attempt it. Reason *relatively* divorced from the emotions and motivations, is a neurotic manifestation. Not only does the neurotic pay a huge subjective price for his vain attempt, but ironically enough, he also becomes progressively a poorer and poorer thinker.

9a. *Because of this fancied independence of values, standards of worth become steadily more blurred.* If means-centering philosophies were extreme (which they rarely are), and if they were quite consistent (which they dare not be for fear of obviously foolish consequences), then there would be no way to distinguish between an important experiment and an unimportant one. There could be only technically well-prosecuted experiments and technically poorly-prosecuted experiments. Using only methodological criteria, the most trivial research could demand as much respect as the most fruitful one. Of course, this does not actually happen in an extreme way, but this is only because of appeal to criteria and standards other than methodological ones. However, although this mistake is rarely seen in a blatant form, it *is* often enough seen in a less obvious form. The journals of science are full of instances that illustrate the point.

If sciences were no more than a set of rules and procedures, what difference would there be between science on the one hand and, on the other, chess, alchemy, "umbrellaology," or the practice of dentistry?

RÉSUMÉ

Means-centered approach to science is contrasted with a problem-centered orientation. Overstress on and too exclusive concern with method, instrument, technique or procedure fosters the following mistakes:

1. Emphasis on polish and elegance rather than on vitality, significance and creativeness.

2. Giving the commanding positions in science to technicians rather than discoverers.

3. Over-valuation of quantification for its own sake.

4. Fitting problems to techniques rather than vice-versa.

5. Creation of a false and pernicious hierarchical system among the sciences.

6. Overstrong compartmentalization between the sciences.

7. Emphasis on the difference rather than the similarities between scientists and other truth-seekers (poets, novelists, artists, philosophers).

8. Creation of a scientific orthodoxy, which in turn (a) tends to block the development of new methods, (b) tends to exclude many problems from the jurisdiction of science and (c) tends to make scientists "safe" rather than daring and unconventional.

9. Neglect of the problems of values, with a consequent blurring of the criteria for judging the worth or importance of an experiment.

31. The Relevance of Laboratory Studies to Practical Situations[1]

Alphonse Chapanis

How relevant to the real world are the results of laboratory experimentation is the question explored by Dr. Chapanis. Using examples from the applied field of human engineering, he lists a number of limitations of laboratory research: (a) the restricting of independent variables in the laboratory; (b) the changing nature of variables when brought into the laboratory; (c) the control over variables frequently producing effects of no practical importance; (d) the dependent variables chosen on the basis of convenience; and (e) the methods of stimuli presentation often being artificial and unrealistic. It is concluded that the results of laboratory experimentation can be generalized to the solution of real world problems only with extreme caution. Dr. Chapanis notes that his investigation of this problem was "a sobering and humbling exercise."

INTRODUCTION

There are a few things in life that, most people would agree, one accepts without question. The exact things that fall into this category depend on who you are and on your momentary position in the moving stream of history. For example, I suspect that most contemporary Americans accept without question *God, motherhood, democracy, freedom* and *baseball*. A Briton would, I am sure, want to modify the list at least to the extent of including *morning tea* and *cricket*. And a Russian would certainly want to see to it that the list contained *Lenin*.

To most working scientists in the behavioural and social sciences *laboratory experiments* occupy such an unassailable position. In our graduate schools we teach our students that laboratory experiments are an infallible way of discovering the truth about the world around us. We rebut popular beliefs about human behaviour by citing the results of laboratory experiments. And in professional and scientific arguments we appeal to the data of laboratory experiments in much the same way

[1] Reprinted from *Ergonomics*, 1967, **10**, 557–577, with the permission of the author and the publisher. This article was prepared under Contract Nonr-4010(03) between the Office of Naval Research and The Johns Hopkins University. It is Report No. 18 under that contract.

that learned men, centuries ago, appealed to the authority of Aristotle or of Thomas Aquinas.

Yet lately I have detected signs of uneasiness, of concern, that perhaps one cannot always rely uncritically on the results of laboratory experiments to tell us how to solve real-world problems. For one thing, there is the fact that your programme committee invited me to talk on this very topic.

Some Recent Critiques of Laboratory Experimentation

Much more impressive, however, are a few articles that have recently questioned the applicability of laboratory findings even when the laboratory studies themselves were originally undertaken to help solve some practical problem. Let me take an example. There is now a considerable body of literature on what has come to be called vigilance and this area of research is, I think it is fair to say, a respectable one in psychology. We have a substantial number of laboratory findings on vigilance and even some fairly sophisticated theories to account for these findings.

I scarcely need remind you, of course, that this whole area of research had an applied origin. It started some twenty or thirty years ago when people tried to understand the behaviour of human beings in systems, such as radar and sonar systems, where the operator had to look for, or listen for, infrequent signals. To a large extent, research in this area still appears to be motivated by applied interests. At any rate, the authors of laboratory studies on vigilance often make at least a token obeisance in the direction of some real-world monitoring job when they write about their work. And, of course, psychologists continually use the results of laboratory experiments on vigilance to try to tell engineers how people will perform in any of a number of monitoring or watch-keeping jobs.

Yet in a recent article Kibler (1965) said in essence that the results of classical vigilance research are not particularly germane to contemporary monitoring problems. Here also is the considered opinion of two other writers, Jerison and Pickett (1963), who have worked in this area of research and have written a critical review of it.

Although vigilance research received its major impetus from practical problems of sustained visual monitoring of radar displays, it does not, at this time, contribute in clear and unequivocal ways to the solution of similar problems in manned space systems or, for that matter, in any systems that are planned for field operation. (Page 235.)

Let us turn briefly to just one other area of psychology. Here is a quotation from a report by Mackie and Christensen (1967).

Research on learning processes represents perhaps the largest single area of investigation presently being pursued by experimental psychologists . . . *However* both academic and practically oriented psychologists agree that a very small percentage of findings from learning research is useful, in any direct sense, for the improvement of training or educational practices. (Pages 4 and 5.)

I am sure you will agree that statements such as these are disturbing enough to shake us from our comfortable complacency about the usefulness of laboratory experiments.

The Results of Laboratory Experiments often Fail to Predict in Real Life

Even more impressive than such evaluations are instances in which the results of laboratory experiments have failed to predict what people will do, or how they will behave, in real-life situations. Sometimes these failures are subtle ones. It turns out that we often cannot confirm in real-world situations what the results of laboratory experiments would lead us to expect. When a failure of this kind occurs, the author of the study almost invariably comments apologetically on the difficulty of doing good experiments in real situations, on the difficulty of controlling variables, and on all the other problems that plague the practical investigator. Other laboratory scientists, in turn, nod sympathetically in agreement. But as with most things in life there is usually more than one way to interpret a particular event. Are failures of this kind the fault of the real-life experiment? Or does some of the fault perhaps lie with the laboratory experiments?

Failures of the kind I have been referring to do not often appear in the literature: and for understandable reasons. Even so, one can find a few such examples in the literature from time to time. To return to vigilance research, here is what Elliott (1960) has to say on this score.

Whenever we have studied real military watchkeeping tasks, we have achieved some results which could not have been predicted from published test data and, indeed, we have often found the published material quite misleading. (Page 357.)

To take another example of a completely different sort, Whitfield (1964) tried to validate the effectiveness of redesigning the console of a digital computer. He found, however, that he could not show any difference in the number of errors made on the old and new machines when programmers and engineers performed five typical operations. His disappointment shows clearly in the article. Although he has a number of explanations for his failure, the conclusion I want to draw is this: he did not get what he expected on the basis of data originating from laboratory studies.

One of the most dramatic examples of all comes from certain experiments performed during the *Gemini* space flights, particularly the flight of *Gemini 11*. To study weightlessness the United States Air Force and National Aeronautics and Space Administration have constructed several flying laboratories. These are specially designed aircraft that, when they fly *Keplerian* trajectories, are able to achieve weightlessness for short periods of time (see, for example, Simons, 1964). Literally thousands of flights have been made with such flying laboratories and the number of experiments performed in them can hardly be estimated. Perhaps you remember the story about the flight of *Gemini 11*. Astronaut Richard

Gordon was to get outside the capsule and tie the *Gemini 11* capsule to an *Agena* rocket with a 100-foot cord. As Gordon himself said about this experience:

All I had done in about 30 seconds *in the laboratory* turned out to be a monumental task of about 30 minutes. It was easy to perform in training, but it was really work in space.

The details of this story have been so thoroughly reported in newspapers and journals that I hardly need to amplify them any further here.

To sum up, then, we often do not find in practical situations the results we would have predicted from laboratory experiments. Such failures are another reason for us to pause and ask, "What's wrong?"

THE PURPOSE OF THIS PAPER

My purpose in this paper is to explore with you some of the difficulties we face when we try to generalize from laboratory experiments to the solution of real-world problems. Oddly enough, this is a topic that is completely ignored in almost all books that deal with experimental design, or the scientific method, in the life sciences. Our methodological textbooks are full of such things as simple randomized designs, matched-groups experiments, factorial designs, balanced incomplete blocks, and latin squares, together with all the statistical manipulations that are appropriate to each of them. But they almost invariably end with a test of statistical significance. They practically never tell you where to go from there. Our inquiries today are concerned with the broader logical question of what an experiment has, or has not, told us in the greater scheme of things.

In the process of finding out why it is that experiments do not solve many practical problems, we shall also be answering two related questions. The first of these is, "Why don't training devices train any better than they do?" The second is, "Why don't psychological tests predict better than they do?" Although I shall not spend any time on these latter questions, I think it will become apparent as we proceed how they are related to our basic query.

Some scientists try to avoid facing the issues I am raising here today by saying that they have no interest at all in practical problems. They may say this in several ways. Usually they say that they are only concerned with *pure* or basic research. Occasionally they may say that they are only concerned with theoretical problems. Or perhaps they may say that they are trying to find out the *truth*. I do not think that such disclaimers have much force. Historians of science (see, for example, Kranzberg, 1967) seem agreed that there is today a unity between science and technology such as has never existed before. Many of our best theoretical developments in the life sciences started with attempts to solve some practical problem. Moreover, a body of basic information, or a theory, that can predict only what happens within the four walls of a laboratory is, in my opinion, an ineffectual science: a science so limited in generality that it gives us a distorted version of reality.

But even if you do not agree with me on these points, you will at least agree that there are large numbers of people who *are* concerned with trying to put scientific information to use in the solution of practical problems. In addition, the average man on the street, and the legislator who votes us our research funds, usually wants to know, "What good is it?" In discussing this topic with you today I hope that we shall all be able to end up with a clearer and more articulate understanding of what good it all is.

Some Boundary Conditions on the Kinds of Experiments to be Discussed

To narrow the field of my discourse, let me make it clear right away that I shall be talking exclusively about laboratory experiments in the behavioural sciences. Laboratory experiments in such fields as physics, chemistry, and the engineering sciences are usually far simpler conceptually, and so somewhat different, in design than those we try to conduct in the behavioural sciences. I want to narrow my topic still further by saying that I shall talk about laboratory experiments that involve the behaviour of intact human beings. I mean by this that I want to exclude all experiments involving animals and all those experiments that might properly be called physiological experiments. In addition, I shall talk about experiments that fall generally within the field of human factors engineering. What I shall have to say about laboratory experiments applies to many fields—education, sociology and economics—but I want to talk about the area I know best. I shall leave it to you to extrapolate my remarks to fields of greater perspective.

The Experiments Discussed Here are Properly Designed and Correctly Analysed

I want next to confine my remarks to laboratory experiments that are impeccably tailored to fit one or another model design. I mean by this that I shall not spend any time finding fault with the technical design of experiments, with such things as counterbalancing, randomization and confounding. Let us also take it for granted that the data of our experiments have been properly analysed and that the results satisfy all the usual criteria of statistical significance. It is true, of course, that scientific journals still publish the results of laboratory experiments that violate one or more of these simple principles of sound methodology. But I want to talk about more fundamental problems. So, for our purposes, let us take it for granted that the laboratory experiments we are looking at meet rigorous criteria of design, form and analysis.

WHAT IS A LABORATORY EXPERIMENT?

At this point, I think it would be a good idea for me to give you a definition of a laboratory experiment in order that you may know exactly what it is I am talking about. There are probably as many definitions of a laboratory experiment as there are experimenters. Still, I think one could probably get agreement from most behavioural scientists that: A laboratory experiment is a deliberately contrived, artificial situation in which the experimenter

(*a*) varies some factors (the *independent* variables), and

(*b*) minimizes the operation of some other factors that are not of interest to him at the moment (the *controlled* variables),

(*c*) in order that he may measure changes in behaviour (the *dependent* variables) that are the result of, or are produced by, the independent variables.

There is a bit more to a laboratory experiment than this, of course, because an experiment does not spring into being fully grown. The experimenter starts with some hypothesis, some question, that he wants to answer. Having formulated his question he must then choose a particular combination of independent, controlled and dependent variables that he hopes will help him to answer his question. Then, too, the experimenter has to decide on the *methods* he will use to vary his independent variables and to measure his dependent ones, that is, the ways in which the independent and dependent variables are to be defined operationally for presentation to the subject. These conceptual aspects of experimental design are an important part of the whole business and we must keep them in mind when we examine the process of laboratory experimentation.

THE LABORATORY EXPERIMENT AS A MODEL OF THE WORLD

In an article I wrote a few years ago (Chapanis, 1961) I said that every laboratory experiment is a model of the real world. I also said that, as representations of the real world, models are *always* incomplete and so are *always* wrong. It follows, therefore, that in so far as they try to represent or model the real world, laboratory experiments are always wrong too. To put this another way, the results of laboratory experiments always fail to give us exact solutions to real-world problems. In some cases, to be sure, the results of a laboratory experiment may be *substantially* correct, that is, it may predict with reasonably good accuracy how people do indeed behave in life. At the other extreme, however, the results of a laboratory experiment may not even come close to predicting human behaviour. And, of course, one can get all possible gradations between these two extremes.

The Complexity of Relationships in the World of Behaviour

Textbooks in the behavioural sciences almost invariably give us an enormously simplified view of the world. It is a neat and tidy world in which a few clearly defined independent variables exert their influences on one or two obvious dependent variables. This is such a simple view of reality that it is misleading.

What, for example, are the independent variables that influence learning, specifically, learning how to drive? The independent variables are so many they almost defy enumeration. To start, we must certainly admit the importance of a large number of physical factors, such as sex, age, physical strength, basic psycho-motor skill and visual acuity. Next, there is a host of intellectual factors that in-fluence learning, things such as intelligence, prior experience with mechanical devices, and motivation. Then, too, consider factors more physiological in nature, things like the general condition of the person when he tries to learn, his condition of fatigue or wellbeing, whether he is taking drugs of any kind, and whether he is suffering from some kind of chronic illness, allergy or other bodily disturbance. You would surely agree that personality factors, such as timidity or aggressiveness, self-confidence and neuroticism must influence learning. We certainly cannot ignore the way in which instruction is conducted, the instructor, his teaching methods, the spacing of trials, and the amount of reinforcement given. Nor can we ignore the learning task itself, the particular vehicle used for learning, its handling characteristics and the environment in which the learning takes place.

But perhaps this is enough to give you the idea I am trying to get across: the number of independent variables that influence something like learning must be a very large number indeed.

Let me also assert, without actually going through a similar tiresome catalogue, that there is always a very large number of *dependent* variables in any real task.

The Laboratory Experiment as a Model

What happens when you do an experiment? From the very large number of possible independent variables, the laboratory scientist selects a very few, usually no more than three or four, to study. He holds some others, perhaps as many as a dozen, constant, and ignores all the rest. Similarly, from all the possible depend-ent variables, he selects one, sometimes two, or possibly three for study, and ignores all the rest. Viewed in this way, the laboratory experiment takes on the appearance of a cramped and stunted model of life.

SOME DANGERS OF LIMITING THE NUMBER OF INDEPENDENT VARIABLES

Reducing the number of variables, in and of itself, might not seem to present any pitfalls. On the contrary, the laboratory scientist can, and usually does, argue that he abstracts from all possible variables those few in which he is interested at the moment in order that he may study them all the better in the laboratory. There is some truth in this, of course. The danger comes when one tries to extrap-olate, or generalize, from the results of a laboratory experiment to the solution of practical problems. Let us start with the independent variables and see where the danger lies.

Hidden Interactions

Like it or not, the real-world of behaviour is full of interactions. When you do a laboratory experiment with one, two, or even three independent variables you never know whether hidden interactions may nullify, or even reverse, the conclusions of your experiment. Let me illustrate.

One of my former students, Lockhead, and I were interested in discovering whether sensor lines on a control panel would help operators respond more quickly to the appropriate controls on the panel. A *sensor line* is a kind of flow line, a heavy line drawn on the panel connecting each display with its corresponding control. The results of a part of that experiment are shown in Figure 31-1. As you can see, there does indeed seem to be a decrease in response time on the panel that had the sensor lines. Does this permit us to generalize and say that sensor lines are good and should be used on all control panels? Not at all. Control panels may differ in many ways—in size, shape, complexity, number of elements and so on—and we have no way of knowing whether the presence or absence of sensor lines interacts with any or all of these other variables.

It so happens that the data in Figure 31-1 were collected from a control panel that contained four displays and four controls arranged in a non-compatible pattern, that is, there was no isomorphism between the location of the displays and their corresponding controls. Lockhead and I also tested another pair of control panels of exactly the same size and shape as the one on which the data of Figure 31-1 were collected. However, the second pair of control panels had a compatible arrangement. In Figure 31-2 you see the results obtained with all

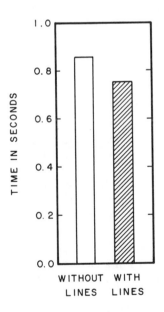

FIGURE 31-1. Average response times for control panels with and without sensor lines. These are data recomputed from the left half of Figure 3, page 223, of the article by Chapanis and Lockhead, 1965.

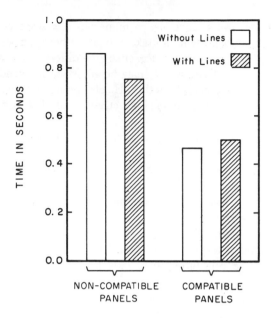

FIGURE 31-2. The data on the left here are the same as those in Figure 31-1. The data on the right are for another pair of panels in which the arrangements of displays and controls are compatible. These are data recomputed from the left half of Figure 3, page 223, of the article by Chapanis and Lockhead, 1965.

four panels. The two bars on the left in Figure 31-2 are the same as appear in Figure 31-1. Here you see a disturbing interaction. The same sensor lines that improved speed of response when the panels were non-compatible actually slow operators down when the panels are compatible. Another way of saying it is that the effect of one independent variable (the presence or absence of sensor lines) may or may not be important. It depends on the value of another independent variable (the compatibility of the arrangements of displays and controls).

If you will allow me to speak immodestly about my own research, I think the results Lockhead and I obtained are interesting and as dependable as one gets from most laboratory experiments. None the less, this experiment shares a common fault with all laboratory experiments. One never knows how many other hidden, or undiscovered, interactions may affect the applicability of the results to any practical situation. The trouble is that in designing our experiment we were able to select only a few from all the possible independent variables. After all, we had to keep the experiment to a manageable size. The other independent variables we ignored. This is what every laboratory experimenter does. But it is those ignored variables, and their possible interactions, that make it so hard to generalize from laboratory experiments to the solution of most practical problems.

Interactions in behavioural science are so numerous one scarcely knows how to pick illustrations from among them. To take only one other example, Broadbent (1963) has shown clearly that the combined effects of different stresses (such as noise, high temperatures and sleeplessness) may be additive, independent, or that one stress may actually partially cancel another. He also points out that, in contrast to the large number of studies we have on single stressors, studies on the effects of combined stresses are rare.

Interactions are the reason we are forced to say, "Well, it depends . . ." when we try to answer practical questions.

"Is it better to present information to the eyes or the ears ?" "Well, it depends . . ."

"Do people learn faster if you space learning trials or group them ?" "Well, it depends . . ."

"Is ten foot candles enough light to see by ?" "Well, it depends . . ."

"Is 95°F a tolerable temperature ?" "Well, it depends . . ."

"Is a carbon monoxide concentration of 0.04 per cent dangerous or not ?" "Well, it depends . . ."

And so you could go through almost any textbook of the behavioural sciences finding general statements that may or may not be true, depending on the particular values or levels of other variables that happen to be operating simultaneously. It is the large number of untested and undiscovered interactions in the behavioural sciences that makes our task so difficult.

A VARIABLE BY ANY OTHER NAME

The second major difficulty we face when we try to generalize from laboratory experiments is that variables in the laboratory are not the same as those in the real world even though they are supposed to be. The very act of bringing a variable into the laboratory usually changes its nature. A variable in the real world contains a lot of elements. When you bring the variable into the laboratory, you lose some of the original elements and add some others that were not in the original. Let us look at an example.

Berkun *et al.* (1962) were interested in studying the deterioration of human behaviour in combat due to the effects of psychological stress. They started out by using some conventional stresses of the type that are often used in laboratory experiments (for example, electric shock) and some stresses (for example, falling from a high, unstable support) that would seem to constitute a clear threat to the subject. In general, however, none of these was successful because, to quote the authors:

. . . *the subjects* usually realized quickly that they were in an experiment, that they were safe, and that they were expected to act "scared." They seemed to recognize that the likelihood of danger in an experiment is very small and that, therefore, there is no reason to actually be "scared." (Page 2.)

Berkun *et al.* also point out that some other kinds of stresses often used in laboratory studies—for example, information overload, achievement failure and frustration of aspiration—are not necessarily similar to, or even representative of, the stresses of combat, catastrophe or major surgery. One essential ingredient that is missing from all such laboratory stresses, these authors argue, is the subject's own belief in their authenticity, based on what he realizes, figures out, or thinks about the situation.

What elements get *added* to variables when they are brought into the laboratory? Well, for one thing, the experimenter. A laboratory experiment is a social situation involving subject and experimenter. The mere presence of an experimenter changes a person's behaviour in certain kinds of experiments (Kintz *et al.*, 1965). There is also good evidence (Kintz *et al.*, *op. cit.*; Rosenthal, 1963; Rosenthal, 1964) that in a large variety of psychological experiments the experimenter himself may subtly and unconsciously bias the way subjects respond in an experiment. In addition to the influence of the experimenter there is the fact that the subject knows he is participating in an experiment. Berkun *et al.* point out that laboratory studies of stress tend to induce in subjects a *test-taking set* or *experimenter-oriented motivation*. They mean by this that subjects in a laboratory expect and are prepared to take a test of some kind. Moreover, in taking the test they may be additionally motivated to please (or occasionally to antagonize) the experimenter. For these reasons, they contend that the only stresses relevant to their kind of problem are those in which the subject really believes he is actually in danger or trouble.

To study stress under more realistic conditions Berkun *et al. op. cit.* devised five carefully contrived, highly realistic, field situations in a military setting. Their results show clearly that the subjects' subjective feelings of stress in the five situations were different. Some of the experimental situations were perceived as highly stressful; others not so stressful. Even more important for our purposes, however, is that performance measures and two physiological measures were clearly related to the subject's evaluations of the five experimental situations. In other words, the results the experimenters got depended on how the subjects perceived the situation.

To sum up, then, I think there is good reason to believe that most variables change when they are abstracted out of real life and brought into the laboratory. What are some particularly unstable variables? I think immediately of such things as anxiety, choice behaviour, decision making, fatigue, information processing, learning, perception, productivity, stress and vigilance.

The difficulty, of course, is that we tend to classify a wide variety of things under a common name. Once having done this we then often make the error of assuming that anything with a particular name is identical to anything else with that name. Broadbent (*op. cit.*), in the article to which I have already referred, points out that those conditions we refer to collectively as *stress* are not at all equivalent. Different stresses have different effects on the body and on performance. They are, in a word, different.

Let me take another example. If you look in the index of *Psychological Abstracts* for a single recent year you will find classified under *decision making* a variety of studies ranging from the behaviour of rats at choice points, through the behaviour of adolescents making vocational choices, to the behaviour of managers in industry. The fact that these are all called *decision making* does not make them equivalent. To be specific, I do not think that choice points in a maze, or the choices offered subjects in laboratory games, are at all similar to the choices offered an industrialist in real life about whether to build a new factory in the U.S., U.K. or Germany. To generalize from either of the former to the latter means taking a dangerous leap unsupported by any solid rules of logic.

THE CONSEQUENCES OF CONTROLLING VARIABLES

The idea that one controls unwanted or extraneous variables in a laboratory experiment has a ring of intuitive correctness about it. Of course. That is precisely what you should do. But let us look at that notion analytically to see what it does to a set of data and what consequences it has for generalizing to broader situations.

Assume an extremely simple kind of experimental design: a randomized-groups experiment involving a comparison of two conditions. The two conditions, call them I and II, might be almost anything: two kinds of dials, two levels of illumination, two kinds of background noise in an office, or two ways of learning binary arithmetic. We pick a group of subjects and, at random, assign each subject to one of the two experimental conditions. The design looks like that in Table 31-1. The X's are scores or measures of each subject's performance. The subscripts, 1, 2, 3, . . ., i, . . . , m, identify the subjects assigned to condition I, and 1, 2, 3, . . . , j, . . . , n, identify the subjects assigned to condition II.

TABLE 31-1

This is a hypothetical experiment to compare
two experimental conditions.

I	II
X_{I_1}	X_{II_1}
X_{I_2}	X_{II_2}
X_{I_3}	X_{II_3}
.	.
.	.
.	.
X_{I_i}	X_{II_j}
.	.
.	.
.	.
X_{I_m}	X_{II_n}
M_I	M_{II}

For many kinds of data we would next compute a mean for each of the two experimental conditions and evaluate the significance of the difference between the means by appropriate statistical tests, usually a t- or F-test. You remember, of course, that when you compare only two means, the t- and F-tests give identical results. For the case we have been talking about, the t-statistic may be written in this way:

$$t = \frac{M_I - M_{II}}{\sqrt{\left[\left\{\frac{\sum(X_{I_i} - M_I)^2 + \sum(X_{II_j} - M_{II})^2}{m + n - 2}\right\}\left(\frac{1}{m} + \frac{1}{n}\right)\right]}}$$

The numerator of this t-ratio is the difference between the two obtained means, and the denominator is an estimate of the random, residual, or unaccounted-for variability among the subjects tested under the same conditions. Table 31-2 shows the results of all these computations performed on a fictitious set of data.

TABLE 31-2

Computations on a fictitious set of data from an experiment
such as that in Table 31-1.

	I	II
	64	79
	67	80
	74	78
	78	89
	80	78
	72	95
	76	97
	85	84
	83	92
	81	88
M	76	86
σ	6.48	6.84

$t = 3.18; p < 0.01$

What every good laboratory experimenter tries to do is to reduce the denominator of the t-ratio as much as possible. If he can cut down the size of the denominator, he increases the t-ratio. And if he can increase the t-ratio, he is more likely to win, that is, come out with a statistically significant result. Most of the stratagems of experimental design, matching subjects, grouping subjects into levels, or controlling variables, have as their single goal the reduction of the magnitude of that denominator. (I hasten to add that some principles of experimental design, for example, counter balancing or randomizing to avoid systematic bias, have other functions and are valid for experiments of any sort whether done in the laboratory or in more realistic situations.)

Now let us suppose that we were to do this same experiment in the real world instead of in a laboratory. We would no longer have control over a large number of variables that would ordinarily be controlled in the laboratory. It might very well be, for example, that we would have no control over the precise conditions of illumination, or of the temperature, or the humidity, or the time of day when subjects reported for the test. The chances are that we might not have precise control over the kinds of subjects we had. Perhaps we could not eliminate those who reported with a headache, hangover, or after having stayed up watching television until the wee hours of the morning. And so on.

What are the statistical consequences of adding the effects of uncontrolled variables to our experiment? These are shown schematically in Table 31-3 and

TABLE 31-3

This is the same experiment as in Table 31-1 but with many more variables uncontrolled.

I	II
$X_{I_1} \pm X_a \pm X_b \pm \ldots X_k$	$X_{II_1} \pm X_a \pm X_b \pm \ldots X_k$
$X_{I_2} \pm X_a \pm X_b \pm \ldots X_k$	$X_{II_2} \pm X_a \pm X_b \pm \ldots X_k$
$X_{I_3} \pm X_a \pm X_b \pm \ldots X_k$	$X_{II_3} \pm X_a \pm X_b \pm \ldots X_k$
.	.
.	.
.	.
$X_{I_i} \pm X_a \pm X_b \pm \ldots X_k$	$X_{II_j} \pm X_a \pm X_b \pm \ldots X_k$
.	.
.	.
.	.
$X_{I_m} \pm X_a \pm X_b \pm \ldots X_k$	$X_{II_n} \pm X_a \pm X_b \pm \ldots X_k$
$M_I \pm M_a \pm M_b \pm \ldots M_k$	$M_{II} \pm M_a \pm M_b \pm \ldots M_k$

numerically in Table 31-4. Uncontrolled variables add (or subtract) some error, or deviation, to a subject's measure of performance. The first subject tested under condition I, for example, earned a score of 64 in the laboratory (Table 31-2). In the real-life experiment he happened to be tested under conditions of illumination that approximated those in the laboratory so that the increment added to his measure of performance from this source in 0 (Table 31-4). However, he happened to report for the test after having been reprimanded for taking too much time out on his coffee breaks. This uncontrolled source of variation subtracts, let us say, 8 from his laboratory performance.

TABLE 31-4

Adding the effects from two uncontrolled variables to the data of Table 31-2 might produce results such as these.

	I	II
	$64 + 0 - 8 = 56$	$79 - 8 - 4 = 67$
	$67 + 2 + 5 = 74$	$80 - 2 + 1 = 79$
	$74 - 1 - 4 = 69$	$78 - 1 - 6 = 71$
	$78 - 6 - 2 = 70$	$89 + 2 - 2 = 89$
	$80 - 3 - 7 = 70$	$78 - 3 + 5 = 80$
	$72 + 0 - 9 = 63$	$95 + 0 - 9 = 86$
	$76 - 2 - 5 = 69$	$97 + 0 + 3 = 100$
	$85 + 7 - 1 = 91$	$84 + 4 - 5 = 83$
	$83 + 1 + 6 = 90$	$92 - 7 + 6 = 91$
	$81 + 3 + 4 = 88$	$88 + 7 - 1 = 94$
M	74	84
σ	11.26	9.66

$$t = 2.02; \ p > 0.05$$

The second subject, on the other hand, is tested under conditions of illumination that are slightly better than they were in the laboratory. This adds 2 to his laboratory score. Furthermore, the second subject came in to the real-life task after having been praised by his supervisor for having done a good job the preceding day. This boost in his morale is so great that it adds another increment of 5 to his basic laboratory score. And so we go through the whole set of data. The final results of such a series of fictitious additions are shown in Table 31-4.

If the effects of uncontrolled sources of extraneous variation are randomly distributed among the experimental conditions the *mean difference* between the experimental conditions is not affected. As you can see, the mean difference in Table 31-4 is exactly the same as that in Table 31-2. What does happen is that the uncontrolled variation all goes into the variability between subjects. If you compare the standard deviations in Table 31-4, with those in Table 31-2, you can see that the former are much greater than the latter. This increase in variability also means that the measure of random error in the denominator of our t-ratio increases. Indeed, as you can see, the difference between the two means in Table 31-2 is highly significant ($p < 0.01$). In Table 31-4, on the other hand, the same difference between the means is not significant ($p > 0.05$). There are exact mathematical equations that show precisely how variabilities accumulate in situations of this kind (see, for example, Chapanis, 1951), but we do not have the time to go into them now. Let me point out only that in the example I have given you in Table 31-4, I have added (or subtracted) the effects of only two additional variables. Life, of course, is full of uncontrolled variables. The more of them one takes into account the greater are the effects I have been talking about.

There is an additional consequence of having uncontrolled variables in an experiment and it lies at the very heart of the problem. One can compute the proportion of the total variability in a set of data that is accounted for by identifiable variables. Although the techniques for doing this are well known (see, for example, Chapanis, Garner and Morgan, 1949, pp. 59–65), laboratory scientists practically never use them. Once having found a statistically significant result, they stop at that. If you look at the total variability in Table 31-2 it turns out that 36 per cent of it can be accounted for by variations between conditions I and II. In Table 31-4, however, only 18 per cent of the total variability is attributable to our primary variable. This reduction occurs not because the difference between the means for I and II decreases. On the contrary, this effect stays the same. What happens is that the size of an effect becomes *relatively* less important as we start adding more and more variables to our data.

Let me summarize what I have been saying. Laboratory experiments try to get the maximum precision possible by controlling extraneous variables and by a variety of design stratagems, all of which are aimed at reducing the amount of error variability. By minimizing unaccounted-for variability a laboratory experiment maximizes the chances of revealing a statistically significant outcome. And therein, of course, lies the power of the laboratory experiment.

Unfortunately, this very power of a laboratory experiment constitutes its major weakness. Behaviour in the real-world is subject to all sorts of uncontrolled variability. Take automobile driving, for example. All sorts of people drive: the young, middle-aged and old. Men and women drive. So do the quick, the halt and the lame. They drive under all sorts of conditions of illumination and traffic. They drive when they are well rested and when they are fatigued or have just taken an anti-histamine pill. The cars they drive range from shiny new vehicles to decrepit pieces of machinery scarcely recognizable as automobiles. And so on through all the conditions that are involved in the practical business of highway transportation. When we try to extrapolate from laboratory experiments on reaction time, or tracking, or steering, to automobile driving what we hope is that the results of the laboratory experiment are large enough to show up when we put them into this huge *mélange* of real-world conditions. And, of course, we should not be disappointed to find that our laboratory findings are often so small they get swallowed up and lost in the avalanche of uncontrolled variables that operate in life.

In focusing on statistical significance a laboratory experiment completely ignores the problem of practical significance. It is a curious paradox: the more successfully a laboratory scientist increases the precision of his experiment, the more likely it is that he will prove statistical significance for effects that are practically trivial. This is, none the less, one of the major difficulties we face when we try to generalize from laboratory experiments to the solution of practical problems. The results of a laboratory experiment may tell us that we are dealing with a statistically significant effect, but they never tell us whether the effect is practically important or unimportant. Indeed, it is possible that a psychological theory based exclusively on the findings of carefully designed laboratory experiments may be nothing more than a theory of the unimportant.

ON DEPENDENT VARIABLES

Let us turn our attention now to the dependent variables of laboratory experiments to see if there are any special problems here. What are some typical dependent measures in human experiments? A good way of collecting a list of these is to go through all the articles in several recent volumes of *Ergonomics* or *Human Factors*. Here are some dependent measures I found in this way.

1. Time, usually the time taken to perform some task.
2. Errors, either the number of errors made in doing some task, or the amount of error measured with reference to some standard of accuracy.
3. Learning, often the time, or the number of trials, needed to learn a task to some criterion.
4. Some sort of psychophysical threshold, for example, an absolute threshold (visual acuity, smallest detectable target) or a difference threshold (smallest detectable difference in contrast, in brightness, or in size).
5. Some physiological measure, such as respiratory-minute volume, heart rate, oral temperature, or sweat rate.

On what basis does an experimenter select a dependent variable to use in his experiment? Even at the risk of alienating some good friends, let us be honest: Dependent variables in laboratory experimentation are most frequently selected for their convenience to the experimenter, rather than for their relevance to some practical problem. I mean by this that the choice of a dependent variable in laboratory experimentation is often made on the basis of what is most likely to yield a significant result, and so a publishable paper. Indeed, I have seen experimenters try one dependent variable after another until they finally hit on one that would give them the result they wanted. Entirely aside from the interesting logical question of what constitutes a statistically significant result under these circumstances, there is the more important consideration that dependent variables selected in this way may have very little to do with what we need to know to solve problems.

Now look at this matter the other way round and ask what kinds of criteria real-world problems demand. What criteria does the systems engineer use, and in what terms does he need to have data presented to him? In the United States the Bureau of Public Roads of the Department of Commerce has for the past several years been supporting an extremely large investigation on mass transportation systems of the future. Supersonic aircraft, automated highways, high-speed individual passenger capsules: you name it, they are interested in studying it. Without any elaboration on my part, I think you can easily imagine that such studies contain human factors problems of almost every conceivable kind. What are the ultimate criteria (the dependent variables) used in assessing the effectiveness of these

transportation systems? They are four in number:
1. Safety
2. Convenience
3. Comfort
4. Cost

But how do you get to safety, convenience, comfort and cost from time, errors, a psychophysical threshold, or a physiological measure? There is the rub.

Let me take an example of the difficulties of translating between ordinary laboratory data and practical criteria. By now everyone is familiar with the condition of anoxia—oxygen lack at high altitudes. Commercial and military aircraft that fly above about 12,000 feet have to be pressurized, or carry supplemental oxygen, if the passengers and crew are to be comfortable, or indeed, survive. Most everyone knows some of the symptoms of anoxia. When unacclimatized but otherwise healthy males are transported to altitudes between 15,000 and 18,000 feet without oxygen, one can demonstrate a variety of effects. Vision and hearing are dimmed, there is an increase in muscular tremor, reaction time is increased, depth perception is impaired, normal powers of reasoning and judgment are affected, and so on (see, for example, McFarland, 1953 and Morgan *et al.*, 1963). What is not so commonly known, however, is that these effects occur at different altitudes. For example, darkening of vision due to anoxia has been demonstrated at altitudes as low as 6000 feet, but impairment of hearing due to anoxia is not ordinarily detectable below about 16,000 feet. Moreover, the onset of effects due to anoxia is gradual. They are certainly worse at 14,000 than at 12,000 feet, but the fact of the matter is that we cannot specify exactly when effects *first* become demonstrable.

Pressurizing an aircraft, or providing supplemental oxygen in a space vehicle, is done at a price, and the price is cost and weight. More pressurization, or more oxygen, means more equipment, more weight, and so less payload. Many interminable arguments between systems engineers and laboratory scientists have occurred, and have remained essentially unsolved, because the two groups simply could not converse in the same terms. The systems engineer can provide the scientist with exact figures about the weight and cost penalty of providing pressurization to keep the interior of an aircraft at altitudes equivalent to 10,000, 12,000 or 14,000 feet. He can tell us how much the payload of the aircraft will be reduced if he has to maintain the pressure at an altitude equivalent to 12,000 feet rather than 14,000 feet. And at about this point, the systems engineer is likely to turn to the scientist with the question, "How much difference will it make to safety if operators are kept at 14,000 instead of 12,000 feet?"

The scientist, unfortunately, is at a loss. He can tell the systems engineer that this 2000-foot difference in altitude will produce about a 5 per cent change in the oxygen saturation of arterial blood, that the operator will need about 24 per cent more light to see, that the operator will be able to recall about 8 per cent fewer words spoken to him in random order, and that the operator's handwriting will become a little unsteadier. But in all the laboratory data that have been collected on anoxia there is nothing the scientist can give the systems engineer to help him compute the costs—the human costs—of providing pressurization for 14,000 feet rather than 12,000 feet. Nor can the laboratory experimenter translate unsteadiness in handwriting, immediate memory for nonsense syllables, or any of his other dependent variables into safety. The equations simply do not exist.

This is a general situation that applies to most laboratory studies: We usually do not know how to translate the dependent variables used in laboratory studies to the meaningful dependent variables of real life.

ON METHODS

Earlier I said that when a laboratory scientist has identified the independent and dependent variables he wants to test, he can define them operationally in many different ways. In this context, operational definitions mean *methods*, methods of presenting independent variables to a subject, and methods of measuring dependent variables. Operational definitions are good. Surely no one will dispute this point. But we sometimes run into trouble because the operational definitions we use in our laboratory experiments are not meaningfully related to what happens in practical situations. Let us look at two examples.

Random Stimuli

How do laboratory experimenters present stimuli to a subject? If he is studying memory he most likely will use random lists of nonsense syllables or words. If he is studying the readability of dials, he will almost certainly use random settings on the dial. If he is studying tracking, he typically uses random inputs to the system. There are, of course, good arguments for using random stimuli. These are so well known that I certainly do not need to repeat them here.

But how often do you find random inputs in real-life? Rarely. When I read my wrist-watch, or the speedometer on my automobile, I am not reading random settings on a dial. In the first place, there is a lot of situational constraint that tells me approximately what the setting is. At the very moment I was typing this material, I knew that my wrist-watch must read very close to noon. My stomach told me so. In addition to such situational constraints, there are sequential constraints in real-life as well. Another reason that I knew my wrist-watch must say about noon is that I had looked at it a short time ago and at that time it had read 11.36 a.m. Similarly, in driving an automobile, we do not track random inputs. Highways do not have random curves put into them. What you do now follows closely on what you have just done. And what you do now is correlated with what you will be doing a minute from now.

When we try to generalize from a laboratory experiment to a practical situation we never know how to assign the proper correction factors to our laboratory data to make them appropriate for the rich and meaningful situations we face in life.

Overloading the Operator

Another variation of method commonly used in laboratory experiments is to overload the operator. The basic idea (see, for example, Chapanis, 1959, p. 215, or Poulton, 1965) is simple enough. In some kinds of tasks error frequencies are so low, or differences in time are so small, that it is difficult to get statistically significant results. What the experimenter sometimes does is to make the job deliberately more difficult than it really is. He may do this by speeding up the presentation of stimuli, presenting them under near-threshold or adverse conditions, or by adding distracting, irrelevant, or annoying tasks to the primary one. Sometimes the experimenter may even measure performance on the subsidiary task rather than on the primary one (see, for example, Brown and Poulton, 1961 and Poulton, *op. cit.*).

What are we doing when we do this? Techniques such as those described above usually create an interaction, an interaction between the primary task and the subsidiary one. Moreover, the experimenter typically uses one part of the interaction (the combined effect of the primary and subsidiary tasks) to argue about a main effect, that is, the effect of the primary variable by itself. In any case, the experimenter under such circumstances is deliberately inflating the numerator of the t-ratio discussed earlier. Put in other words, he is taking an effect that is so small he cannot measure it in a laboratory and is inflating that effect artificially. If an effect is so small that one cannot measure it in the carefully controlled confines of a laboratory, imagine what a small contribution it must make to the total variability we find in real-life situations.

But enough of this. Perhaps my point is clear. The methods (that is, the operational definitions) used to interpret variables in laboratory experiments are often artificial—artificial in the sense that they deliberately distort conditions from what happens in real-life. You will agree that this is another important obstacle to generalizing from laboratory experiments to the solution of practical problems.

CONCLUSION

How can I summarize all that I have tried to say here? Speaking for myself, I have found this a sobering and humbling exercise. It appears that if you want to use the results of laboratory experiments to help solve practical problems, you should do so with extreme caution. Although the results of laboratory experiments sometimes provide you with ideas and hunches that may be worth trying out in practical situations, you would be rash to generalize naively from laboratory findings to the solution of real-world problems.

But perhaps the most important conclusion of all is this one: If we are to have a viable science and a respectable technology we must develop and use techniques that are powerful alternatives to the typical laboratory experiment. What are some of these alternatives? I leave them nameless in the hope that you will invite me back to tell you about them another year.

REFERENCES

Berkun, M. M., Bialek, H. M., Kern, R. P., & Yagi, K. Experimental studies of psychological stress in man. *Psychological Monographs: General and Applied*, 1962, **76** (Whole No. 534).

Broadbent, D. E. Differences in interactions between stresses. *Quarterly Journal of Experimental Psychology*, 1963, **15**, 205–211.

Brown, I. D., & Poulton, E. C. Measuring the spare "mental capacity" of car drivers by a subsidiary task. *Ergonomics*, 1961, **4**, 35–40.

Chapanis, A. Theory and methods for analyzing errors in man-machine systems. *Annals of the New York Academy of Sciences*, 1951, **51**, 1179–1203.

Chapanis, A. *Research techniques in human engineering*. Baltimore: Johns Hopkins Press, 1959.

Chapanis, A. Men, machines and models. *American Psychologist*, 1961, **16**, 113–131.

Chapanis, A., Garner, W. R., & Morgan, C. T. *Applied experimental psychology: human factors in engineering design*. New York: Wiley, 1949.

Chapanis, A., & Lockhead, G. R. A test of the effectiveness of sensor lines showing linkages between displays and controls. *Human Factors*, 1965, **7**, 219–229.

Elliott, E. Perception and alertness. *Ergonomics*, 1960, **3**, 357–364.

Jerison, H. J., & Pickett, R. M. Vigilance: a review and re-evaluation. *Human Factors*, 1963, **5**, 211–238.

Kibler, A. W. The relevance of vigilance research to aerospace monitoring tasks. *Human Factors*, 1965, **7**, 93–99.

Kintz, B. L., Delprato, D. J., Mettee, D. R., Persons, C. E., & Schappe, R. H. The experimenter effect. *Psychological Bulletin*, 1965, **63**, 223–232.

Kranzberg, M. The unity of science-technology. *American Scientist*, 1967, **55**, 48–66.

Mackie, R. R., & Christensen, P. R. *Translation and application of psychological research*. Santa Barbara Research Park, Goleta, Calif.: Human Factors Res., Inc., Tech. Rep. 716-1, 1967.

McFarland, R. A. *Human factors in air transportation*. New York: McGraw-Hill, 1953.

Morgan, C. T., Cook, J. S., III, Chapanis, A., & Lund, M. W. *Human engineering guide to equipment design*. New York: McGraw-Hill, 1963.

Poulton, E. C. On increasing the sensitivity of measures of performance. *Ergonomics*, 1965, **8**, 69–76.

Rosenthal, R. On the social psychology of the psychological experiment: the experimenter's hypothesis as unintended determinant of experimental results. *American Scientist*, 1963, **51**, 268–283.

Rosenthal, R. Experimenter outcome-orientation and the results of the psychological experiment. *Psychological Bulletin*, 1964, **61**, 405–412.

Simons, J. C. An introduction to surface-free behaviour. *Ergonomics*, 1964, **7**, 23–36.

Whitfield, D. Validating the application of ergonomics to equipment design: a case study. *Ergonomics*, 1964, **7**, 165–174.

32. Will Psychologists Study Human Problems?[1]

Nevitt Sanford

In this article, Dr. Sanford argues strongly for a "human problems" approach in psychology to study problems about which people are really concerned. In presenting his case, he takes to task the "fragmented, over-specialized, method centered, and dull" psychology which he believes is predominant today. It is asserted that contemporary researchers have no sensitivity to human experience, have "never had occasion to look closely at any one person," have no idea what it is like to be a research subject, and have no idea "what goes on in human beings." As a remedy for these problems, Dr. Sanford calls for a new kind of theory for the conduct and interpretation of research—a dynamic, holistic, comprehensive, and less concrete theory. These characteristics also imply a different basis for choosing research problems.

This paper started out to be a letter to Joseph M. Bobbitt in his capacity as Associate Director of the new National Institute of Child Health and Human Development. For some time it had seemed to me that certain unfortunate trends in psychology and social science were being aided and abetted by our great fund-granting agencies. Or was it that unfortunate trends in these agencies were being furthered by the "establishment" in psychology? Probably a chicken-and-egg situation. At any rate, it seemed that the inauguration of the new Institute was a good occasion for some analysis and criticism of the disciplines most directly concerned with research in psychological health and development. I warmed up to this subject, and went far enough in criticism so that it seemed I ought to undertake the more difficult task of offering some constructive suggestions.

And so my letter to Bobbitt has grown into an article, the main burden of which is that the new Institute—and other institutes and agencies—ought to encourage

[1] Reprinted from the *American Psychologist*, 1965, **20**, 192–202. Copyright 1965 by the American Psychological Association, and reproduced by permission of the author and the publisher.

psychologists to study problems that people really worry about rather than only problems formulated on the basis of reading the professional journals.

If fund-granting agencies such as the new Institute were to insist that psychologists confront these human problems directly, they would be forced to examine longer sections of behavior, and larger areas of the person, than they usually attend to nowadays; they would have to deal with some really complex processes and, thus, they would be stimulated to devise methods for solving problems—rather than confining themselves, as they do today, to problems to which existing methods are suited.

This would be good for psychology, and I for one am as much concerned about advancing this science as I am about finding a solution to any immediate problem.

Psychology is really in the doldrums right now. It is fragmented, overspecialized, method centered, and dull. I can rarely find in the journals anything that I am tempted to read. And when I do read psychological papers, as I must as an editorial consultant, I become very unhappy; I am annoyed by the fact that they all have been forced into the same mold, in research design and style of reporting, and I am appalled by the degree to which an inflation of jargon and professional baggage has been substituted for psychological insight and sensitivity.

I used to think, when I first noted the trend—10 years ago—that the authors' psychological knowledgeability had simply been edited out in the interests of saving space. I am now convinced that the trouble lies much deeper. The psychologists who are filling up the journals today just do not have sensitivity to human experience, and the fault lies in their training—which is an expression of what academic psychology has become.

We have produced a whole generation of research psychologists who never had occasion to look closely at any one person, let alone themselves, who have never imagined what it might be like to be a subject in one of their experiments, who, indeed, have long since lost sight of the fact that their experimental subjects are, after all, people. (Let us leave the rats out of it for the moment.) They can define variables, state hypotheses, design experiments, manipulate data statistically, get publishable results—and miss the whole point of the thing. Reading their papers you get a strange sense of the unreality of it all; the authors' conceptions of variables and processes seem a bit off; and then you realize that the authors have never looked at human experience, they went straight from the textbook or journal to the laboratory, and thence into print—and thence into the business of getting research grants.

The plain fact is that our young psychological researchers do not know what goes on in human beings, and their work shows it. Not only is it dull, which psychology should never be, but it is often wrong, for that context of processes-in-the-person which they have been trained to ignore is usually doing more to determine what happens in the situation under study than the variables that have been "isolated experimentally."

What has happened is that the revolution in psychology that occurred during World War II, and in the 5 years thereafter, has been over for some time and we are in the midst of the reaction. Or perhaps one might better say that normal operating procedures have been restored, that it is only in times of crisis that the academic disciplines are brought into contact with real life and shaken out of their professional preoccupations.

The revolution reached its high-water mark in 1949 when Erik Erikson was appointed professor at Berkeley. Two years later this would not have been possible; nor has such a thing since been possible in any psychology department in the country. (The appointments at Harvard are special and do not really count. Harvard is special, too, in that it is the only place that can afford to make mistakes.)

The critique is not of the experimental approach in psychology or of general psychology as a discipline; it is of a state of affairs in which the advocates of a particular kind of psychology—psychology-without-a-person—have been able to gain and maintain power through putting across the idea that they are the representatives in psychology of *true science*.

It is quite possible that nothing can be done about the state of affairs I describe. Maybe we are just playthings of social forces that no one can control. The issues underlying the situation are ones that have divided psychologists for a long time. I believe, however, that there is a constructive alternative to the prevailing orientation, one that might be called a "human-problems" approach. It is an approach that has a highly respectable past, but today it is staunchly opposed and falls outside the main current of contemporary work in psychology. It has many silent supporters, but few spokesmen.

THE KIND OF APPROACH NEEDED

Psychology and social science have, of course, always been oriented to action, in the sense that they have proceeded on the assumption that their theories and empirical knowledge would eventually be applied. Psychology, when it has thought seriously about itself, has included among it aims "to promote human welfare." Sociology, traditionally, has been concerned with the solution of social problems and with "building a better society." The National Institute of Mental Health, which has supported so much research in biology, psychology, and the newer social sciences, has been guided by the principle that such research should be "mental health relevant," but in practice any fundamental work in these fields has been considered to have this characteristic.

Yet there is no denying that at the present time there exists a wide gap between research and practice. Psychology participates fully in the trend toward specialization and disciplinary professionalism that dominates in the universities today. The discipline is still much concerned to establish itself as a science, but the psychologists' naive conception of science has led them to adopt the more superficial characteristics of the physical sciences. This has made it difficult for them to study genuine human problems, since quantification, precision of measurement, elegance of experimental design, and general laws are so much more difficult to achieve once one goes beyond simple part processes.

There is, of course, a rationale for all this. It is not without some reason that the National Institute of Mental Health regards the so-called "pure science" of these disciplines as relevant to mental health. Science has always made progress through specialization. It can be argued, and it is argued, that findings concerning simple and isolated processes will eventually add up to systematic knowledge that can then be applied to human problems.

There are two things to be said about this. One is that the "adding up" function is rather neglected today, and the other is that many of these findings just do not add up. Concerning the first, the accent today is on the production of knowledge rather than on its organization. There are few attempts at systematization of the sort that would put particular facts in perspective and show their significance. More than that, there seem to be few attempts to organize knowledge in such a way that its relevance to practice or to policy becomes apparent. A college president might examine a large number of issues of educational or psychological journals without coming across anything that struck him as relevant to his purposes or helpful in the solution of his problems. It is not that all this material is irrelevant, but rather that the task of organizing and interpreting it so that it might be useful is so largely neglected. Scientists write for each other; and when they are looking for a problem to investigate, they turn to their professional journals rather than ask such questions as what might be troubling the college presidents.

When I say that the study of simple, isolated processes does not add up to an understanding of more complex ones, I am assuming that human and social processes are organized on different levels, and that processes on higher (more complex) levels have a character of their own, are just as "real" as processes on lower levels, and must be studied directly. It is just as "scientific" to study, say, self-esteem in its relations to other factors of equal complexity as it is to study the manifold conditioned responses into which self-esteem might be analyzed; it is just as scientific to study conditioned responses as it is to study by physiological methods the nerve processes that underlie them. The student of conditioning who was somewhat contemptuous of the vague globalism of the students of such personality needs as self-esteem could be regarded in the same way by students of the action of the nervous system. I assume, further, that there is *interaction* between processes on different levels. Just as complex phenomena are to be explained in part in terms of the activities of constituent processes, so simple processes have to be understood as partly determined by the larger structures in which they have place. Truth may be discovered by abstracting parts from the whole and studying them intensively, but the whole truth can never be discovered in this way. It is the whole truth, and particularly the truth about wholes, that is needed for practice. Thus it is that one has to be concerned about a trend in science that seems to put all the accent on the study of abstracted part functions. The main reason for this trend is that it is difficult to study complex processes by existing approved methods. In psychology it seems that theory making itself is often guided by consideration of what can be attacked by such methods rather than by an intellectual involvement with the problems of life. The kind of theory that is needed for the understanding of human problems is different from that which guides most laboratory research or is generated from it. Thus, instead of specialized personality theory and specialized social theory, a human-problems approach calls for a more general personality-social theory, a theory that is not formal or mechanistic but dynamic, not elementaristic but holistic, not narrow and specialized but comprehensive, not concrete and tangible but on a level of abstraction that is appropriate to the problem at hand. Each of these aspects of a human-problems approach may be taken up in turn.

Personality-Social Aspects

It seems clear enough that for an effective approach to human problems we must have an integration of personality theory and social theory. This is not as easy as might first appear. Most sociologists seem to get along quite well without giving much attention to the individual personality, and probably the great majority of clinical practitioners rely on an "individual-psychodynamic" approach that gives little attention to social and cultural factors. There is even a certain amount of interdisciplinary rivalry here: In discussions of problems such as prejudice or delinquency there is a tendency to oppose personality factors and social factors and argue about which is more important. But progress toward integration is being made. Certainly personality theory is far more "social" today than it was 25 years ago, and there is evidence, I think, that when sociologists note signs that their psychological colleagues are seeing the light they are willing to go halfway toward rapprochement. What is needed is more knowledge of the articulation of personality systems and social systems. This requires more, rather than less, attention to the relatively autonomous personality structures, and more searching analysis of social structures in terms that are psychologically relevant. The student of personality must, of course, focus on the internal structuring of personality, but he must grant that the hypothetical personality subsystems are not fully understood unless their situational relationships are specified.

Consider authoritarianism and how it might be changed. I assume that there are social organizations that can bring out the authoritarianism in almost anybody; but I would also assume that when it came to changing a particular organization the difficulty—and the strategy—would depend on how much authoritarianism in personality was found in people who occupied the key positions. To put this idea in more general terms: In order to induce change in personality it may sometimes be necessary first to change the role structure in the organization in which the individual lives or works. By the same token, since we deal with a dynamic interaction between personality and social system, it may sometimes be necessary to change certain personalities in order to change the social system. Individuals use their social roles for the expression of their personality needs; hence a change in organizational role structure will be resisted by individuals in the same way that they resist change in internal adaptive devices that have been found to be more or less satisfying. Thus a practicing social scientist needs to be familiar with personality dynamics.

Dynamic Aspects

A personality, or an organized social group, seems best conceived as a system of interacting forces, a going concern in which energy is distributed among constituent parts and between the system (or its subsystems) and its environment. Dynamic organization refers to the way in which these forces or units of energy interact. Personalities and social systems also exhibit formal organization. They may be examined with attention to such overall features as number of different parts or the connectedness of parts, or with attention to such formal relationships among parts as similarity, proximity, or inclusion. In general, the analysis of systems into states, conditions, or arrangements prepares the way for explanation in terms of dynamic theory.

Dynamic theory is essential when it comes to consideration of how a system might be changed. The question here, typically, is how to bring force to bear upon a particular subsystem that one wishes to modify. One might think first of bringing to bear upon the subsystem in question a potent set of environmental stimuli, and this might indeed be effective sometimes. It usually turns out, however, that the particular subsystem is really being determined by other subsystems and by processes of the whole system. The problem, then, is to find out what within the larger system is determining of what, and then to get a purchase on the master processes. To take an example from the field of personality: An individual's prejudice toward minority groups may be due to a nagging but unrecognized sense of weakness in himself; in such a case it would do no good to give him correct information about minority groups; there would be no change in his prejudice until a way had been found to modify his sense of weakness. In an organization it might be generally recognized that a change in one of its processes would increase production without loss in other essential values, but this would not mean that the change would now take place as a matter of course—whoever wished to promote it would still have to reckon with the implicit values of various segments of the power structure.

All this is not to deny the importance of information or of the mechanisms by which it is acquired. It is to say that in dynamic theory information is instrumental to purpose. Just as in an organization the gathering, storing, and communication of information is put in the service of the organization's explicit and implicit functions, so in the individual perception and learning are organized in the interest of strivings. We should not expect learned factual content to be retained for long without becoming integrated with the individual's purposes. But how such integration occurs is a complex question; it could hardly be answered unless individuals were carefully observed over relatively long periods of time—hence, it receives little attention from psychologists.

Programmed learning of academic material affords a nice example of some of the difficulties created when more or less general laws, derived from the study of abstracted part processes, are applied in life situations, without anyone remembering to put the part process back into the living context where it belongs. If the psychologist fragments the person conceptually in the interests of research, many educators, by taking over bodily and applying directly the laboratory findings, seem about to fragment their students for keeps. The advent of the teaching machine, which could be a great boon to education, seems so far to have played into the hands of those educators who believe that the learning of factual content *is* education, that this learning is neatly separated from everything else that might be going on in the student, and that these other things do not matter much anyway. The real educational problem is not "how may students most efficiently learn material well enough so that they can pass examinations at a high level"; the real problem is "how to make academic material meaningful to them, so that it will play some part in the building up in them of the qualities of an educated person." How does the learning of factual material contribute to the development of such qualities as the ability to think well, self-understanding, sensitivity to ethical issues, intellectual integrity? This is the key question for educational psychology.

Holism

The essential idea was introduced above in our discussion of the neglect of complex processes; particular phenomena such as "a perception" or a "conditioned response" are almost always in part determined by—their very nature depends upon—the larger organismic patterns and purposes within which they have a place.

The implications of this are great, and I would like to carry my argument further.

The first point to be made is that few psychologists care to deny, on principle, the holistic premise. It seems to be almost universally understood and agreed that how a stimulus is perceived depends on the context in which it exists at the moment, that whether or not an idea will be assimilated by a cognitive system depends on the degree of that idea's consistency with ideas that are already present there, that the meaning of a particular act depends on its place in a larger pattern of striving. It can be said with perfect safety that all personality theories are holistic in the sense that they are concerned with the relations of particular processes to larger personality functions.

What, then, is the argument about? It is not so much about high theory as it is about what is the best strategy for research. The basic complaint against holistic theory is that it does not lend itself to testing by empirical methods. The very term "whole" suggests something that cannot be analyzed, and American psychologists have been taught to be wary of anything "global." This argument would have force—complete force—if it were true that the study of part-whole relationships were impossible. But to confirm that this is not true one has only to point to the work of Klein (1951) on the relations of perception to the ego control system, of Rogers and his associates (Rogers & Dymond, 1954) on the relations of various attitudes and beliefs to the individual's self-concept, or to the results of Witkin, Lewis, Hertzman, Machover, Meissner, and Wapner (1954) on sex difference in perception. The whole research undertaking that issued in *The Authoritarian*

Personality (Adorno, Frenkel-Brunswik, Levinson, & Sanford, 1950) was carried forward in accordance with a holistic orientation and, indeed, would have been impossible without holistic theory. The F scale for measuring authoritarianism in personality was developed by a process of going back and forth from observed behavior to hypothetical inner structure. The coherence of overt behavior patterns led to the concept of an inner structure of personality, i.e., authoritarianism, and then this concept was used to predict other patterns of behavior.

It cannot, of course, be claimed that research carried out in accordance with the holistic orientation will soon achieve the standards of precision and elegance that are often attained in laboratory experiments involving a few simple variables. Such research can be improved in these respects, but it may never match the best laboratory experiments; it will have to aim at levels of rigor that are appropriate to the task at hand. It cannot be claimed, either, that this kind of research will be other than difficult and expensive. But the criticism of the current strategy of abstracting part functions for experimental study is more serious: It is that because of its very nature it is bound to fall short of the truth. It is not only that it avoids the big problems; it fails to achieve its own chosen goal, which is to establish general laws of behavior. But the main characteristic of such "laws" is their lack of generality. They break down as soon as a new variable is introduced into the picture. And since in real life new variables, or variables not taken into account in the laboratory experiment, are always in the picture, such laws are most limited in their applicability.

One can sometimes carry over into a life situation all the conditions that obtain in the laboratory and show that the general laws still hold. This has been done, for example, in the case of the teaching machine, which enables a student to learn material in just the way that laboratory subjects do. But this involves the dangers suggested above. Unless the educators, and their consultants, are very much aware of the limited role of content learning in education, of its embeddedness in a large context of other processes, the tendency is to transform life into a laboratory experiment. B. F. Skinner, the leading pioneer in the development of teaching machines, is himself fully aware of this danger—unlike many educators and many of his disciples. And yet he is deeply concerned with practice and cannot resist becoming involved with it. He says that his strategy of research is the slow but sure building up of a science from simple beginnings, and that so far he and his colleagues have attacked only the simple problems; but this does not prevent him from remaking school rooms and designing new cultures.

The above is the main argument for holism as the best road to knowledge; there is as strong an argument from the point of view of practice. If parts really are determined by the wholes to which they belong, and one wishes to modify a part, then clearly his best course is to bring influence to bear upon the whole. Thus it is that in the psychotherapy of Carl Rogers (1959) the whole thrust is toward modifying the self-concept, because an inappropriate self-concept is believed to be determining of numerous specific unfortunate attitudes and patterns of overt behavior. The same would be true of a social institution such as a school or college.

Practices with respect to grading, course requirements, the organization of teaching, and so on, are usually integral to the whole system and are not to be changed until after there has been some modification in the general character of the institution. This is far from being a hopeless prospect. Just as one may influence an individual's self-concept as readily as one of its constituent attitudes, so one might initiate a process of change in an institution's general climate with no more difficulty than would be involved in changing one of its most specific part functions. Success would depend upon knowledge of the individual's or the institution's dynamics. By the same token, a holistic approach to individual or social change involves for the change agent a considerable responsibility: He should not seek change in whole structures unless he was prepared for change in numerous particulars.

I have put the case for holism as strongly as I can; yet I do not see how we can do without the intensive study of abstracted part functions. The student of personality, after all, engages in this activity when he undertakes to explain the functioning of social groups. Here he might well be inclined to favor analysis in terms of the personality types of the group's members, but if he is a holist he would not be surprised or put off if a social theorist reminded him that there are things about personality that do not become apparent until the individual is seen in the context of the social group.

At a time when the holistic orientation seems rather neglected in psychology and social science, it seems proper to accent it as is done here. If we must abstract parts from wholes let us be fully aware of the fact that we *are abstracting*, and let us devote as much energy to finding out how special bits of knowledge fit into the larger picture as we do to analyzing wholes in the conventional scientific way.

Comprehensiveness

The holistic orientation requires that we consider in what respects living systems function as units. It says nothing about the size or complexity of the unit. Such a unit might be the context of a perception, a pattern of striving that organizes particular acts, or the self that is expressed in numerous personality characteristics. The argument here is for bigger units; we must examine large areas of the person and of society, and long sections of behavior; and we must have theoretical models that permit us to do this.

The whole that helps to determine a particular personality characteristic may be the whole personality, and not merely the whole self or ego; hence, we need a theoretical model of the personality that permits us to deal with the relations of self to ego, and of these relatively large structures to others of like kind. Similarly for social structures. One may study, holistically, a department of an industrial organization or a classroom in a school, but for full understanding he would have to see the department or classroom in relation to the whole institution, and the institution in relation to the whole society.

Another argument for comprehensiveness is that the determination of human events is almost always complex. Multiple factors are involved, and it is the task of the scientist to find them. This always takes some imagination, but the right kind of theory can be a big help. Consider, for example, the phenomenon of compulsive drinking. A formula for this could be written out in terms of rewards and punishments, and in such a formulation the reproaches of the drinker's spouse might in some cases be put down on the side of punishment. But what about the case of a man who drinks in order to express hostility toward his wife and who welcomes her reproaches as signs that he is achieving his purpose? One could still describe what happens in stimulus-response terms, *after* discovering what the effective internal stimuli are. But in finding the stimuli the usual sort of learning theory and the knowledge that proceeds from laboratory tests of it would be of no help; the quest would have to be guided by theory and knowledge concerning the complex interplay of forces within the personality.

If we are to think comprehensively, it must be with the use of gross units of analysis. The psychotherapist, for example, faced with the task of making sense of vast quantities of verbal material has no alternative to using coarse categories for bringing it all together. And it is thus that when we wish to speak of elements which together make up the whole personality—elements defined with attention to the theoretical structure of the whole—we can do no better today than to use the Freudian concepts of id, superego, and ego.

Suppose—to glance at a relatively broad aspect of the social scene—one wished to compare the culture of San Francisco with that of Los Angeles, a matter that might be of great importance for some aspects of California governmental policy. It would hardly do to employ the highly elaborated schemes and finely calibrated instruments that are used in research on small groups. The investigator who had something less than a lifetime to spend on this undertaking would decide upon a few gross categories that seemed to him important, and then content himself with rough estimates of them.

Most scientists, probably, would dislike the loss of rigor involved in this and would prefer to let George do it. And George, of course, has been very active. Decisions in big and important social matters are still based mainly on the observations and judgments of practical men. No doubt this will always be so to some extent since in practical matters there is a place for wisdom and judgments of value as well as for scientific knowledge. Still, scientists often feel free to criticize the day-to-day decisions that affect us all, and to complain that they are not consulted. This is an admission of their obligation to study complex problems and to show how their findings are relevant to practice. They may do this without being any the less scientific, in the best sense of the word, than the laboratory man. All they have to lose are the chains of respectability. Their procedure should be to suit their instruments to the task at hand, and to make sure that the gross categories used are consistent with what is known at lower levels and lend themselves to reduction and systematic treatment.

LEVEL OF ABSTRACTION

When men are confronted with practical problems, their natural tendency is to focus on the concrete and particular. The psychotherapist, faced with the task of taking action on short notice, has to deal with what is happening to a particular patient in the situation of the moment; he cannot stop to translate his thoughts into the terms of a general theoretical system. The test specialist who wishes to develop an instrument for predicting some practically important pattern of overt behavior does not need abstract concepts to stand for general dispositions of personality; he can go far with a set of concrete test items that correlate with the behavior in which he is interested. And the business man or the administrator of an organization is likely to see his problems as particular, local, and pressing; he seeks solutions through manipulating plainly observable features of the immediate situation.

This kind of orientation to practical problems is a far cry from the most characteristic work of the scientist. The scientist interested in psychopathology must use terms for describing a patient that are sufficiently abstract so that one patient may be compared with others, and with nonpatients. The myriad specific acts of patients must be ordered to a conceptual scheme, so that future observations may be systematic, and general relationships among patients' processes may be established. As for organizations, one might say that we have hardly begun the scientific study of them until we have derived a set of abstract concepts—such as role, communication, power—that apply to organizations generally, so that we can carry over what we learn from one organization to the study of others.

If one uses abstract concepts he must, of course, be able to go back to the concrete, showing that a given concept applies in a particular case; or, to take it the other way around, it must be possible to show that a given concrete phenomenon may reasonably be ordered to the abstract concept. Where everything under consideration is open to direct observation this task is not difficult. "Response," for example, is a highly abstract psychological concept; yet, since it refers to something observable it is not difficult, usually, to get agreement that a given phenomenon is indeed a response. "Unconscious wish," on the other hand, is an abstract concept that stands for processes behind behavior: By definition it is something inside the person that expresses itself in various ways; hence, it is very difficult to show that a given observable phenomenon is a special case of an unconscious wish. We deal here with a hypothetical construct, something conceived or "dreamed up" by the psychologist not to categorize his observations but to make sense of them.

Strictly speaking, no elements or features of personality are observable with perfect directness; all are *inferred* from behavioral indices. But there is a wide variation in the degree of directness or explicitness with which the inferences may be made. The kind of theory that is needed for the study of human problems must necessarily make free use of concepts whose ties to what is observable are highly indirect.

This kind of theory does not go unchallenged by those scientists who consider that the essence of the scientific approach is accuracy of observation and precision of measurement. These "hardheaded" scientists have something in common with the hardheaded men of affairs: Both prefer to deal with the concrete and tangible, with "the facts," with what they can get their hands on; hypothetical constructs smack of mysticism or "untried theory." This orientation gets the practical man into trouble because it leads to too narrow a definition of his problem and cuts off inquiry into the more complex, less observable, patterns of events which may have largely determined his difficulty of the moment. The situation is similar for the scientist who places observability at the top of his hierarchy of values. The highest levels of observability and precision of measurement are attained in the laboratory experiment; but the psychologist who restricts himself to this mode of investigation denies himself the opportunity to study the whole personality. There are aspects of personality that cannot be experimented upon in the usual laboratory situation: For example, there are aspects of the person that become apparent only when he is observed in numerous varied situations, and there are aspects whose meaning cannot be detected unless they are seen in broad context. Also, at the present time it is impossible or unfeasible to arouse in a laboratory situation motives and feelings that equal in quality and intensity some that are common in everyday life. In these circumstances it is natural for the convinced experimentalist not only to limit himself to problems for which his method is suited, but actually to conceive of personality as made up of elements, e.g., measurable performances, that he can get hold of, as it were. He often defeats his own purposes, as we have seen, for those performances owe something of their nature to factors that have been excluded from consideration.

The issue of observable versus hypothetical constructs is an old one in psychology. The early psychology of personality, which stemmed mainly from the clinic, made free use of hypothetical constructs, and this practice was severely criticized by academic psychologists who were eager to establish their discipline as a science. For the latter, objectivity was the watchword, and when Bridgman's "operationism" appeared on the scene in 1927 they embraced it wholeheartedly. It became something of a fashion in psychology to reject, as outside of science, concepts that could not be "defined operationally," that is, in terms of the steps taken to obtain an objective index of a given concept. During the years since the late 1920s, the struggle between the operationists and the traditional personality theorists has continued. The personality theorists have been largely vindicated, but they have been forced to give some ground. Today it is pretty generally recognized that there are practically no theoretical statements that can be completely and directly verified by observation, and that hypothetical constructs are not only necessary to intellectual activity but have led to the best success in predicting and explaining behavior. Modern operationism does not require that every concept be defined in terms of operations; it does require that every concept be connectable, however indirectly, with some kind of observable phenomenon. Personality theorists, while perfectly free to use hypothetical concepts, have had to proceed with more attention to conceptual clarity, to objective indicators of their concepts, and—most important—to the question of just how their theoretical formulations might be proved or disproved by observation.

I am arguing that abstract theory is not only necessary to the development of a science of personality and social systems but also most useful in practice. Personality-social theory that is dynamic, holistic, and comprehensive, as practice demands, must be on a high level of abstraction. It is mainly through its use of hypothetical constructs that science gets beyond common sense, and it is in getting beyond common sense that its greatest usefulness lies. To revert to the example of prejudice: Most of what psychologists and social scientists have said about the situational, social, and economic determinants of prejudice conform well with what everybody knew already; to show that prejudice in some of its aspects springs from a hypothetical deep-lying structure of personality is to go beyond the depth of the man in the street. At the same time it is to state a proposition whose implications for practice are very different from those that flow from the conventional wisdom.

My argument rests most heavily upon a conception of the nature of practical problems and of the role of science in efforts to solve them. We must inquire further into these matters. If we look at the history of psychology, it appears that there was a time when this science was far more concerned with practical problems than it is today, and that the results were not always to the good. For example, the early very practical concern with psychological tests led to many misapplications while contributing little to the advancement of psychology as a science. Again, the experiments of Thorndike and Woodworth (1901a, 1901b, 1901c) on "transfer of training" were carried on in an educational setting, with practice very much in mind. Their major conclusion, that learning was specific, that what was learned in one area of content or skill was not transferred to others, was immediately and very generally applied in the schools. This led to the introduction of all kinds of technical subjects into the schools, the proliferation of courses, the fragmentation of the curriculum. If children had not gone on transferring their training anyway, and if teachers had not continued to use their common sense, the results might have been even more serious. Experiences of this kind led the universities, in time, to become exceedingly wary of practice or "service," which were seen as restrictions upon the scientist's freedom to be guided solely by his curiosity and to look for answers anywhere that he pleased. Hence the present accent on pure science, and the relegation of members of the professional schools to second-class citizenship.

I am arguing that the pendulum has now swung too far in the other direction, that psychology and social science have become too far removed from practice. Many early applications were premature, and science has gained from its period of withdrawal into "purity"; now it can afford to become involved with practice again, and in doing so it will fulfill its obligations and derive benefit for itself.

We have to go at it in a different way from before, however. For one thing, we have to consider that a practical concern involves the setting of goals, and this raises the question of who is to do this setting. When individuals or organizations look to science for help, they are usually focused narrowly upon a problem that seems very pressing, and they often have an overrealistic conception of what they desire. Often in such cases the most useful thing a scientist can do is to bring about a reconsideration of the goal. Psychologists, for example, have been asked to devise tests that will predict success in college and, this being something they are good at, they have gone about it with extraordinary singleness of purpose—and this before the question of what is success was satisfactorily answered. Where grades have been regarded as the only practicable criteria of success the testing has gone forward, usually, without anyone's asking what grades have to do with becoming educated or what success in college, measured in this way, has to do with success in life.

For the scientist to include participation in goal setting within his conception of his role is to interfere in no way with his pursuit of knowledge. On the contrary, this is to open the way for scientific inquiry into complex matters. By insisting that practical problems are complex, interwoven with other problems, and tied to long-range human and social goals the scientist puts himself in a position to ask questions of general scientific interest. He may now adopt the simple rule that no problem is worthy of his attention unless it can be regarded as a special case of something more general, unless it can be phrased in such terms and attacked in such a way as to promise some addition to systematic knowledge. It is thus that he may resist pressure to produce results at once and avoid involvement in local, ad hoc, or fragmentary studies, often called "practical," that contribute nothing to science and do little for the individual or group seeking help.

In the domain of public affairs, where the concern is with such problems as what to do about culturally deprived people or about youthful drinking, there is little reason, save insufficient public enlightenment, for conflict between an interest in solving problems and an interest in advancing social science. Support for both of these kinds of activity comes, ultimately, from the same source—that is, the people, expressing themselves through public agencies. Here the ideal is to build the research function into the planned social actions, and to state research problems in terms of how to induce desired effects. This is to adopt for social and human problems the model of clinical medicine, in which inquiry and action are two aspects of the same humanistic enterprise.

CHOICE OF PROBLEMS

A human-problems approach not only calls for a different theoretical orientation, it implies a different basis for choosing problems. I would like to see the new Institute include something of the following in its program:

1. Accent problems defined in terms of their human significance rather than in the terms of particular scientific disciplines. Study of these will require interdisciplinary theory and multidisciplinary research teams. It may work if the starting point is a human problem and not a disciplinary question or issue. And let us get away for the moment from the familiar psychiatric categories. I have in mind such problem areas as transitional stages, developmental crises, commitment (premature or delayed), institutional dependence, pleasure and play, problem drinking, aging.

2. Look at these problems in the perspective of long-range goals for the individual. If we want people to give up or get over some sort of problematic behavior we have to think of suitable alternatives to that behavior. Think about this for a while and we are bound to come to considerations of what is good for people and of what they might well become. Why not? There are good philosophical as well as practical reasons for this.

3. To think about long-range goals and how they might be reached we have to use a developmental perspective. We have to consider present events with attention to their future consequences. Otherwise we can have no part in the planning of institutional arrangements for the development of young people. Nor can we have anything sensible to say about when is the best time to introduce young people to particular ideas or experiences.

4. If we adopt a developmental perspective there is no way to avoid attention to the whole life cycle. We cannot leave this whole area to Erik Erikson—and Charlotte Buhler. We have to have longitudinal studies, or suitable substitutes for them. At the least we must have studies of lives.

5. But study the conditions and processes of developmental change—in general, at any age. Assume that such changes can occur at any age. It is a matter of the right conditions being present. I say development in general—so I am interested in general laws. I mean organismic laws, which state relationships between part processes and the larger personal contexts in which they are imbedded.

6. This means study the general psychology of personality—particularly the general psychology of personality development. We have to conceive of structures in the person and we have to have theory to explain how these structures are modified through experience. Studies of structures—experimental studies or others—may of course be appropriately investigated in isolation, but there should be awareness of the fact that they *are* being studied in isolation and must eventually be related to persons.

7. Look at various kinds of social settings in which developmental changes occur, particularly settings that have been designed to modify people in some desired way: schools, training programs, correctional institutions, hospitals, psycho-therapeutic programs, summer camps, etc. Or, look at development in unnatural environments, forms of rigid institutionalization, for example, which result in regressive changes or fixations. Let all these settings be described and analyzed in sociological terms, but keep the focus of attention upon developmental change in individuals.

8. Give special attention to youth, but be flexible in defining its boundaries, and of course do not neglect its relation to earlier and later periods. Youth is a neglected area as compared with childhood and old age. It is not so much behavior of youth as development in youth that has been neglected. The theoretical bias has been that little or no development occurs during this period.

The study of development in youth is bound to force a confrontation of theoretical issues. It should lead to the production of new theory concerning the interaction of social and personality variables. If we assume that personality goes on developing, after the age of, say, 16, after the young person has been brought very much under the influence of factors outside the home, then we have to formulate such factors and conceive the ways in which they do their work. Classical personality theory has little to say on this subject—but it can be appropriately modified.

I have listed here special interests of my own. If the new Institute were to show that it really intends to support work of this kind, a great many other psychologists would take heart, believing that their interests would be served also. Proposals would come in from people who have not been heard from in Washington for some time; and new kinds of proposals would come in from scientists who saw a chance to do what they knew was important to the solution of human problems rather than what could be supported.

REFERENCES

Adorno, T. W., Frenkel-Brunswik, Else, Levinson, D. J., & Sanford, N. *The authoritarian personality*. New York: Harper, 1950.

Bridgman, P. W. *The logic of modern physics*. New York: Macmillan, 1927.

Klein, G. S. The personal world through perception. In R. R. Blake & G. V. Ramsey (Eds.), *Perception: an approach to personality*. New York: Ronald Press, 1951.

Rogers, C. R. A theory of therapy, personality, and interpersonal relationships, as developed in the client-centered framework. In S. Koch (Ed.), *Psychology: a study of a science*. Vol. 3. New York: McGraw-Hill, 1959. Pp. 184–256.

Rogers, C. R., & Dymond, R. (Eds.) *Psychotherapy and personality change*. Chicago: University of Chicago Press, 1954.

Thorndike, E. L., & Woodworth, R. S. The influence of improvement in one mental function upon the efficiency of other functions. I. *Psychological Review*, 1901a, 8, 247–261.

Thorndike, E. L., & Woodworth, R. S. The influence of improvement in one mental function upon the efficiency of other functions. II. The estimation of magnitudes. *Psychological Review*, 1901b, 8, 384–395.

Thorndike, E. L., & Woodworth, R. S. The influence of improvement in one mental function upon the efficiency of other functions. III. Functions involving attention, observation and discrimination. *Psychological Review*, 1901c, 8, 553–564.

Witkin, H. A., Lewis, H. B., Hertzman, M., Machover, K., Meissner, Pearl B., & Wapner, S. *Personality through perception: an experimental and clinical study*. New York: Harper, 1954.

33. Prospect for Psychology[1]

Henry A. Murray

In this concluding paper, Dr. Murray presents us with a chilling prospect for psychology. The "long-dreaded Great Enormity" has occurred and the author takes us to the day of judgment for those accused of responsibility (or irresponsibility) for the final catastrophe. In the particular trial we are to witness, the academic psychologists are being judged. Did they use their insights and techniques to try to avert this tragedy? Were their volumes of research results relevant and meaningful to man? Or did they remain aloof and indifferent to man's fate, "satisfied to be superfluous, if not frivolous"? What did they do? What did we do? What will we do?

PROLOGUE

As most of us psychologists are aware, Mr. Aldous Huxley,—long-admired as a gifted and versatile man of letters—has led the way in recent years to a considerable extension of our domain. He has done this by opening with mescaline,—one of today's several psychodelic drugs,—the flood-gates of visionary mysteries. And so, when I was told that Mr. Huxley had decided to reveal the nature of these mysteries to the members of the Congress, and that I was scheduled to precede him on this platform, I came to feel that I was bound by ancient custom to provide a modest *rîte d'entrée* to his hour of enchantment, a passage to that strange-to-us, old world of mind, wherein, we have been told, venturers may gaze with more of wonder than Conquistadors roving through the Aztec glades of Mexico. The fulfilment of this introductory role would necessarily entail,—since, whenever possible, one should speak from personal experience,—at least one intimate transaction with a potent psychodelic substance.

A rather urgent reason for my welcoming a drug with properties of this sort was the fact that since December—when I rashly proposed the announced title for this talk—nothing but banal ideas as to the future of psychology had gained entry

[1] Reprinted in part from G. S. Nielson (Ed.) *Proceedings of the XIV International Congress of Applied Psychology*. Vol. I. *Psychology and International Affairs*, (Copenhagen, Munksgaard, 1962), with the permission of the author and the publisher.

to my ordinary states of mind; and there was ground for hope that an *extraordinary* state of mind would permit the influx of a few far-ranging visions with which I might confront, if not confound, your sanity today. Curiosity and the envisaged possibility that I might revel in a little efficacious lunacy spurred me on to it. Why not?

Happily Professor Leary, who will speak to you this evening—the bravest promoter and accompanist of encounters with the trance-producing essence of a certain Mexican mushroom—happened to be a neighbor and, generous as always, consented to supervise my transition from mundane to preternatural realities.

Here at the outset, I should say that I have no intention of presenting an accurate report of the six hours of my ordeal by mushroom. By adopting a wholly passive set, one becomes the witness of a moving pageant of autonomous hallucinations; but if one allows spontaneously-emerging dispositions and ideas—active fantasies we might call them—to play some part in the transaction—as I so often did—the resulting imaginal display is markedly and variously altered. And so, my visual experience was in part determined by pre-existing as well as by freshly-shaped conceptions, and when later I got around to ordering the medley of impressions— as one does while waking from a dream—there was an inevitable invasion of number- less additional ideas to provide sufficient continuity and coherence for a chain of parables pertinent to my topic—Prospect for Psychology.

ACT I

I shall skip the first, startling thirty minutes of my trance—the stabbing cortical sensations, the hailstorm of brightly colored particles, filaments, and figures, the kaleidoscope of celestial mosaics at the antipodes of mind, the rush of archetypes —and simply tell you that after witnessing the birth in the Near East of the religions that shaped the souls of Western men and women, and after passing down the centuries to the agitations and enigmas of our own day, I found myself on the edge of a dark wood overlooking an existential waste of desolate absurdities with the straightway lost. Then, to my astonishment, I saw, floating down in my direction, an angel clothed in a cloud as white as wool. His countenance was as the sun in his zenith, beaming with encouragement to every benignant form of life. In these features he reminded me so strongly of my cherished friend, Professor Tranekjær Rasmussen, that out of my lonely state I would have hugged him if it had not been for the inhibiting awareness of his far-superior winged status in the hierarchy of being.

"This evening I am to be your Virgil," the angel said, "your appointed guide for the night hours of your journey into future time. Come with me. Over there is the forest path by which we must descend into the abyss of pain and woe and retributive justice."

As we proceeded in the semi-darkness, the angel informed me that the year was 1985 and that the long-dreaded Great Enormity had been perpetrated as predicted.

Barely six months ago a biological, chemical, and nuclear war between the U.S.S.R. and the U.S.A. had been started inadvertently—by the push of a button during a small group's momentary panic caused by a slight misunderstanding—and been concluded within a fortnight, leaving the essential structures of both countries leveled to the ground, their vital centers obliterated or paralyzed, their atmospheres polluted. Demoralized, isolated remnants of both populations, reduced to a mole-like existence underground, were now preparing amid the wreckage to defend themselves with gas against invading forces from China in the one case, and from South America in the other.

"We are approaching the subterranean courthouse of posterity," announced the angel, "where those accused of responsibility for the Great Enormity—or of irresponsibility—are being tried before the gods, of whom there is a multiplicity, I should say, in case you have not heard the news. On trial this evening is a host of academic psychologists of all breeds and nationalities."

In a minute the two of us were entering a crowded underground cavern, constructed like the Colosseum, all parts of which were preternaturally illuminated. The tiers of seats that constituted the sides of the amphitheater were arranged in sections, each of which, the angel pointed out, was occupied by a different denomination of psychologists. At the opposite end of the oval arena on a raised platform was a long judges' bench behind which sat a row of unmistakable divinities. One of these bore a striking resemblance to Aphrodite and another to Dionysius, but the majority were essentially androgynous. I was informed that all of them had recently been created in man's image as visible representors of the major determinants of human personality, society, and history. Attracted by a masked figure that sat near the center of the bench, I was told that that was *Alphaomega*, the influential and often-propitiated god of Chance, whose unpredictable operations could result in either good or evil fortune. The angel informed me that several pagan deities, after a period of sincere repentance and character reformation, had been admitted to this high court and named anew; but that most of the more imperious deities of antiquity had been rejected—Zeus for juvenile delinquency, Jehovah for narcism and delusions of infallibility, Allah for ferocity. Sitting at desks on both sides of the broad open space in front of the supreme court bench were the lawyers with their consulting sages. I recognized Buddha, Confucius, Moses, Thomas Aquinas, and a dozen more, engaged in whispered conversations with each other. One moody isolate was obviously Kierkegaard. As we took our seats, Socrates, attorney for the prosecution, was about to terminate his indictment of psychology.

"And now, divine judiciary," he said, "as I approach the slippery task of summing up my argument, I am assailed by the mutterings of sundry doubts. I have much fear of erring. To appraise the activities and the retailed wares of these most learned and industrious psychologists is a perilous and presumptuous undertaking for an untutored, rusty man like me. And yet, were I to permit cowardice to silence the voice of my in-dwelling daemon, ye gods and ancient sages would rise up in judgment to denounce me as a traitor to what light I have received from you, as one who would buy smiles from men at the price of sinning against conscience,

against you, Oh *Va!*" Here Socrates punctuated his speech with a deferential
bow to one of the chief jurists. "*Va*, supreme arbiter of the better and the worse,
who can discern differences, imperceptible to ordinary mortals, between fine
gradations of beauty, love, and truthfulness; and of sinning against *you*, immortal
Co, god of creativity in nature and in man."

"And so, ye gods, because I dread your odium more than anything I can name,
I shall go on, despite my qualms, and inquire whether these most eminent psychologists did anything or endeavored to do anything which might luckily have modified
the course of events that finally brought about the Great Enormity? When the
world's dire strait called for the full investment of rational imaginations, did or did
not these privileged professionals remain aloof, virtually indifferent to man's fate?
Did they, or did they not, behave as if they were quite satisfied to be superfluous,
if not frivolous? Had they, or had they not, acquired any knowledge, or were they,
or were they not, seeking any knowledge which might have served in any way to
stop the instinct-driven rulers of this earth from pursuing their fatal foreign policies
or to help them reach a more creative and humane solution of the world's ills,
instead of letting loose the fury which at this moment—1985 A.D.—seems to be
heading toward the termination of millions of years of evolution?"

"As you have surely noted, revered justices, I am an inept fumbler in the man-
sions of the social sciences, and, though I shall have to use it, correctly or incorrectly,
from now on, I have no stomach for their lingo, so noxious to a Greek. But, in spite
of these impediments and others, I shall perform the duty with which I have been
charged to the best of my ability."

"If we were to state, for short, that the crux of the world's dilemma consists of
a conflict between two different ideologies, thesis and antithesis, represented by
two blocs of power-oriented social units, would not a miniature paradigm, or
analogy, of this condition—susceptible to direct and detailed psychological investigation—have to include at least two interacting hostile personalities or groups,
each astringently attached to a contrasting set of social values, or religion? If the
answer is yes, I should like to ask what proportion of psychologists were observing
and conceptualizing on the level of two or more conflicting personalities, each
operating as a directed system of beliefs, emotions, wants, and higher mental
processes? Did, or did not, a goodly number of extremely intellectual psychologists,
insisting on the utmost scientific rigor, shun the complexities of personality, and
in search of higher pecking status, plant their minds in biology, physiology, statistics,
symbolic logic or methodology per se? And, among those academic psychologists
who observed and tested persons, did, or did not, a rather large percentage conceive
of personality as a galaxy of abstractions in a vacuum—a mere bag of traits, a profile
of scores on questionnaries, a compound of factors without referents, or, perhaps
some elaborate formulation of a conflict between oedipal hate and fear of punishment—giving little indication, in any case, of how the person would proceed and
with what outcome in a vehement transaction, let us say here, with a specified type
of ideological antagonist?"

"I have been told that a large number of more statistically-disposed American psychologists—social psychologists you might call them—constructed their propositions wholly in terms of the conforming majority of the population studied. If this is true, did, or did not, the conformists who confirmed their theories (and therefore behaved lawfully in the scientific sense) become equated in the minds of these psychologists with what was functionally right and proper? Since their results relegated to limbo the responses of the better-than-average members of the population mixed with the responses of the worse-than-average, did not the publication of these results reinforce, with the authority of science, the complacence of mediocracy? Did, or did not, these psychologists conceive of any better standard of values than was provided by the relatively well-adjusted, happy exemplifiers of the so-called 'dominant' culture patterns of their country?"

"And here, divine jurists," said Socrates with special emphasis, "comes the crucial question, which my daemon is impelling me to ask, harsh though it may seem: did the psychologists see, or fail to see, that the dominant majority in pretty nearly every sovereign state had been rendered obsolete in certain critical respects by the discovery of genocidal weapons? Suddenly the old rules of evolution had been drastically revised. Were, or were not, the psychologists aware of this? And, if aware, did they, or did they not, bring their minds and hearts to bear on the problem of specifying what kinds of personalities would be fit to govern the nations of both blocs under these harrowing new conditions, as well as what kinds of men and women would be fit to support fit governments?"

"To discover in what ways unfit personalities can become fit, could, or could not, psychologists have studied relevant transformations in depth of a few self-converted persons? The psychologists' models of a human being were various and ingeniously contrived—an electronic mechanism for the processing of symbolic information, an empty animal reacting in a standard cage, a self-centered, solipsistic atom in a social void, and a dozen other imaginal concoctions amazing to an old Athenian. An elegant side-show, I would hazard, of cleverly-contrived freaks. But if you, divine jurists, could ever bring yourselves to look at any one of these models in the eye, would you, I wonder, be convinced that man is worthy of survival, or, if not worthy in his present state, capable of becoming worthy? Were, or were not, a majority of clinical psychologists—Western not Soviet psychologists—so attracted by odors of decay, by neurotic illness, degradation, criminality, and what-not, that they were blinded to all else? And did not the constant advertisement of their brilliantly-analyzed cases of psychological decreptitude only serve to generate, through imitation, more of the same thing? In short, immortal judges, would you, or would you not, declare that quite a few psychologists—with no terminology at all to represent better-than-average personalities—added what influence they had to the general trend of denigration which reduced man's image of himself to the point of no revival, stripping it of genuine potentiality for creative change, the only ground there was for hope that people could do anything but what they actually did do? This brings me to the end of my queries as to possible explanations of the non-entity of academic psychology outside the minds of its own practitioners. With these I rest my case."

At this point, *Yu*, one of the jurists—god of charity and forgiveness—intervened. "Socrates," he said, "all you have done so far is to chide the all-too-human darkness in the minds of these distinguished scientists. Are you not capable of kindling a little light? What would *you* have done?"

"Oh," exclaimed Socrates, "I foresaw, in dread, that one of you venerable deities would challenge me precisely on this point, and, after consulting with myself, I discovered that the senescence of my faculties had rendered me incapable of complying with your imperative request. Instead, I have a little parable to offer —the idle fancy of an aging cortex—which begins with a miniature world-model, that is quite close to the personal experience of every one of these admirable psychologists, and also so compact that it lies within their sphere of feasible investigation. For this model, the scope of concern is not the world at large, but a single, purely hypothetical department of psychology marked by an on-going, bitter competition between two contrasting scientific ideologies represented by two blocs of faculty members, each with its ambitious, rivalrous, charismatic theorist-leader. One competing ideational system is derived from Existentialism and the other from Behaviorism. The two systems, the two faculty blocs, and the two prime protagonists are competing for the minds of the uncommitted students as well as for power and prestige, the directorship of the department."

"In due course, the two ideological protagonists, Asa and Bede, by name, become involved in an over-heated argument which ends in a sworn compact to settle their differences with pistols in the morning. There is no law against duelling in this area, and since each theorist has nerves of iron and a pistol loaded with nuclear material, the death of both is certain, and, since the members of each bloc feel that the grandeur of their theory demands that they too defend it with their lives, the elimination of the whole department is inevitable."

"Here, in a nutshell, is the problem which faces the psychologist—in this instance a visiting Danish scholar whose scientific curiosity and prudence have kept him securely in the role of a nonparticipant observer. What can he do? First, do as he was trained to do: produce a flock of promising hypotheses. If he applies method 27 to Asa and Bede, the existing high level of belligerent emotions will be lowered; and if he uses method 39, under conditions of lowered tension, Asa and Bede will agree to a postponement of the duel, and so forth and so on. But suppose that the psychologist's entire structure of smartly-conceived manoevres collapses at the very start, when a private talk with Asa and then with Bede unambiguously reveals that the whole pride system—the ego ideal—of each of them is glued to the conviction that his particular ideology is the complete, perfect, ultimate, and saving truth, and also glued to the moral imperative that a man must be prepared to kill or be killed whenever the survival or expansion of the authentic truth is endangered by the falsehoods or heresies of others. Asa and Bede are not deterred from the duel because each is supremely confident that he is quicker on the trigger and can kill the other before the other can discharge his weapon."

"The situation is clearly beyond remedy, and the visiting scholar, realizing that all his bright hypotheses have been invalidated, stumbles back to his room in a state of such abysmal melancholy that he turns to an extract of mushrooms for relief. Within an hour, Eureka! He has had a vision that engenders hope, and although it is long past midmight, he rushes out, calls on a few of his foreign-student friends, gets them to dress up in the semblance of constables; and then at dawn, disguised as a sheriff, he conducts them to the selected spot outside the city limits. They reach it just in time to inform the two protagonists, with an ample show of authority, that a law against duelling was signed on the previous day, and that if any man is alive after the shooting, he, the sheriff, will hang that man from the nearest oak tree. Faced by the absolute certainty of death, Asa and Bede, after a little hemming-and-hawing summit conference, agree to call off their war and return to the city with their two blocs of allies."

At this point, Socrates, as if talking to himself, queried: "Is there no hint here of the power and advantage of world government?"

"The parable ends with the staunch friendship of Asa and Bede, and with their joint production of a grand synthesis—an experiential-behavioral system of psychology—which integrates the inner and the outer aspect of a personality in action. Both Asa and Bede acknowledge their indebtedness to the Danish scholar, without whose beneficent intervention they never would have reached their present peak of solid satisfaction, justified in each of them by his proved capacity to understand and to encompass an ideology that is opposite to his own. As for the young Dane, his energies have been spent from first to last in recording and conceptualizing the stages of affectional and intellectual transformation experienced by Asa and Bede as they progressed from a monocentric to a dycentric pride-and-value system. The final climax of the fable comes with the Danish psychologist's publication of a generative book of postulates, theorems, and graphic illustrations which represent one validated way to a solution of ideological antagonisms, a book which promises to mark a turning-point in the history of inter-personal and inter-ideational relations."

Socrates' whole oration—his charges against psychology and his concluding mythic narrative—had been delivered in the gentlest fashion, words dropping from his mouth as leaves from trees. His benign manner was such as to intensify the guilt aroused by my awareness that his accusations were, in large part, applicable to me. As this noble philosopher took his seat, the defense attorney—none other than the formidable Aristotle, I was glad to see—came forward and immediately commenced his argument, pacing back and forth before the judges' bench with measured gestures.

"Honored deities," he said, "I trust you have not been deceived by the wiles of Socrates, his seductive way of mixing fact and fiction, comic and tragic flavors. I myself shall rely on simple, referential language to convince you first that this generally-wise old man has been unjust in overlooking the tender age of academic psychology as science, still in its adolescence in the years preceding the Great Enormity. Look at the giant strides it took from the days at the turn of the century when its sphere was virtually restricted to the sensations and perceptions of healthy, educated, adult European males."

"Second, I shall show that Socrates has little understanding of the differentiated modes of science-making, of the garnering of data, here and there, particle by particle. He is attentive only to the over-arching generalist who struts on the stage at some timely moment to devour and digest the spread-out produce of the toil and talent of numberless single-minded specialists. Academic psychology was approaching but had not yet reached the timely moment for a great, integrative generalist. Give this young science twenty years more and you shall witness, I predict, the emergence of a creative thinker of the first order—a Newton, Darwin, Marx, Frazer, Freud, Pavlov, Jung, Einstein, or Niels Bohr."

"You might suppose, honored jurists," continued Aristotle, "that these psychologists were a bit retarded in their growth; and I must confess that occasionally in private I have thought that they would have moved more surely toward their destined goal, if they had been less patronizing toward me and toward other anticipators of some of their recently vaunted concepts. Quite a few of them, I noted, failed to heed my irrefutable affirmation that it is the mark of an educated man to know the degree of precision—precision of observation and of statement—that is most appropriate to each stage in the development of each realm of knowledge. In this sense, many psychologists, mostly American, were not educated, in so far as their zeal to approximate the technical perfection of the more exact sciences led them away from the phenomena which psychologists, and only psychologists, are expected to study and to elucidate by the fittest scientific means. Their tolerance of uncertainty was too low," said Aristotle with finality.

"I shall persuade you, however, that this methodological compulsion was a necessary expedient in effecting the emancipation of their discipline from the enclosing husk of one or another brand of idealistic or speculative philosophy. Give psychology another forty years and you shall see one great embracement and extinction of all separate schools. Monocentric schools, as Socrates has suggested in his preferred mythic mode of speech, are symptoms of adolescence. Medicine has no schools."

"The last and more agreeable part of my task will be to prove by reference to works and names how close psychology had come to an impressive status in the house of intellect, not only by way of its excellent technology but because of the genuine importance of its ordered knowledge."

Then Aristotle, starting at the beginning of his announced plan of defence, proceeded systematically and logically, step by step, to annul the validity of each of Socrates' accusations. Though his performance was in no respect spectacular, the evidence he marshalled in our behalf was so copious and his presentation so lucid and concise, that within less than thirty minutes my guilt had turned to pride. This pride in my profession soared to even greater heights when Aristotle came to the last part of his oration in which he made it apparent, by pointing to specific researches and results, that Socrates had not read the literature of the four decades preceding 1985. He mentioned more than forty names, at least one from every nation represented in this hall. But since the bearers of a large proportion of these names are members of this Congress and some of them may be present in this audience, I shall not risk embarrassment all round by singling them out.

Aristotle's masterful exposition of psychology's achievements was followed by a short inaudible debate among the gods. They had been visibly impressed by the great Stagirite's facts and figures, and I had no twinge of apprehension in regard to the decision that was on the lips of *Va*, the chief justice, when he stood up and faced the tiers of psychologists on trial. Unspeakable, then, was my dismay when, in one shocking sentence, he proscribed for all of us a period of purgatorial probation!

Upon the pronouncement of this verdict, the smoke of our collective shame swirled upward. The atmosphere became too dense for sight, and in a second I was elsewhere, wrapped in utter darkness without angelic guidance. Then, before my passive eyes there passed a startling succession of horrendous scenes: a bottomless abyss of fire and brimstone out of which emerged the notorious beast of the Apocalypse; then thunder, lightning, and a hurricane of deafening explosions; then a great expanse of scorched earth strewn with rubble and cadavers: and finally, a colossal earthquake which swallowed up the residues of all the wrecked creations of centuries of human toil and faith, all the damning evidences of man's inhumanity to man.

EPILOGUE

All of us fully realize that, like the inhabitants of Herculaneum and Pompeii just previous to 79 A.D., we are living on the slopes of a simmering volcano. Except that in this instance the volcano is of human origin, and we have received abundant warnings, and it is by no means absolutely certain that there is *nothing* that any of us can do which might play some part in preventing its eruption. The problem is that of coping with the possibility of an impetuous or deliberate decision in the *minds* of certain men or in the mind of one man, as the climatic consequence of beliefs, aims and policies resident in the *minds* of men. This being the case, how many of us, I wonder, can comfortably accept the prospect that we—whose designated and selected province is the *minds* of men—are destined to be futile, to fiddle with irrelevancies while the giant powers multiply their infernal weapons, threats, and provocations? Collectively, we psychologists have faced and solved many formidable problems; but we have been singularly disinclined to face up to this one. Will we get round to it?

If yes, will we be vouchsafed the necessary time and opportunity? If yes, is there, distributed among us all, enough drive and genius? What can we say now except that the answers to these questions hang by a thread on what succeeds in unknown fate?

THE HOPE OF A
SCIENCE

If one were to attempt a verbal portrait of the contemporary science of psychology (perhaps drawn to caricature-like proportions for emphasis), the result, based on the ideas presented in this book, would not present a flattering resemblance. Of course, staunch "defenders of the faith" might argue that it would not bear any resemblance at all, but then they would probably not have read this far and are presumably busy writing criticisms of the criticisms.

What is the picture that emerges? We have a psychology whose metaphysical framework or foundation is outdated, based on a philosophy of science discarded decades ago by physics (long the model for psychology). Not only is this foundation obsolete, but the concepton of its subject matter, man, is no longer appropriate if indeed it ever was. We have findings that are irrelevant and meaningless to man, based upon experiments that study nonrepresentative, atypical samples of subjects who don't believe what we tell them and who respond in terms of their own perception of what the experimental situation is all about. Our data are often analyzed and interpreted incorrectly, and conclusions drawn without legitimate substantiation. Psychology lacks relevance and scientific and philosophical sophistication, conducts trivial and technically incorrect experiments, and presents a demeaning and defeating image of man.

The portrait is not excessively overdrawn, depressing though it may be, for each of the charges has a firm basis in reality as each of the authors has stated here. When one looks at the quantity and the quality of such criticisms, and the stature of those who propose them, one is apt to be overwhelmed by a feeling of futility.

Have we progressed appreciably since 1892 when William James said that when

we talk of "psychology as a natural science," we must not assume that that means a sort of psychology that stands at last on solid ground. It means just the reverse; it means a psychology particularly fragile, and into which the waters of metaphysica criticism leak at every joint, a psychology all of whose elementary assumptions and data must be reconsidered in wider connections and translated into other terms. . . . *This is no science, it is only the hope of a science. The matter of a science is with us* [editor's italics].[1]

The "matter of a science" is indeed very much with us for psychology surely must retain a scientific approach to its subject matter. As Maslow[2] reminds us, "scientific methods (broadly conceived) are our only ultimate ways of being sure that we *do* have truth." Poets, artists, prophets and others also investigate the human condition but however intriguing their insights may be and "however sure *they* may be, they can never make mankind sure. They can convince only those who already agree with them, and a few more. Science is the only way we have of shoving truth down the reluctant throat. Only science can overcome characterological differences in seeing and believing. Only science can progress."

To turn around an earlier phrase: *Psychology's only hope is science*!

The task, commitment, and direction of psychology must then be not to discard a scientific approach but to enlarge upon it, to expand psychology's narrow definition and scope of science. Psychology must become more flexible, open, and experimental in its choice and use of experimental methods. As McGuire[3] advises, we must remember the etymologically correct meaning of "experimental": to test, to try. It does not refer exclusively to laboratory manipulative research, although this is the narrow definition it has come to have in scientific psychology. By using such restrictive definitions, psychology excludes a wide world of meaningful, empirical data that can be just as scientific (in the true sense of the term) as the data collected in the most modern, well-equipped, computerized, sterile laboratory.

Despite the vast array of criticism presented here, or perhaps precisely because of it, it is possible to conclude this book on an optimistic note. The growing body of thoughtful criticism and reflection indicates that a revolution of some sort is developing in psychology—a movement away from the mechanistic, behavioristic psychology that has been dominant for so many years.

New winds of change are blowing, new ideas being expressed and heeded, and new approaches being tried. As Koch[4] notes: "for the first

[1] W. James, *Psychology: Briefer Course* (New York, Holt, 1892). Republished: New York, Crowell-Collier, 1962, p. 463.

[2] A. H. Maslow, *Toward a Psychology of Being* (Princeton, N. J., Van Nostrand, 1962), pp. iv, v.

[3] W. J. McGuire, "Some Impending Reorientations in Social Psychology: Some Thoughts Provoked by Kenneth Ring," *Journal of Experimental Social Psychology*, Vol. 3 (1967), pp. 124–139.

[4] S. Koch, "Epilogue," in S. Koch (Ed.), *Psychology: A Study of a Science*, Vol. 3 (New York, McGraw-Hill, 1959), p. 783.

time in its history, psychology seems ready—or almost ready—to assess its goals and instrumentalities."

The words of William James, quoted earlier, echo as clearly and forcefully as they did in 1892. However, due to the kinds of inquiries and criticisms presented in this book, perhaps psychology's hope of a science is nearer reality than ever before.

INDEX